1 Carl Reiner

2 Mel Brooks

3 Albert Brooks

4 Morey Amsterdam

5 Buddy Lester

6 Eddie Cantor

7 Groucho Marx

8 Harpo Marx

9 Jerry Seinfeld

10 Jerry Lester

11 Bob Odenkirk

12 Robert Smigel

13 Conan O'Brien

14 Henry Morgan

15 Dick Cavett

16 Don Rickles

17 Lenny Bruce

18 Chico Marx

19 George Schlatter

20 David Brenner

21 Sid Caesar

22 Louis C.K.

23 Richard Pryor

24 Jack Paar

25 Larry David

26 Richard Lewis

27 Harry Einstein

28 Jonathan Winters

29 Pigmeat Markham

30 Phyllis Diller

31 George Carlin

32 Moms Mabley

33 Milton Berle

34 Joan Rivers

35 George Burns

36 Ellen DeGeneres

THE
COMEDIANS

THE

COMEDIANS

DRUNKS, THIEVES, SCOUNDRELS
AND THE
HISTORY OF AMERICAN COMEDY

KLIPH NESTEROFF

Grove Press
New York

Published simultaneously in Canada
Printed in the United States of America

FIRST EDITION

ISBN 978-0-8021-2398-5
eISBN 978-0-8021-9086-4

Grove Press
an imprint of Grove Atlantic
154 West 14th Street
New York, NY 10011

Distributed by Publishers Group West

groveatlantic.com

15 16 17 18   10 9 8 7 6 5 4 3 2 1

For Marc M—
thanks for the boost

CONTENTS

PREFACE

I'm sitting in a greenroom across from Mel Brooks on a Tuesday afternoon in February. Here on the Warner Bros. lot he is idling, waiting to be brought onstage by Conan O'Brien for a taping of the TBS program *Conan*. The loss of his beloved wife nine years ago seems to have hushed his backstage tones, but in a half hour when his name is announced, Brooks will summon his unique comic energy and annihilate a young audience on the very lot where he made *Blazing Saddles* forty years ago.

Jokes have been made about Brooks and his longtime comedy partner Carl Reiner gaining on the 2000 Year Old Man, but at eighty-eight and ninety-two, respectively, they remain astoundingly perceptive. Like time travelers, they have transitioned from one generation to another. Reiner's first TV gig was in 1949 and Brooks had his in 1950, a time when owning a television was a luxury. Now Reiner has lived long enough to use Twitter as compulsively as a teenage girl and Brooks is hustling Blu-Rays and appearing on podcasts. Mel Brooks and Carl Reiner: seminal links to comedy's past living in the world of the future.

Today Brooks is wearing a white-collared shirt and a rumpled black blazer. He drags his right palm across his face like a washcloth, a nervous tic of sorts. Comedian Jimmy Pardo speed-walks through the greenroom, reknotting a necktie, preparing for the audience warm-up. Tonight's episode of *Conan* is a tribute to Sid Caesar, the legendary comic actor who had recently died at the age of ninety-one.

In the 1950s Caesar was not just a top sketch comedian, but a revolutionary one. His two programs, *Your Show of Shows* (1950–1954) and *Caesar's Hour* (1954–1957), employed the most influential comedy writers of the twentieth century, including Brooks, Reiner, Larry Gelbart and Neil Simon. Conan O'Brien said Sid Caesar was the whole reason he got into comedy:

> *When I was a kid growing up in Brookline, Massachusetts, my father took me to the Hearthstone Plaza in Brookline Village to see something called* Ten from Your Show of Shows . . . *He said, "You've got to see this." He took me, lights go down, I watch this, and when it was over I thought to myself, "I don't know what that guy is doing—but I want to do that."*

Mel Brooks was the wunderkind behind the Sid Caesar sketches, and when the program went off the air in 1954 Brooks was a hot commodity. Over on a different comedy program, *The Red Buttons Show*, the ratings were plunging, and NBC thought Brooks might be able to help. Mel was hired to write and direct the sinking show. It would have been his directorial debut, fifteen years before *The Producers*. Instead Brooks quit after only six days. I had always wondered about the reason, and since we were both idling in the greenroom, I asked him.

"Mel . . . I've always wondered . . . In 1954 you were hired to direct *The Red Buttons Show* . . . It would have been your directorial debut, but it never happened . . ."

"Buttons, yeah. I don't think I ever did it."

"He had a reputation for being difficult . . ."

"Oh, yes. Yeah, there was only one comedian worse, only one person more difficult to work for."

"Who's that?

"Jack Carter."

Back in 1950 Jack Carter had been Sid Caesar's Saturday night lead-in as the star of *The Jack Carter Show*. Another iron man of show business, Carter recently died at the age of ninety-three. He was a nightclub powerhouse during the 1950s and 1960s, and a ubiquitous TV personality on everything from *The Judy Garland Show* to *The Odd Couple* to the *Dean Martin Celebrity Roasts*. Carter's first stand-up gig was in 1943, and he still appeared on programs like *New Girl* and *Shameless* until his death in 2015. Mel's suggestion that Jack could be difficult was accurate, and I knew it firsthand. Over the course of chronicling stand-up history I interviewed Jack Carter several times. I learned that his curmudgeon exterior masked a gentle but insecure man. Not long ago as I was leaving his home he shouted at me, "How does a total fucking nobody like *you* get a book deal?" It made me laugh. He was seldom happy about anything, but I couldn't help but love the guy.

I'd grown fond of many elderly comedians over the course of my research: some famous, some obscure, some funny, some cringe-worthy. I respected them all. I found their stories of Mob run-ins, hopeless bombs and triumphant evenings altogether fascinating. In the case of Brooks and Carter they were among the only men alive from whom I could get firsthand information about forgotten venues and faded comics.

One month after Mel Brooks and I chatted in the *Conan* greenroom, we faced each other again, this time at the Cinefamily theater in Los Angeles. I'd convinced Brooks to join me for an onstage interview about Sid Caesar followed by a 35mm screening of *Ten from Your Show of Shows*, the sketch film Conan O'Brien cited as his primary influence. I was pacing backstage when my phone rang. "Hi, it's Mel! We're driving down the alley. Where is it? Is this it? Is that you? What? Where? Okay!" Brooks hopped out of a Town Car with his unlikely companion for the evening, the owner of Elvis Presley's Graceland. We casually went over some talking points while he sipped from his ginger ale and vodka and conversed about old, forgotten acts like Borrah Minevitch and His Harmonica Rascals. We were fully warmed up come showtime. The executive director of the theater welcomed the crowd and gave a preamble while we waited in the wings. Brooks whispered to me, "You gonna talk first?"

"Yeah," I said. "I'll set it up and talk about Sid Caesar for three minutes . . ."

"Do five," said Mel.

I laughed. "What—now I'm opening for you?"

"Yeah, you're opening for me!"

"Ladies and germs!"

INTRODUCTION

Just tell the truth and people will laugh.

—Jonathan Winters

A comedian's success is almost always the result of a long, arduous struggle. Whether it was at a vaudeville theater in the 1920s or a Mafia-run nightclub in the 1940s, a coffeehouse run by filthy beatniks in the 1950s or a comedy club used as a cocaine front in the 1970s, the comedian's struggle was remarkably similar through the generations.

An obstacle always seemed to lie in the way of achievement. Opium habits and corrupt managers plagued the vaudeville comedian's life. Nightclub curfews, conscription, anti-Semitism and mankind's impending doom hampered comics during World War II. In the 1950s there were comedians arrested for "lewd and obscene" material. In the late 1960s there were comedians listed as enemies of the state for their political opinions. No matter who you were or to which generation you belonged—you had to pay your dues. If you were launched into stardom without first putting in your time, you were sure to pay your dues later, when your career faded away.

While the facts of struggle were a constant in comedy, the style of performance was not. The art form evolved and shifted shape over a hundred years, so much so that comedy fans of the current generation find it nearly impossible to relate to comedians who dominated only decades before.

*   *   *

Familiar tropes have corrupted literature devoted to comedy. The "tears of a clown" idea has dominated comedy discourse even as giants like Johnny Carson and Jerry Seinfeld rejected the idea. "There are a lot of unhappy people driving bread trucks, but when it's a comedian people find it very poignant," said Seinfeld. "Some of them are in pain but I don't see that as a thread." Carson said, "There have been volumes written about why comedians are lonely, depressed, rejected, hostile, within themselves. They say you must be suffering. I don't adhere to that philosophy."

Comedy writers were often more morose, miserable and angry than the comedians for whom they wrote. Philip Rapp spent decades writing for comedy stars like Eddie Cantor and Danny Kaye. He spoke bitterly in his unpublished memoir: "The dusty corners of comedy are littered with the trash of the stand-up comics who have fallen on their faces. The stand-up comic is a special breed of non-comedian who reads jokes, such as they are, to an audience who rarely pays to see or hear him. He is indigenous to television and nightclubs, borscht circuit hotels and weddings, places to which people would go even if he wasn't there. His earnings may be microscopic or astronomical, depending on his 'drawing power,' which has nothing in common with talent. There are the talented few who are genuinely funny in their approach, but finding them is like looking for grapes in a field of thistles. In the main the stand-up comic belongs to a sub-literate group. The stand-up comics and their one-liners—they might just as well be reading from a joke book."

And for decades they pretty much were. Prior to the 1950s the vocation of stand-up comic was not far removed from being a door-to-door salesman. One learned the basics, memorized some routines, found an agent at 1650 Broadway and called himself a comic. "There were so many bullshit comics back then," says Jack Carter. "Frauds! Just frauds! When I was coming up there were a million of them and there were lots of clubs for them to work." A 1946 book called *From Gags to Riches* praised comedians who used lines like "I know there's an audience out there, I can hear you breathing" and "Is this an audience or a jury?" It's amazing anyone earnestly used lines now associated with Fozzie Bear, but the Willy Loman approach worked for decades. Eventually men like Lenny Bruce, Mort Sahl and Jonathan Winters came along and led a revolution by developing their own material, derived from their actual personalities.

For decades, being funny was not even a prerequisite for a career in comedy. *High Anxiety* scriptwriter Ron Clark remembers a comedy writer named Buddy Arnold. "Buddy Arnold's big claim to fame was that he was Milton Berle's writer, but he was more like a *researcher*. Arnold was not a funny guy at all. He would remember an old joke and find a way to switch it. There were a lot of those guys. They weren't funny, but they were good at piecing it together. It is amazing they earned a living."

For decades most stand-up comics relied on material written by others, seldom writing their own words. New comedians started to question that method for the first time in the 1950s. "If he's a chap who needs writers, he's not a comedian," said Lenny Bruce. "He's an actor—whom I respect as a craftsman."

It was a new attitude in comedy. By the time Robert Klein entered the business in the mid-1960s, the attitude was an accepted one. The William Morris Agency wanted Klein to write for London Lee, a regular on *The Ed Sullivan Show*, but Klein was adamantly opposed. "I have no respect for London Lee or guys that use writers. There was no way I would *ever* use writers." It was a maverick change.

Back then you could categorize the style of comics based on what they smoked. In the 1960s the new comedians like Dick Gregory and Bob Newhart chain-smoked cigarettes and hipsters like Lenny Bruce and George Carlin smoked pot. Established old-school giants wouldn't go anywhere without burning a giant cigar. Milton Berle, George Burns, Sid Caesar, George Jessel, Ernie Kovacs, Groucho Marx, Red Skelton and Danny Thomas were cigar aficionados long before it became the trademark of an asshole. "It gave you time to think," said Marx. "You could tell a joke, and if the audience didn't laugh you could take some puffs on the cigar. Sometimes that would give the audience a chance to think about the joke and give them time to laugh before you went on to the next joke." Mel Brooks nearly suffocated while working at *Your Show of Shows*. "Carl [Reiner] smoked a cigar, Sid [Caesar] smoked a cigar, [staff writer] Mel Tolkin smoked a cigar. I think [staff writer] Lucille Kallen smoked a cigar! I couldn't stand it." Comedian Alan King started smoking cigars because he was told he had to. "Milton Berle chided me, 'If you're gonna be a comedian, you gotta smoke cigars.' So I started smoking cigars in my act [and] didn't stop until they took out half my jaw."

Plagiarism, stolen jokes and lifted ideas have been another familiar narrative in the history of stand-up. Jack Benny's early years were plagued by threats of lawsuits after he plagiarized from better-known vaudeville performers like Phil Baker and Ben Bernie. More recently were the disputes between Denis Leary and Bill Hicks, Dane Cook and Louis C.K. Producer Robert Morton said the program *Mind of Mencia* was canceled because Comedy Central didn't want to jeopardize its reputation among comedians after Carlos Mencia was accused of widespread joke thievery. It's an unresolved issue that goes back to the earliest days of stand-up.

It's common to hear older comedy fans complain that comedians *used* to be funny. In comedy, generational considerations are everything. As time passes, the comedy from another era fails to resonate with the new generation. Key and Peele fans are laughing at something relevant to them, whereas the sketches of *The Carol Burnett Show* are mostly relevant to those who were weaned on such comedy. George Carlin influenced Louis C.K. and Lenny Bruce influenced George Carlin—yet very few Louis C.K. fans connect to the material of Lenny Bruce. It's not a matter of one being funny and the other not, but a relation to one's time. Veteran comedian Jan Murray said, "Comedy—every era—as it dies, people bemoan it. 'Oh, these new comics aren't like *those* guys!' But it's wrong, because every generation breeds its own generation that talks to that generation." Shecky Greene agrees. "People say to me, 'You guys were better in the old days.' Fuck the old days!"

Vaudeville comedy now seems out of date and out of touch, incapable of creating reflexive laughter. To our modern sensibility the jokes are little more than an intangible abstraction. Epes W. Sargent, a veteran critic who died in 1938, predicted that vaudeville comedy was not going to age well: "It must be remembered that old vaudeville was more a matter of style than material. It was not so much *what* they said and did—as *how* they said and did it. The compiler can give the words. He cannot add the saving grace of personality." Viewed through a contemporary prism, vaudeville comedy can be rather painful, but this doesn't mean it wasn't legitimately funny in its day.

And yet the actual experience of the comedian remains similar to that of the vaudeville comic, transcending the generations. Then as now, countless stand-up schleppers toiled in the trenches, learned their craft, bombed before hostile audiences and killed in front of anonymous drunks. The struggle of the funny performer has remained a symbiosis of drive, jealousy, heartbreak and triumph— existing then as it exists now. Perhaps the only other constant is comedy's unfailing popularity. Phyllis Diller once said, "There will never be enough comedy. Comedy is at a premium always."

A NOTE ON SOURCES

The show business trade paper *Variety* was the most important source for showbiz news for nearly a hundred years. Likewise it was the most important source for this book. In many instances its reviews and editorials—which were published six days a week—are the only surviving accounts of many comedians, radio performers and television shows. For this reason *Variety* is cited in these pages frequently.

More than two hundred interviews were conducted for *The Comedians*. Where a quote is derived from an original interview, it is indicated with the present tense "says." Where a quote is derived from a preexisting source, it is indicated with the past tense "said." Some quotes have been condensed for length.

THE
COMEDIANS

CHAPTER ONE

VAUDEVILLE COMEDIANS

At the start of the twentieth century, the United States had close to five thousand vaudeville theaters. There were small houses with less than five hundred seats, medium theaters seating a thousand and large palaces that accommodated anywhere from fifteen hundred to five thousand people. The result was an immense working-class circuit, an underbelly where future stars learned their craft.

The theaters were owned and operated by a small handful of moguls, greedy men of massive wealth with a pathological need for profit. Benjamin Franklin Keith was one of them. The father of vaudeville's largest circuit, Keith got his start in the 1880s selling tickets to exhibitions of "prematurely born Negro babies." Other money-hungry weirdos copied the idea and the industry hailed Keith as the groundbreaking innovator of the "incubator baby shows."

The Keith circuit controlled the majority of vaudeville theaters west and south of Chicago. "It is a very rich corporation," said a 1905 profile. "Its Chicago offices resemble those of a New York financial institution." And it was every bit as ruthless. Corners were cut to maximize profit: The heat was turned off, the dressing rooms were unkempt, and the comedians' pay was low. Travel tickets, if covered at all, were the cheapest possible. The front of a major vaudeville house might look ornate and dazzling, but behind the curtain it was a parade of literal rats and figurative rodents.

At the turn of the century parishioners attacked vaudeville as a sinful venture. Organized boycotts adversely affected ticket sales. Keith's wife was deeply religious and prodded her husband to follow church directives. Comedian Fred Allen said, "Mrs. Keith instigated the chaste policy, for she would tolerate no profanity, no suggestive allusions, double-entendres or off-color monkey business." Keith realized it would be wise business if he could get into the good graces of the church; receiving its endorsement while the competition suffered a boycott would be a great advantage. Keith aligned himself with religious types and entered a financial partnership with the church. Soon it was bankrolling Keith's larger shows and had made him the most dominant vaudeville force in the Midwest.

Edward Franklin Albee was another mogul and an early partner of Keith's. Together they conspired to crush all competition. They triumphed through intimidation. If it was an independent theater they wanted to take over, they publicly smeared it as a merchant of sin. Its reputation tarnished, they swooped in and "saved" their acquisition with a clean Keith-Albee bill.

They could dish it, but they couldn't take it. If anyone criticized Keith-Albee, there was trouble. *Variety* was the show business paper of record, and when it dared publish objective criticism of Keith-Albee shows, Albee banned *Variety* from his property. Any performer caught reading it was immediately fired from the circuit.

"Edward F. Albee became an almost dictatorial figure in American vaudeville," wrote vaudeville scholar Charles W. Stein. "Our appraisal of him lies midway between unmitigated ogre and enlightened despot. He gobbled up one chain of theaters after another, built huge new ones and succeeded in merging Keith-Albee with the Orpheum circuit."

The Orpheum circuit had been Keith-Albee's largest competitor, with theaters in Calgary, Champaign, Davenport, Decatur, Denver, Des Moines, Duluth, Fresno, Kansas City, Lincoln, Los Angeles, Madison, Memphis, Milwaukee, Minneapolis, New Orleans, Oakland, Omaha, Portland, Rockford, Sacramento, Salt Lake City, San Francisco, Seattle, Sioux City, Springfield, St. Louis, St. Paul, Winnipeg, Vancouver and Victoria.

Once a comedian was contracted to a class circuit, his standard of living went up. "Circuits were signing vaudeville acts to three- and five-year pay-or-play contracts that guaranteed the acts forty or more weeks each year," said comedian Fred Allen. "These contracts could be used as collateral . . . A vaudeville performer could present his five-year Keith contract at any local bank and borrow enough money to buy or build a home."

Keith-Albee and their Orpheum theaters had almost total control of vaudeville. Stein wrote, "Their virtual monopoly in the field of vaudeville was akin to that of John D. Rockefeller's in oil or Andrew Carnegie's in steel." It was an apt comparison. The working conditions of vaudeville were not unlike that of industrial age factories, with few benefits offered its working class. "I played *dumps*," said Milton Berle. "I toiled when I first started to play all the vaudeville theaters. Terrible theaters. I played small towns. One town was so small the local hooker was a virgin."

Three small circuits contentiously fought Keith-Albee during the first twenty years of the twentieth century: the Pantages Circuit of Alexander Pantages, the Loew's Circuit of Marcus Loew and the Sheedy Time Circuit of Michael R. Sheedy. Keith-Albee eventually decided they posed no threat and let them endure. As the magazine *The American Mercury* explained, "It was dollar-and-a-half vaudeville against twenty-five-cent stuff, with the difference in price about equal to the difference in material offered." Comedian George Jessel said of the Sheedy Time Circuit, "It should have been spelled *shitty* . . . I'll never forget the opening in Gloucester, Massachusetts, in the dead of winter at a little theater at the end of a pier. The dressing rooms were afloat with sea water and we had to put boards and boxes on the floor to make up and dress . . . It was a tough time, all right."

Theater owners dodged construction costs, cutting corners and employing nonunion labor. Shoddy methods caused the death of vaudeville comedian Rube Dickinson in Kansas City. Booked at a brand-new venue, Dickinson stepped outside to have a smoke and was standing underneath the large wooden marquee advertising him when it collapsed. As the marquee caved, so too did his head—killed under the weight of his own name.

Vaudeville houses had poor ventilation. "The vaudeville seasons would end by summer because there was no air conditioning in those days," said Groucho Marx. Moe Howard of Three Stooges fame remembered the Kansas City Orpheum, where "the dressing rooms were unclean, unheated, unventilated and rat-infested. In some of the theaters, the manager used the dressing room as a storeroom, often filled with bags of unpopped corn, sometimes up to the ceiling. The bottom bags usually had holes where the rats were nibbling."

W. C. Fields was popular in vaudeville as a comic juggler as early as 1900, but he still referred to his vaudeville days as "the most miserable [time] of my life. I would never have gone through with it if I had known what it was going to be like . . . mental torture is too high a price to pay for anything."

Early vaudevillians had no defense if they got stiffed on pay. "We were completely at the mercy of local managers and booking agents," said Harpo Marx. "If they ran off with the share of the receipts they had promised us, we had nobody to appeal to. There was nothing we could do except pick up our bags and start walking to the next town before we got thrown in the jig as vagrants."

It was decades before the Jet Age, and the means of transportation available to a small-time vaudevillian were brutal. "The cities and towns could seldom be reached by any one railroad," said Fred Allen. "There never seemed to be a direct way the actor could go from one date to another without changing trains once or twice during the night and spending endless hours at abandoned junctions waiting for connecting trains. Through the years I have spent a hundred nights curled up in dark, freezing railroad stations." Harpo Marx said, "Looking back, I simply don't know how we survived it. Those early days on the road were sheer, unmitigated hell."

Some acts subsidized a meager income doing odd jobs in showbiz rooming houses. "Many of the acts did light housekeeping in little flats and others lived in boardinghouses where for a buck you could get three meals a day and a room with a window," said comedian and vaudeville historian Joe Laurie Jr. Silent comedy pioneer Mack Sennett lived in vaudeville boardinghouses "along with midgets, fat ladies, tap dancers, carnival entrepreneurs and unemployed snake charmers." He said his audiences were full of "prostitutes, pimps, touts, beggars, sneak thieves and pickpockets."

Comedians built a kinship with prostitutes and drug dealers living a vagabond lifestyle not vastly different from their own. "The Saratoga in Chicago was that kind of spot," said Laurie Jr. "You could buy anything—a double routine, parody, tip on a horse, hot jewelry or even some 'nose candy' right in the lobby. The only rule strictly enforced in this type of hotel was 'No smoking of opium in the elevators.'"

The opiate of the vaudeville people was opium. Morphine was a close second. Trade publications were full of reports like that of vaudeville actress Edith Peck, who was arrested for morphine possession. Peck said, "Late night work made me an addict."

Narcotics addiction was so common that vaudeville comedian Lew Kelly became famous for a dope fiend *act*, with comedy derived from his character's stoned hallucinations. It was successful enough that it created a dope fiend genre. "There have been many imitators of Kelly in his dope characterizations," wrote the *Pittsburgh Press* in 1915, "but none of the imitators have succeeded in getting the originality and the genuine worth into the part that Lew Kelly imparts to it."

Drug dealing was a way to subsidize a small-timer's income. Some comics were in demand not for their act, but for their connections. Ray Ripley was a small-time comic who dealt drugs on the side until he was imprisoned in 1921. Comic Joe Perryfi dealt to burlesque acts until he was busted in Pittsburgh, his four thousand dollars in cash confiscated when he was charged with unlawful possession and transportation of ten ounces of morphine.

Booze was a tragic undercurrent for many vaudeville comedians, and when Prohibition started in 1918, drunks acquired their alcohol from unregulated sources. For an alcoholic touring the country, it meant panic if you didn't have a hookup in each town. Fred Allen said, "Prohibition posed great problems for the drinking vaudeville actor. He had to find a bootlegger in a strange city and take the word of some newly made acquaintance as to the quality of the hooch available. Usually, the stagehands could be depended upon for this information. Some of the stagehands were themselves bootleggers."

The lower-end vaudeville audience often comprised passed-out drunks. Allen recalled the Jefferson Theater in Manhattan, where "alcoholics of all sizes and in varying conditions used the Jefferson as a haven from the elements and a slumber sanctuary. At some performances the Jefferson took on the appearance of a flophouse that had put in vaudeville."

Vaudeville comedians and burlesque comedians flourished during the same era, but in separate, parallel worlds. The main burlesque circuit was the Columbia Wheel, cofounded by Harry Abbott, the father of Abbott & Costello's Bud. The Abbotts lived in the Coolidge Hotel, a New York SRO that accommodated "burlesque people, pimps, prostitutes, and purse snatchers." Abbott started the Columbia Wheel using the money he made from his Coney Island attraction Midget City—a community for little people built to scale.

Burlesque comedians struggled for attention, as naked women were the main draw. According to groping expert Irving Zeidman in his book *The American Burlesque Show*, strippers like Betty Duval and Bubbles Yvonne "would be mauled by the comics in the bits, and as the star strippers of the shows, would exhibit their well-proportioned breasts in full view, then their well-developed buttocks in full view, all the time shaking whatever was exposed, and smilingly walk off after four or five encores—a hard day's work well done."

Burlesque comedy relied on stock routines and characters. Its most common comedy conventions, according to Zeidman, were "rampaging husbands and racial caricature, both holdovers from the turn of the century. Also standard in all burlesque shows was the use of odd descriptive names for the cast of characters [like] A. Grafter, Stockson Bonds, Ima Peach." Standard burlesque turns had names like *Under the Bed* and *Suck a Lemon*. According to journalist Bill Treadwell, "The old vulgar gag where the policeman swung his club between his legs was done in every show."

Burlesque's primitive vulgarity brought inevitable police shakedowns. Morton Minsky of the successful Minsky's burlesque said, "The aggravation we had from the self-appointed moralists started almost at the beginning and haunted us to the very end."

Burlesque comedy was risqué, while vaudeville had pathological sanctimony. Vaudeville houses posted warnings backstage about
verboten subject matter. References to sex or Christianity were out,
as was any cussing—although restrictions varied from town to town
and year to year. The phrase "working blue" came into usage at the
time. If a representative of the Keith Orpheum circuit objected to
the content of an act, a request to cut the material was sent backstage
in a blue envelope. So-called blue material was considered prob-
lematic enough that vaudeville listings in local papers noted which
shows were "Clean Bills." Some of the restrictions had no obvious
logic. The Keith circuit had its list of seventy-three objectionable
topics including "Mayor Jimmy Walker, Fiorello LaGuardia, Aimee
McPherson, Herbert Hoover and Arabs." Fred Allen said, "Long
after Mr. Keith's death, the circuit was still waging its campaign
against suggestive material." Albee was delighted when a woman
wrote him a letter saying she could attend his theaters "on the Sabbath and still feel in direct communion with God." The arbitrary
Keith-Albee rules carried over into postvaudeville media. Long after
vaudeville died in the early 1930s, the Keith-Albee restrictions still
informed the censorship bureaus of radio.

Vaudeville may have been clean, but it bred cruelty. The method
of using a giant hook to yank acts from the stage seems like an
invention of cartoons, but the basis for the cliché was real. A showman named Henry Clay Miner invented it for his amateur night at
Miner's Bowery Theatre in the 1880s. If the act was deemed rotten,
a stagehand was cued to remove the performer with a massive hook
and a violent tug. The sheer rancor of this spectacle turned Miner's
amateur nights into a profitable draw.

George Burns once relayed the story of a theater owner in
the 1920s whose cruelty surpassed the hook, using an even more
humiliating instrument—the hoop. "A man with a hoop would sit
in the front row during the performance, and if he thought the act
was lousy he'd use the hoop to pull the performer right over the
footlights."

If the crowd thought you stunk, they had their own props to show their distaste. "If an audience didn't like us we had no trouble finding out," said Harpo Marx. "We were pelted with sticks, bricks, spitballs, cigar butts, peach pits and chewed-out stalks of sugar cane."

Just as the hook was nestled in reality, so too was the cliché of chucking rotten tomatoes at the stage. But this was less a product of dissatisfied patronage than of vaudeville promoters looking for another gimmick. Turn-of-the-century vaudeville impresario Oscar Hammerstein came up with the idea of erecting a screen and encouraging the hordes to pitch overripe groceries. Likewise, impresario Billy Rose ran newspaper ads for his Casino de Paree exclaiming, "Sunday Nite—Amateur Nite. Come and throw vegetables at actors!"

The attraction of rotten food matched the attraction of so-rotten-they're-good performers. George Burns loved an act called Swain's Rats and Cats, which he claimed "consisted of several cats dressed as horses being ridden by several rats dressed as jockeys." Most notorious were the Cherry Sisters, a group of singers promoted by their vaudeville hosts as the worst act in showbiz. Audiences were encouraged to treat them accordingly. For those with a sense of humor, the Cherry Sisters were a must-see. *Variety* observed in 1924: "As terribleness, their skit is perfection. The manager, who happens to be punished by having them placed on his bill, has only one opportunity—that of billing them as a comedy duo."

Some of the most influential comedy figures of the twentieth century entered vaudeville as children. Child acts featuring Groucho Marx, Phil Silvers and Buster Keaton were among the most popular forms of vaudeville comedy.

Buster Keaton was part of the most controversial act in showbiz when he was a toddler. The Three Keatons featured patriarch Joe Keaton concentrating on a serious task at the start of each comedy sketch. He would be calculating taxes or changing a flat tire when his tiny son Buster would enter the scene, prodding and annoying his father. Buster would harangue his father over and over, incessantly, until Joe Keaton snapped with rage. What followed was a mesmerizing session of acrobatic brutality.

Joe Keaton punished Buster with violence while Mother Keaton played straight, screaming at her husband to have mercy on the boy. Buster was thrown through the air and slammed against backdrops. The pratfalls Buster deployed would have busted the spine of a layman. He wore a specially designed outfit with a suitcase handle sewn to the back of his coat, allowing his father to easily catch, grab and toss. During one performance, the elder Keaton misjudged a move and accidentally kicked Buster in the head, knocking him unconscious for eighteen hours.

The Society for the Prevention of Cruelty to Children tried to put them out of business. Buster said the Society's grievances were misplaced. "What most burned up Pop was that there were then thousands of homeless and hungry abandoned children of my age wandering around the streets of New York, selling newspapers, shining shoes . . . Pop couldn't understand why the S.P.C.C. people didn't devote all of their time, energy, and money to helping them." The family spent much of their earnings on legal fees, fighting foes who yearned to shut them down. The Three Keatons usually won. "The law barred children only from performing on a high or low wire, a trapeze, bicycle, and the like," said Buster. "There was not one word that made it illegal for my father to display me on the stage as a human mop or kick me in the face."

The Three Keatons were an original standout compared with the majority of vaudeville comedy featuring children. Most kid comics participated in the schoolroom sketch craze, which enjoyed a heyday from 1905 to 1920. The schoolroom was the perfect arrangement for a flurry of fast punch lines springing from one simple setup. A staid schoolmaster played straight to a collection of schoolchildren giving joke answers to their teacher's queries. According to Joe Laurie Jr., schoolroom acts "were always surefire. Their inevitable hand-raising, kid-writing gags had the important advantage of being highly inexpensive. The only props were a few desks and chairs. A vaudeville census in 1913 counted sixty-two such acts playing vaudeville across the country."

Gus Edwards was the most successful producer of schoolroom acts. He was constantly auditioning children, and many reviled him as an exploiter of child labor. Comedian Joe Frisco used to have a line in his act, "Hide your children—here comes Gus Edwards." Future comedy stars who started in schoolroom sketches included Larry Fine of the Three Stooges, Eddie (father of Teri) Garr, Eddie Cantor, George Jessel and the Marx Brothers.

The Marx Brothers toured as the Six Mascots, and like many schoolroom acts, their characters were defined using racial caricature. Such racial stereotypes were common in vaudeville. Jack Sobel, father of comedian and television director Howard Storm, was in a Gus Edwards road company. "It was called School Days with the Crazy Kids," says Storm. "My father did what in those days they called 'the Jew comic.' They had the Irish comic, the Dutch comic, the Jew comic."

Joe Laurie Jr. argued that in those days "nobody took exception to the billings of The Sport and the Jew, Irish by Name but Coons by Birth, The Mick and the Policeman, The Merry Wop, Two Funny Sauerkrauts. It was taken in good humor by the audience. There were no pressure groups and no third generation to feel ashamed of immigrant origins."

Laurie Jr. said nobody found it offensive, but a better interpretation is that *fewer* found it offensive. Many felt uncomfortable with racial stereotypes, but there were few places for their grievance to be heard. Vaudeville comedians Harry Hershfield and Peter Donald made their livings with racial caricature. When former schoolroom players Groucho Marx and Walter Winchell, now a newspaper columnist, found themselves in a position of power years later, they waged a battle to have racial caricature erased from vaudeville. They used Hershfield and Donald as examples of undesirable comedy. Hershfield and Donald defended themselves, telling the press that racial caricature "if done well is not offensive." In an open letter to *Variety* they argued, "The most dialectically used and abused nationals were the Scots and the Swedes—who have never complained." Groucho Marx shot back angrily, "The Sandy McPhersons and Yonny Yohnsons were not a minority being subjected to oppression, restriction, segregation or persecution."

Groucho's perspective was informed by the racism the Marx Brothers had faced while playing the road. "We had to brazen our way into strange towns in the Midwest and down South," said Harpo Marx, "where we knew we had three strikes against us. One: we were stage folks, in a class with gypsies and other vagrants. Two: we were Jewish. Three: we had New York accents." Comedian Benny Rubin remembered vaudeville in the Deep South. "There were the hate towns, which you found down South where they hated Catholics, Blacks and Jews. So anybody like that didn't have a chance."

The protests against racial caricature made gains in the final years of vaudeville. Laurie Jr. wrote, "Gradually each burlesque Irishman, Jew, German and Italian gave way on the stage to the 'neat' comic—one well-dressed and attractive, who relied on his wit and talent for laughter and applause."

One element that did not disappear until after the Second World War was blackface. Everyone from Fred Allen to W. C. Fields to Mae West spent early days smeared in burnt cork. More than any other racial bit, blackface persisted. It was less a matter of race prejudice than conformity. "Nearly all the singles [solo acts] started to do blackface," said Laurie Jr. "But it wasn't like the old-time minstrels who tried to portray a character; these new minstrels just put on black and talked white. No dialect, didn't even try, in fact some of them told Hebe stories in blackface! For what reason they blacked up will never be known. It became a craze. People figured you were an *actor* when you had black on. And besides, working in white face demanded a personality, which many of the guys didn't have."

Bob Hope was a blackface comedian. He abandoned it only because he was late for a gig. "I missed the streetcar to this theater one night and I didn't have time to put the blackface on. Mike Shea, who booked all the theaters, said, 'Don't ever put that stuff on your face anymore because your expressions after a joke are priceless.'"

Ted Healy, comic straight man and creator of the Three Stooges, started as a blackface comedian. He left an imprint on American comedy, influencing performers like Milton Berle. "He was one of my idols," said Berle. "I loved his style. He was flippant. He was ad-lib. Threw one-liners. The audience talking back. He was the [Don] Rickles of his day."

Ted Healy hired Moe Howard for an act called the Annette Kellerman Diving Girls. "There were six girls and we four boys," said Howard. "We did a thirty-foot dive into a tank. We wore long bathing suits, the one-piece variety. We quit after a pretty young lady named Gladys Kelly misjudged the tank, broke her neck and was killed instantly."

Ted Healy hired Moe Howard and his brother for a new act. "[Healy] found these three guys and he put them as his assistants," said Berle. "That was the Three Stooges. He brought them out, he lined them up and—this visual bit—he would smack them all at one time."

The cat was initially billed as Ted Healy and His Three Southern Gentlemen, and the assistants were Moe Howard, Shemp Howard and violin player Larry Fine. When first offered the gig, Larry Fine was beholden to his contract with producer Fred Mann and his Rainbow Gardens nightclub. "A few nights later, fate stepped in when the police closed the Rainbow Gardens for violation of the Prohibition laws," said Moe Howard. "Not only was the Gardens shut down, but Fred Mann committed suicide. Now there was no contract problem and Larry was in the act."

The New York Times captured Healy's essence with a review by theater critic Brooks Atkinson: "Mr. Healy is one of those loud, rough, hustling fools who make the most satisfactory comedians. When he tackles a refractory close-harmony singer, murder burns in his eye. When he assaults from the rear, he kicks to kill. When he stuffs two eggs in a bumpkin's mouth, he does not temper the artistic effort with gentleness. Sex does not abash this democratic buffoon; he tackles women around the neck quite as roughly as men. It is a refreshing thing to see. He is dangerous." Healy's onstage violence was an outgrowth of his brooding offstage demeanor. Moe Howard said, "While under the influence, he became a foul-mouthed vicious character."

Healy was drunk the night he tried to kill comedian George Jessel. Jessel supposedly invented the Bloody Mary while trying to concoct a tomato-based hangover cure and named it after Healy's girlfriend, Mary Brown Warburton. The next day Walter Winchell made mention of it in his column. Healy read it backstage at a Chicago vaudeville theater and flew into a rage. "Ted turned white," said Jessel. "What the hell are you doing making a pass at my girl you son of a bitch! He pulled out a pistol and tried to shoot me. I ducked and the shot missed, but as the pistol went off within a foot of my right ear, I was completely deaf for a week."

The Three Stooges started accepting film offers in the early 1930s. Tired of Healy's erratic behavior, they moved on without him. When the Stooges found solo success, Healy filed a lawsuit that laid claim to all poking, slapping and *nyuk nyuk nyuking*. He lost the suit and tried a new act with replacement Stooges, but nothing worked as long as booze controlled him. "Ted was suffering from a bad case of the DT's," said Moe Howard. "We found Ted in his room, screaming. He insisted there were firemen coming through the walls of his room."

Healy died in 1937, and his death became a Hollywood mystery: part reality, part urban legend. "It seems that Ted was at the Trocadero, the famous nightclub on the Sunset Strip," said Howard. "Drinking up a storm, he got into an argument with three patrons. The men went outside and, before Ted had a chance to raise his fists, they jumped him, knocked him to the ground and kicked him in the ribs and stomach. Ted passed away a few days later of a brain concussion."

MGM screenwriter Harry Rapf claimed it was actor Wallace Beery who bashed Healy, but the coroner was adamant that the cause of death was "chronic alcoholism." Some said it was a cover-up. Healy's ex-wife complained, "Police are not investigating the right people." Curly Howard, who five years earlier had replaced his older brother Shemp in the Stooges, said, "It can't be on the level." Healy wasn't long for the world either way, but in creating the Three Stooges and influencing Milton Berle, he had a lasting effect on comedy.

Until the 1920s, most vaudeville shows were without a master of ceremonies. The idea of a host never crossed anyone's mind. Placards with performers' names were the only emcee necessary. San Francisco–born Frank Fay broke that tradition and became renowned as the first of the great comic emcees—and in many minds the first stand-up comedian. Journalist Abel Green witnessed the revolution and said, "Fay pioneered the emcee and made him important."

Fay was a long-standing emcee at the crown jewel of American vaudeville theaters, the Palace. If you played the New York venue in the 1920s, it meant you had made it to the top. To succeed at the Palace was to be a star, the equivalent of a Las Vegas headliner in the 1960s. It was at that venue that Frank Fay not only became a bona fide celebrity, but developed the idea of an emcee. For several years vaudeville used only painted signs with the name of each act to announce who was coming to the stage. Fay changed this common practice, becoming one of the first people to actually emcee a show. His role as an introducer and extroducer was another revolutionary shift in stand-up. He wasn't just introducing, but entertaining as he did so. If the previous act bombed, he warmed the crowd back up, and if the momentum was good, he just kept the show going.

Frank Fay didn't care for physical shtick. He got his laughs by standing in one place and speaking. Strange as it seems now, this low-key convention was unheard of at the time. He stood and talked—no gimmicks. And he held comics who relied on gimmickry in contempt. He would address Bert Lahr, a comedian who utilized facial mugging and costumes: "Well, well, well, what's the *low* comedian doing today?"

Fay had once participated in low comedy himself. Veteran comic Johnny Dyer goaded Fay into showbiz while regularly hustling him in billiards. Dyer wrote an act in which Fay wore baggy pants, roller skates and a fake nose, circling Dyer as he made wisecracks. The eight-minute performance ended with Fay's pants tearing in half. It was a kind of humiliation Fay vowed never to repeat. Out of this embarrassment he blazed a new path as the first pure stand-up comedian.

He hit the circuit in 1917 as "Frank Fay, Nut Monologist," and resistance was immediate. *Variety* critically stated, "Fay needs a good straight man, as before, to feed his eccentric comedy." A comedian standing *alone* onstage? Unheard of. Doesn't this guy know anything about showbiz? To stand still and tell jokes was a foreign move. To perform without some kind of gimmick was considered amateurish. "A comedian without a prop can't click," said actor Wesley Ruggles. "I learned that back in the days when I pushed the props around for Charlie Chaplin. Great pantomist that he is, Chaplin realizes the necessity of props."

Fay succeeded without props and without a partner. He slicked back his hair and put on a well-tailored suit. His act grew stronger and, as people started to respond to his style, his ego ballooned. Other comedians sharing the bill became the targets of his condescending put-downs. Milton Berle once challenged Fay "to a battle of wits." Fay replied, "I never attack an unarmed man." Fay and Berle had one of comedy's great rivalries. It wasn't without reason. Comedy writer Milt Josefsberg said, "In a business known for its lack of bigotry, he [Fay] was a bigot. This was no secret, but widely known and well substantiated." In a business known for its many Jewish comedians, the goyish Fay was vocally anti-Semitic.

Fay performed at the Palace one evening as Berle stood in the wings watching. Fay gestured to the stagehands and yelled, "Get that little Jew bastard out of the wings!" Berle fumed. "I had picked up a stage brace," said Berle. "I reached out and spun him around. Before he knew what was happening, I hit him right across the face with the brace. It ripped his nose apart."

Fay's views were common knowledge in industry circles. "Everybody criticized Frank Fay because of the anti-Semitism," says comedian Will Jordan. "Everyone was on Berle's side, but in actual fact Fay was much better than Berle. When they went onstage Frank Fay would just cut him to pieces."

Fay was so disliked by his fellow performers that jokes at his expense became famous. Fred Allen said, "The last time I saw Frank Fay he was walking down Lover's Lane holding his own hand." When Fay married movie star Barbara Stanwyck, the joke went:

"Who is the actor with the biggest prick in Hollywood?"

"Barbara Stanwyck."

Despite his unlikable offstage demeanor, Fay turned into the most consistent stand-up comic of the late 1920s and essentially changed the art form. Crowds and critics eventually came to accept a man standing alone, cracking wise. No longer did Fay bill himself as a "Nut Monologist." Now he used egomaniacal monikers like "The Great Fay," "The King" and "Broadway's Favorite Son." One snide reporter wrote, "Fay forgot to mention who made the appointment."

Those who could overlook his racism and narcissism held him in extraordinary regard. "Frank Fay was something else," said Bob Hope. "He was just a sensational man that could do more with *nothing*, with attitude, than any man I ever saw on the stage."

As influential as Fay was to stand-up, the Marx Brothers were to comedy as a whole. When they entered show business at the start of the century, vaudeville was already a family trade. Their mother, Minnie, was sibling to Al Shean, part of the famous comedy team Gallagher and Shean. So vast was the popularity of Gallagher and Shean that they spawned low-rent knockoffs, and the Keith circuit sent down the directive: "Only one Gallagher and Shean imitator allowed per show."

Minnie Marx managed her sons, the well-remembered Groucho, Harpo and Chico and their less beloved brothers Zeppo and Gummo. Groucho remembered an early gig they did at the Henderson Music Hall on Coney Island. "That's where Harpo appeared on stage for the first time. At the opening performance he shit his pants."

The Marx Brothers crisscrossed North America for twenty-five years, sharing the bill with struggling unknowns like Jack Benny, W. C. Fields and Charles Chaplin. Groucho first saw Chaplin while killing time between performances in a small Canadian town. "It was a real dump. Chaplin was doing an act there called "A Night at the Club." I never heard an audience laugh like he made that audience laugh. I went back to tell the boys about him. I told them, 'I just saw the greatest comedian in the world. I don't know who he is, but you have to meet him.' We had to leave for the next town but we managed to get acquainted with him there. He was getting $25.00 a week and was dressing with five other guys in one room . . . Chaplin would wear a high neck shirt. He'd wear it for two weeks, then wash it and put it on again. He only had one shirt! . . . Five years later I went to California and he was living in a huge home and fucking all the leading ladies."

Chico, Groucho, Gummo, Harpo and Zeppo received their stage names from monologist Art Fisher, who equated them with comic strip characters. "At that time there was a very popular comic strip called Knocko the Monk," said Harpo. "As a result there was a rash of stage names that ended in 'o.' On every bill there would be at least one Bingo, Zingo, Socko, Jumpo or Bumpo."

Future comedian Jack Benny was playing in the orchestra pit when they passed through Illinois. Minnie Marx asked him to join the Marx Brothers as their accompanist. "She was impressed by my playing and sight reading and offered me fifteen dollars a week plus transportation and room and board to travel with her young sons," said Benny. But his mother felt he was too young and nixed the idea immediately. Benny was somewhat relieved to keep a distance. "We weren't very close. In fact, I never knew whether I liked them or not. I was always a little afraid of them."

Benny crossed paths with them later when he became a professional vaudeville comedian. He hated how they disrupted the balance of the bill. The Marx Brothers had a fast, manic act and it was hard for the methodically paced Benny to compete. "Benny didn't know what kind of a living hell he was headed for," said Harpo Marx. "For thirty solid weeks he had to follow the Marx Brothers on the bill." Benny said, "The thing was that *nobody* could follow the Marx Brothers." W. C. Fields experienced the same nightmare. "Most of the time Fields would find himself playing to only half a house because a lot of people would leave after our act," said Groucho. "One day Fields went to see the manager of the theater and told him he had to leave for New York. He said, 'You see this hand? I can't juggle anymore because I've got noxis on the conoxsis and I have to see a specialist right away.' He just made up a word because he didn't want to continue following our act."

In 1924 the Marx Brothers took their vaudeville act to Broadway and opened in a legitimate show called *I'll Say She Is*. It brought them to a new breed of audience and furthered their status. When they returned to vaudeville they feuded with Edward F. Albee over budgetary allotments. Albee, angered, fired them and pressured theater operators not to hire them. "We had kicked ourselves smack off the pinnacle of vaudeville," said Harpo Marx. "Too late, we learned that Albee's power ranged far beyond his own empire. When you were on his blacklist, doors were closed in your face all over town."

The Marx Brothers were relegated to a B circuit and no longer encountered Jack Benny. Benny knew he wasn't capable of the madcap pace of the Marxes and instead took cues from low-key, post-Fay monologists like Julius Tannen.

Benny was influenced by Tannen just as Tannen was the first to emulate Frank Fay. It was still a fresh phenomenon. "Julius Tannen [was] for years one of the most brilliant monologists in vaudeville and revue," wrote historian Marian Spitzer. "His humor was based on ideas, not gags. He was a witty comedian, a quick mind and an economy of effort." Comedian Joe E. Brown said, "The thing that impressed me most was that he just put on his hat and walked on stage, took it off, chatted awhile, then put his hat on again and walked off." Benny admitted he "deliberately copied" Tannen while still an amateur comic. When a newspaper columnist saw Benny perform he wrote, "Evidently he has seen Julius Tannen . . . but not often enough."

Benny suffered many rough gigs billed as Ben Benny—Fun with a Fiddle, a shameless way to cash in on the popularity of violin-playing bandleader-comic Ben Bernie. Dim-witted bookers confused Ben Benny with Ben Bernie and the amateur Benny got a lot of accidental work. Ben Bernie's lawyers sent a cease-and-desist letter. In order to appease them he added a middle initial and started performing as Ben K. Benny: Fiddle Funology. The minor amendment wasn't enough and threats of legal action persisted until he changed his name from Ben to Jack. With the new clarification, Benny saw his bookings fall by half.

When Benny saw vaudeville comedian Phil Baker—a former partner of Ben Bernie's—he stole from his act as well. Blatantly performing Baker's material, he diverted potential criticism by billing himself as Jack Benny: Phil Baker's Brother. A review of Benny's act from March 1920 said, "Benny says that he is the brother of Phil Baker, who was here last week. And since he is quite as amusing as Baker and has all his tricks of voice and expression, why dispute him?"

Phil Baker had a cast of characters that insulted him and he would deadpan to the audience in response. It was the template for the eventual Jack Benny mold in which a wisecracking group made fun of his shallow vanity. Benny developed on the shoulders of others—but he was no chump. He knew a career could not be sustained on theft alone. So rather than continue stealing from Baker, he hired Baker's head writer.

Al Boasberg was an influential comedy writer who focused on format and persona rather than jokes. Not only was he Baker's main writer, but he essentially created the comic personalities of Jack Benny, Milton Berle, George Burns and Bob Hope.

He also created a common vaudeville convention in which hecklers were planted in the audience. Boasberg wrote a sketch for Phil Baker in which comic Sid Silvers sat in a theater box seat and shouted carefully written barbs. It became a popular conduit for straight man/punch line banter. Bob Hope took the idea and used female hecklers in the box seat, to great comedic success. The gimmick was resurrected years later on *The Muppet Show*.

Boasberg crafted the persona of the Ben Bernie Orchestra, turning them into a wild group of carousing, drunken party animals (the same persona later adapted for the Phil Harris Orchestra on *The Jack Benny Program*). Boasberg also wrote a routine for George Burns and his wife, Gracie Allen, called "Lamb Chops," in which he forced George Burns to play straight to his clueless spouse for the first time. He wrote a monologue for a teenage Milton Berle in which Berle proclaimed proudly he wrote all his own stuff and would never steal a routine—and then rattled off a series of trademark jokes identified with others.

Boasberg designed a persona for Jack Benny as a vain man who didn't realize he was the butt of the joke. Humorist Robert Benchley caught the new act in 1924 and found it hysterical, but other critics missed the put-on and criticized Benny for "egotism and aloofness."

After eighteen months using the Boasberg blueprint, Benny enjoyed his first real wave of success. He absorbed the influence of Phil Baker, Ben Bernie, Julius Tannen and Al Boasberg. In doing so he became one of the most successful comedians of his generation.

When Ben Bernie sent his lawyers after Benny, it demonstrated one of vaudeville comedy's biggest problems. Thievery was a reality and it was difficult to prove who originated what. "Comedy acts were always the targets of the pirates," said Fred Allen. "If a comedian was original and wrote his own material, he soon found that other comedians were stealing parts of his act. For many years performers had no way to protect their gags, parodies or bits of business."

The vaudeville term for a joke thief was a "chooser." The National Vaudeville Artists (a company union started by Albee in 1916 to circumvent actual labor unions) put together a plan to stop choosers. Fred Allen explained, "Any member could protect his act. All he had to do was enclose a copy of his material in a sealed envelope and deliver it to the NVA office. The envelope was placed in the files of the Protected Material Department. Later, if a plagiarist was brought to bay, the envelope was opened and the NVA officials dispensed justice. Hundreds of acts protected their material through this service." But when vaudeville died, so did the National Vaudeville Artists—and the enormous archive within the Protected Material Department. According to Allen, "Before the members vacated the clubhouse on 46th Street, some official, by whose authority nobody will ever know, sold the entire contents of the NVA Protected Material files to [comedy team] Olsen and Johnson."

Fred Allen was noted for not having an enemy in the world. But in the case of successful 1920s Broadway comic Eddie Cantor he made an exception. Cantor's mother died of lung disease when he was a toddler and his father abandoned him shortly thereafter. It created a lifelong insecurity that manifested in difficult behavior. "Cantor was a sneaky little man," says comedian Jack Carter. "He was never liked by the others."

Cantor's enormous fame came from the lavish Broadway revues of Florenz Ziegfeld. Ziegfeld made stars out of several comedians, including Fanny Brice, W. C. Fields, Bert Williams and Ed Wynn. Known as the *Ziegfeld Follies*, these revues were essentially vaudeville shows in disguise, featuring many of the same people and material, but admission was three times the price and the production was placed in a bourgeois setting. "Producers found that with the proper amount of glittering costumes, they could turn a vaudeville bill into a $2 legitimate stage revue," said Joe Laurie Jr. "The raids on vaudeville talent began and [they] had to struggle to keep their acts from deserting. Vaudeville comedians became harder to find, and harder to hold."

The *Ziegfeld Follies* had gorgeous showgirls doing elaborate dance numbers. Between those numbers were comedy sketches with top comedians. For Ziegfeld they were a necessary evil. "Ziegfeld loathed comedians," wrote *Life*, "and tolerated them merely as time-fillers in his shows to enable the girls to make their costume changes."

Ziegfeld signed Eddie Cantor for the *Ziegfeld Follies* in 1916. Comedy writer Gene Buck wrote his sketches and Cantor worked hard to make them a hit. Contemporaries said his work ethic covered for a lack of talent. "Eddie Cantor had to fight for his laughs," said Milton Berle. "He wasn't born a funny man." Broadway luminary George S. Kaufman said, "Cantor's humor is painted on like his blackface."

One of Cantor's costars was Bert Williams, considered by some historians as the greatest African American comedian who ever lived. When Ziegfeld hired him as his star comic a few years earlier, a racist band of actors informed the impresario they would abandon the show in protest rather than perform alongside him. "Go if you want to," Ziegfeld told them. "I can replace every one of you—except the man you want me to fire." Cantor said Williams was the "best Negro comedian to trod the boards. The best teacher I ever had. Working alongside him in the *Ziegfeld Follies* I studied his extraordinary powers as a pantomist, his incomparable way with an audience—manipulating their emotions as if they were puppets on strings. A moment of silence as they watched his gestures, his shuffle, his expressive face and hands—then—thunderous applause."

Williams was in a turn-of-the-century comedy team with straight man George Walker. In 1911, when Walker died, Williams went solo and found success with signature songs that he talk-sang. He got his laughs with under-the-breath comments (not unlike comedian Jim Gaffigan a hundred years later), as the songs themselves were not meant to be funny. His signature routine was a melancholic song called "Nobody," all about a lonely loser. It was a sad bit of humanity that audiences demanded, and Williams grew sick of it. "Before I got through with 'Nobody' I could have wished that both the author of the words and the assembler of the tune had been strangled or drowned or talked to death. For seven whole years I had to sing it. Month after month I tried to drop it and sing something new, but audiences seemed to want nothing else. Every comedian at some time in his life learns to curse the particular stunt of his that was most popular."

Bert Williams was the most popular African American comedian of his time. There were others, like Eddie Green, a writer of Black comedy revues who later hit it big on the radio sitcom *Duffy's Tavern*; Miller & Lyles, popular sketch comedians between 1910 and 1925 who accused the creators of *Amos 'n' Andy* of plagiarism; and 1920s dancing hipster comics Buck & Bubbles, who kidded each other with jazz slang and smooth moves. Williams had the greatest crossover success, but despite being a Broadway star he was treated with contempt when he walked offstage—as were most of his brethren. "Conditions outside of New York were not too rosy for the sepia-skinned," wrote Laurie Jr. "[This] was made evident by a convention of Negro actors held in Washington, D.C. . . . to improve conditions of the colored circuit. Negro thespians also banded together in an organization called The Frogs, a Negro version of The Friars."

During vaudeville the Friars Club grew into the most famous comedians' fraternity in history. Noted for cigar-smoking comics and profane roasts, it was founded under bizarre auspices in 1904. New York press agents were swindled by scam artists posing as journalists, doing so in order to score free theater tickets. The tickets were scalped and the swindlers cleared a profit. Thus, the Press Agents Association was formed to distinguish legitimate journalists from the bums. Eventually showmen and others in the Broadway realm were nominated for membership and it became known as the Friars Club. It accepted all creeds, in contrast to "restricted" showbiz fraternities like the Lambs Club, which initially had racist membership rules.

The very first Friars Roast, or the closest thing to it, took place in 1921 under the name "Friars Insult Night." It was a fund-raiser for the Relief Fund, at five dollars a seat. The Friars themselves were a charity case, usually in arrears, unable to pay bills or wages. Their early Manhattan home was auctioned to cover their debts, and their membership roll of fifteen hundred became depleted; by the 1930s the club was all but dead. Indeed, for a long time, the only notoriety the Friars Club enjoyed was death itself. Famous agent William Morris had a heart attack on its premises while playing pinochle. William Morris dead at the Friars Club—must be some kind of showbiz metaphor.

Vaudeville grew throughout the 1920s, and Albee invested heavily in new ventures. He did not foresee the stock market crash, nor was he concerned about the ascendence of radio or talking pictures. Vaudeville enjoyed one last hurrah in its naiveté. Laurie Jr. said Albee shelled out for "beautiful lobbies with oil paintings that cost thousands of dollars, rugs that cost more thousands, dressing rooms with bath that compared to the finest hotels, and he even furnished Turkish towels to the actors. A green room that a millionaire's home could boast of." However, the elaborate theaters were not always full and the comedians who had "made it" often felt as if they had not. "Performers usually worked three or four shows a day for very little money," said George Burns. "Sometimes, at the five o'clock show, there would be fifteen people sitting in a 1200-seat house."

By the 1920s the most important theater in vaudeville was the Palace, at Broadway and 47th. If you headlined the Palace, it was understood you were among the highest-paid performers in show business. Phil Baker got five thousand dollars a week, Eddie Cantor eight thousand, and the Marx Brothers ten thousand for a six-day engagement. It was a time when the average weekly American salary was one hundred dollars.

Milton Berle, George Burns, Bob Hope—the comedians who dominated comedy in the decades to come—received their vaudeville breaks at the Palace, and they got those breaks just in time. "Just as we were becoming stars, vaudeville was dying," said Burns. "Movies, vaudeville, burlesque, the local stock companies—all survived together. Then radio came in. For the first time people didn't have to leave their homes to be entertained."

The vaudeville moguls panicked. Albee-Keith-Orpheum had seven hundred theaters and twenty-five thousand performers under contract in 1929. Weekly attendance was an estimated twelve million. The moguls funded a widespread propaganda campaign to warn about "the dangers of radio." They funded newspaper editorials bemoaning the hearing loss radio caused and the house fires started by receiver sets. Vaudeville financed aggressive lies, but it was no use. RCA had developed the all-electric receiving set in 1925 and a year later released the "perfected radio tube," which operated with alternating current. "This was a revolutionary advance," said radio columnist Ben Gross. "It did away with the need for those cumbersome acid-seeping batteries which had disfigured millions of American living rooms. Radio now was so simple that even a child could tune it in without fuss, mess or bother."

General Electric and RCA advanced technology and became more powerful than the vaudeville tycoons. They used radio to further their own means and circumvent their adversaries. Historian Erik Barnouw wrote that GE and RCA, "born of a military establishment, and still closely linked to it, had now also acquired a special relationship to a wide spectrum of big business and its advertising agencies. No such constellation had ever planned and controlled a nation's popular culture. Most programs were being produced by advertising agencies, as an activity parallel to the planning and designing of billboards and magazine advertisements." Vaudeville would lose out to newer, more powerful business interests.

Joe Laurie Jr., much quoted here, was the most credible of all vaudeville historians. In 1950 and 1953 he published two massive books chronicling the history of vaudeville. His masterwork—a total of fifteen hundred pages—took eleven years to complete. For him it was not merely radio that killed vaudeville, but a betrayal of its roots. "The backbone of vaudeville was low comedy. Albee dressed up vaudeville fit to kill and it committed suicide. It became something that was neither variety, burlesque nor revue. The performers, forced to dress to match Albee's million-dollar theaters (which were too large for comedy), looked no different to the audiences who could see tuxedos anywhere. Anyway, the customers stopped coming."

The Great Depression was no help. The stock market crashed and people lost their disposable income. New genres like the "endurance contest" lured away vaudeville patrons with a chance to win cash. "They flocked to watch who could sit on ice longer, who could hurl rolling pins further," said Laurie Jr. Vaudeville profits dwindled and star comedians fled to radio. The medium reaped large profits while other businesses crumbled. Radio paid comics massive sums, and vaudeville no longer could.

As vaudeville died, so too did its perverted cousin. "A whipped dog, the burlesque industry retreated into the shadows," wrote Irving Zeidman. "Most of the houses in operation in the rest of the country went back to the side streets and obscure locations. When these, in turn, were censored out of business, the operators withdrew still further—to Skid Row. Many of the operators were bankrupt."

Investors turned to radio, as did the crowds. It became impossible to get Wall Street backers for a vaudeville show. Its death was never so absolute as when the ornate Palace fell into disarray, unable to pay its bills. It was "no longer the pinnacle of the entertainment world," according to Phil Silvers. "This was no living."

CHAPTER TWO

RADIO

Vaudeville sputtered in denial at the start of the new decade, but by 1933 it was clearly dead, its old theaters canceling the stage shows and replacing them with movies. But in radio the vaudeville gags and gagmen lived on. There were three million radio sets in 1923 when vaudeville was still humming. By 1936 there were thirty million radio sets in American homes and everyone had forgotten vaudeville ever existed.

Radio's golden age was rather brief—the mid-1930s through the early 1950s—but it lasted long enough to create some beloved comic personalities that endured for the rest of the century. Radio made millionaires out of comedians who had toiled for years touring the vaudeville circuits and performing in Broadway revues.

Eddie Cantor was one of radio's first major comedians. By the start of the 1930s Cantor was a bona fide star, having triumphed on Broadway and in vaudeville, movies and books. The final medium for Cantor to conquer was radio—and he did, to the amazement of many. His broad motions and brash speech pattern were designed to reach large crowds in massive theaters and seemed out of place in the subtle medium. His writer, Philip Rapp, said, "Possibly because there was very little to listen to in those days, the Cantor program remained on top of the rating services."

Cantor was paid a hundred dollars a minute for his first radio guest shot, a five-minute monologue on *The Eveready Hour* in 1931. It led to a hosting job on *The Chase and Sanborn Hour,* and his following grew. Mel Brooks was a young fan at the time. "Eddie Cantor was very important to me. Very influential on my work. The

sketches were fast and furious—and Cantor was great at supporting the other guy in the sketch. It was Cantor who was making it
all work for me."

The comedy community at the time was less impressed. "Cantor was the first man to wear costumes for a radio audience," said
Rapp. "Laughs were mystifying to the home listener. Laughs were
provoked by gestures and other means. When script lines were cut
we wound up with nothing but trash." Physical shtick and funny
costumes played the same role as laugh tracks did years later; if
the people at home heard an audience laughing they figured it
must be funny—even if the laughter had little relation to what was
being said.

Radio critics treated Cantor's show harshly, and he was sensitive to their scorn. Ben Gross and Abe Greenberg gave Cantor
unfavorable reviews and Cantor called them out over the air. In
response Gross and Greenberg filed individual libel suits against
him—and won.

Cantor's ego ballooned, to the detriment of those around him.
Irving Fein, the veteran manager of Jack Benny and George Burns,
said, "The cast of the Eddie Cantor program always complained that
whenever one of them got a big laugh at rehearsal, Cantor would
immediately change the dialogue so that he could take the funny
line." Comedy writer Mort Lachman said, "He begged for laughs
and that bothered me. He was a difficult man to work with, a very
limited talent, but he got the most out of what he had."

The disparity between Cantor's onstage persona and offstage
personality was an issue. He was sold to the public as a family man
with five daughters, but within showbiz circles he was considered a
sexual harasser and philanderer. "Cantor liked the girls," said radio
actress Jean Vander Pyl. "And he liked to goose them. He would
wait until they were on the air, so that they couldn't protest and no
one would know. On one occasion, he goosed Billie [Bellport], who
was a sweet naive thing. She was so unprepared she went, 'Oh, Mr.
Cantor!' and he had to quickly cover. Cantor was fuming. He came
storming off the set, 'Don't ever use that girl again.'" Comedy writer
Bob Weiskopf said, "He was chasing women around while poor Ida

[Cantor's wife] would sit in her room crying. But all the mothers loved him. My own mother refused to believe he wasn't a nice man."

Cantor was eventually knocked off the air by the competition— *Major Bowes Amateur Hour*, a forerunner to *American Idol* type of programming. Philip Rapp relished the poetic justice: "The world's greatest professional toppled by amateurs."

As radio progressed, so did methods of marketing. Advertising agencies controlled the early radio shows. They dictated the content and packaged the talent. The advertising agencies provided the money and as such filled the airwaves with Madison Avenue hucksterism. The success of comedian Joe Penner was such a creation.

Penner was an early radio comedian whose popularity was based on gimmickry. He toured with an exotic dancer named Sheikee in the late 1920s, but an obscenity bust scared him off the circuit. Influenced by fellow comic Al Reeves, who segued gags shouting, "Give me credit, boys," Penner created his own catchphrases. Penner became a hit repeating the phrases "You na-ah-asty man!" and "Wanna buy a duck?"

While playing vaudeville with dancer-actor Russ Tamblyn's father, Penner was signed by a scout from the Rudy Vallee radio program. His 1933 guest shot went over well enough that the J. Walter Thompson marketing agency felt it could manufacture a spin-off. Penner was paid seven thousand dollars a week as star of *The Baker's Broadcast*.

Penner had a whiny, childlike voice that annoyed adults and appealed to children. The style of his program was juvenile but undeniably popular, a sort of *Gilligan's Island* of the air. His catchphrase "Wanna buy a duck?" was merchandised shamelessly. Rubber ducks with the Joe Penner seal of approval polluted department store shelves. Moronic songs like "Doin' the Ducky-Wuck" were sold as Joe Penner sheet music. As the merchandisers cashed in, so too did Hollywood. Film studio RKO starred Penner in several cheap movies alongside comedians Jack Oakie and Harry "Parkyakarkus"

Einstein. He toured the country making personal appearances in an all-white suit. The color was a necessity. "Wherever we went, we were invited to the swankiest restaurants," said lead Penner writer Parke Levy. "The owners always thought they had a novel publicity idea when they would have Joe Penner hold a live duck. They gave him a live duck for the photographers to snap, and the ducks always shit all over him—all over his pretty white suit. The suit would be immaculate and he would have that smile and the duck would be shitting all over him."

Like any career based on a gimmick, Penner's dissipated as quickly as it rose. After his show had been on the radio for two and a half seasons, the public grew tired of hearing "Wanna buy a duck?" He was a marginal figure by the 1940s, when he accidentally overdosed on sleeping pills at the age of thirty-six.

It was singer Rudy Vallee who gave Penner his first radio shot. Vallee was the Johnny Carson of his day, introducing new acts and turning them into stars. He was immensely popular. "During the span between 1928 and 1933, the king of crooners won a degree of feminine adulation," wrote radio critic Ben Gross. "The Vallee fans were the original fanatics of radio." George Burns & Gracie Allen, Edgar Bergen, Milton Berle, Fanny Brice and Bert Lahr all had their radio debuts with Vallee. An unknown comic named Victor Borge was his audience warm-up man. But while Vallee got credit for introducing many future giants of comedy, the actual booking process had little to do with him. "Rudy Vallee's great claim to fame was that these stars were on his show," said one of his writers, Paul Henning. "That was none of his doing—they were all chosen for him—he just fronted the band."

"He never wrote a line, never edited a line and never really could tell a joke," said Norman Panama, another of Vallee's writers. "He had absolutely no talent and the show deservedly went off the air." Comedy writer Jess Oppenheimer was frustrated by Vallee's lack of comic savvy. "We once wrote a long sketch that ended with Rudy delivering a great punch line. It was met with uproarious laughter.

In the middle of the following week's show, Rudy suddenly turned to the audience and ad-libbed the same punch line—this time by itself, without any of the preceding material. The audience just stared at him. Rudy later told me he couldn't understand why last week's audience thought the line was so much funnier."

Comedian Ed Wynn entered radio in 1932 and pioneered the idea of a studio audience. The Ziegfeld veteran was terrified of an audience he couldn't see. His son, Keenan, said, "He got so scared about his ability to keep an unseen audience laughing that he was the reluctant dragon of Madison Avenue when it came to signing a contract." A Texaco advertising executive attended four Ed Wynn performances with his back turned to the stage. He wanted to see how Wynn's act played without the visual element. Wynn was signed by NBC for five thousand dollars a week, with his contract stipulating the need for a live audience. Texaco footed the bill to have the radio studio renovated, and the studio audience was invented.

Ed Wynn, like many vaudevillians, had a great memory for old jokes. That mental reservoir came into play when a radio writer tried to pass off an old gag as new. "Snag Werris worked for *The Ed Wynn Show*," says comedian Jack Carter. "He gave Wynn a joke [in the writers room] and Wynn said, 'Come with me!' They left the theater, got in a cab, went to Ed's home, went up to his office. Ed had walls of boxes and crates. He pulled them out and pulled out pages and and pages! And there was the joke. Ed said, 'There! There's the joke you gave me today! You see? Don't *ever* do that to me again.'"

The Kate Smith Hour was an important radio showcase for comedians. It revolved around the famed singer's introducing different guests, including a comic who'd Americanized his family name, Jungmann. "I put thirty guys in business," said Henny Youngman. "When I was on *Kate Smith* I had six writers, so every week I told twenty-six jokes. A lot of comics started from those routines. They couldn't afford routines. They were all amateurs at the time. Buddy Hackett. Jan

Murray. Red Buttons. All of these guys started in the business with my jokes."

Paramount studio executives offered him a contract based on his *Kate Smith Hour* appearances. Not wanting to screw over a show that had given him his break, Youngman scouted for a replacement. He went to New Jersey with his friend Pat Cristillo, who wanted Youngman to see his brother's act. The brother was Lou Costello. "So we went out there and that's where I first saw and met Abbott & Costello," said Youngman. "They were working in burlesque and because burlesque comedy had by that time become filthy to keep up with the stripteasers, Bud and Lou were working very dirty."

Despite their salacious material, Youngman recommended Abbott & Costello to Kate Smith's manager. The hiring of Abbott & Costello was controversial in the burlesque community. Burlesque had stock routines and it was no big deal if one comic had the same act as another. But no one expected interchangeable burlesque routines to find a home on a national broadcast. Other comedy teams like Wheeler & Woolsey and Howard & George had done versions of "Who's on First?" prior to Bud and Lou, but Abbott & Costello now got all the credit.

Regardless of where they got their style, Abbott & Costello influenced future comedians. "Bud Abbott was a genius," said Mel Brooks. "Lou Costello was one of the greatest comics in movies. Together Bud and Lou were sublimely funny."

Abbott & Costello would become the most successful comedy team in movies, but in radio the distinction belonged not to Abbott & Costello, but to two white guys pretending to be black—Charles Correll and Freeman Gosden.

Amos 'n' Andy was a serialized sitcom with established characters. Its radio competition was joke-driven, while *Amos 'n' Andy* presented season-long sagas with the arc of a soap opera. Historian Elizabeth McLeod said, "While minstrel-style wordplay humor was common in the formative years of the program, it was used less often as the series developed, giving way to a more sophisticated approach to characterization."

Remembered for controversy rather than content, *Amos 'n' Andy* was one of the most prolific comedies in broadcast history. Airing for fifteen minutes, five days a week, it had broadcast 4,091 episodes by 1943, when it became a weekly half-hour broadcast.

There were objections to the audio blackface of Charles Correll and Freeman Gosden as early as 1930. *Radio Digest* published a complaint from a listener: "I have never heard negroes (and I was 'fotched up' among them) talk as these two comedians talk." An accompanying article said, "Similar protests have been received from dwellers in Virginia, Louisiana, Mississippi and elsewhere. Particularly do the correspondents say that 'Andy' Correll's use of [malapropisms] are out of place." *The Pittsburgh Courier* called *Amos 'n' Andy* a racist program in May 1931 and published letters of support: "I am glad to know that there is one paper that is willing to take up the fight against the two 'crackers' from the South. If Amos 'n' Andy and the rest of their kind would spend a little of their time broadcasting about the lynching and burning of Negroes in the South, I am sure that we could get some benefit and America could hold her head up. Please don't give up the good fight."

To offset the controversy, Correll and Gosden became one of the only network shows to hire nonwhite cast members. In 1938 African American actress Ernestine Wade was hired to play Andy's girlfriend and Asian American actress Barbara Jean Wong was hired as Amos's daughter. Four years later James Baskett, Ruby Dandridge, Jester Hairston, Lillian Randolph and Ernest Whitman—all African American—were added to the cast. While Correll and Gosden did audio blackface through the war years, they employed more black actors than any other show.

When *Amos 'n' Andy* moved from radio to television in 1951, the executive director of the NAACP called the program a "gross libel on the Negro and a distortion of the truth . . . The picturization of Negroes as amoral, semi-literate, lazy, stupid, scheming and dishonest perpetuates a harmful stereotype which departed with the old minstrel show." There was less stomach for racial comedy after the days of Hitler. *Amos 'n' Andy* faded away.

The Jack Benny Program featured the most prominent African American comedian in radio. Eddie Anderson played Benny's valet, Rochester Van Jones. His raspy voice and sarcastic comments frequently upstaged the star. Anderson and Benny had the chemistry of a great comedy team—but with one being black and the other white, no one dared describe them as such.

Benny was one of the most enduring comedians of the twentieth century, and he managed to do something no other comedian could boast of. His persona as a miserly penny-pincher was established in the 1930s and became so ingrained in the American consciousness that it made setups unnecessary. Whenever a store clerk told him the cost of a piece of merchandise, Benny could evoke and then milk a laugh by simply remaining silent. These were punch lines in 1959 that had been set up in 1939, a remarkable feat that was never again equaled.

Benny's penurious character emerged on his first series in 1932, sponsored by Canada Dry. "The president of the advertising agency representing Canada Dry Ginger Ale thought I was funny," said Benny. "His client wanted to be in radio with a variety program and he talked them into making me a star." Comedian Bobby Ramsen explains, "During that first sponsorship, Canada Dry decided if they could get their hands on the empty bottles, offer a deposit of two cents, they could reuse them. The writers started to give Benny lines like, 'I'm so excited. Today is the day I'm bringing back four bottles of Canada Dry and I'll get eight cents!'" Canada Dry eventually objected to being ridiculed and canceled the show.

Chevrolet was Benny's next sponsor, footing the bill for two years. The critics named Benny the best radio comedian of 1934, but Chevrolet president William Knudsen decided Benny wasn't funny and pulled out. A lot of people were tricked by the program's unconventional structure; the majority of the laughs went to his supporting players and were derived from Benny's hesitant silence. Nothing he actually *said* got laughs, and people like Mr. Knudsen felt he was a lousy comic. As critic Gary Giddins wrote, "He may be the only great comedian in history who isn't associated with a single witticism. He was the ultimate reactor—and it made him a comedy star."

Eddie Anderson joined *The Jack Benny Program* in 1937. The *Benny* cast was going by train from New York to Los Angeles in his first episode and the script called for a porter. "He was a traditional Negro dialect stereotype," recalled Benny. "He had a molasses drawl and he yassuh-bossed me all over the place. He was such a drawling, lazy, superstitious stereotype that even the original Uncle Tom would have despised him." Benny Rubin was initially slated for the part, but writers figured a white actor doing a black drawl would not win the same laughs as an African American actor doing the same. Eddie Anderson was hired and he would soon be the highest-paid African American actor in the world, but first he had to shed the caricature. Racist stereotypes were not uncommon prior to the Second World War, but as Benny writer Milt Josefsberg said, "Jokes of that insensitive sort tapered off during the war years, and when Jack's new quartet of writers joined him in 1943, such punch lines were at a minimum and soon became non-existent."

European fascism changed comedy in America. Benny explained, "During World War II, attitudes changed. Hitler's ideology of Aryan supremacy put all ethnic humor in a bad light. When the black man's fight for equal rights and fair play became an issue after the War, I would no longer allow Rochester to say or do anything that an audience would consider degrading." Benny's attitude toward race relations was enlightened. Starting in 1940 he refused to play any segregated venue. In the 1960s when his agent scheduled a world tour, Benny chastised him for booking a gig in apartheid South Africa and refused to appear.

Although he is increasingly forgotten, Benny was influential in his time. When Kraft Foods sponsored his show starting in the late 1930s, Jell-O was the company's worst seller. After a season of plugs on the Benny program, it was Kraft's number one product, and "Jell-O" remains a household word. He influenced subsequent comedians from Bob Newhart to Albert Brooks. "The biggest influence was Jack Benny," said Brooks. "He was at the center of a storm, he let his players do the work, and just by being there made it funny."

American neutrality in the face of European fascism in the late 1930s was a concern for many Jewish comedians, and seemed to embolden anti-Semites. Jack Benny and George Burns received an onslaught of vicious, anti-Semitic hate mail—and it was only amplified after they were indicted on charges of international jewel smuggling.

"Jack Benny and I were arrested for smuggling jewelry," said Burns. "It really shook up Gracie [Allen]. We were having dinner at 21 one night with a charming man named Albert Chaperau and his wife. She was wearing an unusually wide diamond bracelet. I admired it and told them I'd like to buy one just like it for Gracie. 'I'll tell you what,' Chaperau said. 'I'll sell you this one.'"

Benny's wife, Mary, was known in the Beverly Hills social scene for her petty jealousies. Eyeing Gracie's new bracelet, she goaded Benny into purchasing jewelry from Chaperau as well. "What none of us knew was that the jewelry had been smuggled into the country," said Burns. A few months later Chaperau got into an argument with his German maid. When Chaperau spoke ill of the Nazis, the maid took offense and tipped off local customs agents to his smuggling ring, leading them to Benny and Burns. "After a brief investigation," said Burns, "Jack and I were charged with possession of smuggled jewelry."

Chaperau was a bona fide con man. The *Los Angeles Times* reported that Chaperau was "his name at the moment. Investigation revealed that his claims of being a Nicaraguan diplomat, his ploy for getting baggage through customs without inspection, were utterly false. In fact, Chaperau was born Nathan Shapiro and under that name had served eighteen months after being convicted of mail fraud." Chaperau pleaded guilty, and there was a real concern this would end the careers of the comedians. "Under a strict interpretation of the law, we were guilty," said Burns. "I pleaded guilty on a misdemeanor in Federal Court." The papers reported Benny was "pale and nervous [as he] pleaded not guilty to the smuggling charge. He faces a maximum of six years in prison."

The Burns and Allen Show lost its sponsor in the panic and NBC radio was nervous, quietly coaxing New York State prosecutors to resolve the matter. "The executives at NBC, General Foods and the advertising agency were in a state of hysteria," said Benny. "They kept talking about 'public relations' and 'strategy' for handling the press and what kind of statements I should make. The main problem was how would this influence the sales of Jell-O? At that moment I was probably the single most popular radio star in the country. I didn't want to plead guilty."

They received a suspended sentence of one year and one day and were fined fifteen thousand and ten thousand dollars, respectively. It was little more than a week's salary for them, but reputations were hurt as newspaper editorials decried the "special treatment" allotted these celebrities.

John Cahill was the U.S. district attorney grilling Benny during the case. Ten years later when Benny's contract was up with NBC, it sent its legal team to renegotiate. One of the lawyers was Cahill, who had switched from public to private service. According to Benny the memory was so sore that rather than renegotiate with Cahill, he took his whole operation to CBS.

The maid who squealed on Chaperau received an award of nine thousand dollars. She was an avowed Nazi, but the U.S. government was still a neutral observer of the German situation and had no problem handing a Nazi a generous check.

Criticism of the Nazis was not allowed on American radio prior to 1941. Powerful radio sponsors frowned on anything that might offend German consumers. "One sponsor would own the whole show, so therefore he was very powerful," said radio writer Sol Saks. "They were very tough. The radio writers were looked down upon. We were all young, we were all in our early twenties, most of us were Jewish." The American Tobacco Company had been wary of its client Eddie Cantor ever since he raised eighteen thousand dollars to help five hundred Jewish children escape Nazism in 1935. When Cantor spoke out against Hitler in 1938, American Tobacco wanted to cancel his show. Fascist sympathizers harassed Cantor in his own studio audience. According to his April 1939 FBI file, "After the conclusion of a recent broadcast in Hollywood, Cantor made some remarks about Hitler and an individual in the rear of the studio arose and left and was followed by two persons, who are reported to have attacked him after engaging in a verbal dispute outside the studio. Apparently the incident, as well as Cantor's remarks, were very disgusting to the broadcasting company officials and he is becoming increasingly unpopular in radio circles."

Booked by a women's group for a speaking engagement, Cantor told his audience that Hitler was the "murderer, kidnapper, and number one gangster of the world." The ad agency in charge of the Cantor account, Young & Rubicam, sent a memo to the network and sponsor: "We are all of the opinion that we should present Cantor to the public strictly as a funny man and try to avoid any publicity that would indicate that Cantor ever has a serious thought or is guilty of a serious deed."

While radio sponsors appeased fascist Germany, Hollywood's ruling class appeased fascist Italy. Harry Cohn, head of Columbia Pictures, was an admirer of Benito Mussolini and in 1933 released *Mussolini Speaks*, a pro-fascist documentary. *The New York Times* said the film was so good "that even those in the audience who are not Italians cannot resist a surge of patriotic feeling." In gratitude, Mussolini flew Cohn to Italy. Cohn was so impressed with the fascist headquarters that on his return to Hollywood he had his own office remodeled in its image.

Hal Roach, the mogul who produced countless Laurel & Hardy films, entered a partnership with Mussolini and the fascist leader's son Vittorio. Roach said, "He looked at all the good American movies and he looked at all the bad Italian movies and he went nuts. He said, 'Why, with the great literature of Italy, the great paintings, the great music, are we so behind in motion pictures?' The Cinecitta Studio was turned over to me, as well as eight million dollars in credit from the largest bank in Italy. I owned fifty percent of the company and the bank owned fifty percent. Young Vittorio Mussolini was to be my partner." They formed RAM (Roach and Mussolini) Productions in October 1937. Roach said, "As our trademark we decided to use the head of a ram in the way MGM used the head of a lion."

It appalled many in the Hollywood community, who objected to the rise of European fascism and Vittorio's recent hand in Ethiopian slaughter. Still, Roach hosted a lavish reception for him on the tennis court of his home. "I gave a large party for him. Some Jewish people who were in the motion picture business called other people and asked them not to come." A Hawaiian orchestra played as the Mussolinis and Roaches entertained an audience that included Cary Grant, Ray Milland and Spencer Tracy. Bette Davis attended wearing a "red and gold metal cloth." Roach said his collaboration with Mussolini would benefit Hollywood "from a business and diplomatic angle . . . [and] help Italy's good will toward Hollywood."

Among the Hollywood figures who vocally objected were Charlie Chaplin, Joan Crawford and screenwriter Donald Ogden Stewart. They signed their names to an open letter of condemnation sponsored by the Hollywood Anti-Nazi League. Meanwhile, J. Edgar Hoover ordered FBI agents to protect the visiting fascist. Mussolini's trip was cut short when the protest became too vocal, Roach accompanying Vittorio to his plane. They continued their partnership discreetly. RAM was rebranded Era Productions and Roach quietly sent a surrogate, Warren G. Doane, to Italy as his studio representative. However, when the United States officially entered World War II, RAM was officially aborted. Still, the man responsible for Laurel & Hardy and so much early film comedy defended Mussolini for the rest of his life, calling him "a good dictator."

Anti-Nazi film comedy became a mini-genre at the start of the 1940s. Hitler was apparently devastated when Chaplin parodied him in *The Great Dictator*. Elwood Ullman, a comedy writer at Columbia Pictures, said the Three Stooges were on Hitler's "death list" because of their two-reelers *You Nazty Spy* and *I'll Never Heil Again*. Jack Benny was apparently on the same death list for his part in Ernst Lubitsch's anti-Nazi comedy *To Be or Not to Be*.

World War II had a major impact on nightclub comedy. Top comedians were either in the military or busy performing on its bases. Future giants Sid Caesar, Don Knotts and Jack Paar were enlisted men and got their first taste of showbiz performing in camp shows, and Zeppo Marx of the Marx Brothers left showbiz for the lucrative world of war contracts. "I had a very large manufacturing company that employed five hundred people. We made the clamping devices that carried the atomic bombs over Japan."

War curfews were imposed on nightclubs and most joints were required to close by midnight. Comedians enlisted, and the domestic entertainment vacuum propelled some comics who would never otherwise have had headliner status. "Most of the American comedians were in the army," said comedian Alan King. "So suddenly there was a lot of work for an underage hopeful."

Lenny Kent and Jackie Miles were two unlikely comics who became substitute stars. "Lenny Kent and Jackie Miles were the big New York comedians during the war," says one of their contemporary comics, Stan Irwin. "They toured the circuit, although they were more concerned with the perks of show business than the business itself." Comedian Bobby Ramsen explains, "They became names because they were the only ones around. Kent didn't even have that much talent. Their popularity lasted until just after the war and then it was over."

World War II created a genre of army comedians: fellows who remained in uniform after the war, doling out punch lines about army life. There were a ton of them making the rounds in the 1940s. Army comics capitalized on the country's goodwill toward soldiers, but as the 1950s approached, the adoration faded and people started asking these hacks, "Why are you still performing in uniform?"

"Nobody was half as good as the G.I. audiences made him look," said Harpo Marx. "For this reason a lot of young comics I knew became war casualties. They made it big doing camp shows. They made it too big. When the war was over they didn't know, or had forgotten, how much hard work it took to win over a club full of drunks."

One of the most successful was Corporal Harvey Stone. After the armistice he played New York houses and Miami Beach nightclubs.

"His whole act was borrowed from a guy named Johnny Burke—
Soldier Burke," says Jack Carter. "He used to do all the old army
jokes. We *all* did them. I used to kiss my discharge button. That was
my running gag." Stone succeeded on the coattails of Burke, but soon
that karmic circle was complete. "Everybody that came out of the
army stole Harvey Stone's act," says comedian Van Harris. "There was
one agent that had a performer named Sands. He had him change his
name to *Harvey* Sands. People would call up saying, 'We want what's-
his-name . . . that guy . . . that G.I. comic . . . Harvey . . . uh . . . Harvey . . . uh . . .' This agent would say, 'Oh, yes, you mean Harvey Sands!'
And they would say, 'Yeah, yeah, that's the guy.' And he would get all
the work that was meant for Harvey Stone."

"At that time the thought of becoming a motion picture personality was big in the mind of those in comedy," says comic Stan
Irwin. "Harvey had his nose done, and very bad, made it even worse.
It put him in a state of depression. He considered suicide and barely
got work as a stand-up comedian." Stone and his botched nose job
played out their days doing out-of-date army jokes on a cruise ship.
Jack Carter says, "Harvey died at sea, and at the time he and his
wife were estranged. The cruise ship called and said, 'Your husband,
Harvey, died. We have the body on ice. Should we hold it or should
we fly it back to New York?' Harvey's wife wasn't too thrilled and
said, 'Oh, well, few people knew this, but Harvey always wanted to
be buried at sea.' She got rid of him that way! Here's a Jew from
Detroit who never saw a boat in his life. They dumped him in the
ocean. And that was the end of Harvey Stone."

Comedians died in weird ways—none more so than Harry Einstein,
the father of comic actors Albert Brooks and Bob Einstein. Popular
throughout the war years, his move into show business was like
something out of a movie. Einstein insulted a star comedian to his
face and it led to a network radio contract, a series of motion pictures
and a permanent place at the Friars Club roasts.

In the early 1930s Harry Einstein was making a good living in
Boston. In charge of advertising for Kane Furniture, he was friendly

with local radio stations. He appeared on regional airwaves promoting Kane Furniture, but ended up as a comic of sorts, using the platform to orate as a blustery know-it-all. Calling himself Nick Parkyakarkus and speaking with a bastardized Greek accent, Einstein mastered the art of the put-on. He spoke mangled English and got laughs with his malapropisms. For a few years Einstein did shows at civic gatherings posing as an expert in a given field, the put-on confusing the crowd until they eventually caught on—by which time they turned hysterical.

Eddie Cantor came through Boston in February 1935 for a charity dinner. Einstein was booked to do his shtick at the function. After Cantor spoke and earned a good number of laughs, Parkyakarkus was introduced as an important Greek dignitary. Everyone but Cantor was familiar with the local put-on master, and they relished the look on his face as Parkyakarkus spoke: "You Americans are such children when it comes to humor. No sophistication. No subtlety. The simplest little things amuse you. I could hardly believe my ears when I heard you all laughing so heartily at this man Cantor just now. If you Americans pay this man a million dollars a year, as I have heard you do, all I can say is, you must be crazy."

Einstein looked at Cantor, but couldn't sustain the deadpan; the look of terror in Cantor's banjo eyes was too good. Einstein started laughing. It brought down the house. When Cantor got back to New York he sent a telegram asking Einstein to appear on his radio show. Einstein was astounded: "I never for a moment dreamed that such a part would ever be handed me on such a program." He sent word back to Boston that as of February 1935 he was done with the furniture racket.

Einstein became a program regular and Cantor introduced him to all the right people. He became a Hollywood staple. Cantor cast Einstein in his next motion picture for Samuel Goldwyn, *Strike Me Pink*. In July 1936 RKO signed Einstein to a long-term contract. The film studio had plans to make a comedy team out of Parkyakarkus and Joe "Wanna Buy a Duck?" Penner.

Einstein was invincible with the powerful Eddie Cantor guiding his interests. Comedian George Givot did a dialect act in the dying days of vaudeville called the Greek Ambassador of Good Will. When he claimed Einstein was succeeding on his heels, Eddie Cantor reversed the accusation. Cantor said he would punish anyone emulating Parkyakarkus to the fullest extent of the law. In spring 1936 voice actor Bill Thompson started doing a comical Greek on the *Fibber McGee and Molly* radio sitcom, but the sponsor objected, fearing a lawsuit from Cantor.

After two years of service, Harry Einstein asked for a raise. Cantor refused and Einstein left his benefactor. Al Jolson hired Einstein for the requested amount and Parkyakarkus joined *The Rinso-Lifebuoy Program*, starring Al Jolson and Martha Raye, in January 1937.

RKO teamed Joe Penner and Parkyakarkus for the first time in *The Life of the Party*, a brisk motion picture written by Marx Brothers collaborators Bert Kalmar and Harry Ruby. It featured Parkyakarkus dialogue indicative of the era:

> **Boss:** Parkyakarkus!
> **Parkyakarkus:** Oh, good morning!
> **Boss:** Good morning? This is afternoon. What do you mean sleeping on the job?
> **Parkyakarkus:** I can sleep on a dime. If you ain't got a dime, I can sleep on two nickels.
> **Boss:** Someday you'll sleep yourself out of a job.
> **Parkyakarkus:** I can sleep there too!
> **Boss:** Well, sleep at *home*!
> **Parkyakarkus:** My wife sleeps at home!
> **Boss:** I don't care about your wife!
> **Parkyakarkus:** Me too!

In reality, Einstein's wife was the key to his legacy. Thelma Leeds was a radio songstress on a number of programs in the first half of the 1930s. RKO used her in the Ginger Rogers–Fred Astaire musical *Follow the Fleet* and in the latest Einstein-Penner pairing— *New Faces of 1937*. A romance blossomed on the set of *New Faces* and Einstein asked Leeds to marry him. Einstein fathered four sons, three with Leeds, and all had remarkable careers. Charles Einstein, his son from a previous marriage, was a reporter and Willie Mays's biographer. Second son, Clifford Einstein, became a touted Beverly Hills art collector. Bob Einstein wrote for the Smothers Brothers and produced variety shows for Redd Foxx and Sonny & Cher, finding fame as characters Super Dave Osborne and Marty Funkhouser. The youngest child conquered stand-up, comedy LPs, short films and features under the name Albert Brooks.

In 1945, ten years after he first appeared on network radio, Parkyakarkus got his own radio show—*Meet Me at Parky's*. Originally a summer replacement for the *Harold Lloyd Comedy Theater*, it lasted on NBC for a year and a half, moving to the Mutual Broadcasting System in October 1947. It featured fine comic actors Elliott Lewis, Frank Nelson and Sheldon Leonard. *Billboard* assessed it positively: "It's funny. Not inspired humor, nor delicate. Still it's funny in a purely low comedy vein that, regardless of whether one likes aural pratfalls, pays off in laughs."

In the summer of 1947 Einstein was plagued with serious back pain. He checked in to Cedars of Lebanon on August 27, 1947. Doctors conducted a routine procedure on his spine to alleviate pain—but it went horribly wrong. "I'm sure my doctor had no expectation of any such serious consequences," said Einstein. "All he intended to do was cut away an overgrowth of bone on my upper vertebrae that had caused me considerable pain during the previous five years. 'Don't worry,' was my last admonition to my wife, Thelma. Well, I was mistaken. Something went wrong during the operation." Einstein was now confined to a wheelchair.

More aware of his mortality, Einstein started investing. He sunk money into the Hollywood Palladium, the major Hollywood big-band venue for the likes of Tommy Dorsey and Artie Shaw. He invested in the Boston Braves, a major league team. He incorporated an independent production company with plans for *Meet Me at Parky's* film shorts. He partnered with New York philanthropist Charles Hendrickson to produce educational films for grade school students called *Parky Talks*. He planned a record of children's novelty songs and announced publishing schemes: one a history of mimicry, the other a collection of jokes he had amassed over twenty years.

Albert Brooks recalled his father's cumbersome days. "He was so sick . . . He couldn't walk. And so he gained weight. Nothing about him was healthy. Every time we were alone and he called me, I thought he was dying." His condition worsened in 1949 and most of his planned projects were abandoned. Inactive, he took up coin collecting and sat helplessly by as another comedian stole his act. "George Givot went on the air once when we were watching a telethon locally," says Bob Einstein. "I'm watching with my father, and the guy says, 'And now, ladies and gentlemen . . . Parkyakarkus!' And George Givot came out. He used my dad's act and name. My dad was furious."

As he lost mobility in the last ten years of his life, Einstein relegated his show business appearances to the Friars Club roasts. The roast format was ideal for Einstein's condition, as he could remain seated at the dais for the duration and lean on a podium during his set. Confined to the Friars, he honed a new persona as a roaster. Throughout the 1950s, he roasted Sammy Cahn, Eddie Cantor, Nat King Cole, Eddie Fisher, Jackie Gleason, Tony Martin, George Raft, Phil Silvers and Glenn Wallichs of Capitol Records. On November 23, 1958, he was asked to join the Friars roast of Lucille Ball and Desi Arnaz at the Beverly Hilton. It was a fund-raiser for a Burmese leper colony and the tenth anniversary of the Friars Club of California. The ballroom was packed with twelve hundred people, the largest crowd in Friars roast history. It was the final time Parkyakarkus would ever perform.

Art Linkletter was the roastmaster. Actor-turned-senator George Murphy went first. Next, Tony Martin sang a song about the Desilu cash cow. Milton Berle followed with a rapid succession of old gags. The crowd was cooking. Dean Martin had the unenviable position of following Berle and cracked, "I wouldn't give this spot to a leper." George Burns went up and killed. Linkletter then set the stage for Parkyakarkus: "With his Greek dialect [he] has done for the Greeks what Desi has done for the Cubans—set back the United States' relations with them about a century. I want you to meet a great guy and a fine Friar: Harry Einstein—Parkyakarkus." Einstein went up and destroyed the crowd with a routine that lasted around eight minutes. (It must be heard to be appreciated—and luckily you can find the audio on the Classic Television Showbiz website.) Parkyakarkus finished to a loud ovation. Linkletter returned to the podium and said, "I've seen Harry at a dozen of these Friars benefits and affairs and every time he finishes I always ask myself, 'Why isn't he on the air in prime time?'" The audience applauded again.

"I remember helping him with his monologue the night before," said Albert Brooks. "He went to the banquet and when he got up, he was as funny as could be, and they just roared. They just banged the table, so you hear the silverware jumping up and down. And he finished to this thunderous applause."

Milton Berle was seated directly beside Einstein. Roastmates encouraged Harry to stand and take another bow. "As he sat down for the third time, I looked at him and his face was turning colors," said Berle. "He took a breath and went boom and hit my shoulder. I heard a lot of 'oohs' and 'ahs' from the audience. They guessed what had happened. I never saw so many pillboxes thrown out from an audience. So I said, 'Ladies and gentlemen, take it easy, just a little accident here.'" Art Linkletter tried to calm the audience, repeating, "He's all right, he's all right."

Ed Wynn rushed the stage yelling, "Put his head down! Put his head down!" Thelma Leeds ran to her husband and shoved nitroglycerine tablets—used to treat his arteriosclerosis—under his tongue. "Milton and I each took an arm of the chair and pulled him back," said Friar Barry Mirkin. "I tried to get Lucy to unclamp her hands from the table, and she couldn't do it." Einstein was carried backstage. "Desi was crying," said Berle. "He was beside himself, and so was Lucy, and so was everybody. Tony Martin was on the dais, so I told him to sing a song, and what do you think he sang? 'There's No Tomorrow.'"

Dr. Alfred Goldman, chief surgeon from the City of Hope hospital, was in attendance. He cut open Einstein's chest with a pocket scalpel. Electric shocks were administered to Einstein's heart using a raw cord ripped from a nearby lamp. "When we saw the doctors come out, their shirt sleeves rolled up, glum, everyone knew," said Mirkin. After they'd worked on him for eighty minutes, Einstein was pronounced dead of myocardial infarction.

"If he had been eighty-five, it would have been *a movie*—a joy—a great thing," says Bob Einstein. "This was not good. It was weird. Someone once said to me, 'Well, at least your dad died doing what he loved.' My dad was fifty-four! I said, 'What does your mother do?' He said, 'Oh, she's a housewife.' I said, 'Let's go over to her house while she's doing the laundry and I'll blow her fucking head off. At least she will have died doing what she loved.'"

"The interesting thing to me was that he finished," said Albert Brooks. "He could have died in the middle, but he didn't. He finished and he was as good as he'd ever been in his life."

Advertising agencies continued to control radio in the 1940s. The profits brought in during the 1930s made them only more powerful in the following decade. Radio gave the hard sell for Geritol "for tired blood" and evaporated milk "from contented cows" while "nine out of ten doctors" recommended Lucky Strike cigarettes. Few comedians dared defy this atmosphere. The two who did exemplified the great disconnect between comic cynicism and sponsor deceit.

Fred Allen was a quiet subversive, an armchair intellectual and a beloved comedian. In an era when radio comedians were sold to the public as cheery good sports, Allen was the dour opposite. He once said, "I have high hopes I'll be able to withdraw from the human race." He objected to the rules and restrictions imposed by the sponsor, concluding, "Radio is a repugnant medium of entertainment." His good friend Jack Benny said he was "a bitter, frustrated and unhappy man. He thought life was some sort of miserable trap." His attitude was funneled into a unique persona that appealed to those listeners tired of radio hucksterism. As an insubordinate he thrived in the very environment he held in contempt, a voice for the cynical voiceless.

Fred Allen was a network radio star from 1933 to 1949, fighting his superiors from the start. The concept of the studio audience was entrenched by 1935, but Allen fought against it. "The worst thing that ever happened to radio was the studio audience. Somebody like Eddie Cantor brought these hordes of cackling geese in because he couldn't work without a bunch of imbeciles laughing at his jokes. Would anybody with a brain be caught dead in a studio audience? Would anybody with a sense of taste stand in line to watch a half dozen people in business suits standing around reading into microphones?"

Still, the live audience gave birth to an Allen trademark. Whenever a line didn't go over he veered off script and referred to the lack of response. It showcased a quick wit, and the "savers" made him worth listening to when the script was lackluster.

Allen believed he was more in line with *New Yorker* humorists than radio comedians. "I wonder what thoughts are rampant in the minds of the morons who bark the same jokes over the networks week after week," said Allen. "The only way I can figure it out is that the listeners have the same mentality and do not discriminate." Allen griped about radio writing in general, but stopped short of insulting his own writers. He lamented that an original comic didn't have a chance against the bandits of the air. "Radio comedy is the most painful form of entertaining. This pressure for new ideas drives every comedian on the air into becoming a vulture. I don't blame them. I blame their gag writers. You can't copyright a joke. You can't tell a new joke on the radio without hearing it in almost the same version on almost every other comedy show during the week."

The vitriol aside, he treated his writers well. "Fred was better, kinder, and more liberal and generous with writers than anyone else—even though publicly he used to complain about them," said comedy writer Bob Weiskopf. Among those who got their start writing for Allen were *The Caine Mutiny* author Herman Wouk and the creator of *The Phil Silvers Show*, Nat Hiken.

Allen was the first comedian to call out network executives, making jokes at the expense of NBC suits: "A conference of radio executives is just a meeting at which a group of men who can do nothing agree collectively that nothing can be done." Allen was censored live on the air when he spoke of "gray flannel junior executives who wear tight suits so they can't make a move without a conference." NBC told Fred Allen to cut this line out of the script. When he delivered the line anyway, the NBC chimes cut him off mid-joke. The following week he addressed it on air while bantering with his costar and wife, Portland Hoffa. "Why were you cut off last Sunday?" asked Portland. "Who knows?" said Allen. "The main thing in radio is to come out on time. If people laugh, the program is longer. The thing to do is to get a nice dull half-hour. Nobody will laugh or applaud. Then, you'll always be right on time, and all of the little emaciated radio executives can dance around their desks in interoffice abandon."

Radio critic Jack Graver observed in 1945, "More and more things have become taboo in the last half-dozen years until it is almost useless to think of making satirical comment along these lines on radio. The networks are taking no chances . . . All of which is a sad blow to a person of Allen's penetrating wit. The advertising people are also the bane of Allen's existence."

Allen reflected on corporate influence in radio. "Men who ran oil companies, drug, food, and tobacco corporations, were attending auditions, engaging talent and in too many instances their untutored opinions adversely influenced the destinies of artists."Allen said that if radio comedy was lousy, it was because the sponsor wanted it that way. "Practically everything is taboo. We end up with ersatz subject matter and ditto humor." He told the story of one network censor who marked up every page of his script, crossing out the transitional instruction "segue." The censor in question was under the illusion that the word "segue" had "immoral overtones."

In the fall of 1948 the ratings for *The Fred Allen Show* took a nosedive due to the rising popularity of quiz shows. Programs like *Break the Bank* and *Stop the Music* eviscerated their competition by promising listeners cash prizes. Allen said, "Radio's slogan is, 'If you can't entertain people, *give* them something.'"

On June 26, 1949, *The Fred Allen Show* was thrown off the air. "*Fred Allen*, hardest hit program because of the direct competition opposite *Stop the Music*, led radio stars in ganging up in a campaign to laugh the giveaway shows off the air—and failed," wrote *Variety*. "Their gags were more than good-natured humor; they had a sarcastic, always frustrated bite. Allen's insurance policy, purporting to compensate any lucky listener who called while tuned in to his show, had a reflex effect—in that it focused even more attention on the jackpot program."

Radio comedy of the 1940s was mostly hokum. With the sponsor dictating the tone, the least likely to offend was most likely to air—even if it was least likely to make you laugh. "Rabid radio fans have begun to display an apathy toward the high-priced comedy program, and even a sporadic listener can detect a certain shabbiness creeping into the top-ranking shows," said radio writer Philip Rapp. "Little or no regard is given to originality, imagination in most cases has been entirely dispensed with, and the theory seems to be that if the studio audience laughs, the program is a success." Fred Allen had been the antidote to the creeping shabbiness, but now he was gone.

Heavily influenced by Fred Allen was the new satirical curmudgeon Henry Morgan. He was far crankier than Allen could ever dream of being, and *The Henry Morgan Show* had a successful run on NBC as a "sustaining" program, meaning it aired without a commercial sponsor. Morgan was different from his contemporaries in the sense that he was willing to offend—and likely to do so. But he had a healthy run thanks to a fervent cult of listeners and Fred Allen's support. Members of comedy's next generation—Sid Caesar and Mort Sahl among them—considered Henry Morgan a hero.

Morgan's whole persona was born of insubordination. Working as a weatherman in Chicago, he was given his own show to stop him from sabotaging the weather report with his sarcastic comments. He moved to the New York market in 1940 and WOR implemented the same strategy of appeasement. Morgan was as much a saboteur as he was a talent; it was better to give him his own show than have him ruin someone else's.

Williamson Candy, makers of Oh Henry!, sponsored his first program, a daily fifteen-minute show called *Meet Mr. Morgan*. The sponsor thought they had a clever gimmick by sponsoring a comedian named Henry. Instead they were disturbed when Morgan said, "If children eat enough *Oh Henry* bars they'll get sick and die."

Morgan buried himself in his show, creating a world of his own. He ranted as a cast of one—complaining about the world. "Morgan is likely to ramble on about anything in his fifteen minutes," said an early *Variety* review. "[He] did a goofy yarn about the code used by lunch counter waiters, meandered through a ludicrous piece about barrooms and football predictions, answered a couple of letters from outraged listeners." He burned through his sponsors, refusing to read ad copy without editorial. A cough remedy sponsored his show for six weeks. Morgan announced on the company's last segment, "Thank goodness the contract for this is concluded so we won't have to hear that announcement anymore."

Despite his cult following, Mutual Radio decided to cancel Morgan after many regional complaints. Morgan regrouped with the national *Here's Morgan* in 1942, sponsored by Adler Shoes. He promoted its line of footwear, which helped small men look taller. Morgan again defamed the product, but president Jesse Adler saw sales soar in remarkable fashion. Morgan even wrote a new slogan, which bugged Adler but moved his product: "Wake up your lazy liver bile with a pair of Adler Elevators."

Edward Noble, president of Life Savers candies, owned ABC. He made *Here's Morgan* one of its flagship programs in the postwar years, Wednesday nights at 10:30. Morgan told his listeners not to buy Life Savers because the candies were missing their middle. Despite the insults ABC stuck with him, since the three other network comedies—starring James Gleason, Bill Thompson and the forgotten Ray Wencil, respectively—were abysmal failures. ABC increased Morgan's budget and gave him a full orchestra, a stooge named Arnold Stang, a Bing Crosby lead-in and a new sponsor—the Schick razor company. It was the most successful run of his career.

A full writing staff was hired for the new season, including Joe Stein, who later wrote *Fiddler on the Roof*. He specialized in the fast banter between Morgan and Stang:

Arnold Stang: Say, Henry, I heard your show last night.
Henry Morgan: How'd you like it?
AS: Great, great. It was all I could do to keep from laughing.
HM: Thanks a lot, I guess. By the way, I heard *your* show last week . . .
AS: Oh yeah? I'm glad you caught it . . .

HM: Yeah, I was at a party. You know how it is . . . everybody
drinking . . . some *drunk* turned it on . . .

AS: Well, what did you think of it?

HM: Well, there was a lot of noise. It didn't come in very well . . .

AS: What kind of noise?

HM: I was talking.

AS: Oh.

HM: But, say, that was a good joke you had there about Sinatra
and the pipe cleaner.

AS: Sinatra and the pipe cleaner? That's Bob Hope's . . .

HM: Yeah, that's right, but I like the way *you* told it. By the way,
how's your Hooper rating?

AS: Well, it's uh . . . ah, that rating doesn't mean a thing.

HM: Mine is not so good either. As a matter of fact, you see, the
trouble with me is . . . I've got a terrific listening audience
that can't *get* phones . . .

AS: Sure. Say, Henry, did you have a studio audience last night?

HM: Why, certainly!

AS: I *knew* it! I could swear I heard breathing . . . but my wife
read somewhere you got asthma.

Schick lost patience with Morgan during the season when he
said of their razors, "They're educational. Try one. That'll teach you."
A *Life* magazine profile showed Morgan's face covered in bandages,
praying to a razor. Despite strong ratings, Schick dropped Morgan,
and his season was aborted.

Morgan was one of the first to remark on the insipidity of
radio commercials, and his success made ridicule of corporate deceit
marketable. His niche as the anti-advertising iconoclast was copied
by others. Radio WINS hired Dayton Allen as its version of Henry
Morgan and Radio WCAE hired Irene Cowan to be "a female Henry
Morgan." Future *Tonight Show* hosts Steve Allen and Jack Paar mod-
eled their radio shows "in the Henry Morgan fashion." When future
Match Game host Gene Rayburn entered radio he was criticized as the
poor man's Henry Morgan. It was a testament to Morgan's popularity, but overall it didn't cool corporate apprehension.

Luster-Creme Shampoo put him back on the air in February 1948, but by then the quiz craze had exploded and Morgan suffered the same fate as Fred Allen. *The Henry Morgan Show* indicted quiz programs with the sketch "Take It, for Heaven's Sake, Take It," in which the studio audience applauded maniacally whenever the name of a city was mentioned. The bitterness was real. Morgan's own sponsor ditched him for a game show. While sponsors and listeners fled, Allen and Morgan supported each other. Starting in March 1949 each episode opened: "*The Henry Morgan Show!* Brought to you by . . . *The Fred Allen Show!*"

Morgan did not have much success in subsequent decades. His show canceled by the end of 1949, Morgan returned only sporadically to radio, usually regionally and often playing novelty records with surly commentary. Just like Fred Allen, he complained that he wasn't getting a fair shake, but at the same time he did nothing to ingratiate himself to those who could help. "He was ahead of his time, but he was also hurt by his own disposition," said radio announcer Ed Herlihy. "He was very difficult. He was so brilliant that he'd get exasperated and he'd sulk. He was a great mind who never achieved the success he should have." His sidekick Arnold Stang said, "He was a masochist, a neurotic man. When things were going well for him, he would do something to destroy himself. He just couldn't deal with success." Morgan was one of the first to lash out against corporate advertising, but in the end it did him in. "I grew up thinking it was American to be outspoken. I've since learned it's un-American."

CHAPTER THREE

NIGHTCLUBS

If Fred Allen or Henry Morgan criticized their overlords, the worst that happened was cancellation. While cancellation was indeed awful for a comic, it did not compare with the perils facing comedians who performed in nightclubs on a regular basis.

Organized crime and nightclub comedy coexisted. Mob-run speakeasies employed entertainment during the days of Prohibition. When Prohibition was repealed in 1933, vaudeville was dead and the speakeasies turned into legitimate nightclubs and became the primary venues for comedians. If you were a stand-up comedian, you worked for the Mob.

The Mob essentially created the term "stand-up comic"—according to eighty-six-year-old comedian Dick Curtis. "The Outfit used to manage fighters. A stand-up fighter is a guy that is a puncher. A stand-up guy was a guy who was tough and you could depend on. The Outfit managed fighters and they managed clubs that booked comics, so the term found its way into the lexicon of nightclubs. A guy who just stood there and punched jokes—joke, joke, joke—he was a stand-up comic."

Comedians playing Chicago during the dying days of vaudeville found themselves victims of Mob shakedowns. "Lou Holtz, Georgie Price, Ted Healy, all paid off for this so-called protection," said George Jessel. "If they didn't, they were told, they would get hurt. 'Remember Joe E. Lewis?' was the usual admonition." That admonition would never work today, as nobody remembers Joe E. Lewis.

From 1935 until his death in 1971, Joe E. Lewis was the comedian at the forefront of the Mob's nightclub network. He was everywhere: El Rancho in Las Vegas, Ciro's in Hollywood, the Copacabana in New York. Lewis was possibly the most prolific nightclub comedian who ever lived. But he almost didn't live at all. Lewis defied the Mob—and paid the price in gore.

In 1927 he'd already been booked for a lengthy engagement at a small Chicago club called the Green Mill Cocktail Lounge when he was lured down the street for a gig at the New Rendezvous. Both venues were run by the Mob. Unfortunately for Lewis, they were rival factions.

The Green Mill was co-owned by Machine Gun Jack McGurn, an Al Capone associate. Taking a gig elsewhere without permission was an act of treason, but Lewis was a show business novice who thought nothing of it. Three Mob enforcers came to his hotel room to teach him a lesson. What happened next became a symbol for the decades-long relationship between comedians and the Mob. As described in the 1958 biography *The Joker Is Wild* by Art Cohn:

> *A horrendous blow struck him from behind. He turned as he fell and saw the man with the .38 raising his arm to hit him again. The third assailant was unsheathing a hunting knife. Pain coiled around his brain, tighter and tighter, and sank its fangs deeper and deeper. The knifeman went to work. He punched the blade into Joe's left jaw as far as he could, ripped his face open from ear to throat, and went on cleaving impassively, like a butcher. He was lying on the floor, his face immersed in a pool of blood.*

It took three years for Joe E. Lewis to regain the ability to talk. As a comic, words were his trade. The average comedian building an act from nothing had it tough enough, but now he had to do it while relearning how to speak.

Years later mobster Sam Giancana admitted he had been involved: "Jack [McGurn] sent me, Needles [Gianola] and another punk over to pay him a visit. We beat him to a pulp and pistol-whipped him real good. Shit, we cut his fucking throat from stern to stern. His goddamned tongue was hanging by a string out of his mouth when we got done with him. It's a fucking wonder the guy lived. One thing we didn't count on was how other entertainers would react. There isn't a star alive now who'd turn us down."

When Lewis staged his comeback in the early 1930s, crowds got a look at the fleshy scar that started at his left ear and curved across his neck. They heard the obvious rasp and struggle to establish command. The fact that Lewis survived and recovered was remarkable. More incredible, by the time Prohibition was repealed he was a headlining professional. Adhering to the code of the street, he refused to comply with police and name the men who sliced him. Back from the dead, refusing to squeal, Joe E. Lewis now had the respect of every Mob outfit in the United States. As a result, his career was set for life.

Alcohol was legal and vaudeville was dead. Milton Berle was oscillating between the half-empty vaudeville houses and the post-speakeasy nightclub world, trying to determine how to make a living without the power of Keith-Albee behind him. Nightclubs required comedians to have longer acts than in vaudeville. The average vaudeville turn was anywhere from eight to eighteen minutes; in a nightclub a comedian needed forty-five. Berle didn't have that, so in order to stretch his time, he would ridicule the crowd. He picked on a random table at the Vanity Fair club in New York, but was unable to evoke any laughter. It is a typical nightclub story of the time.

"A mobster nicknamed 'Pretty' Amberg had a fondness for puncturing people's faces with a fork," said columnist Earl Wilson. "Milton Berle, then a young comic, didn't know Amberg was sensitive to remarks about himself. Glancing at Amberg's table one night at the old Vanity Fair, Berle said, 'Oh, it's Novelty Night—you're with your wife.'"

Berle recalled, "When the show ended I went straight to my dressing room. 'Table twelve wants to see you.' Nobody at the table nodded or said hello or even smiled at me. When the waiter left no one spoke. I was getting very nervous, so I said, 'Did you like the show?' 'No. It stunk.' He yanked my face close to his."

"Amberg grabbed Berle's throat and began pulling on his tie," said Wilson. "Berle was choking helpless. Then Amberg reached for a fork ready to tear Berle's face with it."

"He jabbed the fork straight into my chin," said Berle. "[Mobster] Marty Krompier stepped in and grabbed his wrist and forced his hand open . . . I got the hell away from that table as fast as I could. Krompier pushed me into the street, pushed me into a cab, and gave the driver the name of a doctor the local Boys had on call. I got two stitches for each prong of the fork, eight stitches in all."

"Amberg was later found dead in cement," said Wilson. "His penis had been cut off and jammed in his mouth. This was the mobster's way of saying that a victim had talked too much."

For a good forty years the Mob controlled American show business. "It was always 'Outfit' to us," says comedian Dick Curtis. "Never the Mob or Cosa Nostra or any of the other names you might have heard. These guys were the Outfit." From the 1930s through the end of the 1960s every city in America had at least one glamorous supper club, if not four or five, featuring the top headliners in every showbiz genre. Furthermore, it didn't matter if these clubs were in Cleveland, Portland, Corpus Christi or Baton Rouge—if it was a nightclub, the owners were the Mob.

"The clubs were owned by bootleggers and even a few killers," said actor George Raft, who had worked as a dancer in New York supper clubs. "In my time I knew or met them all. Al Capone, Joe Adonis, Frank Costello, Vito Genovese, Dutch Schultz, Machine Gun Jack McGurn, Lucky Luciano, Vinnie Coll—most of them were around."

"The Mob was very, very good to me," says ninety-one-year-old comedienne Rose Marie, best known as Sally on *The Dick Van Dyke Show*. As a nightclub performer in the 1940s she was regularly booked at the Beverly Hills Supper Club in Newport, Kentucky, a Mob venue that was intentionally burned to the ground on two different occasions.

*   *   *

Insulting the Mob-connected was a common problem for comedians. As Milton Berle learned, you had to be cautious. In New York five caustic insult comics—Vince Curran, Frankie Hyers, Fred Lamb, Pat Harrington Sr. and Jack White—figured out a way around the risk. In 1938 they opened Club 18. Its whole mandate was insult comedy. It was known in advance that patrons would be ridiculed, thereby downplaying the risk of the wrong person being angered. Club 18 was named for its address on West 52nd Street, the former domain of Red McKenzie, a preeminent comb-and-wax-paper soloist. Taking over the jazz joint, Curran, Hyers, Lamb, Harrington and White made it the bailiwick of angry comics for ten successful years.

"Jack White was a wild kind of guy for those days, a leader of comics," says Pat Harrington Jr. "By the second year of Club 18, everybody knew what the place was about. If a guy looked like he was from the Midwest, then you treated him that way and insulted him. But if he had any kind of a broken nose or scarred forehead, your instinct was to avoid him."

Jack White was the first modern insult comic. He had balls like no other. Comedians Bob Hope, George Jessel and Rags Ragland sat in his audience as willing targets. It was a comic's room where comedians actually laughed rather than sneered from a back table. The five comedians simultaneously berated patrons. From backstage Frankie Hyers would shout, "And ah-*way* we go!" and, with individual mics, they'd prowl the crowd. "They are all masters of insult," wrote *Life* magazine. "When a well-dressed guest arrives, Jack cordially invites him to stand up and bow. Then Pat yells, 'Sit down, you bum!' And Frank adds, 'That's no bum. Bums take baths!'" Arnold Shaw, chronicler of 52nd Street, wrote, "No small part of the club's audience consisted of would-be comics, as well as the leading comics of the day. In fact, there were so many gagsters around that it was difficult to know who was part of the act and who was just sitting in."

Club 18 occasionally used guest comedians when one of the primary five was on the road. Jack Waldron was a good fit. He honed his insult shtick at Lambs Club Lambastings, a rival offshoot of Friars Club roasts. Comic Benny Rubin said Waldron was "the first Don Rickles and Jack E. Leonard. His task was a little more difficult, however, because he insulted guys who would shoot you."

Agent Willie Weber asked Fred Lamb to use a comedian he represented, a fat kid who usually played Queens. His name was Jackie Gleason and he became a regular. Gleason said, "Every time someone like Frankie Hyers or Pat Harrington or Jack White couldn't make it, it was little Jackie boy who stepped in and always saved the day." Gleason picked up some of his familiar phrases at Club 18. "Frankie Hyers was the guy who invented the phrase 'And ah-*way* we go,'" says straight man Peter Marshall. "It was his catchphrase—and then Jackie Gleason took it."

Gleason, Harrington and Hyers eventually became regular performers in Miami Beach. The same could be said of almost every comedian of their era. Dominated by the Mob element, there were more nightclubs in South Florida than anywhere else in the country. In the words of comedian Alan King, "Miami Beach was the Vegas of the 1940s."

Lax laws in regards to gambling and prostitution made it an attractive vacation spot. South Florida was transformed into America's playground during the Great Depression. To buoy the sinking economy, restrictions on pari-mutuel gambling were erased. Desperate people flooded the region and wasted their meager dollars at new dog tracks, horse tracks and casinos. Construction boomed, with forty new hotels opening in 1940 alone. "Early Miami was marvelous, and there were big gambling places way out past Miami toward Hollywood, Florida," says comedian Jack Carter. "There were places like Greenacres and the Colonial Inn and they would play four people on one bill: Sophie Tucker, Harry Richman, Joe E. Lewis, Milton Berle—they'd all be on one show. It was big, big-time showbiz."

"They had dice games going on and stuff like that, all on the QT," says comedian Woody Woodbury. "You'd go into the back room and it was like walking into a showroom in Vegas. You couldn't believe the gambling there in the old days." At midcentury *Time* called Miami Beach "the prime destination for Americans on the make, on the lam, or on a pension." It was also the prime destination for comedians. The Beach was a place where total nobodies like Jackie Clark, Artie Dann and Frankie Scott could make a living reciting their joke book hackwork. At the same time they could brush shoulders with giants like Milton Berle, George Burns and George Jessel. Everyone did the Beach. It had the largest concentration of stand-up comedy in the United States.

Comedian Bobby Ramsen got his break in Miami Beach playing the Nautilus Hotel. "I jumped at the chance to be playing Miami Beach. Every year they put up a new hotel. When World War II was over, America had a party. We had won the war, people were working, money was no object, people were going out every night. Every town in America—every other door in every small town in America was a nightclub! Comics were working. Marimba players opening the show! Dance teams! Contortionists! Everybody had a job in show business."

During the winter of 1950, the region had more than three hundred hotels in operation. The number of hotels operating in Las Vegas at the same time was four. It was a hedonistic culture where tourists indulged in booze, drugs, gambling and girls. A comedian could do a show at midnight, seduce a woman at three, wander into the Five O'Clock Club and drink till dawn. Jack Carter says, "The people that stayed at the big hotels would go early to the Colonial Inn or the Copa City. The Five O'Clock Club stayed open for the late mobs. You really had to be on your toes to work that crowd. That's when Murderers' Row came in."

The Five O'Clock Club was a compact joint at 22nd and Collins Avenue. When it first opened it meant *class*. Leo Lazaro and his Continentals played sultry waltzes and Lady Vine belted out the standards. The advertisements boasted that it was elaborately decorated in the modern manner. But like so many class nightclubs, it drifted into depravity; the Five O'Clock Club frayed and lost its allure. In an attempt to boost business, Martha Raye was offered a piece of the club if she would allow her name to appear above the sign. The scheme worked and Martha Raye's Five O'Clock Club reopened as a party spot where high society shared space with drug addicts.

"I went down there and Martha Raye was a big star, supposedly," says Shecky Greene. "This guy named the club after her and it was successful for a while. I went in and I really didn't know what was happening . . . strange people hanging out at the bar . . . all of a sudden I smell this stuff. They were all hitting on amyl nitrate. The whole club. Errol Flynn came in. He was on amyl nitrate."

It was the kind of place where comedians, no matter how bad their act was, could always find a stripper to lay. The kind of place where rim-shots were born and backstage babies conceived. "The Five O'Clock Club brought in comedians and Martha would take their stuff," says Greene. "I would come back to work for her and the bandleader would say, 'Don't do your French routine—she's doing it.' Well, it was *my* routine!"

Another compact venue was the Vagabond Club, a joint named for a musical novelty act with a stoned accordion player. "I worked with the Vagabonds on and off for seven years," says Woody Woodbury. "They were a tremendous hit down there. They opened up their own place, a real plush place." Jack Carter says, "They were a good act. Atillio Risso played the accordion and created a lot of the hippie-stoned jokes." The Vagabonds, like all the others, were connected to the Mob. Vagabonds member Babe Pier says, "The Mob was always good to us. They were great guys—to *us*."

Miami Beach was stand-up comedy's busiest city, but the whole country was littered with club dates. "When we say a 'club date,' we mean a one-nighter," says old-time comic Milt Moss. "An organization would send out a singer, a dancer, a comedian for a club date. Today that has faded out. But there used to be tremendous work between New York, Chicago, Boston, Philadelphia, Miami and Houston."

Many of them had back rooms with casinos or bookmakers. By the end of the 1940s Democratic senator Estes Kefauver of Tennessee was going after them. A mild-mannered Machiavelli-in-disguise, Kefauver railed against Mob-run gambling rooms and rode the issue to prominence. Perfectly timed with the rise of television, Kefauver became the first celebrity-politician of the televised age.

Kefauver's attack on the Mob officially started January 5, 1950, when he introduced Senate Resolution 202. It called for an investigation of organized crime in the United States. The committee started work on May 10, 1950. Kefauver launched the U.S. Senate Special Committee to Investigate Crime in Interstate Commerce. Suddenly people knew the name Frank Costello as well as they knew the name Kefauver.

Kefauver's battle was a touchy one. The Mob's power was concentrated in the big cities of America, which were overwhelmingly liberal. Consequently, the majority of the politicians in the pocket of the Mob were Democratic officeholders—and their Democratic colleague Kefauver was about to expose them. By default the liberal senator became a hero to Republicans and a pariah in his own party.

The committee held hearings in fourteen different cities. The first stop was Miami. It listened to several hours of testimony. Florida governor Fuller Warren refused to cooperate with the commission and by doing so implied guilt—ending his political career. Warren said Kefauver "is an ambition-crazed Caesar who is trying desperately and futilely to be a candidate for President of the United States."

Kefauver's next stop was Chicago. A former Chicago police officer was slated to testify, but he was murdered first. Two days later the lawyer amassing the information for the sheriff's office was killed. Lenny Bruce joked that Chicago was the only city where death certificates listed a cause of death as "He wouldn't listen." Bruce played small Chicago coffeehouses like the Cloister, but even they were run by the Mob. Comedian Dick Curtis says, "The Cloister was an Outfit joint. Of course it was! All of those places were."

The Chez Paree was Chicago's primary nightclub. "It was the most important club and the biggest stars played it," says singer Monica Lewis. "They had a wonderful orchestra, wonderful food and a wonderful line of dancing girls. They'd have a comic as an opening act and a singer or a dance act. It was always a big show." Mike Wallace, long before hosting *60 Minutes*, did a radio talk show from its lounge, and the Mob ran a secret casino in the back. Peter Marshall says, "You needed a gold key to get in the back room, with gambling and broads and all of that."

Chicago had a collection of lobbyists that defended Mob interests. A Mob front called the Chicago Cafe Owners Association represented their concerns. It flourished during the war years, but ended when its president, John Comise, was convicted of assault with a deadly weapon.

Variety usually signed its nightclub reviews with the nickname of the author—but in Chicago the bylines were left anonymous. "It was emphatically chancy," said one editor. "Two staffers in the Chicago office narrowly escaped bone fractures or worse for pans."

When Kefauver arrived in New York, the hearings became high drama. Frank Costello, éminence grise of Manhattan's Copacabana nightclub, was the star witness. Brought before the committee, Costello would not allow his face to be shown on television. In a compromise, the committee instructed cameras to focus solely on his hands, adding an expressionist flourish to the broadcast. Costello's statement "I refuse to answer that question on the grounds it may incriminate me" became a familiar refrain that entered the American lexicon. As Costello was grilled, the names of nightclubs and comedians entered the public record.

The Copacabana was the most important of all the Mob-run nightclubs. "The Copacabana was a front for Frank Costello," says comedian Lou Alexander. "I mean, all of those places were racket guys. All of them. If you worked nightclubs and these guys didn't like you—then you didn't work." The Copa hosted successful runs of comedians like Sid Caesar, Jack Carter, Myron Cohen, Pat Cooper, Jean Carroll and Martin & Lewis. It opened in 1940 at 10 East 60th Street in New York City, directly below the Hotel Thirteen. It was accused of being a Mob front as early as 1944. "In those days, any of the nightclubs were being run by that *element*," says Bobby Ramsen. "It was a natural flow of ownership and leadership [because] these guys, during Prohibition, were the ones running speakeasies."

Dean Martin and Jerry Lewis made their reputations at the Copa. Jerry's shtick had him running through the aisles, knocking things from tables, shouting in the faces of patrons. As always, berating the audience was a dangerous approach. "An incident took place in the Copa lounge," said Lewis. "I heard this gruff-sounding voice, 'Why don't you knock off that shit and be quiet?' I halted in my tracks. I figured he was either kidding or too drunk to appreciate who I was." Rather than lay off, Lewis upped his antagonism. The voice turned out to belong to Albert Anastasia, of Murder, Inc. "The bull slowly rose from his chair. Snorted, sauntered up and stuck his finger under my nose. 'That's not funny, you son of a bitch. If you open your mouth once more it'll be without your teeth.' Dean came between us, trying to calm him down."

It was rare for a comedian to deal with Anastasia or Costello at the Copa. It was the house manager, Jules Podell, who had the job of handling comics. Podell was a former speakeasy bouncer, a thickheaded hulk, loyal and gruff, with no criminal record: a perfect front man for the Mob. He was a replacement for the outgoing Jack Entratter, whom the Mob had sent to book shows in Las Vegas. "Podell worked for these guys and ran a very tight club," says Bobby Ramsen. "People would come there and see—Jimmy Durante! Frank Sinatra! Rosemary Clooney! Louis Prima! The *biggest* stars in America. Most of the time you would find Podell in a high chair, sitting at the exit of the kitchen, looking at the plates of food that were going out to the customers. He once threw somebody out of the club because they sent a steak back. He said, 'I serve only the finest food. It's *always* done perfectly—*leave* and don't ever come back.'"

"When I played the Copa, I never said a word to Podell," says comedian Don Sherman. "They told me, 'Never talk to him!' Finally after a week I got my check and I needed some money. I said, 'Excuse me, Mr. Podell? I have this check and I would like to know if you could cash it.' He said, 'This look like a fucking bank? You see tellers here? This is a fucking nightclub! We *take* money! We don't *give* money!' Then he said to the bar, 'Cash his check.'"

Friar's Club patriarch Freddie Roman remembers Podell. "He was an absolute tyrant. I did a joke opening night: Fella goes to the doctor. He says, 'Doctor, I have a problem. I can't pee anymore.' Doctor says, 'How old are you?' 'I'm ninety-four.' Doctor says, 'You've peed enough.' After the show the maître d' said, 'Mr. Podell wants to see you.' I walked over and he looked up and said, 'Nobody pees at the Copacabana!'"

"The Mob got you the right jobs," says comedian Frank Man. "This guy said to me, 'You come in here tomorrow and put five thousand dollars on this desk and you'll be playing Vegas in a week.' He was the head of AGVA—Jackie Bright."

The performers' union AGVA—the American Guild of Variety Artists—represented nightclub comedians. Naturally, it was in the pocket of the Mob. "AGVA always was a garbage union," says Jack Carter. "It was on the take."

Comedian Joey Adams worked up the AGVA hierarchy and headed the union when a congressional subcommittee looked into "the alleged link of AGVA personages with hoodlum-dominated niteries and stripperies." Adams and his coexecutive, former comedian Bright, felt the heat. *Variety* editorialized: "The end-result is a black eye for the performers union and perhaps for show business. The image will remain negative, protestations by Joey Adams notwithstanding. Coercing AGVA members, chiefly femme, into 'mixing,' B-girl drink-hustling and suggestions of even more sordid avocational pursuits, have made the national headlines."

One of AGVA's most vocal board members was Penny Singleton, the former Blondie Bumstead of the movies. She attacked the union's Mob connections. "I have made considerable headway in correcting the union's evils. The primary obstacle is Mr. Bright's domination through the control given him by thirty members of the national board who are obligated to continue his policies." She campaigned for reelection and a campaign advertisement said, "No one wants to or should be pushed around! I am voting for Penny Singleton because Penny Singleton is Racket-Free! Because Penny Singleton has no 'STRINGS' attached to her and therefore isn't afraid to speak the truth!"

Controlling both nightclubs and the union, it made sense for the Mob to have contacts within the major agencies. The Mob had an inside man at William Morris. Agent George Wood was the liaison between organized crime and legitimate showbiz. Wood handled comedians Marty Allen, Danny Thomas and Ed Wynn. John Bonomi of the New York District Attorney's Office said, "You could identify any entertainer as Mob-controlled by virtue of the fact that Wood was his agent." Frequently this meant that Wood's clients had to be at the Mob's beck and call. In the case of Joey Bishop, he had no choice when he was asked to emcee the wedding of Sam Giancana's daughter.

Bernie Brillstein got his start in the business working as Wood's secretary. "By the time I joined the agency Wood had been there for almost fifteen years, booking nightclub acts like Berle, Durante, Sinatra, Joe E. Lewis and Sophie Tucker at Mob joints all over the country." The day mobster Albert Anastasia was knocked off, Brillstein ran into Wood's office to tell him. Wood calmly looked at his watch and said, "That's right."

Comedy writer Sol Weinstein wrote for three Mob-connected comedians—Joe E. Lewis, Allan Drake and Jackie Kannon. "Allan Drake married a woman who was a Miss New Jersey. She ended up being murdered. I wrote for Allan Drake for quite a few years and I had to cut my relationship with him. A lot of things that he did were scary and immoral." Miami Beach comic Lou Marsh knew Drake. Now in his late eighties, Marsh is still too nervous to speak about him. "Allan Drake was just a comic and . . . I'd rather not talk about the rest."

Journeymen comedians like Dick Curtis spent half their careers working the smaller Mob clubs. "I worked a strip joint in Baltimore called Eddie Leonard's Spa. Eddie Leonard was an ex-boxer. When he retired from the ring, the Mob owned him. They gave him a nightclub and some slot machines around town as his retirement. I opened at Eddie Leonard's Spa in Baltimore on Christmas Eve. Can you imagine who would go to a Baltimore strip joint on Christmas Eve in 1952?"

Howard Storm was a comic playing the low-level rooms. "There was always danger. I worked a club in Johnston, Rhode Island, on the outskirts of Providence. The owners were brothers and they were evil guys. They didn't want to pay me the full week. There was a dispute and the guy, Gino, said to me, 'Okay, you stay the week. But every night when you go out to your car—you better look over your shoulder.'"

Some grew fond of the mobsters. Comic Orson Bean says, "I spent a lot of time with them when I was breaking in. I found the Mafia guys to be interesting and pleasant. If you crossed them you'd wind up with your feet in cement, but if you didn't cross them they were generous."

Small-time comedian Artie Dann saw his wife lured away by a mobster who made a play for her while he was onstage at the Roosevelt in New Orleans. After his show the mobster came backstage: "Great set, kid. And . . . your wife . . . she's leaving you. Give her a divorce."

"You're crazy, I'm in love with that girl."

"If you want to work again, you get a divorce."

Artie Dann got divorced.

Milton Berle said Dann encountered the mobster again years later. "The hoodlum burst into his dressing room . . . 'I'm gonna kill you, the hoodlum threatened. Kill you and dump you into Lake Pontchartrain. Son of a bitch, why didn't you tell me she was a nympho!'"

Comedian Sammy Shore was almost killed in Danville, Illinois. "It was $125 a week—Dan's Supper Club—with a stripper. I'm working and all of a sudden in the middle of the show these guys get in an argument at the ringside table. Mob guys. Guy takes out a gun and shoots the other guy in the head. People were screaming and running out. I started singing, 'Oh when the saints! Come marching in! When the saints come marching in!' I played the trumpet and finally the cops came. The owner came over to me and said, 'Sammy, I'm holding you over for another two weeks.' There were things like that happening wherever I worked. You knew they were the Mob. And they were just the greatest guys in the world."

To be a comedian in the 1930s, 1940s or 1950s was to be an employee of organized crime. Henny Youngman said, "If they like you they'll take anything. If not, you'd get your head broken somewhere. I heard them plan kidnappings, but I kept my mouth shut and minded my own business. Yeah, they weren't bad fellas—although they were murderers and thieves."

Estes Kefauver did not end Mob rule, but he stymied it. William Morris complained that Kefauver inflicted suffering on the clubs it booked with his "excess law enforcement." Clubs that ran clandestine gambling were increasingly busted, and this process became known as "Kefauverization."

Many of those shut down during Kefauverization found solace in an emerging new city in Nevada. Dick Curtis says, "The Outfit figured, 'Oh, let's stop fighting this. Let's take our money to Vegas.' And they did. They built the bottom floor of what is there now."

Moralists often outdid Senator Kefauver when it came to harassing nightclubs. They often attacked supper clubs for the "immoral" comedians they presented. While Lenny Bruce was the famous martyr, several other comedians were arrested before he came along.

Burlesque comic Jimmy Savo was arrested by plainclothesmen in 1942 after an organization called the Catholic Theatre Movement complained about his performance at the New York Ambassador Theater. The summons said "the show violates the penal law prohibiting indecency on the stage." Comedians Mickey Diamond and Jack High were arrested for obscenity in 1946 in Philadelphia. They were removed from the stage at the Silver Fleet Inn and held on bail. The same year comedian Marty Wayne had problems with a Philadelphia judge who said "nightclub operators should compel comedians to submit scripts before allowing them to go on." An arresting officer read portions of Wayne's act and Judge Harry S. McDevitt called the material "an affront to public morals." The details of that have yet to surface, but for the charge of "lewd entertainment," Wayne served six months in prison.

In 1949 comedian Lenny Ross was arrested in Atlantic City on charges of being "smutty." The State Department demanded Ross be "dismissed and barred from working," based on a previous conviction "for using blue material and obscene language in his act, for which he served a prison term." Ross told the judge, "I resort to smut only because patrons demand it." He started billing himself as "The Most Shocking Act in Show Business."

The definition of lewdness was completely arbitrary. The offending material was never quoted in the newspaper, so it's hard to determine what was actually said. Knowing the restrictions of the time, it's unlikely it would be considered offensive today. *Variety* pointed out at the time, "Under the present attitude, any routine except tap dancing is eligible for the tag 'lewd entertainment.' The local police, with a series of hit-and-miss raids, have been clamping down. The arrests in almost every instance have been promptly tossed out of court."

A club owner in Oakland was sentenced to five days in jail in December 1956 for staging an indecent show. The comedians playing his club—Charles Castle and Will Maso—were fined three hundred dollars and put on probation. Comedian Tom Melody was arrested in a Waikiki nightclub in 1957 after people complained that the "jokes, and actions, in his nitery routine are immoral." A warrant was issued and Melody was charged "with lewd conversation and lascivious conduct." On April 14, 1961, at the Jester's Club in Stanton, California, an audience member objected to the language of comedian George Hopkins and placed him under citizen's arrest. Police followed up and arrested Hopkins officially.

The most famous of the so-called lewd comics was B. S. Pully, a creature of Miami Beach strip clubs and Catskill roadhouses often billed as The Comic Who *May* Make You Laugh. "B. S. Pully—boy, was he tough," says comic Jackie Curtiss. "You ever hear about his penis-in-the-cigar-box bit?"

Pully was a kindred spirit of Joe E. Lewis. Both hard-drinking horse bettors, they became fast friends. If Lewis was offered a gig he couldn't accept, he recommended Pully for the job. Lewis elevated him from his strip club habitat, but Pully's subject matter imposed limitations on his career. Milton Berle called him "a legend in the annals of raw filth." When Rodney Dangerfield was starting out he shared the stage with Pully. "I'd heard plenty about B. S. Pully before I met him. People said he was a low-class, filthy, dirty maniac. When I met Pully, I learned that they had all been too nice." Peter

Marshall says, "B.S. would come out onstage. 'My name is B. S. Pully. B.S. don't stand for Boy Scout. It stands for bullshit.' That was his opening. In those days you couldn't say 'damn' in a club, but B.S. sure did."

Pully stood onstage with diminutive straight man H. S. Gump, whom he abused and knocked about. "Gump was a cute little nebbish," says Jack Carter. "Pully used to slap him around: 'Bleed, Gump, bleed!'" Occasionally they performed with a third partner named One Ball Barney. "Those two guys were really off-color," says Sammy Shore. "In those days you didn't work off-color, but because they were so damn funny they got away with it. They were incredible characters. They'd say 'shit' or 'fuck' and they'd do dirty things on stage with props and stuff."

Pully was arrested at the Frolics in Greenwich Village in 1942 and jailed for indecency. He and the club operator were detained until someone arrived with the five-hundred-dollar bail. In October 1946, Pully was again arrested in New York. He was put on trial for obscenity, but a grand jury refused to indict him.

Pully's act wasn't limited to verbiage. He often got laughs by being physically offensive. "I saw him do something horrendous one night," says comedian Freddie Roman. "There was a young girl singer, one of her first jobs. He walked up behind her and started grabbing her breasts while she was singing. The audience was laughing. The girl burst into tears and ran off the stage." Pully did things that would be considered bad taste even today. Lou Alexander says, "As a joke he used to walk around with a cigar box down by his crotch. He'd say, 'Hey, lady, would you like a cigar?' His dick would be in there with the cigars!"

Miami Beach was a sanctuary for the dirty comics. "'Dirty' was the thing after midnight in Florida," says comedian Rip Taylor. "They booked 'em specifically for those people that stayed up late, and they did more than 'hell' and 'damn' jokes." Pully's home base in Miami Beach was a strip club called Place Pigalle, where dirty comedienne Pearl Williams also played. Trumpet player Chris LaBarbera says, "You would walk in and Pearl Williams would be by the door insulting everybody. If a fat guy came in she'd say, 'How long has it been since you've seen your dick?'" Williams sat at a piano and delivered sex-related commentary and suggestive songs. She had been shut down in New Jersey for "lewd, indecent and immoral entertainment." The head of the New Jersey Alcoholic Beverage Control wrote a seventeen-page report in which he chided her "obscene and vulgar references to sex and sexual behavior, geared to a pornographic level with dirt for dirt's sake."

Comedian Ray Bourbon was arrested many times. He was safe in Miami Beach, but elsewhere he was customarily raided, civic authorities unplugging his microphone mid-performance. Bourbon was what the era called a "swish" performer. Objections to his act came from clerical voices, activating vice squads to action. Los Angeles police raided a gig of his way back in 1936. He was put on trial "in municipal court for allegedly putting on an indecent performance." The charges against Bourbon did not stem from dirty words, but from his onstage admission that he was homosexual. "There was a place he worked in Miami called the Jewel Box—what they called in those days a queer nightclub," says Woody Woodbury. "I guess it was a stigma if you were seen going to it, but we showbiz people, we used to go watch him."

Plagued by various levels of harassment, Bourbon invested his bank account in a one-man show at the Ivar Theatre in Hollywood in the early 1950s. The show was a failure, a victim of snide reviews panning its "obnoxious results" and "smutty allusions." Bourbon owed creditors and teetered on the verge of bankruptcy. In 1956, out of financial desperation, he initiated a publicity stunt. Inspired by the famous sex change operation of Christine Jorgensen, Bourbon visited surgeon "Emerick Szekely," or claimed he did, and returned to Hollywood in a blitz of triumphant sex change publicity. Stories about the procedure generated new interest in his act. Booked into the Melody Room on Sunset Boulevard for a one-man/one-woman show, it got the attention of the aggressive Los Angeles vice squad.

"The age old showbiz injunction to change your act led Ray Bourbon into court yesterday," wrote one news report. "Bourbon underwent a sex change operation in Mexico some months ago and announced that henceforth the act would be Miss Rae Bourbon.

Under that billing the performer was booked into the Melody Room. Seated at ringside Monday night for the first show were three uproarious gentlemen. And when the act was over, they followed (Miss) Bourbon into (his ... her ... check one) dressing room and flashed their buzzers. Sheriff's deputies. The charge—impersonating a woman."

Bourbon was outraged by his arrest. He shouted from the courthouse steps, "I *am* a woman!" He was held at the county jail, where deputies spent an hour conferring on whether to detain him in the male or female wing. While the details were hashed out, Bourbon sulked on a bench in a velvet gown before being released on bond. Melody Room proprietor Jack Gordon honored the remainder of his engagement, but adhering to the bizarre law, Bourbon was henceforth obligated to wear pants.

One week later the Los Angeles County Public Welfare Commission labeled Bourbon an "undesirable performer," granting sheriff's deputies the authority to close the Melody Room for "presenting an indecent performance." Overseeing the commission was Reverend Andrew F. Griffin, who categorized Bourbon as "obscene and profane." On November 1956, he was convicted in municipal court and sentenced to thirty days in prison for impersonating a woman. With nightclubs unwilling to take a chance on him, Bourbon started his own record label and released twelve comedy records. One was titled *Let Me Tell You About My Operation*.

Likewise, comedienne Belle Barth found records to be a good avenue for her risqué comedy. Barth was hounded by the authorities for decades. She based her act on another bawdy saloon singer named Annette Mitchum. According to author Lee Server, Mitchum "textured an act that mingled music with intimate conversation, verse, anecdote, some clever and charming lines with which to greet the crowd." Mitchum's brother wrote her material, and Barth hired him as well. "For ten or twenty dollars per piece, he would write a song, or satiric new lyrics to a hit tune," said Server. "Much of it was risqué stuff, packed with off-color implications and double entendres, going as far as the law or a club's management would allow." The writer was future movie star Robert Mitchum.

Barth established herself in 1940s Catskill roadhouses. They were stand-alone venues dotting the highway from Manhattan to the Catskill Mountains; places to get hammered, as opposed to the Catskill resorts, where people played tennis and ate latkes. By the early 1950s Barth was well known as a comic songstress who laced her lyrics with sexual innuendo. She was busted in 1953, 1954 and 1955 "for staging an obscene show."

The arrests furthered her legend, and her LPs moved solely based on reputation. Her first album—*If I Embarrass You Tell Your Friends*—was banned outright in New York City. *Billboard*, the trade journal devoted to record industry trends, wrote of Barth: "A curious anomaly in the disk business, she has sold close to 300,000 records on the After-Hours label but has yet to appear on any best-selling record chart. Her material is blue, and in many towns district attorneys or vice squads have raided her act or kept her records out of stores, or removed them from under the counter."

Her records were a boon to her nightclub business, but there was always the risk of overzealous law enforcement. Barth was playing a gig on the Sunset Strip in Los Angeles when sheriff's deputies arrested her "on suspicion of performing a lewd show liberally sprinkled with four-letter words." The charges were thrown out of court.

Charges of obscenity and lewd performance were dismissed more often than not, the interpretation of the law being highly subjective. Authorities in Atlantic City threw a fit when Barth played Irv Kolker's Le Bistro. The state's Alcoholic Beverage Control chastised Kolker for permitting "lewdness and immoral activity and foul, filthy and obscene language." A year later Barth was arrested in Buffalo for "disorderly performance." She released a maudlin statement: "If it's breaking the law to make people laugh, then I'm guilty."

It took a long time for social strictures to loosen. A pair of female schoolteachers watched Barth perform at Harry's American Bar at the Eden Roc Miami Beach Hotel in 1964 and were so offended by Barth's performance they sued her for $1.6 million, claiming the evening "corrupted them morally."

* * *

The church and the Mob held sway over subject matter, but the Catskill Mountains were insulated—and isolated—from such considerations. There were Mob-run roadhouses along the highway leading to the Catskills, but the Mountain resorts themselves were family operations. The demise of vaudeville allowed the area to gain traction as unemployed vaudevillians chased a paycheck. A solace from the Great Depression, with affordable prices and like-minded people, it earned the famous nickname "the Borscht Belt." Jerry Lewis said it was because "you'd have borscht and dairy products at lunch and meat products at dinner." Comedian Henny Youngman said it was "an area of maybe fifty square miles. And luckily for the entertainers, it was where a lot of squares came to have fun." Lewis disputed the square mileage, but agreed about, and was grateful to, the squares. "The Borscht Belt was a community within thirty square miles of a hundred and thirty hotels. For fifty-five dollars you could have room and board for an entire week. Plain people could come up from New York and have a wonderful week's vacation for very affordable prices. They had shows at night and they had three meals a day and beautiful accommodations. There was boating and swimming and golf. The food was magnificent. We had the opportunity of working a hotel at seven o'clock and driving to another hotel for an eight-thirty show, and another show at eleven . . . You'd get fifteen bucks for one of those shows, you do three of 'em you've got forty-five bucks. Pretty good for a fourteen-year-old kid."

Lewis was in the Mountains because of his parents. His father, Danny Lewis, was a longtime song-and-dance schlepper. "All he wanted to do was sing. He even showed up on vaccination lines. In those days the city hired entertainers to perform for the schoolchildren while they received smallpox shots."

The main attractions for most Catskill attendees were the food and finding a future spouse. Comedians were far down the list of enticements and, contrary to popular belief, Catskill crowds could be difficult. Sid Caesar started in the Catskills and found it difficult to fit in. "Every summer, as the comedians arrived at the hotels, they would open an old trunk and take out even older material. The shtick that was being used to entertain was familiar and tired. Catskill audiences were *tough*. Some of them didn't laugh at anything." Playing a resort called the Avon Lodge, Caesar worked with a marginal Catskill veteran named Jackie Michaels. A reporter from *Collier's* said the material was so old it "originated in pre-caveman times."

> **Jackie Michaels:** What do I have in my hand? An egg or a
>   tomato?
> **Sid Caesar:** An egg.
> (Jackie Michaels smashes a tomato into Sid Caesar's face)
> **Jackie Michaels:** Wrong, it's a tomato!

Determined to reject this "pre-caveman" comedy, Caesar was forced to create. "It was there, in an attempt to do something new, that I first started developing sketch comedy."

The Catskills were dominated by one major booking agency. "Charlie Rapp was the office that booked the Catskills," says comedian Norm Crosby. "He was the boss. He was the king of the Mountains." A booker for MCA in the 1930s, Rapp amassed a large network of showbiz connections and went independent in 1942. He circumvented war rationing by founding Rapp's Farm, which supplied Mountain hotels with scarce supplies like gas and tires . . . and comedians.

"He is the Ziegfeld of the Catskills," reported Earl Wilson in 1949. "He sends his acts rushing from one hotel to another, and they may work five or six spots a night, being hustled around the circuit by auto." Rapp brought his nephews into the family business, and Charles Rapp Enterprises monopolized the Mountains, booking talent for the largest and most important Catskill resorts—the Concord and Grossinger's.

Grossinger's and the Concord conjure a specific lifestyle and time. "It was like you 'made it' if you headlined the Concord," says comedienne Marilyn Michaels. "Big place. At the time they had these 'knockers' to applaud. They didn't use their hands, they used these wooden sticks with wooden balls at the end of them. If they really liked you *then* they used their hands." The Concord was a modest resort that grew larger and larger as the economy recovered during Roosevelt's presidency. It became almost too big a room for a comedian to succeed in.

"I did the Concord several times, and every time it was an ordeal," says Jack Carter. "It used to be a cute little job when it was a couple hundred, but then it became a massive arena and it was really tough to handle. Thirty-five hundred seats. You had to have a powerful act to capture that group. They had big signs along the highway when someone was playing the Concord—always major stars, major names, and it paid big money."

Many professional comedians who did well in the Catskills never bothered to leave. "Larry Best and Larry Alpert were two comedians whose prominence was only in the Catskill Mountains," says Freddie Roman. "Ninety percent of their income was up there." Comedian Jackie Wakefield remained in the Catskills out of fear. Comedy writer Marshall Brickman sold him jokes. "He never went on television. He just had his twenty minutes and did his Mountain circuit and never had to write anything new." Comic Art Metrano rattles off Catskill names: "Jackie Miles, Jackie Winston, Mal Z. Lawrence. These guys never really made it, but always worked the Mountains." Another in their group was Morty Storm. Comedian Pat Cooper said Storm "stood on stage and garbled a bunch of jokes that no one could understand. He wore big, thick-rimmed glasses. He had a hairpiece that sat on his head like a dead raccoon. Morty would wear the same suit for a week and never bathe. When he performed in the Catskills, there were certain maids who would not do his room."

The Catskills endured for several decades. Cerebral comedians in the early 1960s played the Mountains—even if they were out of place. "The summer I graduated from high school, I had a job in the Catskill Mountains at a small, reasonably dumpy resort called the Almanac Hotel and Country Club," said comedian Robert Klein. "'Country Club' was an appellation frequently affixed to second-rate hotels in the area, to add the panache so lacking in the rickety buildings and the bumbling staff." Klein was often astounded by veteran comedians. "At times they would throw in jokes with Yiddish punch lines, mystifying and confusing those of us who did not understand the language."

The Catskills endured as a phrase, a description and a put-down. If a comedian was referred to as a "Catskill guy," it was a euphemism for old-fashioned and out of touch. Some say working in the Catskills was a way of life, but for most comedians it was just another job. The majority of comics didn't stay there any longer than they had to. The cliché goes that the Catskills shaped modern comedy, but the majority of the stars who went through the Mountains actually made their mark in the bustling media capital of Manhattan more so than the Catskills.

New York City remained the most important place for a comedian in the 1940s and 1950s. Hollywood was reserved for movies, while New York was the epicenter of radio and television. The mammoth presentation houses along Broadway gave important career boosts to Jack Carter, Jean Carroll, Myron Cohen, Phil Foster, Alan King, Jack E. Leonard, Jan Murray, Larry Storch and Henny Youngman. The venues brought comedians to the attention of influential newspaper columnists, radio advertisers and television executives. These comedians were too young to have done vaudeville, but not yet confident enough to write their own material. They were the bridge between old-fashioned vaudeville and the intellectual coffeehouse comics soon to emerge. Nearly all the comedians who populated television in the 1950s came out of Manhattan's presentation house scene.

Broadway presentation houses seated anywhere from one to five thousand people. The pay was good, performances were frequent and engagements were long. They showcased "band shows" with the likes of the Count Basie, Tommy Dorsey and Duke Ellington orchestras. Accompanied by a girl singer, a dance team and a comic, the live performance would run under an hour, followed by a new motion picture. Each presentation house was owned by—or had a deal with—a major film studio.

The major New York presentation houses were the Capitol, the Music Hall, the Paramount, the Roxy, the Strand and Loew's State. A comedian performed a set averaging twelve minutes anywhere from four to six times a day. Morning shows started at ten o'clock, attracting derelicts who needed rest after a night in the cold. For a quarter they could buy a ticket, sit down and snore through the show. "Sidney Piermont was the booker for the Capitol and Loew's State, and he liked me," says Jack Carter. "Loew's State was kind of a bum theater. A lot of bums would come in and hang out. It was tawdry."

The mammoth Roxy presentation house seated 5,500 people; this could be deadly for a novice, but if you had a strong routine the sound of 5,500 laughs was exhilarating. Comedian Joe Frisco had a famous line about its vastness: "Don't get lost on the Roxy stage without bread and water." Comic Leo DeLyon says, "At the Roxy you did four shows a day. As a rule, the first show was pretty good reaction-wise. The second was a bit of a letdown, a little tougher and a little thinner. The best was always the evening show, the last one, when they were the most receptive."

According to New York columnist Earl Wilson, a celebrity headliner playing a presentation house could command an astounding fifty thousand dollars for a weeklong engagement, whereas a typical nightclub paid one-tenth that amount. Before Las Vegas, it was Broadway presentation houses that offered the comedian's largest payday. Still, it was hard work for even competent veterans. "Those presentation houses became terrible grinds, even though the salaries were better than bigtime vaudeville," said comic Benny Rubin. "There was nothing artistic about what you did, but it was a lot of money. We did four shows a day along with a movie. When you walked on the stage of a presentation house, there was always a band, usually set on the stage in full view of the audience. During the first show the band laughed at the jokes. The second time around, they'd heard the jokes and don't laugh so much. Well, the audience is looking at them. The audience says, 'If they're not laughing, why should I laugh?' By the third show one guy is cleaning his trumpet and the other is fixing the slide on his trombone and another guy's writing a letter and by the fourth show they hated your guts."

Before the existence of comedy clubs, the presentation house was where an aspiring comic went to observe and learn. Jerry Lewis was a teenage usher at the Paramount. Woody Allen, Jack Carter, Pat Cooper and Will Jordan all attended presentation houses as children, absorbing the entertainment, dreaming of participating in it. "I saw Milton Berle as a kid at the Paramount," says Carter. "My sisters would take me and I'd see him onstage and think, 'Jesus, that's amazing.' I'd try to memorize every joke. I had no idea that he was doing the same jokes every night, all rehearsed."

The Paramount was arguably the most important of the houses, with its fifty-five-cent admission slightly higher than the others. Harry Kalcheim of William Morris booked the talent while Bob Weitman produced the shows from 1935 through the early 1950s. The Paramount was where Frank Sinatra became an idol to sexually inchoate bobby-soxers, solidifying its reputation as one of the most important venues in town.

Singers were the primary draw on a band show; the comedians existed in their shadows. Comedian Don Sherman says, "It was tough because you came out and the audience was waiting for the singer. When I got my first job with Johnny Mathis they'd announce, 'And now . . . bump-bada-bumm! Don Sherman!' And a thousand people would groan. I mean actual groans. They groaned every place I went. I jumped on that groan, man. 'You sons of bitches! What about me? I'm a human being!'"

Jean Carroll was a prolific presentation house comic in the 1940s and the only female stand-up comic around. As a femme joke slinger, she predated Phyllis Diller and Joan Rivers, and unlike those who came before she wasn't comical in appearance. She didn't wear a funny costume or a frumpy hat, but took to the stage in an elegant dress and evening gloves. She was the first of a new breed.

"There weren't very many 'comediennes' in those days," says 102-year-old Connie Sawyer, who did sketches and parodies in the late 1940s. "Jean Carroll was like Bob Hope. She did stand-up jokes. Jokes, jokes, jokes. As far as comediennes—that was *it*."

Jean Carroll worked with Marty May, a son-in-law of Olsen & Johnson's Chic Johnson, during the dying days of vaudeville. Their billing was "Marty May Annoyed by Jean Carroll." Their only historical distinction is giving Bob Hope his big break. Marty May was offered a starring role in the Broadway show *Roberta*, but since May and Carroll had contractual obligations with presentation houses, he turned it down. In his place producers cast the unknown Bob Hope, and it gave him his first taste of stardom.

Jean Carroll married dancer Buddy Howe, and he became her new straight man. Then came World War II and Howe enlisted, leaving Carroll to perform alone. Just as many women entered the traditional workplace during the war, taking occupations usually filled by men, Carroll took advantage of the vacant slots at presentation houses and got a lot of the stand-up work previously reserved for dudes.

"Jean Carroll, petite and dark-haired miss, comes on cold, introduces herself as mistress-of-ceremonies," read a review of a November 1943 engagement. "She tells some stories, does a good impression of various radio announcers delivering trite commercials." Five months later at the Hippodrome in Baltimore, "Jean Carroll, a single this time, has the emcee assignment in addition to her own slot. Does a very credible job and shows considerable possibilities." Three weeks later in Newark, "Jean Carroll gives a hint of stellar material. She needs better gags, but does remarkably well with what she has [and] the audience liked plenty."

She had those better gags by 1945, and over the next three years she played Loew's State, the Capitol, the Palace, the Paramount and the Strand multiple times. No other comic played as many presentation houses. Unlike the few other comediennes, she did not do sketches, characters or song parodies, nor did she work as part of a team. She stood onstage alone and rattled off punch lines every twelve to fifteen seconds. She was a joke machine:

Love! Does anybody know what love is? That's a moot question. So I asked Moot. Moot was my first boyfriend. I was crazy about him. Our romance was one of those triangles. You see, he and I were both in love with him. Then there was Jack. Oh, let me tell you how I met Jack.

I was standing on a corner—as usual. We went out and lemmee tell
you something, he was a real sport. Money? Money meant nothing.
Nothing! He didn't have any. I shouldn't make fun of him. After all,
he's so sweet. Nothing bothers him . . . He drinks. Well, he doesn't drink
because he likes it. He drinks to steady his nerves. The other night his
nerves got so steady he couldn't move at all.

Carroll became the first female stand-up to headline major night-clubs like the Latin Quarter and the Copacabana. CBS starred her in an early sitcom with Art Carney. In a way she was a poster child for the independent working woman, but when her husband was named head of the massive talent agency General Amusement Corporation, she retreated. In typical 1950s fashion, after several appearances on *The Ed Sullivan Show*, she abandoned her trade and became a housewife. Carroll was forgotten in her lifetime, but she should be noted for her influence on Phyllis Diller, Minnie Pearl and Joan Rivers. As a child Lily Tomlin played dress-up and pretended she was Jean Carroll.

The biggest comedy act to come out of the Manhattan presentation house world was Martin & Lewis. Just as young girls had shrieked for Sinatra, the fervor surrounding Dean Martin and Jerry Lewis at the Paramount was enormous.

Lewis started in clubs with a "record act," a common convention used by amateur comedians with no material. A popular song was played offstage on a record player while a comic mugged expressions and gestures in time to the track. British-born actor Reginald Gardiner was said to have originated the idea. One tally had it that by 1940 there were more than two hundred such acts in the biz. Comedy writer Philip Rapp recalled seeing the early Jerry Lewis: "It was in a downstairs café somewhere on Broadway and business was brisk. He had a mop on his head and was going through the motions of conducting an orchestra while a phonograph record played in the background. He also walked on his insteps and imitated a spastic. I was not impressed."

Dean Martin was a struggling crooner with a massive schnoz. The Jersey native was connected to comedians from the start. His roommate in the early days was a struggling Alan King, who also did a record act. One of Martin's early boosters was Lou Costello of Abbott & Costello. "I even advanced him enough to have his nose bobbed," said Costello. "He hasn't even bothered so much as to call me."

Dean Martin and Jerry Lewis were occasionally booked on the same shows. They had a nice chemistry and their interactions turned to shtick. Suddenly they were a team, acccelerating at an incredible pace, scoring choice bookings at Bill Miller's Riviera in Fort Lee, New Jersey, and Slapsy Maxie's in Los Angeles. Martin was calm, cool and suave while Lewis was gawky, obnoxious and animated. Martin would sing a song and Lewis would run through the crowd knocking over dishes and chairs. Club-goers ate it up.

Their spell at the Paramount established them as stars. *Life* magazine encapsulated it with a classic photo spread. Accompanying newsreel footage showed the duo being swarmed by fans and hounded by screaming girls tearing at their shirts, the closest thing to Beatlemania comedy has ever had. Frequent collaborator Norman Taurog said, "The response was almost orgiastic."

They became so big so fast that veteran comedians complained bitterly. "They're using all my best bits," complained Milton Berle. Comedian Jack E. Leonard said, "This is a nothing act. What Martin & Lewis do isn't basically funny, but nobody else has the gall to do it in a sophisticated café where they're paying you twenty grand a week. When you figure other comics have struggled all their lives to perfect an act, it burns you up that here's a couple of characters that come out and do nothing but tell some old chestnuts and the customers are crazy for them."

They were a smash in Hollywood and Manhattan, but outside the big cities people had to take the word of syndicated newspaper columnists. It wasn't until NBC hired them for *The Colgate Comedy Hour*, a primitive television variety show, that the country understood the fuss.

The Colgate Comedy Hour had a rotation of hosts. A sentimental Eddie Cantor emceed the debut episode on September 10, 1950. Martin & Lewis hosted the second episode. Poor Fred Allen had the misfortune of following them on week three. Beside Martin & Lewis, everyone else looked like they were moving in slow motion.

Future names like director Arthur Penn and writers Ed Simmons and Norman Lear worked on *The Colgate Comedy Hour*. They had difficulty with the twenty-four-year-old Lewis, who, as one of the biggest stars in comedy at such a young age, had an enormous ego. "We were rehearsing our first show," said Lear. "Jerry, who was supposed to be the 'funny one,' couldn't stand it if Dean got any laughs. Dean could be insanely funny with a line. Any morning that Dean would start being funny, Jerry would wind up in a corner on the floor someplace with a bellyache. And a doctor would have to come. Whenever Dean was very funny, strange physical things happened to Jerry." They worked together well, but jealousy was always an issue. "Dean would come up with these great lines in rehearsal," said comedy writer Bud Yorkin. "Then Jerry would do them on the air as if they were ad-libbed and get an ovation. It was down and dirty for a while." When *TV Guide* called Simmons and Lear "the brains behind the success of Dean and Jerry," Lewis had an immediate response. He fired them.

It is unlikely Lewis would have experienced such enormous success at such a young age if not for the New York presentation house scene. Manhattan was the place to be if you were ambitious. Midtown was dense with show business. Not only were there the presentation houses, but there were a number of small clubs to try out new material, like Leon and Eddie's on 52nd Street.

Leon and Eddie's hosted a popular "Celebrity Night" on Sunday evenings, where baby-faced comics stood at their tables and lost themselves in improvised routines. The nights were a way around Manhattan's "blue laws," which prohibited performances on Sundays. Singer Eddie Fisher said, "The greatest performers in show business would stand up right in the audience and sing and tell some jokes. Even after the blue laws were modified these celebrity nights remained a show-business tradition."

Co-owner Eddie Davis was a vaudeville veteran who did song parodies. Like many venues of the time, it was a former speakeasy.

Forgotten today, it was one of the top comedy venues of the late 1940s. "I don't know whether it was planned that way to get a lot of free talent, but every Sunday there used to be a sort of happening at Leon and Eddie's," said Henny Youngman. "Everybody would drop in to show off their stuff and catch the competition. With guys like Alan King, Jack E. Leonard, Jerry Lewis, Joey Adams, Milton Berle, all hanging around looking for a spot to zap in a yock, you can imagine the heckling that went on." Ed Sullivan and writer Robert Benchley were Leon and Eddie's regulars. Marlon Brando and fellow actor Wally Cox were too, until Brando was barred for defying the dress code.

Leon and Eddie's inspired another freewheeling room, this one run by comedian Morey Amsterdam. "It was called the Playgoers Club," says comic Bobby Ramsen. "It was on Sixth Avenue and it was downstairs. It was the subbasement of the building. Morey always said, 'I get most of my customers because people think this is the subway.'" Jack Carter says, "That was my hangout. Morey would get up and do an hour and a half. I'd either heckle him or I'd get up and do something with him. Art Carney would get up at the club too. Carney did the funniest routine of President Roosevelt taking a crap, squeezing it out and trying to talk at the same time."

Morey Amsterdam was one of the few comedians of his generation to write his own material. He was prolific and could rattle off jokes—of varying quality—at will. "He was a joke machine," says comedy writer Bill Persky. "No taste. He wasn't necessarily vulgar, but he made up jokes that didn't have any substance." It didn't matter, because Amsterdam had a lot of time to fill. He had his own marathon radio show called *The Gloom Dodgers*, described in trade-speak as "a marathon ad-lib stanza." It was loose comedy, from 1 to 5 P.M., five days a week. "Morey was on for four hours—everything off the top of his head," says Ramsen. "He would kid around with the orchestra leader and he would kid around with people in the studio. Morey would ask the audience for subjects and he would tell a joke on any: carpenters, maids, landlords—he had a joke for every one of them."

Another comic fronting a Manhattan nightclub in the late 1940s was Milton Berle. Rookie impresario Nicky Blair, a Broadway associate of showman Billy Rose, ran a club called the Carnival. The room, at 53rd and 8th, opened its doors two months after the war. It was enormous, seating nearly eight hundred people. America was experiencing prosperity, and Blair was able to pay Berle ten thousand dollars a week. Berle had been a success in vaudeville, a failure on Broadway, a triumph in nightclubs and a mediocrity in radio. Joey Adams' 1946 book *From Gags to Riches* dismissed him as "the poor man's Bob Hope." At the Carnival he honed the emcee tricks he used for the rest of his career.

Milton Berle at the Carnival Club, Morey Amsterdam at the Playgoers Club, everyone else at Leon and Eddie's: These venues, along with the presentation houses, laid the foundation for early television comedy and were where future comedy stars found their way. And beyond them there were the New York delicatessens like Lindy's and drugstore counters like Hanson's, which were perhaps the most important meeting grounds of all.

New York comedy had a class system. Your stature in the business determined where you hung out. If your career was lower than low you spent your time at the B-G Coffee Shop, the Horn & Hardart automat, Hector's Cafeteria or Kellogg's Cafeteria. You cooked up a grotesque tomato soup by mixing hot water with a free paper cup of ketchup. You sat down with Sam Newgold, the agent who exclusively represented losers and used the automat as his office. "During the day at the Theatrical Pharmacy he books the acts," said comedian Joey Adams. "At night in Kellogg's he waits for his commission. Sam claims he is the biggest booking agent of the best comedians in the low-priced field."

The hierarchy of Lindy's, the Stage Delicatessen, the Carnegie Delicatessen and Hanson's Drugstore still has meaning for an old-timer. "Hanson's was for the nothing comics," bristles Jack Carter. "The third-raters! I would never step foot in Hanson's! *Never*. It was Lindy's for me."

Lindy's was king. Mentioned in countless magazine profiles of the time, it permeated the pages of *Collier's*, *Esquire* and *TV Guide*.

It was mentioned in the radio jokes of Fred Allen and the wry comments of Oscar Levant. If chronicler Richard Gehman was writing a profile of a top comic, Lindy's was where they met. If Abe Lastfogel wanted to inform a client about a deal William Morris had closed, he did so over the matzo ball soup at Lindy's. When a columnist was on a deadline with nothing to say, inevitably the atmosphere of Lindy's itself became the story.

In 1914 Leo Lindemann was waiting tables next door to the Palace Theatre. His affection for showbiz types blossomed at the Palace Café. He absorbed their tastes, nuances and idiosyncratic aspirations, and incorporated all of it when he opened his own spot seven years later.

There were two locations. The first opened in 1921 at Broadway and 49th. "The old Lindy's was where the songwriters, music publishers, horseplayers, bookies, hoodlums, hustlers and high rollers used to hang out," said writer Maurice Zolotow. "It was where [gangster] Arnold Rothstein was wont to transact his business and it was at the old Lindy's that he got the mysterious phone call which summoned him to a rendezvous with death."

The second location was the larger and more famous. It opened in 1929 at Broadway and 51st. "Songwriters, song pluggers, show folks and even eminents like the late Bernard Baruch and J. Edgar Hoover were frequent diners," wrote columnist Louis Sobol. Song-and-dance man Sonny King, a sidekick to Jimmy Durante, had his wedding at Lindy's. It was at the Lindy's entrance that mobster Abraham Telvi threw acid in the eyes of journalist Victor Riesel, blinding him for life.

More than anything else, Lindy's was known for its comedians, who'd crowd in around midnight after their final shows. To sit at the center front table meant you were at the top of the comedy world. Those with a modicum of success were seated closer to the revolving door. If you were a bum by Lindy's standards—someone who performed at Leon and Eddie's but never the Copa—you were stuck way in the back, out of view, a reminder of your insignificance. Milton Berle was the leader. "One seldom sees him at Lindy's without a retinue of assorted hangers-on who laugh every time he utters a syllable," wrote columnist Ben Gross. A classic Al Hirschfeld drawing gave a sense of the atmosphere, rendering Berle, Fred Allen, Morey Amsterdam, Ben Blue, Red Buttons, Phil Foster, Jack E. Leonard, Joe E. Lewis, Red Skelton, Arnold Stang and Henny Youngman.

The newspaper columnists hung out at Lindy's in hope of snagging an entertaining quip. With circulation at an all-time high, newspapers were often vital to a comedian's career. It was great publicity for an up-and-comer to get a mention from Frank Farrell, Hy Gardner, Leonard Lyons, Louis Sobol, Ed Sullivan, Walter Winchell or Earl Wilson. "There were so many columns then, and you had to feed them," says Jack Carter. "In New York there were millions of them." Comedians hired press agents whose sole job was to get the comics' names in the columns. Bobby Ramsen says, "Press agents used to get a client and place something like, 'Gene Baylos was at Jack Dempsey's last night. He said the crowd at Madison Square Garden must be dressed in Saks Fifth Avenue . . .' That press agent would have Gene Baylos as a client, Jack Dempsey as a client, Madison Square Garden as a client, Saks as a client."

Writers like Maurice Zolotow loved Lindy's. "Lindy's was where we went after midnight. There was a talented, a frantic, a hedonistic, a beautiful generation of show people. The clinking and clattering of silverware and dishes reverberated and the babble of conversation became amplified so much it was deafening. At Lindy's the service would completely break down during such crises and it was then that the waiters became arrogant, nasty, insulting. Many out-of-town diners seemed to enjoy being browbeaten by one, especially if he spoke ungrammatically and with a rough New York accent."

Lindy's had a famous waiter named Jaegger, a snide bastard who thought nothing of insulting the biggest stars in the business. "Milton Berle popularized him," says Jack Carter. "He was a waiter who was snotty with Milton and treated him like garbage. 'Vot do you vant, you low-class comic?'"

One rung down from Lindy's was the Stage Delicatessen, which was smaller in stature, smaller in size and inhabited by comedians with smaller careers. *Tonight Show* host Jack Paar said, "It's a small place so crowded that dining there is not only an adventure in eating, but in self-defense. The place seats just seventy people or, as Max puts it, with mink coats—thirty." The Max in question was owner Max Asnas. Comedians ridiculed the bald, squat proprietor. He was famed for his broken English and malaprop-filled philosophy. Fred Allen dubbed him Broadway's Corned Beef Confucius. Jack Carter says, "He had a lot of Max Asnas–isms. He thought anything he said was memorable and he thought he was a great wit, but nothing he said made sense. He'd say things like, 'You know, a man is like salami: Once you eat it—you don't want it.' 'Life is like a boiled potato. If you don't eat it—you never got it.'" Fred Allen was so taken with the Asnas malapropisms that he integrated them into a character on *The Fred Allen Show*. He switched the gender, but kept the character Jewish, naming her Mrs. Nussbaum. Fred Allen would greet her, "Why, Mrs. Nussbaum!" She would respond with a Yiddish inflection, "You were expecting Cecil B. Schlemiel?" Jack Paar joked, "Max is a man of many words. All of them hard to understand."

The Stage entered popular culture. An episode of *The Joey Bishop Show* took place in the deli and Asnas played himself. Noted showbiz manager Jack Rollins proposed a television series about the Stage. It never came to be, but the Woody Allen film *Broadway Danny Rose*, which Rollins produced, had a similar theme.

The Stage gave birth to a delicatessen gimmick that exists to this day. Sandwiches had titles like "the Milton Berle," "the Henny Youngman" and "the Jack Paar." The delicatessen was named in the routines of several comics. When Youngman appeared on *The Merv Griffin Show* he was introduced, "Direct from the Stage Delicatessen!" The atmosphere radiated Broadway excitement. Bobby Ramsen says, "When you walked into the Stage Delicatessen at ten or eleven o'clock at night—you could *feel it*."

Hanson's Drugstore was near the bottom of the class system, but it hosted the most comedians of all. A narrow rectangle of a pharmacy with a long lunch counter, wooden telephone booths and a small loft, it smelled of general desperation. Beside the old Wintergarden Theatre, across from the Roxy, it was where comedy's unemployed spent their afternoons. Comic Stan Irwin called it "the poor man's Friars Club."

"It was the oldest show business building in New York—1650 Broadway, at 51st and Seventh," says Don Sherman, a comic who schlepped through immortal obscurity. "All the offices above it— fourteen stories—were agents." Hanson's back entrance took you to the 1650 lobby, the agency directory and an elevator. "There were phone booths at the back of Hanson's that were constantly busy," says comedy writer Ron Clark. "Comics stood there waiting for their agents to call them." Jerry Lewis hung out at Hanson's before his success. "Jerry Lewis was still in his teens, wasn't married," says Will Jordan. "He wasn't even that successful yet, but he would get girls in that loft and he'd make it right in Hanson's."

"We were working two days a week," says comedian Lou Alexander. "If we got a job on Friday or Saturday it was a big deal. We'd get fifty dollars for the two days. I hung around Hanson's from 1952 through 1953. It was enough to pay our rent, enough to pay our phone, enough to pay our food. Fifty dollars a weekend—we lived on it. And enough to hang around Hanson's all day long."

Comedians too poor to afford the signature cheesecake at Lindy's could settle for Hanson's not-so-famous grilled cheese and loiter all day. "The guy who ran it, Hanson, was Danish," says Will Jordan. "When Victor Borge came to town he let Borge get behind the cash register. Hans Hanson had this expression, 'All yuh comedians, kvit hangin round!' We'd clutter up the store and no one ever bought anything. Then he sees me on *The Ed Sullivan Show* and says, 'Vas dat you last night?' I said, 'Yeah.' He says, '*You* can hang round.'"

The most notable of all the Hanson's Drugstore regulars was an impressionist in an all-white suit—Lenny Bruce. "Comedians would stand around Hanson's and banter dirty jokes back and forth," says Bobby Ramsen. "But you would never think of repeating that dirty joke at the nightclub. You'd tell those kinds of jokes in front of Hanson's and laugh, but then Lenny Bruce came along and had the guts to go out and do that kind of material on a nightclub floor."

Bruce's mother, Sally Marr, managed a handful of comedians, and she held court in a back booth. She got Bruce his first broadcast gig. Appearing on *Arthur Godfrey's Talent Scouts* in 1949, he scored with his James Cagney, one of the most common impressions of the day. "*Arthur Godfrey's Talent Scouts* was as important as *American Idol,*" says comedian Leo DeLyon. "It was coast-to-coast radio on CBS. Three contestants. They were actually mostly professionals, but they were early in their career. Everyone who went on got a hundred dollars no matter what. They had a big applause meter projected on a screen for the studio audience. If you won then you would be on the Godfrey morning show for the next four days, and from that you would get nibbles from various agents."

"Some of the amateur nights that I did, Lenny Bruce did too," says Will Jordan. "We were not booked the same nights because we were too similar. We did the same things and the same amateurs beat us the same amateur nights." Jordan and Bruce swapped impressions back and forth at Leon and Eddie's. "When Lenny Bruce first came by he looked like an Arab pimp—very pale, mustache, big white coat and everything. I didn't know that years later he would be a terrible thief. I came up with all these bits; Lenny Bruce stole them, and it hurt me. It partially ruined me. He stole a bit I did about [film actor] Sabu and a bit about Hitler." Lenny's former manager, Frankie Ray Perilli, confirms that Bruce stole some of Jordan's material. "Will Jordan has reason to be mad at Lenny Bruce, because that is true."

It was a transitional time for Bruce. He wasn't happy with the material he was doing or the showbizzy results of his *Arthur Godfrey* appearance. He was booked at the Strand, his largest gig to date, but the presentation house gave him a cool reception. "I didn't get one goddamn laugh. The audience knew it was dishonest. It wasn't me."

Bruce briefly joined the merchant marines, where his pot habit expanded. When he returned to New York he longed for greater highs. Bruce met up with the diminutive burlesque comedian Tommy Moe Raft, who introduced him to his wife. "I had to figure out a way to really meet this Lenny Bruce," said Honey Harlow, the future Mrs. Bruce. "I asked Tommy if he had any ideas. Tommy laughed and told me not to worry. He'd bought a matchbox of grass so he invited Lenny and the chorus girls to his hotel room for a J. The five of us piled into Tommy's room and passed a couple of J's around.

By the time we'd finished smoking them, Tommy's tiny room was a mellow haze of smoke and everyone was smiling."

According to Frankie Ray Perilli, Harlow introduced Bruce to heroin at this time. Bruce was booked for a five-week engagement at the China Doll, a short-lived venue directly across from Hanson's, which became his place to score dope. *Time* magazine wrote about Manhattan's drug trade in 1951 and mentioned the China Doll and Hanson's Drugstore. "It is a city where 'pushers' peddle their wares almost as casually as sidewalk balloon vendors, . . . where an innocent-looking drugstore or cafeteria may be an addicts' hangout . . . [An addict] named scores of drugstores, bars, restaurants, hotels, night-clubs . . . where she had purchased a fix. The famed China Doll night-club off Broadway was a good spot: 'Two or three peddlers hang around there on a quiet basis.' So was Hanson's Drugstore at 51st Street and Seventh Avenue in midtown Manhattan . . . 'You just walk in, get a cup of coffee, put your money down, pick up the drugs and leave.'"

Lenny Bruce used heroin with Harlow, but for the rest of the com-ics it was strictly marijuana. Jack Roy, who would change his name to Rodney Dangerfield, relied on a pal of Lenny's named Joe Ancis to supply him. Smoking pot was a common ritual for the Hanson's crowd. Buddy Hackett, Jackie Miles, Joe E. Ross—even big names like Huntz Hall and Phil Silvers—loved to get stoned. "All those Brooklyn guys were big pot smokers," says Jack Carter. It passed the time, it absolved the problems and it heightened the laughs.

Jack Roy's first time stoned was a life-changing experience. "One night in Kellogg's Cafeteria I was sitting with a couple of show folk—a comic named Bobby Byron and my friend Joe E. Ross. Bobby and Joe E. decided that they wanted to get high. They invited me to join them. So we walked back to the Belvedere Hotel. Bobby took out a joint. He and Joe E. took a couple of hits off that joint, then offered it to me. I felt relaxed, peaceful, everything was okay. That night I found a friend for the rest of my life."

The Hanson's crowd couldn't stand Jack Roy if he *wasn't* high. "He had a reputation for being angry," says Bobby Ramsen. "They called him Angry Jack. When Jack Roy was working it was with an *edge*." Comedian Pat Cooper agrees: "He was very depressed and *angry*." Jack Carter shouts, "Yeah, he was a bum! He'd hang around Hanson's. He *tried* to come into Lindy's."

"Jack Roy was performing in Queens," says comedian Art Metrano. "He wasn't very good, but he knew how to tell jokes. We always thought he was like a young Henny Youngman. 'My wife is such a bad cook, the dogs beg for Alka-Seltzer.'" Indeed, Jack Roy sat through consecutive shows at the Paramount in order to study Youngman's act and emulate his prolific rate of punch lines.

Jack Roy bombed more often than not. It wasn't that he had bad material, but his persona was combative and unlikable. It didn't matter how funny the material was—the audience despised him.

For all the talk of a postwar nightclub boom, if you couldn't ingratiate yourself with club owners, your peers, or the Mob, then stand-up was an impossible pursuit. "It was rough," he said. "Even then, with hundreds of clubs in New York, no one would take a chance on a kid. All day I walked around in the heat, going from agent to agent trying to get a job in show business."

Jack Roy's marriage added to his frustration. His wife persuaded him to quit stand-up so that he could spend more time with his family. He had just been offered a gig at La Martinique, a major nightclub, but instead acquiesced to his wife. It filled him with resentment.

"He married her twice and divorced her twice," says comedian Robert Klein. "I knew her as a frightened, pale-skinned woman." Comedian Van Harris says, "It was a very bad marriage. One day he walked into the club after they had been married awhile. I swear, she must have been forty years old, but she *looked* sixty. It was a terrible marriage. Her family *hated* him." According to Art Metrano, "Rodney had *tremendous* hate for his wife."

Jack Roy left comedy and entered the world of aluminum siding. "I needed a steady income. So I went into the home improvement business. I sold aluminum siding and paint on a commission basis at a place called Pioneer Construction in Newark." Comedian Stan Irwin literally rented Roy's act when he left the business. "I said,

'Your act fits mine. I'll rent it from you for X amount of dollars per week and put it with mine, since you're not using it.'" Roy didn't abandon show business completely. In order to retain a connection, he and Joe Ancis drove to Hanson's in the morning to get high and sell jokes to other comedians. Irwin says, "Jack had a file of jokes in the trunk of his car that he would sell to you for five dollars apiece."

Years later he claimed he was successful in home improvement and changed his name to erase the memory of his initial stand-up career. The reality is that Jack Roy changed his name to erase the stigma of a criminal record. "I sold aluminum siding," he once said. "I made a decent living . . . but I wasn't *living*." The decent living he made was not as a salesman per se, but as a con man.

"They called them tin men," says Van Harris. "After World War II, a lot of the guys would sell home repairs to people. These guys would all wear the Ruptured Duck [honorable service button] on their lapel and people would see they were veterans. He'd say, 'I just served in the army. Now I'm making a living thanks to the United States government—and I can get you repairs for your home. If your roof leaks or if you need new windows . . . I can get these things for you for cheap.' They would sell these things to the mothers of veterans, and it was a *scam*. A big scam!"

Roy enlisted struggling comedians to join him. "Everybody was doing it, including me," says comic Howard Storm. "They were scamming people, and I hated doing it. I quit after the first week. They kept calling me to come back. I said, 'No, if I need money I'll come back. I don't want to do it on a regular basis.' They were charging people three or four times what it was worth."

One morning the comedians at Hanson's were waiting for Jack Roy to arrive with his carful of jokes—and he didn't show up. Nobody knew why until the paper was delivered the following day. The FBI had been hipped to the tin men and had been monitoring Jack Roy. "In a series of midnight and pre-dawn raids, the FBI today collared 15 men accused of faking $600,000 in home repair loans," reported the *Long Island Star-Journal* on October 22, 1955. "According to James J. Kelly, special agent in charge of the Manhattan FBI headquarters, loans granted by banks and insured by the FHA were used to consolidate debts, pay off autos and other purposes. Kelly charged that the high-pressure operators—known in the trade as 'suede shoe boys' and 'shingle bums'—worked their racket through a kickback arrangement. Top executives in the four firms [include] Jack Cohen, also known as Jack Roy."

What happened next is fuzzy, but Roy somehow finagled his way out of the situation. "The charges were all dropped," says Robert Klein. "It had to do with the federal housing something or other, but it never came to court. He was never in jail." But he would never go back to the siding racket either. Drummed out of home repair by the law, he got back in the stand-up game. An FBI sting resulted in Jack Roy becoming Rodney Dangerfield.

Stanley Dean of forgotten comedy team Norman & Dean has a unique perspective on the transformation. "When I first came to New York, a friend told me, 'If you want to get good comedy material I know a guy that lives out in Long Island.' We called Jack Roy and he invited us out. I asked if he would write for me. He said no. I said, 'Well, then why the hell did you make us come all the way out here?' He had barely performed and couldn't make enough money. Years go by. I'm in the Stage Delicatessen. In comes Jack Roy. He was looking to connect with the show folk. You could see he was wandering. He didn't know how to approach anyone. He was not a very nice character. He was a very difficult kind of guy. He said, 'Hey, do you know an agent that will get me a club date?' I said, 'Well, go see the agents. Go talk to them.' He said, 'I went to all of them! They wouldn't do anything for me.' It was the way he approached people. He wasn't likable in the least. I said, 'I've never seen you perform.' He said, 'Can I come to your house?' The following day he comes over. He starts doing his material and I'm thinking, 'Boy, this is funny stuff.' He came back the next day and did another fifteen. Every day—at least five days a week—for a month. I said, 'I can't be spending this much time with you. I've got my own problems. Here's what I'm gonna do. You pick up the other phone and listen in. I'm gonna call Nat Kalcheim at William Morris.' I called and said, 'I have a guy who is a tremendous comedy talent. I think your office would do well to meet him.' I told Rodney, 'When we walk into the office shake his hand and say, "Pleasure to meet you," and walk to the back of the office. I'll sit with him at his desk. Say hello and nothing else.' Because this guy, Jack Roy, could destroy himself in a hurry.

"Nat Kalcheim said, 'Where can we see him work?' I said, 'A place in the Village.' A little club that seated twenty-five people at the most. I walked in there with Rodney. I went up to the manager [Jan Wallman] and said to her, 'You see that guy sitting over there? He is a very funny comedian. Would you let him do a few minutes? If you see him work you'll want him for a few weeks. Take my word for it. You won't be sorry.' 'Five minutes. That's all.' She loved him. He was an animal. To see him up close—it had a great effect and the jokes were sensational. His material, without question, one of the top ten comedians I had ever heard. Material, jokes, delivery . . . but as far as the person goes . . . well, there wasn't much to talk about. But as a performer! You could *sense* it."

Jack Roy searched for a manager and approached Jack Rollins, the legendary force behind Woody Allen, Harry Belafonte and Nichols & May. Rollins passed on him because he was "tasteless." Roy settled for Will Jordan's manager, Roy Duke. "Roy Duke was with Rodney all the way in the beginning," says comic Frank Man. "He told him to change his name." Rodney claimed to have picked the name at random from the Manhattan telephone directory, but it was actually copped from *The Jack Benny Program*, which used "Rodney Dangerfield" as a gag name whenever it referenced a matinee idol. "I knew him only as Jack Roy," says Will Jordan. "I never thought of him as Rodney. I remember when I heard that name I groaned. I said, 'Rodney Dangerfield? It sounds so completely contrived.'"

CHAPTER FOUR

TELEVISION

In the early 1950s there was a new force in the lives of the delicatessen comedians, and it brought hope to old vaudevillians, fading radio stars and the new comics looking for a break. It was the emerging television industry—and it was a boom.

Television boosted dormant careers, from Olsen & Johnson to Buster Keaton. TV desperately needed content, and even the stalest routines made it to air. Television was an exciting new novelty and a fascinating piece of magic, but beyond its status as a technological experiment it was offering little entertainment value. Things like boxing matches and baseball games came across best. But anything that required premeditation, such as a drama or comedy, came across very poorly. Even in the rare instances where the content was exceptional, viewers were often stuck with a grainy image that disserviced quality content. Much of it was lost amid the amateurish technology. Comedian Fred Allen called television "a device that permits people who haven't anything to do to watch people who can't do anything."

In the days of radio comedy, a program could play in the background while folks ignored it. High ratings could be deceiving. Milt Josefsberg, a veteran writer for Jack Benny and Lucille Ball, considered the differences between radio and television: "Radio was a much more casual medium that demanded less of the listener's attention than television, thus making it wear better and longer." Television asked the viewer to sit down and focus—and when they did they discovered that what they were focusing on was mostly shit.

In 1948, the year that Milton Berle and Ed Sullivan first aired, there was a total of nineteen television stations in twelve cities.

The markets were Baltimore, Chicago, Cincinnati, Cleveland, Detroit, Los Angeles, Milwaukee, New York, Philadelphia, St. Louis, Washington, D.C., and Schenectady-Albany. Two hundred different advertisers purchased airtime and 750,000 television sets were manufactured.

The motion picture industry was disturbed by the popularity of television. TV was a threat to the profit margin, and studios were openly hostile. MGM took the hardest line. *The Jack Benny Program* had satirized films on radio for years, but when it did a television takeoff on the Oscar winner *Gaslight*, the result was an expensive lawsuit. The court action lasted nearly a decade, motivated only by MGM's antitelevision vendetta.

AT&T was in the process of linking coaxial cable countrywide so that television viewers could watch the same live program simultaneously. It was an elaborate process that took several years. Most television production was concentrated in New York, as the coaxial was linked first in the East.

Ed Wynn was the first comedian to star in a television show from the West Coast. Debuting in 1949, he quickly used up all his old vaudeville material. "For one season, *The Ed Wynn Show* saw him dig out every old gag and prop he'd ever devised," said son Keenan Wynn. "For nine months Dad was on top of the pile again. But just as it drained [others], television killed Dad as a clown. His audience began to dwindle, but he was tied hand and foot to his format, doomed like a dinosaur because he couldn't think of changing it."

"The show lasted only a year," said director Ralph Levy. "I think the audience was getting too sophisticated for his silly puns. The next thing we did out there was a pilot for an Edgar Bergen show. The funniest thing about that show was we couldn't use the rushes because the men on the mic booms were so carried away with [ventriloquist dummy] Charlie McCarthy they turned the mic heads toward him, so every time the dummy 'spoke' we had no sound."

Levy next went to work on *The Alan Young Show*, the second television comedy to be done from Hollywood, which he called "one of the funniest shows ever on television." Alan Young, a former star of Canadian radio, won the first Emmy for a lead comedy performer. One of the only comedians on television without a vaudeville background, he was awestruck during his time at CBS. "It was all the same one washroom for everybody at CBS," says Young. "Jack Benny was in there. I was washing my hands, and it was such a thrill when Red Skelton walked in. 'Hiya, Jack.' There I am washing my hands and I hear these two comedy legends talking. Going to the bathroom was a real thrill."

Among the more significant comedians during television's first full decade were Milton Berle, Red Buttons, Sid Caesar, Jackie Gleason and Phil Silvers. Berle and Buttons were loud nightclub comedians with immediate success. Caesar, Gleason and Silvers came on the scene and added a new dimension with their brilliant abilities as comic actors.

Berle was fresh off his stint at Nicky Blair's Carnival when he hosted *Texaco Star Theater* for the first time in June 1948. William Morris heavily promoted the debut episode. "Just as radio carried acts cradled in the vaudeville tradition, *Texaco Star Theater* [will be] the Palace of television," read the press release. "The sixty-minute program will be laid out like a vaudeville bill and will be paced by the emcees much as Frank Fay used to emcee the yesteryear two-a-day bills at the Palace on Broadway."

The premiere was a success. "Parlaying the best in camera techniques with sock [effective] trouping in the best tradition of old Palace days on Broadway, Milton Berle socked over his standard nitery-stage routine and brought to his emcee role one of the best showmanship lifts yet given a television show," wrote *Variety*. Initially the program rotated hosts. Berle took a turn once a month, along with Jack Carter, Morey Amsterdam and mimic Georgie Price. He was hired permanently in the fall. The program was packaged in a new way. Agent Lou Weiss explained, "In 1948, [William Morris] made the deal with Berle. We also got someone we represented to book the show, a producer, writers and talent to put on the show. That's a package. The whole concept of an agent changed in those years. An agent used to be a guy in a derby with a cigar. All of a sudden an agent's input and his knowledge of the business was needed."

Berle's ratings were big, although with countrywide coaxial cable not yet synched, twenty-four cities in the East saw the program live, while everyone else viewed a fourteen-day-old kinescope. Every Tuesday night at eight o'clock, America was transfixed by two different episodes. The Detroit waterworks offered the best indicator of Berle's popularity. The city's water reservoir dropped to alarming levels at nine o'clock every Tuesday. Technicians couldn't deduce why until a strong-bladdered comedy fan explained the phenomenon.

A classic Joe E. Lewis joke made the rounds at the time. Lewis first told the joke in 1947 at the expense of Berle's radio show and adjusted it for the television age: "Milton Berle is responsible for the sale of more television sets than any other performer . . . I know I sold mine and my brother sold his."

Production meetings were held every Wednesday, and they were an ordeal. Berle had a paranoid fear of cold drafts. Every window was sealed at his request, intensifying the cigar smoke. He rejected every idea his staff pitched, sending writers and producers into a panic. "He had Hal Collins following him around with a gag file," said comedy writer Charlie Isaacs. "He started inserting old jokes [into the script]. Berle didn't use his judgment, didn't understand he was ruining the next couple of jokes."

Show folk were fascinated by Berle rehearsals. They'd sit on the Studio 6B bleachers at Rockefeller Center and watch Berle berate his coworkers. Berle's rehearsal uniform was a gray sweatsuit, a towel around his neck and a whistle he blew frequently to stop an act or stagehand: a gym coach on a rampage. "For a reporter, the afternoon preceding the show afforded a fascinating study of a man who knew he was the top dog," wrote columnist Earl Wilson.

"The rehearsals became a Broadway institution, and all sorts of people managed to get in. With a cigar in his kisser, Berle would show a chorus girl how to wiggle or explain to great tap dancer Bill Robinson how to deliver a joke." Phil Silvers said rehearsing with Berle was like "being stuck in an air raid with a paper hat." Berle's guest stars always had difficulty. The Three Stooges appeared on one episode. "With all due respect to Milton's talent, I guess I'm spoiled," said Moe Howard. "I don't like being on the receiving end of slapstick. Especially since Berle came across with a slap in one routine which cracked my front tooth."

Jack Carter was doing a show for NBC at the time. Of his guests he says, "I got Basil Rathbone, I got David Niven, I got William Bendix. I got everybody that ran away from the Berle show. Milton would abuse them, manhandle them, and they'd quit. The Morris office would call us, 'Would you like to have David Niven? He's in town.' 'He's not in town—he came in to do Berle and he walked!'"

The reputation made Berle defensive. "That whistle got me bad publicity throughout the business. The word that went around was that Berle had no respect for other performers, he treated them like circus animals with himself as the trainer blowing his whistle. That's a lot of crap! I used that whistle for one very good reason: to save my voice. But nobody ever thought of that, or even bothered to ask me why." Director Greg Garrison was hired midway through the show's run. He was one of the few willing to bully back. "Milton is a coward. I took the whistle away from Milton the day I started."

Ernest Lehman was assigned by *Cosmopolitan* magazine to profile the behind-the-scenes workings. He chronicled Berle's bombastic abuse of stagehands, writers and his brother-producer, Frank. Lehman submitted it to his managing editor, only to be told there was no way they could run it; it was too salacious and potentially slanderous. Lehman changed all the names and published it as fiction. *Cosmo* ran it as a short story titled "The Comedian." Five years later Rod Serling adapted it for a *Playhouse 90* teleplay starring Mickey Rooney, directed by John Frankenheimer. The relationship between Rooney and Mel Torme, playing the brother-producer, was its darkest piece of business. Everyone in the industry knew it was based on Milton and his browbeaten brother.

Years later Milton excused the behavior that had been the basis for the drama. "I was under pressure. I adored my brother Frank. He was my manager, and before you know it, we got into an argument up at the rehearsal studio and I forgot it was my brother. He pushed me and I pushed him back and I hit him with a left hook and knocked him down. I just went berserk. Under pressure, pressure, pressure. Then all the newspapers—just like today—the dirt comes up. They're there right away. 'Did you and your brother have a fist-fight?' Everyone tried to say no. But it was obvious."

Mike Kirk of the Kudner advertising agency had the job of implementing the sponsors' wishes and added to the anxiety. Kirk was considered "arrogant, demanding and hard to please." One of his primary chores was ensuring that no Communist, suspected or otherwise, was in any way associated with the show. Every guest star had to be vetted by Kirk. This vetting sometimes extended to the rejection of Black guests for fear it would upset sponsors in the Deep South.

Texaco integrated its advertising into the Berle variety format, blurring the line between commercials and entertainment for the first time. The man doing the advertisements, Sid Stone, became a star. Stone used the defunct vaudeville template of "comic pitchman." It was based on vaudevillian Charles Kenna, a onetime vendor with a fast comic patter, who became a sensation at Hammerstein's Theatre. Kenna knockoffs became popular and he had to place full-page ads in trade papers: "Please let me know what stuff of mine you are using, so I won't have to follow you in with the same material.—Charles Kenna, Comedy Pitchman." When Kenna died his material was up for grabs. W. C. Fields claimed Kenna's catchphrase, "Go away, boy, you bother me," and Sid Stone adapted Kenna's act for *Texaco Star Theater*. With his sleeves rolled up, Stone gesticulated and exclaimed, "Tell you what I'm gonna do, folks," giving a fast yammer about Texaco products. A 1951 episode had Stone give his spiel to a young Mel Brooks in an uncredited walk-on.

Berle's first three years on the air were his most triumphant. By 1951 there was talk that New York City would erect a statue in his honor. Fred Allen joked to a friend, "It will be the first time *people* shit on a statue."

Milton Berle frequently opened his shows in drag, wearing a dress, blonde wig and grotesque makeup. Cross-dressing became a trademark of *Texaco Star Theater*. Berle learned it from the experts. "Jackie Miles, Lenny Kent and Milton Berle were some of the better comedians who visited the she-hes to get first-hand information on their swish characterizations," said Joey Adams. Frequenting New York's gay nightclub scene, Berle co-opted the approach. "I got the idea from the annual drag balls they used to have at a place called the Rockland Palace. The gay guys would work for months on the fancy dresses they showed up in. It was a wild evening and people would come from all over the city, not to take part, but to watch. I first realized there was humor, if you played it right, in playing gay."

While Berle became a national icon for cross-dressing, less famous performers were persecuted for the same reason. LAPD vice squads were arresting drag performers like Ray Bourbon while Berle was being idolized for the same thing. Berle hit the cover of *Time* magazine while Bourbon was in prison for "impersonating a woman."

Berle was on the air for seven and a half seasons, his popularity diminishing as the rest of early television improved. The competing comedian who surpassed his ratings was Phil Silvers. The two comics had known each other for years. Berle's mother insisted her teenage son hang out with Silvers, whom she believed would be a good influence. Their first time together, Silvers took Berle to a whorehouse to lose his virginity.

The Phil Silvers Show premiered on Tuesday nights at 8:30, up against the second half of the Berle show. The first several episodes were ignored. Then CBS put *The Phil Silvers Show* head-to-head with Berle at 8, and Silvers stripped Berle of his Mr. Television appellation. "We reached twenty-three million," said Silvers. "Knocked Berle off the air." Berle returned home after his final broadcast and stared into space. He sat in his darkened living room all night. "I felt drained, finished, washed up and terribly tired. To end up axed, out . . . I was really working my way down to the depths."

In the 1940s Phil Silvers was a Hollywood regular. He was under contract to Fox, where he appeared as a comic sidekick in a succession of musicals. Eventually he found work behind the scenes at MGM as a backlot tutor with friend Rags Ragland, and he performed a nightclub act at Slapsy Maxie's on Wilshire Boulevard. He returned to New York, starring in Broadway productions *High Button Shoes* and *Top Banana*, and was a made man at Lindy's. He was a major star—without major fame. *Variety* called him "one of the most likeable comics in show biz and one who has always been more highly regarded by the trade than by the general public." He was an insular draw, playing Friars roasts and AGVA fund-raisers, but his life changed forever when he played the White House Correspondents' Dinner on February 6, 1954. Silvers brought down the house that night, and CBS executive Hubbell Robinson Jr. was among those in attendance. He immediately entered negotiations with Silvers.

Alternately known as *You'll Never Get Rich* and its shorthand, *Sgt. Bilko*, *The Phil Silvers Show* featured a sitcom protagonist unlike any other on 1950s television. Nat Hiken, a former radio writer for both Berle and Fred Allen, created the *Bilko* program. Hiken had just left Martha Raye's variety show, where he had hired marble-mouthed pugs like Rocky Graziano to deliver comedy lines. Poor cue card reading and inept acting *became* the comedy, and Hiken's inept cast members became stars. Throughout his career he spun gold from the mugs of Rocky Graziano; his manager, Jack Healy; lowlife comedians Maurice Gosfield, Joe E. Ross and B. S. Pully; and even Jake "Raging Bull" LaMotta—all unlikely comedy talents.

Hiken put together a $30,000 pilot and screened it for Robinson, who was "immensely impressed." Jack Benny tried to talk Silvers out of it. "Don't get into that TV trap. They're going to be after you for television, that's the wave of the future, but it's a drain. Stay in theater." Silvers arranged a screening of the pilot for Benny, who immediately changed his mind and concluded, "He's going to be the new big guy."

Sgt. Bilko led a platoon of sweaty, disheveled slobs whose military mandate was to avoid work. Bilko was a scheming con man who voraciously gambled, aggressively womanized and compulsively lied. He was the only sitcom protagonist of the decade embodying such flaws. For those tired by domestic 1950s comedies like *Father Knows Best* or *Ozzie and Harriet*, it was a revelation. "Most of those family shows [of the 1950s] sickened me," said sitcom writer Everett

Greenbaum. "*My Little Margie* was stupid. *Father Knows Best* and *Danny Thomas* with that sermon at the end. These shows represented American life in a dishonest way." With its cynicism and selfishness, *The Phil Silvers Show* was the antithesis of competing sitcoms. It was an archetype not seen again for many years. "My all-time favorite show is *Bilko*," said *Curb Your Enthusiasm* creator Larry David. "*Sgt. Bilko* holds up. It's just a *hilarious* show—starring a bald man with glasses, by the way."

Buddy Hackett was cast in *The Phil Silvers Show*, but landed a role in *Lunatics and Lovers* on Broadway simultaneously. Actor Harvey Lembeck took his place. Small-time comedians Mickey Freeman, Jimmy Little, Allan Melvin and Billy Sands joined the initial cast, while Silvers hired his former vaudeville pal Herbie Faye in a supporting role. Silvers said he learned everything about comedy from Faye. "He nursed me along. Cajoled me, taught me the fundamentals of stage comedy [and I] became more creative."

There was one supporting player who upstaged all of them, and he was a typical Hiken casting choice. Maurice Gosfield had a great look and questionable ability. He had knocked about show business for years without success. When Gosfield auditioned for the *Bilko* show he presented a litany of credits that could not be verified. His inability to deliver lines with conviction, let alone proper pronunciation, made it clear the résumé was fraudulent. The role of sloppy Private Doberman was intended for Maurice Brenner, a distinctive actor with Coke-bottle glasses, but when Gosfield walked in wearing a suit covered in stains, Hiken gave him the part. Essentially playing himself, Gosfield got laughs as a larger-than-life buffoon. His *Bilko* colleagues were shocked when he was nominated for—and won—an Emmy Award. "He began to have delusions," said Silvers. "He did not realize that the situations in which he worked, plus the sharp lines provided by Nat and the other writers, made him funny." Instead Gosfield gloated, "Without me, the *Bilko* show would be nothing."

Gosfield became close friends with second-season cast member Joe E. Ross. It made sense that they bonded. Both were uneducated comedians, slobs with a lowbrow sensibility. Hiken cast Ross as a mess hall cook with appalling hygiene. He stole scenes with his guttural catchphrase, "Ooh! Ooh! Ooh!" He used it as a delay tactic while trying to remember his lines. The success of *The Phil Silvers Show* gave Ross an expendable income and he became a darling of the prostitutes he patronized. "He was married eight times and they were all ex-hookers," says comedian Hank Garrett. "The one I knew was number eight. He introduced her as his dialogue coach."

Ross and Gosfield decided to cash in on their television popularity and form a comedy team. *The Ed Sullivan Show* was their first and last booking. Silvers watched the performance. "Their sketch was painful. Not a laugh. Monday, Ross eased himself into the rehearsal hall, embarrassed. He received an enthusiastic phone call from Doberman, 'Baby, we're the talk of the town!' Gosfield never accepted the realities."

The Phil Silvers Show was critically acclaimed. The rare voices of dissent complained about its distracting laugh track. One review griped, "Someone apparently didn't have much confidence in the ability of the material and cast antics to get the required reaction from viewers, so the show played off to the irritating accompaniment of an unnecessary titter track." Other detractors were members of the armed forces. The Veterans of Foreign Wars blamed *The Phil Silvers Show* for President Eisenhower's intention to slash veterans' benefits: "[The president] has been overly influenced by the weekly television program poking fun at the Army starring comedian Phil Silvers. May we express the hope that the armed forces are not being measured by the platoon of characters commanded by Sgt. Bilko."

Bilko the character loved to gamble. When he lost money the laugh track cackled, but in real life Silvers suffered the same addiction, and it was calamitous. "He was a terrible insomniac and he gambled all the time," said *Bilko* writer Aaron Ruben. "That ruined his life. He would come in around seven A.M. for makeup, purple bags under his eyes. I felt sorry for him. His head would be slumping down. Then, 'Okay, Phil, we're ready for you,' and the guy who a moment ago looked like he was near death, the face, the eyes, and the teeth would light up as if he had just been plugged in. When they said, 'Okay, cut,' he would just flop down again." Like many of his generation, Silvers battled an undiagnosed anxiety disorder. Cramps, headaches and stomachaches overwhelmed him. Silvers lamented, "People don't understand the special kind of hell a comic goes through."

Nat Hiken himself was exhausted. He wrote most of the series by himself while overseeing ancillary Bilko projects: paperbacks, comic books and a brief talk show spin-off hosted by Harvey Lembeck in New York with Allan Melvin and Maurice Gosfield as sidekicks. Hiken explained, "I'm getting out. It doesn't come easy any more and the fun is gone." He hired new writers to take over the workload. Arnie Rosen, Coleman Jacoby, Billy Friedberg, Leonard Stern and Tony Webster worked to emulate the Hiken style. Rosen and Jacoby had just finished the screenplay for *The Joker Is Wild*, a biopic based on the autobiography of Joe E. Lewis. Stern had just left Universal, where he and Lenny Bruce were punching up screenplays. Hiken met with Carl Reiner and offered him a job as chief director of *The Phil Silvers Show*, but Reiner chose to remain with Sid Caesar.

The Phil Silvers Show aired for four seasons with a cynical tone unlike that of any other sitcom. Jack Benny made a callback to the "TV trap" after *The Phil Silvers Show* won Best Comedy, Best Actor, Best Directing and Best Writing at the 1956 Emmys. He sent Silvers a telegram: "You son of a bitch, you wouldn't listen to me."

Berle was TV's first comedy star and Silvers reached the top of the sitcom heap, but it was Sid Caesar who brought a new dimension to television. Myron Kirb was head of the television division for the Kudner advertising agency. He had closed the Berle deal and was looking to keep NBC's momentum going. Kirb entertained clients at the Tamiment Resort, a progressive version of the Catskills near the New York–Pennsylvania border. On a weekly basis it presented elaborate revues produced by "the Ziegfeld of the Borscht Belt," Max Liebman.

Liebman was the Lorne Michaels of his era. He put together an original comedy-variety show for Caesar every single week and made stars out of unknowns. Lucille Kallen and Mel Tolkin were his head writers. "I met Max in 1948 when he was recruiting people for Tamiment," said Kallen. "Every week that summer, Mel and I turned out a two-hour original revue, music, lyrics and sketches." Pat Carroll performed in the next round of shows, which were written by Danny and Neil Simon. "Tamiment was wonderful. You were doing an all-original revue every weekend! I worked at Tamiment with Neil Simon, who was then known as Doc, and they wrote the best sketches I had ever seen."

During the war Liebman directed a military revue called *Tars and Spars*. It starred comedian Marc Bolero. In the same show Sid Caesar did a supporting part and completely upstaged Bolero. Liebman was hip to the reaction and guided Caesar through a new sea of opportunity.

Columbia Pictures offered Caesar the starring part in *The Jolson Story* and he opened for Joe E. Lewis at the Copa, but the attention made him uncomfortable. He feared being exposed as a straw man. Caesar was in demand as a comic—but he was an actor without an act. Liebman reassured him, having built stars out of nothing before, as in the case of Tamiment graduate Danny Kaye. Liebman worked with Caesar, mapping movements and emphasizing key lines, readying him for his Copa debut on January 1, 1947. Mountain friend Don Appell came backstage to congratulate Caesar on his success and brought a fellow Mountain employee—Melvin Kaminsky. It was the first time Caesar met the man who would become his voice—Mel Brooks.

Caesar was booked at the Roxy presentation house when Leo Lindemann, owner of Lindy's, caught his act. When producer Joseph Hyman dined at Lindy's shortly thereafter, Lindemann convinced Hyman to cast Caesar in his Broadway show *Make Mine Manhattan*. It ran from January 1948 to January 1949, with Caesar playing twelve different roles. "He was imitating pinball machines," says Mel Brooks. "He could imitate people or slot machines or a gumball machine. He really could do anything and he talked fast. He was doing the Danny Kaye stuff only quicker and better and sharper." Caesar's reputation as Broadway's hot new comic was solidified.

Kirb met with the head of the Admiral appliance company. In less than twenty minutes he sold the executives the idea of a televised Tamiment series. Liebman went backstage to give Caesar the good news. In the dressing room Caesar introduced Liebman to Mel Brooks for the first time and told him he wanted Brooks to write on the show. Liebman considered Brooks an unfunny hanger-on. He refused to hire him, so Caesar started paying Brooks under the table.

According to Caesar, the debut was a marathon of advertising: "The premiere episode was virtually one long commercial for the sponsor's products—refrigerators, ranges, phonographs and television." Roy Atwell, Admiral's answer to Sid Stone, did the commercials in a comedic stammer and one of the sketches took place in an Admiral appliance store.

Subsequent episodes were bogged down by a pet obsession of Liebman's: long, elaborate dance numbers choreographed by James Starbuck. Liebman believed that ballet—not comedy—would be the key to his success. Critics complained about it from day one: "Fundamentally the weakness of this first in the Admiral series was in the songs and dancing. A dancer spends weeks working on a routine. Then a camera moves up on him, cutting his body off at the waist and turning him into a twisting torso, a pair of gesticulating arms and a perspiring face."

The Admiral Broadway Revue lasted four months. Caesar wanted out of his contract. The workload was too much, he said, as he was doing nightclub engagements at the Waldorf-Astoria simultaneously. In addition, he was fielding an offer from Fox to star in a film with Paul Douglas, but only if he would quit television. He was also stressed over a pair of lawsuits. Caesar was being sued by a small-time agent for a quarter of a million dollars over a contract he naively signed back in 1945. Furthermore, while preparing *The Admiral Broadway Revue*, Liebman instructed Tolkin and Kallen not to write original material, but to rework sketches from *Make Mine Manhattan* and the revue *Small Wonder*. When those sketches appeared on *The Admiral Broadway Revue* without permission, comedy writer Devery Freeman took legal action and named Caesar, Liebman and NBC in the lawsuit.

The Admiral Broadway Revue left the air, but the primary players involved—Sid Caesar, Mel Brooks, Lucille Kallen, Mel Tolkin, diminutive actor Howard Morris and former two-reel comedienne Imogene Coca—returned the following year with a better version of the same thing.

A new, key player was hired. Carl Reiner was a young, journey-man sketch actor. He and Buddy Hackett toured in a road version of *Call Me Mister*, Harold Rome's satire of military bravado. He played in *Pretty Penny*, a failure from the legendary George S. Kaufman. He did a creaky TV show called *The 54th Street Revue*, sharing screen time with mimic Al Bernie and comic Billy Vine. Lastly there was *Alive and Kicking*, a troubled revue that was neither alive nor kicking, but resulted in the biggest break of his career. Liebman was asked to doctor *Alive and Kicking*. Despite its ruptured state, it featured sketches written by great comedy minds like I. A. L. Diamond, Sid Kuller, Henry Morgan and Joe Stein. Liebman tried, but ultimately decided it could not be salvaged. Instead he raided its talent pool and hired Stein and Reiner for his own project.

Mel Tolkin and writer Abe Ginnes were preparing a Sid Caesar sitcom called *Great Caesar* when Young and Rubicam executive Pat Weaver asked Liebman to do a revamp of *The Admiral Broadway Revue*. It was to be called *Your Show of Shows* and Weaver wanted it to fill a massive two and a half hours every Saturday night. Lieb-man dismissed the idea as unworkable and they compromised with a weekly ninety minutes. *Your Show of Shows* debuted February 25, 1950, starring Sid Caesar, Imogene Coca, Howard Morris and Carl Reiner.

Weaver created the catchall title *The Saturday Night Revue* and placed two comedy shows under its banner. The first hour consisted of Jack Carter's sketch program, *The Jack Carter Show*, followed by the ninety-minute *Your Show of Shows*. While the Caesar staff hypo-thetically had six days to write a show, the script needed to be ready by Wednesday, as the archaic mimeograph machine literally took days to produce copies. "The time pressures were so great I took the telephone out of the room," said Caesar. "I literally ripped it out of the wall and threw it into the hallway."

Neil Simon replaced Lucille Kallen when she went on maternity leave. He recalls Caesar being tense, but supportive. "There was an enormous amount of anger, but it would all come out in comedy. When he was angry, he could be very funny about it. Sid loved the writers and paid them better than anyone else."

The pressure of carrying a ninety-minute live show every week turned Caesar into a boozer. "I once saw him drink a whole bottle of gin before the show and he was wonderful on the show, but he was an alcoholic," said writer Joe Stein. "The very first day I was there was very peculiar. I was sitting around chatting with the guys when suddenly I heard a lot of vomiting. I said, 'What's going on?' They said, 'Oh, Sid just came in.' He usually came in and threw up his breakfast."

The Jack Carter Show suffered as the lead-in. Max Liebman wielded a great deal of power at NBC, whereas Carter producer Ernie Glucksman did not. *The Jack Carter Show* could not book guest stars or submit scripts until *Your Show of Shows* had done the same. Liebman was adamant there not be any redundancy in the shows, and to this day Carter is upset about it: "It was always Sid Caesar, Sid Caesar, Sid Caesar! Sid Caesar everything—and I was treated like crap."

Ben Starr was a writer on *The Jack Carter Show*. He says Carter was his own worst enemy. "The writers were myself, Larry Klein, Marvin Marx and the producer Ernie Glucksman. We'd pitch all day, go for lunch, come back until eight o'clock at night. Jack would turn *everything* down. By Wednesday, Ernie Glucksman was a basket case. We would have to pitch it *and write it* and bring it in Thursday morning to start rehearsal for Saturday broadcast. Almost every Saturday, the morning of the show, Carter, Glucksman and Weaver would be there with the union guy for all the guys that build the sets. Nobody would be building any sets. Why? Jack had insulted all the hammer guys and we were waiting for someone to arrive with a case of champagne. The case would arrive and they would give it to the steward. *Then* everybody would go in and start rehearsing."

Your Show of Shows had a writers room that became the subject of essays, panels, a Broadway play and a TV movie. It holds legendary status. "For nine years I presided over what was arguably the best collection of comedy writers ever assembled in the history of television," said Caesar. They were the highest-paid comedy writers in the business, and it gave Mel Brooks a complex. "When I was listed as a regular writer and my pay went to $205 a week, I began to get scared. Writer! I'm not a writer. Terrible penmanship. And when my salary went to $1,000 a week, I really panicked . . . It was unreal . . . It was like I was stealing and I was going to get caught. Then the year after that, the money went to $2,500 and finally I was making $5,000 a show and going out of my mind. In fact, the psychological mess I was in began to cause a real physical debilitation. To wit: low blood sugar and under-active thyroid."

Brooks was a writer in the shadows, not yet the star he would become. The one time he appeared on air he was petrified. "We put him on the show once," said cast member Howard Morris. "We wanted him to do this cat sound he does because he has this space between his teeth. He came over to the corner where the mic was, and I have never seen anyone paler in my life. He was petrified. I said, 'You son of a bitch, just do the fucking cat sound.'"

But in the writers room Brooks had no fear. "I was aggressive. I was a terrier, a pit bull terrier. I was unstoppable. I would keep going until my joke or my sketch was in the show. I didn't care if anybody else's was in or out. All of us writers were like a litter of pups, and we all fought for our little tit and struggled and screamed. Sid was God, and if we could get his ear and he would smile on us—that was important."

Although Liebman had finally deferred and put Brooks on the payroll, he always considered Brooks a distraction. "Max would fire Mel at least once a week," said Caesar. "Sometimes once a day. When Max would yell at him, 'You're nothing, all you'll ever be is nothing!' Mel would respond, 'And you're the boss over nothing!' Max tried to manage Mel's enthusiasm by throwing lit cigars at him."

When they entered television, comedians like Berle, Cantor and Wynn relied on stuff they'd done a thousand times before. Caesar had the opposite approach, and as a result he stood out. "Caesar's material is all around him and inexhaustible," said Fred Allen. "Caesar running out of material would be like NBC running out of vice-presidents." Caesar's success created some backlash against Berle.

A couple years earlier people thought Berle was the best television could offer—and now they felt rooked. "If Berle is the King of Television," commented Sid White of *Radio Daily*, "then Sid Caesar is the Emperor." *The Chicago Tribune* wrote, "Sid Caesar doesn't steal jokes; he doesn't borrow ideas or material. A gag is as useless to Caesar as a fresh situation is to Milton Berle."

Television made stars out of Berle and Caesar, but for regular nightclub comics the best forum was *The Ed Sullivan Show*. Comedians who couldn't carry their own show had immediate credibility with a *Sullivan* shot. And while it may not have made them overnight stars, it increased their drawing power in clubs and their financial value. *The Ed Sullivan Show* ran from 1948 to 1971 and gave much of America its first glimpse of Lord Buckley, Rodney Dangerfield, Totie Fields, Alan King, Moms Mabley, Pigmeat Markham and Joan Rivers. Most of the comics considered Sullivan an anomaly. They kissed his ass in person, but made fun of him behind his back. Comedian Irwin Corey yells, "Ed Sullivan was a very dull person—no fucking talent at all!"

The comedians booked most frequently reflected the taste of the host. Though few clamored to see them, Jack Carter, Myron Cohen and the comedy team of Wayne & Shuster were paraded before the cameras nearly every month. "I became a favorite of his," says Carter. "He used me as a barometer for what he wanted. He'd yell at the other comics, 'Why can't you be like Jack Carter?' He had this clean-cut American image, but was filthy off-camera. You went to his dressing room while he was being made up and he would curse. 'You can't do that fucking shit on my show, Jack. That's bullshit. That's fucking shit.'"

The early version of the *Sullivan* show was called *Toast of the Town*. Premiering June 20, 1948, it was a creaky affair made worse by the bland style of Sullivan himself. "Ed Sullivan was one of the most boring, untalented men on the planet," says comedian Pat Cooper. "If Ed Sullivan was around today he wouldn't get on *slides*. But we didn't know any better! Television was still in its infancy, so we didn't know."

Sullivan was notorious for making comedians cut their act shortly before they walked onstage. Henny Youngman had such an experience. "He calls me upstairs. 'Take this joke out. Take this out. Take *this* out. Take this out.' I got onstage and I didn't know what I was doing. He broke up my rhythm. He broke up my routine. I came off and I said, 'You amateur-night son of a bitch! How *dare* you do this to me!'"

The Ed Sullivan Show did a full run-through the day of the show to determine the length of the broadcast. *Sullivan* director John Moffitt says, "The run-through had an audience that was all stragglers that hung around Broadway. I don't know how you could ever get a good take on how good a routine was, but Ed made judgments because of that audience." Bobby Ramsen says Sullivan seldom had a reason for the cuts and merely wanted to exercise his power between rehearsal and air. "You'd do your routine for the rehearsal and nine times out of ten, 'You're not going to do that routine on my show tonight.' So you'd give him something else. And whatever else you gave him, 'That's what you'll do on my show tonight.' No matter what you did."

Will Jordan became a comedy star doing the very first impression of Ed Sullivan. Jordan came on the program, exaggerated Sullivan's mannerisms and got laughs with the phrase "really big shoe." The caricature he created soon became a signature of every hack comedian in the business. "I first imitated him in 1953 on his show. I did what many mimics had done before—I invented. I *invented* the character. He never said 'really big shoe.' That was *me*." Jordan cashed in with a novelty recording of the Everly Brothers hit "Bye Bye Love" done in the voice of Sullivan. "When the record came out Ed Sullivan said, 'You can't release this.' I asked him why. He said, 'Because of all those lewd things you made me say in the song!' I said, 'The song? It's a *real* song. It's "Bye Bye Love" by the Everly Brothers.' He thought, 'There goes my baby, she's got someone new . . .' He thought that was bad taste! Ed Sullivan was not the brightest person."

Sullivan would frequently ask notable audience members to stand up and take a bow. According to Carter this led to the occasional faux pas. "He asked this group of GIs to get up and take a bow. 'Come on, you guys, get up! Get up here! Stand up and take a bow, you wonderful GIs!' They were all in wheelchairs. Paraplegics."

A last-minute Sullivan cut could make a comedian seem worse than he was. Likewise, the development of a brand-new technology attempted to make television comedy seem funnier than it was. Canned laughter became a staple of the American viewing experience.

Insulting the home audience and reassuring the insecure comic, the laugh track was an indelible American trademark that created an aural homogeneity. The laugh track was used on almost every television comedy and variety show from the mid-1950s through the 1970s, and it made every show sound the same. Laughter was often dropped into programs at inappropriate moments, leading viewers to wonder what the disembodied laughs were laughing at.

Charley Douglass developed what he called the "Laff Box" in 1953. It came into general use in 1955 and looked like a Dadaist invention. "While dialogue, effects and music was being put in [during postproduction], there was a fourth person with a laugh machine," said audio engineer and Douglass assistant Carroll Pratt. "All four items would funnel into the final product. Ours were cued by a series of keys that we [installed in] a Royal typewriter. They were in banks of four based on the sex of the laugh, the size of the laugh and so on. In the basic machine there were thirty-two keys. You could program and play as many as you wanted."

Contrived laughter was a radical development. When comedy first started on radio a studio audience of any kind was forbidden. George Burns said, "They were worried their laughter would spoil the show for listeners at home."

Ed Wynn lobbied for the studio audience in radio and won. Twenty years later the laugh track had replaced most live bodies, and it would be decades before comedy consistently broadcast without aural assistance. Critics like Kenneth Tynan complained America lived "in an age when canned hilarity has all but usurped the viewer's right to an autonomous sense of humor."

Insecure comedians like Milton Berle romanced the laugh track. "That machine was his answer to every prayer he ever had," said comedy writer Mel Diamond. "He didn't need the fucking audience anymore—which he didn't like anyway because he couldn't depend on them. To me, the machine is as fraudulent as the phony quiz shows, but the comedians saw it as the answer to their worst fears."

In the wake of the 1950s quiz show scandals, in which a government investigation revealed that popular game shows were rigged in advance, CBS president Frank Stanton announced that CBS programming would be "what it purports to be." Erik Barnouw wrote in *Tube of Plenty*, "Canned laughter and applause would have to be identified as such. However, this radical idea was abandoned a few weeks later."

Any comedian who opposed the laugh track was overruled. "Television executives insisted that a comedy show had to have a laugh track so the audience watching at home would know when to laugh," said George Burns. "I told them we didn't need one on our show because the audience knew when something funny had happened. They still insisted we use the laugh track."

Charley Douglass almost sold motion picture studios on the use of the laugh track. The Lee Marvin–Jane Fonda film *Cat Ballou* actually had a laugh track added and was sent out to a handful of drive-in theaters to gauge response. Naturally, the response was negative. Further use of laugh tracks in feature films was abandoned, but it had been a serious consideration for half a second.

Douglass and Pratt were frequently ordered to insert heavy laughter where it didn't belong. "That was always a bad situation and it happened a lot," said Pratt. "It got to the point where [executives thought] the louder the laugh was—the funnier the joke was. But that wasn't the case. That's why the press, the media and the public in general came down on us."

The laugh track dominated 1950s television comedy. At the same time the Cold War dominated American discourse. The Red Scare affected several comedians in the late 1940s and early '50s. Among them were Lucille Ball, Charlie Chaplin and Groucho Marx.

Marx joined the quiz show craze that had brought the end of Fred Allen and Henry Morgan. Their demise was seen as a lesson. If you can't beat the quiz show craze, join it. Comedians George DeWitt, Hal March and Jan Murray all became better known as game show hosts. Groucho joined their ranks as the host of *You Bet Your Life*. "I wasn't particularly proud of doing a quiz show," said Marx. "It was like slumming."

You Bet Your Life premiered on radio in October 1947, formatted to fit Marx's personality. It became an excuse for Marx to ridicule civilian contestants with trademark snipe. Fans were impressed with how often Marx's quips hit the mark—but the audience didn't know he was the first beneficiary of magnetic tape. Unlike competing programs, the show was not live. For every half-hour episode, there was an extra hour the public never heard or saw. "The ability to edit was a very important thing," said director Robert Dwan. "If it wasn't funny at all, it wasn't used. We gave Groucho crutches to lean on."

Each segment featured two eccentric civilians "selected by our studio audience before the show." In reality, they were heavily vetted and rehearsed by the production staff. They looked for people with outrageous occupations or personalities—easy fodder for ridicule. After Marx interviewed them and scored a good number of laughs, he'd resort to the quiz and ask four questions on a given subject, allowing the contestants to win some money.

The anti-Communist hysteria was at its height during *You Bet Your Life*'s television run from 1950 to 1961. The Senate Permanent Subcommittee on Investigations hoped to remove left-wing influence from American life. Groucho's show was caught in the mix. According to an internal FBI memorandum from August 17, 1953: "Groucho Marx contributes heavily to the Communist Party." To this day the rest of that memorandum is blacked out and the majority of the file heavily censored.

You Bet Your Life musical director Jerry Fielding was fired for his political activity. The House Un-American Activities Committee subpoenaed Fielding. "I was very much involved in politics and all kinds of crusades. One of the things that bugged me most was that we had two [musicians'] unions in this town [Hollywood], a Black one and a white one. The white union had a higher scale than the Black union and a higher death benefit, and a lot of other things. There had never been a Black musician on the West Coast playing network shows on the radio. I joined to form an amalgamation committee to break this law down. We were going to put two Black guys on the Groucho Marx show. Groucho felt the idea was very good, and when I got noise from NBC, I went to him and he backed me up pretty strongly. But at the time I was told in no uncertain terms that if I kept this up, they were going to get me. The amalgamation finally happened. It was on account of the Groucho Marx show that this happened. Otherwise, there'd still be two unions here."

You Bet Your Life's sponsor, Chrysler, was convinced only a Commie would dare promote racial equality. Fielding couldn't find work for ten years. "After that I couldn't get Groucho, I couldn't get my agent, I couldn't get NBC. It was as though I didn't exist. I never saw any of them again." Marx conceded a few years later, "That I bowed to the sponsors' demands [to fire Fielding] is one of the greatest regrets of my life."

Abbott & Costello were filmdom's most popular comedy team at the start of the Red Scare. Lou Costello was influenced by his friendship with right-wing film producer Robert Arthur. "Lou was very much, as I was, a supporter of Senator McCarthy," said Arthur. "Lou felt very strong about this and tried to do his part to protect the freedom of America." Costello complained about the high taxes leveled on his massive income, but conceded, "We have to keep taxes high to pay for the fight against communism."

Lou Costello's daughter said, "Joe McCarthy was a demagogue, but to my father he was a man in shining armor." Costello's enthusiasm for McCarthy affected the atmosphere of his shoots. At one point he drafted a loyalty oath and asked everyone working with him to sign it. John Grant, writer of special material for Abbott & Costello, was offended when Costello presented him with the loyalty oath. "Lou, after all these years do you have to question my loyalty?" Costello said, "If you really are a true-blue American, you won't mind saying so. Just sign the paper, John. Are you gonna sign or are you gonna let people wonder if you might be pink?" Grant quit and stormed off the lot.

Costello was a star attraction at a McCarthy testimonial. Some warned it would impact his popularity. "That reasoning doesn't make any sense to me," said Costello. "Since when is it more important to have good box office appeal rather than be a good American?"

McCarthyist hostility affected those who already had paranoid delusions. Steve Allen was an early champion of civil rights and was a target of death threats. A cancer victim wrote Allen, "I will be dying in three or four weeks and was thinking of what I could do in my last few days to make up for all my sins. [I have decided] to exterminate some of the Communist fifth column. That is why I write to you, Mr. Communist Allen . . . I have nothing to lose taking my revolver, going down to your home, or better yet, to your office in Sherman Oaks, and, on the whim, firing two or three bullets into the head of the biggest liar, cheat, humbug and Communist in this country."

Radio satirist Henry Morgan received a letter from *Red Channels*, the pamphlet that named suspected Communists in the entertainment industry. Morgan was one of 151 people cited in the original pamphlet, including comedy writers Abe Burrows and Nat Hiken. *Red Channels* and its publisher, the journal *Counterattack*, could kill a career with one swift mention, even if the accusation was false.

> *Dear Mr. Morgan:*
>
> *As you know, I am the originator of* Red Channels. *I enclose a confidential memo listing reported affiliations on your part with Communist fronts and causes. If you care, in your interests, to comment on these to me before I publish them, I shall be glad to hear your side of the story.*

Red Channels named Morgan for his participation in a 1947 radio special called *Hollywood Fights Back*, a variety show mounted to fight the House Un-American Activities Committee. Guests included

Lauren Bacall, Myrna Loy, Edward G. Robinson and Artie Shaw. *Red Channels* also noted a joke Morgan told at the 1947 White House Correspondents' Dinner: "Whenever it is quiet in Washington, you can count on the Un-American committee to issue a report. Maybe sometime later, when it has a chance, it will start gathering the facts."

Morgan's employment fell sharply. He worked in regional New York radio for a couple of years, but had no exposure beyond Manhattan. He bought space in the 1952 New Year's edition of *Variety*, most of which was filled with celebrities' season's greetings. Morgan's space said, "Whatever happened to Henry Morgan? Signed, Henry Morgan."

Red Channels and *Counterattack* enriched themselves through intimidation. "I worked for *Counterattack*," said informer Harvey Matusow. "Besides the newsletter, for five thousand dollars we also set up security systems for companies. If a company bought our services, they would send us lists of names and we would check them out in our files and let them know if they were acceptable or not." Ira Skutch directed Henry Morgan on various panel shows. He remembers the vetting racket. "The guys who came to see us said if we subscribed to their service, they'd clear everybody we called, so this whole business of clearing people was a blackmailing scheme."

The anti-Communist blacklist was greatly motivated by a desire to destroy showbiz labor unions. A number of sitcom writers and actors were blacklisted, the majority of whom were involved in union politics. "Most of us were not Sam Gompers types," said comedy writer Charlie Isaacs. "Nevertheless we decided to start a union. I was made president. Jess Oppenheimer was the vice-president. Immediately we got into a terrible jurisdictional fight with the Screen Writers Guild. Some clique over there decided they couldn't beat us because we had most of the TV writers, so they began smearing us, saying we had Communists in our group."

Blacklisted comedy writers included Reuben Ship (*The Life of Riley*), Leo Solomon (*The Alan Young Show*) and Frank Tarloff (*I Married Joan*). Danny Thomas hired Tarloff to write on his sitcom, but had to credit him under a pseudonym. "Two of our best writers were Frank Tarloff and Mac Benoff . . ." said Thomas. "Frank and Mac were on the list—God knows why because I never heard them say anything more subversive than 'Richard Nixon is a jerk.' But they couldn't work anywhere else in the industry . . . We had to use pseudonyms for them, or we might have been blacklisted too."

According to comedy writer Herb Sargent, Steve Allen intentionally booked blacklisted talent. "On the early *Tonight* shows, he'd book people like Zero Mostel and Jack Gilford, who were blacklisted. The network would say, 'Wait a minute, wait a minute,' and Steve would say, 'No, if they don't go on, I don't go on.' He was terrific that way."

Jack Gilford was a constant presence in Broadway sketch revues, certain to be a major player in television comedy until the blacklist. Ezra Stone was directing a television show for Fred Allen when they tried to book Gilford. "Pat Weaver came down personally to the rehearsal hall and took Fred and me aside and said, 'We've got to let Gilford go. We can't clear him.' Fred turned absolutely crimson. He was so incensed and humiliated." Gilford's wife, Madeline Lee, was also blacklisted. *Red Channels* was confused by her name and blacklisted three different performers named Madeline Lee rather than let one Commie squeak past.

Jane Wyatt, the wife on the sitcom *Father Knows Best*, was blacklisted from the film industry in 1950. "I had gone to Washington with the group that protested the Hollywood hearings. I also was seen wearing a Russian costume at a meeting during the war to push for a second front, which President Roosevelt was pushing for too." Wyatt had been costarring in motion pictures with Gary Cooper and Cary Grant, but was kept out of movies for the next several years. Before she was cast in *Father Knows Best*, the sponsor required she narrate anti-Communist documentaries for the Central Intelligence Agency's Radio Free Europe.

The family sitcom *The Goldbergs* was popular, but had its life span shortened by the blacklist. Male lead Philip Loeb supported the End Jim Crow in Baseball Committee, an attempt to integrate the major leagues. It made him unpopular with the sponsor, General Foods.

Jack Wren of the advertising agency BBDO told Henry Morgan he would remove him from the blacklist if he would defame Philip Loeb in return. Morgan said, "He sent for me to talk about my blacklisting. Wren says there's an AFTRA meeting to consider the case of Phil Loeb. 'Here's the speech I want you to make.' I say, 'I can't read that.' It was slander. I said, 'I'll make a speech, but not this one.' I didn't know Phil. At the meeting . . . I went up to the microphone, trembling. I start to read my version of this, which was that Phil Loeb shouldn't bring his case to AFTRA. Wren called me after the meeting. He wanted me to write him a letter saying he cleared me 'to show the evenhandedness' of his office. I prefer to think I didn't write the letter, but I did. He [Loeb] killed himself not too long after I made my speech to the union."

Some comedy figures promoted the blacklist by creating a Hollywood committee in support of McCarthy. While it was no surprise that Hollywood reactionaries John Wayne and Ward Bond were involved, other signatories included Marx Brothers screenwriter Morrie Ryskind, Laurel & Hardy director Leo McCarey and silent comedy legend Harold Lloyd.

The biggest supporters of the blacklist were the newspaper columnists. Their reactionary rants resonated with readers. Ed Sullivan wrote in his column, "The entire industry is becoming increasingly aware of the necessity to plug all Commie propaganda loopholes. Network and station heads, with a tremendous financial stake, want no part of Commies or pinkos." Sullivan welcomed blacklisters into his home. Theodore C. Kirkpatrick of *Counterattack* was invited to vet the guests of *The Ed Sullivan Show* in person. Sullivan said, "Kirkpatrick has sat in my living room on several occasions and listened attentively to performers eager to secure a certification of loyalty."

Columnist Hy Gardner accused Charlie Chaplin of being a Communist and pointed to his pallbearing at the funeral of novelist Theodore Dreiser as proof. Chaplin's status as a noncitizen especially bugged his detractors. When asked why he remained a British subject, Chaplin told the *New York Herald Tribune*, "I'm an internationalist. I do not believe in nationalism because that makes for war." Gardner wrote, "I will be proud to take a bow for encouraging the government to refuse [Chaplin] readmission to this country without first putting him under an Immigration Service microscope used on all foreign objects likely to spread a disease."

Walter Winchell attacked Lucille Ball at the height of her fame. On his low-budget television show, Winchell read his scoops to the rhythm of a ticker tape. "While the House Committee on Un-American Activities was holding secret sessions in California, the most popular of all television stars was confronted with her membership in the Communist Party." Newspapers aligned a photo of Lucille Ball with Winchell's words. Television critic Jack O'Brian drooled over her potential demise: "Lucille Ball announces in the current *Silver Screen* magazine that she intends to retire in five years. It may be a lot sooner than Lucille plans."

The American Legion organized a protest against *I Love Lucy* and in September 1953 Ball was called before the House Un-American Activities Committee to testify. The FBI unearthed her 1930s voting record, in which she was registered as a Communist. She explained that her grandfather was a socialist and she registered as a Communist to please him. This admission would have been enough to sink a union activist, but true to the name of her sitcom, Lucy was well loved. J. Edgar Hoover defended her as one of his favorites. Republican HUAC member Donald Jackson held a press conference to prevent runaway smearing: "She had never had a role in the communist party," but not wishing to contradict his colleagues he added, "The investigation is continuing [and] no case is ever closed."

The next *I Love Lucy* taping was tense, and Desi Arnaz eased the studio audience. "Welcome to the first *I Love Lucy* show [of the season]. Before we go on, I want to talk to you about something serious. Something very serious. You all know what it is. The papers have been full of it all day. Lucille is no communist. We both despise the communists and everything they stand for." Arnaz introduced Ball to the studio audience as "my favorite redhead. That's the only thing red about Lucy—and even that is not legitimate." The audience cheered.

When the campaign against Ball went nowhere, angry columnists claimed that even that had been part of the Communist conspiracy. "The commies themselves had a big part in breaking the Lucille Ball story and here's why," wrote Mike Connolly in *The Hollywood Reporter.* "They feel that when Miss Ball proves she was never a Red it'll tend to discredit charges of commie membership still to be lodged against others. Fiendishly clever, these fiends."

One of the only major newspaper columnists not beating the drum was acerbic television critic John Crosby. The red he detested was Red Skelton, and that had strictly to do with his program, not his politics. Crosby wrote at the time, "The blacklist is one of the things our generation is going to have to answer for to succeeding generations."

While some comedy writers were blacklisted, NBC drafted a plan to mentor new ones. NBC had good luck with comedy—Milton Berle, Sid Caesar, Martin & Lewis—and the network wanted to keep that winning streak going. It created an in-house classroom called the NBC Writers Development Program, with a mandate of shepherding newbies into professional positions. Playwright Tad Danielewski and comedy writer Joe Bigelow were tutors. Executives Ross Donaldson, Leonard Hole and Les Colodny were scouts. One of the more notable students in the program was Woody Allen.

Allen was assigned to shadow comedy writer Danny Simon during the dying months of *The Colgate Comedy Hour.* Allen called Simon one of the "most important people to my career . . . for teaching me the fundamentals of how to construct sketches and, even more, for the psychological boost of having someone that *accomplished* believe in me." Simon was widely respected in 1950s television, but when his brother Neil "Doc" Simon became the most popular playwright of his generation, a chip developed on Danny's shoulder. He was no longer the picture of confidence; his brother's great success made him question his own ability. Comedy writer Ron Clark says, "He would turn out a funny sketch, but he would just keep rewriting and rewriting and rewriting and the sketch would get less funny and less funny and less funny." A prime example was his play *Only the Shadow Knows*. It was originally about two brothers, one living in the shadow of the other, and was based on the relationship between him and Neil. Danny rewrote it so much that the finished version was about a gentile woman who converts to Judaism.

Bill Dana joined the NBC Writers Development Program with his partner Gene Wood. They were assigned to *The Kate Smith Show*, and Dana eventually blossomed into one of Steve Allen's primary writers. Student Paul Keyes was assigned to a Kaye Ballard pilot and was placed on Jack Paar's brand-new *Tonight Show*, eventually becoming head writer of *The Dean Martin Show* and *Laugh-In*. Despite the blossoming of students Woody Allen, Dana and Keyes, the network disbanded the development program after twenty-four months, disappointed with its results.

After 161 episodes, NBC broke its successful *Your Show of Shows* into three separate pieces, believing it could have three successful shows by splitting up the ingredients. The three programs included *The Imogene Coca Show*, *Caesar's Hour* and a series of dance-laden "spectaculars" produced by Max Liebman. *The Imogene Coca Show* debuted October 2, 1954, with no real premise. Lucille Kallen oversaw the variety show, which shifted to a sitcom format and then back to a variety show when things weren't working. In an attempt to help the aimless program, Mel Brooks was hired, but he and Kallen did not get along. Brooks reportedly yelled at Kallen, "Don't tell me what's funny—just *type*." Kallen refused to work with him and gave the network an ultimatum: "It's either him or the rest of us." It was all of them. Despite a supporting cast that included Bill Dana, Don Knotts and Hal March, *The Imogene Coca Show* was canceled. Coca said the network forced her into it: "I wanted my own show like a hole in the head."

Caesar's Hour, on the other hand, was a success. It was a chance for Caesar's gang to focus solely on comedy, without the interference of dance numbers. Additions like Larry Gelbart added to the legendary status of Caesar's writers. Milt Kamen, a struggling stand-up comic, was hired as Caesar's stand-in. Kamen brought a nebbish he'd met in the Mountains named Woody Allen to meet the group, and Allen was soon writing television specials for Caesar.

Caesar's Hour had three successful seasons. It ended in May 1957 when Caesar had a financial dispute with NBC and broke his seven-year contract. Gelbart claimed its demise was due to low ratings, in a factually inaccurate but amusing assessment: "Do you know the competition that finally knocked Sid off the air? *The Lawrence Welk Show*. Sid got into television on the ground floor, when television was new. In the early years, most of the TV sets were owned by affluent people, and affluent people tend to be the most educated people. By the time Lawrence Welk came around, a lot of far-less educated people owned sets. And these people would have much rather seen bubbles coming out of Lawrence Welk's ass than Sid Caesar doing a takeoff on *Rashomon*."

CHAPTER FIVE

LATE NIGHT

NBC invented another important comedy franchise, one that introduced more stand-up comics to a national audience than any other. The influence of *The Tonight Show* cannot be overstated. The first three hosts—Steve Allen, Jack Paar and Johnny Carson—introduced America to everyone from Don Rickles to Nichols & May, Bill Maher to Roseanne. Almost every major comedian of the last sixty years cracked wise in its late night time slot.

NBC's development of late night television happened concurrently with the success of Berle and the rise of Caesar, but took longer to evolve. The very first late night show was called *Broadway Open House*. It debuted on NBC on May 29, 1950. "When it got to be ten or eleven o'clock at night, television just showed a test pattern," says *Broadway Open House* bandleader Milton Delugg. "Pat Weaver of NBC decided he wanted to put entertainment on late at night." It was the template for every late night show in the years that followed.

A prop comic named Don "Creesh" Hornsby was hired to host *Broadway Open House*. In nightclubs he wore a crash helmet and doused his nightclub audience with dry ice from an extinguisher. As he sprayed patrons he told them, "Don't worry, it won't hurt you. It will only burn holes in your flesh."

NBC put Hornsby's face on billboards, but by the time they were erected Hornsby was dead, a sudden victim of polio. The husband-and-wife radio team of Tex McCrary and Jinx Falkenburg were emergency replacements for the 11:30 slot. They hosted the very first episode of *Broadway Open House*, which *Variety* called "unfortunate" and "embarrassingly pedestrian."

NBC searched for yet another host, and this time settled on prolific comedian Jerry Lester. He was a favorite at major nightclubs and a regular in New York presentation houses. "He worked the Paramount, the Strand, the Roxy," says his contemporary Van Harris. "They'd announce, 'And now a surprise for you, ladies and gentlemen. Here is the star of our show, Jerry Lester . . . *with* the Ink Spots!' Jerry would come down in a worn white dinner jacket with big blotches of ink all over it."

Lester had a glib persona, a toothy smile and a fast mind, all of which served him well in television variety. He'd been fired from a previous variety show, *Cavalcade of Stars*, for spitting on the stage. Producer Joseph Cates said, "He came out to do a monologue. He tells a joke. It doesn't work. He tells another joke. It doesn't work. He says, 'You know what I think of the writer of that? *Thpt*.' He spits. 'That's too good for him—*thpt, thpt, thpt*.' Two days later, the president of the drug chain which owned the show said, 'Look, we don't interfere with how you do the show, but spitting on the runway is not appropriate.'" The following episode Lester swaggered onstage and told viewers about the comment. "You know what I think of the people who told me that? *Thpt, thpt, thpt*." Lester was promptly fired.

But the brief spell proved Lester knew how to host a television show. It was a talent few comedians possessed in 1950. With the sudden death of Hornsby and the on-air drudgery of Tex and Jinx, an unemployed Lester was a natural choice. They tried him out for three nights. "He did anything that came to his mind," said his wife, Alice. "He wrecked the place. He jumped up and down on the couch like a monkey. He poked fun at the cameraman. He kidded everybody in the audience and kidded the show. He just had himself a good time. The next day they made a deal."

Lester was signed as the permanent host, but five nights a week was an enormous workload. At Lester's insistence, NBC divided it between two comedians. Lester hosted Tuesday, Thursday and Friday while Morey Amsterdam hosted Monday and Wednesday. It aired only on New York flagship WNBT, which later became WNBC. "He did it one night and I did it the next night," said Amsterdam.

"It wasn't like the late-night shows now where they have guests. It was like a little stock company stuck together with spit."

"We started off alone and Jerry later hired writers," says Delugg. "Initially [the script] was like: Jerry opens door. Delugg walks out wearing accordion and says something." Eventually NBC hired Cal Howard, a former gagman from Disney cartoons, to write sketch outlines. To supply him with nightclub material, Lester hired a freelancer—a future star of comedy records, Allan Sherman. As the first late night show, it enjoyed favorable ratings, but Delugg admits there was a specific reason. "We were such a hit—but nobody stopped to think that the real reason we were a hit was that we were the only thing on."

Airing live as it did, it was difficult to procure a studio audience at nighttime. "The toughest part was getting a studio audience from eleven to twelve at night," said Amsterdam. "I went down to the Greyhound Bus Company. They had all these tours of New York and I said, 'As you go around in the nighttime, ask the people in the buses if they would like to see a television show.'"

A buxom sidekick was hired, and it made *Broadway Open House* a sensation. Virginia Egnor, also known as Jennie Lewis, adopted the stage moniker Dagmar. Lester had worked with her in nightclubs and hired her as a comic foil. "Boy, was she *stacked*," says Delugg. They devised a joke to introduce her to viewers.

> **Delugg:** Jerry, this is the new chick with the band. She's going
>   to sing with us.
> **Lester:** How does she sound?
> **Delugg:** Who cares!

Broadway Open House exceeded expectations. Naysayers said nobody would watch television at a late hour, but it became a star program on the NBC roster. And it enamored future comedians, including a kid in Morningside Heights. "I never missed *Broadway Open House*," said George Carlin. "That one really got my attention."

Lester took advantage of his sudden success, demanding a higher salary and a better time slot. NBC gave him a raise, but negotiations broke down when he demanded a prime-time show. NBC gave him a daytime radio program as placation. Such fringe benefits didn't sit well with Amsterdam, who didn't get the preferential treatment. Feeling slighted, Amsterdam quit, and a number of comics—Ben Blue, George Conley, Wally Cox, Mickey Deems, Lenny Kent and Hal March—got their first television exposure filling in.

Lester's demands were his downfall. He and his business manager tried to sign supporting players to secondary contracts and insisted on a percentage of Dagmar's personal appearance fees. When Dagmar failed to go along, Lester fired her and replaced her with another blonde—Barbara Nichols. And then NBC went and did the same thing, firing Lester on May 25, 1951. "Jerry Lester did a terrible thing," says his friend Shecky Greene. "He tried to make demands on NBC and they just plucked him out. His show was one of the forerunners of all of that late night shit, but his ego got the best of him."

Broadway Open House revealed an untapped late night audience. NBC executive Pat Weaver wrote a memo expressing further late night intentions, a more ambitious network-wide version of the *Broadway Open House* format: "We have plans for a strip show [five shows a week] late at night, shot on an ad-lib basis as in the early radio days . . . We'll run for an hour with fun and songs and jollity and featured unrehearsed gimmicks. The idea will be that after ten or eleven at night, a lot of people will still want to see something funny." The memo is often used as evidence that Weaver created *The Tonight Show*, although program hosts Steve Allen and Jack Paar both disputed that claim. "He didn't invent programs," said Paar, "but wrote great memos."

Steve Allen, a horn-rimmed jazz fan with a gift for wordplay, got his showbiz experience out west, doing a regional radio program called *Smile Time* with announcer Wendell Noble. Inspired by Henry Morgan, the two men satirized radio advertising:

When you cross the street at a busy corner against the red light—do you get that run-down feeling? When somebody slugs you—do you wake up feeling sluggish? When you lose your grocery list or your laundry list—do you get that listless feeling? Then you ought to try Ovaldeen! Believe it or not, folks, before I drank Ovaldeen, I had circles under my eyes. After drinking it for six weeks—I've got ovals under my eyes.

After five years Steve Allen was at the top of his radio market. NBC put his name on its short list of potential *Tonight Show* hosts along with Jack Carter and Alan Young. Knickerbocker Beer was the first sponsor, and it favored Steve Allen. The original *Tonight Show* debuted as the *Knickerbocker Beer Show* on WNBT and was renamed *The Steve Allen Show* thirteen weeks later.

The early production staff forced ideas on Allen against his will. Allen fired producer Johnny Sterns after yelling, "Don't tell me what's funny!" NBC hired regional producer Bill Harbach as a replacement. "I was directing cooking shows," says Harbach. "They told me, 'The new guy is not getting along with the producer. We think you can handle him.' My first show—at the end of it Steve said, 'I would like to read a letter. It's from a bigot.' Lena Horne had been on the show a couple weeks earlier and at the end of her number he kissed her on the cheek and said, 'Please come back again, you're marvelous.' He reads this unbelievable letter on live television: 'How dare you kiss this nigger.' He reads the letter exactly as it was written, with all the awful words. It went on and on. The audience was silent and my mouth was wide open. There was dead silence. He looked at the camera and took his glasses off. He said, 'If anybody happens to know who wrote this letter—he didn't have the guts to sign his name—find him a doctor. He's the sickest man in America.' The house came down with applause. I fell in love with Steve Allen that night."

The first broadcast on a national basis under the name *The Tonight Show* was September 27, 1954. The guests were Wally Cox and Willie Mays. The advertising buildup was enormous. It received added publicity when shortly before the network debut Allen was threatened by the Mob.

Allen was scheduled to host a WNBT special about the influence of organized crime. Threatening phone calls started coming in that said if Allen named names, he would pay the price. Milton

Berle's Mob-connected manager, Irving Gray, phoned Allen directly and demanded the deletion of several references. Allen complied and names were changed to "Mister X." During a broadcast a few nights later, Allen's studio was bombarded with stink bombs.

The opening week of *The Tonight Show* had no further controversy. Those who watched were surprised by Allen's casual, improvised confidence, and *The Tonight Show* grew into a successful late night franchise, primarily because of his ability. After two profitable years of late night television, NBC gave Allen a Sunday night prime-time program. Allen was hosting *The Tonight Show* five nights a week for 90 minutes (in some regions it ran 105 minutes, although the extra 15 minutes were mostly advertising). NBC convinced Allen to do an hour-long scripted variety show to compete with Ed Sullivan. Allen explained the reason for taking on an even greater workload. "I'd have six million people watching *The Tonight Show* and on Sunday night I'd have thirty million watching. Also, the money was five times bigger in prime time, which had a lot to do with it."

The Steve Allen Show premiered June 24, 1956. There would be several different programs in the coming years with that exact same name, but this initial series was by far his most significant. It featured a cast of recurring sketch comedy players who became, if not household names, at least household faces. Among the Mighty Allen Players were the son of a Club 18 comic—Pat Harrington Jr.; a product of the NBC Writers Development Program—Bill Dana; a former Bowery Boy actor—Gabe Dell; an actor who attended the American Academy of Dramatic Arts with Don Rickles—Tom Poston; one of radio's early Henry Morgan rip-offs—Dayton Allen; and the elastic faces of Louis Nye and Don Knotts.

Bill Dana got Knotts the job. "Don and I had done little bits with Hal March on *The Imogene Coca Show*. I was walking through Times Square and here comes Don Knotts looking sad. I said, 'What's wrong?' He said, 'Oh, I can't do anything. I'm going back to Morgantown, West Virginia, and get a good job.' I said, 'What are you talking about? I'm writing this show and Steve would love you!' I physically took him to our rehearsal at Dance Players Studio. He went in and did his nervous man routine. Steve loved him and he was on his way."

The Steve Allen Show required actual scripting, as opposed to the mostly improvised *Tonight Show*. When the workload started overwhelming him, Allen vacated *The Tonight Show* on Mondays and Tuesdays. A number of people took his place twice a week, among them cartoonist Al Capp, Dick Van Dyke, Ernie Kovacs and Betty White. In January 1957 Allen left *The Tonight Show* altogether to focus on his Sunday night program. NBC offered the permanent job to Ernie Kovacs, but he turned it down. Rather than search for another comedian to continue with the established, successful template, NBC revamped the format and renamed it *Tonight! America After Dark*. In a matter of weeks the successful *Tonight Show* franchise was run straight into the ground.

Tonight! America After Dark had an altogether different premise, promising to show "the nightly glamor" of American cities as moderated by a top showbiz columnist in each town. Syndicated newsmen Paul Coates, Bob Considine, Hy Gardner, Irv Kupcinet and Earl Wilson took turns, in the words of one review, "looking ill at ease and nerved up to a point of embarrassment." Earl Wilson interviewed George Gobel and Joan Crawford from the Beverly Hilton in the first episode while Bob Considine bored viewers with a report about a baby born at midnight. The only notable moment was a Hy Gardner interview with Dean Martin, in which Dino spoke of the fresh Martin & Lewis split: "What I'd say about Lewis, [the tabloid] *Confidential* wouldn't print."

Earl Wilson admitted *Tonight! America After Dark* was "a disaster from the first, eventually nicknamed *America* in *the Dark*. We undertook stunts and we tried to be different. One night I went to an all-night beauty parlor and got my hair dyed red just to show what Broadway actresses go through. All our gruesome mistakes were there—live—to be winced at and ridiculed by millions."

NBC affiliates dropped the show en masse after five brutal months. So awful was *Tonight! America After Dark* that *Variety* speculated it would spell the end of late night programming altogether. Comedy writer Walter Kempley said, "*America After Dark* was so bad viewers went next door to turn it off."

* * *

The man who made *The Tonight Show* an entity was Steve Allen. But the man who turned *The Tonight Show* into a talk show was Jack Paar. He emerged from the ashes of *Tonight! America After Dark* and was arguably the most important tastemaker in comedy in the late 1950s and early 1960s.

Paar was an unlikely guy to have influence. He started as a low-key comedian, a talker who was similar onstage and off. He cited Frank Fay as his biggest inspiration. "I met and became friendly with Frank Fay. Unlike the baggy pants comedians, he wore a dark suit with a carnation on stage, and he had a most imperial manner. Fay was known as a 'talking gentleman'; he just stood quietly and said the most outrageous things. I used him as my model."

Paar got his start as a war comedian like Johnny Burke and Harvey Stone. Stationed in the Pacific with fellow showbiz types Hy Averback and Hans Conried, Paar wore his uniform and stammered army jokes at field hospitals. Over the course of the war he honed his craft, and an embedded journalist from *Esquire* took notice. The write-up jump-started Paar's postwar career:

> *This Jack Paar was not a USO entertainer—he was just a G.I. himself. He was part of one of these Special Service units made up exclusively of G.I. talent. They went on month after month, untouted, unheralded, like the foot-slogging infantry itself, doing a job that had to be done, making men laugh in some of the most laugh-proof places in the world. Jack Paar was a comic in one of those troupes.*

The profile went on to call Paar one of the most fresh and original young comics in quite some time. The write-up landed him a Hollywood contract with RKO. However, the studio was only looking to profit from the sudden attention, and Paar's time in B-movies didn't amount to much. But the write-up also brought Paar to the attention of comedian Jack Benny. It seemed like Paar hit the big time when he was hired as the summer of 1947 replacement for *The Jack Benny Program*.

The Jack Paar Show opened with a topical monologue followed by satirical sketches based on the same topic. After its first few episodes it was criticized for being "patterned too closely after Henry Morgan." If Morgan influenced Paar, he was not flattered. Morgan said of Paar: "I hope he is as funny as he thinks he is."

Morgan was not alone in his contempt. "I won't dwell on the daily difficulties of Mr. Paar," said comedy writer Milt Josefsberg. "He hired and fired more writers during his first few weeks than Jack Benny used in his entire lifetime." When Benny returned in the fall Paar returned to scraps. He joined the showbiz purgatory of daytime quiz programs and lamented, "Did you ever have one of those days where everything seems to go wrong? I had several *years* like that."

One of his more notable gigs was the *CBS Morning Show*, which he hosted three hours at a time, five days a week, from 1954 through 1955. "The program that CBS wanted me to do was a tough one, I think perhaps the most difficult of any television show on the air," said Paar. "Three hours a day, five days a week, practically all ad-lib. This was before the perfection of tape, and so the first two hours, from seven to nine, were sent to the East and Midwest, and then at nine we had to do an extra hour for the West Coast." When Paar took a vacation in the spring of 1955, his substitute was a barely known Johnny Carson.

In June 1956, after Steve Allen abandoned Monday and Tuesday *Tonight Show* broadcasts, Paar filled in. He shone and was hired as sole guest host from July through September, setting the stage for his assuming the chair the following year.

The network frequently altered the name of *The Tonight Show*. It made *TV Guide* listings and the program's historical record incredibly confusing. At different times it was known as *Tonight!*, *The Tonight Show*, *The Steve Allen Show* and *The Jack Paar Show*. Allen and Paar hosted other programs with similar—and sometimes identical—titles, muddling things further.

On July 29, 1957, the first official episode of Jack Paar's *Tonight Show* aired, taking over for the crippled *Tonight! America After Dark*. *Variety* wrote, "This looks like the last stand, the make-or-break outing for *Tonight*. Jack Paar [has] the near-Herculean task of restoring it to its former prestige. Paar's got a chance to make it—a slim one, but a chance."

NBC had ideas for restoring *The Tonight Show* after the *America After Dark* debacle, but had little credibility when it made suggestions to Paar. Paar said, "Their main thought was to split the program into three separate half hours and to have a different game show in each thirty-minute segment." Paar resisted. He fought to turn it into an actual talk show—and won.

Paar was an unsanitized personality, veering in unscripted directions. He thought nothing of crying on air or throwing a tantrum. "He was uniquely neurotic in a way that made him special to me and those who got addicted to watching him," says Dick Cavett, a Paar writer. Frequent guest Orson Bean says, "He was a very odd guy, very complicated, strange and moody." The press treated him with resistance. He wasn't amiable like other 1950s hosts like Ralph Edwards or Garry Moore, and initially his ratings were poor. Of 131 different programs on the air, both the Crossley and Nielsen ratings placed Jack Paar at 131st. Boston, Cleveland, Houston and Pittsburgh all refused to carry Paar when he first started.

Paar conducted interviews in a casual manner and altered the norm of booking practices. The common approach, then as now, was to have a several-month space between appearances. But Paar brought back successful guests multiple times a month, from the ditzy Dody Goodman to the cynical Oscar Levant to the free-spirited Jonathan Winters. Author Alexander King became a regular guest, talking humorously about his addictions, and Paar dubbed him the "Junkie Mark Twain." By bringing these characters on air time and again, he turned them into stars, and the show became a hit.

Paar's fights were many. He endorsed Fidel Castro, which brought condemnation from the Hearst press. Mickey Rooney, full of liquor, told Paar he couldn't understand why people watched him and that Ava Gardner was "more woman than you will ever know." Paar bickered with catty columnist Dorothy Kilgallen. He engaged in a booking war with Ed Sullivan. And he missed no opportunity to attack his predecessor, Steve Allen. "He is the most self-promoted thing," said Paar. "Steve is the greatest living nonauthority on comedy. Whenever there is a scholarly discussion of humor, Steve raises his hand. I wish he'd just leave the room."

Paar took a vacation at the end of May 1958 and Johnny Carson filled in, hosting *The Tonight Show* for the very first time. It was a historical moment that at the time was dismissed. "With Carson navigating, it was wholesome, intelligent and mostly dull," wrote *Variety*. "The experience of his helmship will never go down as memorable either for a Carson appearance or for an edition of the show."

The American public adjusted to Paar's bizarre personality and soon embraced it. Fortunately, NBC did not concede to dissatisfied affiliates, and by the summer of 1958 Paar's ratings had doubled. A merchandising blitz followed. RCA released novelty singles like "Blue Wiggle"—a slow rockabilly jam with Paar muttering, "Blue. Wiggle. Blue. Wiggle." He published his first of four memoirs, and George Jessel optioned the rights for a Jack Paar motion picture, which was described as "a mystery comedy using Paar stalwarts Charlie Weaver, Genevieve and others." Jack Benny did an impression of Paar on *The Jack Benny Program* and comedy duo Bob & Ray did the same on a promotional LP. By the end of the year, Paar averaged thirty-five million viewers each night, the most successful late night host in history. It set the stage for his power as a starmaker. With the eyes of the nation on his show, he introduced Jonathan Winters, Nichols & May and the Smothers Brothers to a massive audience for the first time. All three acts embodied comedy's new coffeehouse style. All pressed comedy LPs with excellent sales, thanks to the Paar promotion.

Regardless of popularity, a five-night-a-week grind was exhausting and Paar told the press he would quit in July 1959. Paar said if NBC denied his wish he would "get a doctor's certificate in order to quit." He also made a number of demands. His biggest peeve was the length of the show; it varied from affiliate to affiliate, airing anywhere from 90 to 105 minutes. Paar asked for a manageable 60 minutes, but affiliates were beholden to their advertisers and presold airtime. In protest Paar vacationed more and more—giving guest host Johnny Carson more and more experience. Finally, NBC and Paar negotiated a new deal. For a substantial raise Paar would continue hosting *The*

Tonight Show Mondays through Thursdays, with a rerun airing every Friday. He had the most profitable show on NBC, reaping sponsor dollars with his no-budget setup, allowing him to whine, complain and act like an ass with impunity.

Jack Douglas and Earle Doud were the comedy writers crafting Paar's opening monologues, in which he stood center stage and talked to the audience about whatever was going on in the world. It became a *Tonight Show* template. On February 11, 1960, he used his opening monologue to criticize NBC. His beef was about the previous night's monologue, which had been cut by network censors. Paar made reference to a "WC," an old British slang term for the bathroom. It was considered profane by network suits, the piece was cut and rumors spread that Paar had told "an obscene story," the collective imagination assuming he said something much worse than "WC."

Paar explained, "I felt the implication that I had told an objectionable story was harmful to me and the show. When I learned that the network had cut it out of the show without even telling me, I was angry. It was a tacky story, I must admit, and it was told at midnight. Innocent story. And somebody made the mistake of cutting it. And I objected to it. They had admitted it *was* a mistake." NBC tried to placate its star by conceding he was right. Paar said great—let's air it. "They said, 'No, no. If you do that, Jack, it will look like you're running the company and it's a corporate decision.' And I said, 'No, my reputation is more important. You say it was not obscene? Show it—or I will walk off.'" The following night, in place of his opening monologue, he delivered a rambling speech that attacked his detractors in the press:

"I have been wrestling with my conscience all day . . . Now I have made a decision about what I'm going to do. Only one person knows about this. It's [*Tonight Show* sidekick] Hugh Downs. I'm leaving *The Tonight Show*. There must be . . . a better way . . . of making a living than this." Paar shook the hand of Downs and walked off the show. Talk about a drama queen.

That evening's guests included comedians Orson Bean and Shelley Berman. "When Paar walked off the show I was in my dressing room," says Berman. "I thought, 'What should I do?' I did not know how to side. I [went] on that show instead of walking out [in solidarity]. He never forgot it. He would make unpleasant remarks about me from then on." Bean took Paar's side and criticized NBC, but found himself on Paar's shit list anyway—just like Berman. "I stuck up for Paar and I heard there was a suit that was pissed off at me for badmouthing NBC. Paar did not appreciate my sticking up for him. I couldn't understand it."

The suits conferred about whether to air Paar's walk-off or not. "It was seriously discussed to run a movie and not to run that tape," said Hugh Downs. Not wanting to take heat for censoring Paar on consecutive nights, NBC allowed his tantrum to air. The media circus was instantaneous. "For days my home was surrounded by press cars, television crews, and police to protect the property," said Paar. "Bob Hope and Jack Benny called and said it was the damnedest publicity stunt ever in show business. This really hurt, as there was no thought of publicity. The truth was that I became quite ill. My wife knew we had to get away somehow, but for two days we could not open our front door."

One month later, at the urging of his wife, Paar returned. He'd achieved his objective of humiliating NBC and received a loud ovation as he walked back through the *Tonight Show* curtain. As the applause calmed, he spoke—and got an enormous laugh. "As I was saying before I was interrupted . . ."

Paar's return did not last long. NBC was preparing a replacement, with Johnny Carson a top candidate. Paar soon moved to an hour-long Friday night prime-time show called *The Jack Paar Program*, where he introduced new stand-up comedians like Dick Gregory and Woody Allen. While Paar is now little known in comparison to Steve Allen and Johnny Carson, he invented most of the conventions associated with late night talk shows during his run. Pretty impressive for a guy who hosted *The Tonight Show* for only five years.

CHAPTER SIX

THE EMERGENCE OF LAS VEGAS

Throughout the 1950s Senator Kefauver tried hard to influence America, but he couldn't hold a candle to the power of a television personality like Jack Paar. When Kefauver first took on the Mob he seemed like the most influential man in America, but Democratic Party power brokers, furious at him for sabotaging his own party, ended his chances of achieving greater influence. Party members were told not to cooperate with Kefauver's investigation, and few of his recommendations were implemented. "Of the first twenty-two contempt cases arising from the crime hearings, not one was upheld," wrote scholar Joseph Bruce Gorman. "By 1953, forty-five citations had been disposed of; the results showed three convictions, twenty-two acquittals, ten dismissals and five convictions reversed on appeal."

Kefauver's biggest achievement was unintentional. During the height of the Kefauver hearings, local officials were harassing nightclubs, and the Mob spent a fortune fighting back. Tired of the harassment, Mob outfits from Cleveland to Miami Beach moved their operations to the safe haven of Nevada. Thanks to Kefauver, Las Vegas as we came to know it was created.

Vegas had been a sleepy hamlet. Alan King was one of its earliest comedians. "Those were the Ben [Bugsy] Siegel days. The days when everybody I worked for got killed. When I arrived in Las Vegas, it was a small town in the desert." Comedian Woody Woodbury was also there. "There was no Strip at all. It was called the L.A. Highway. Beldon [Katleman] had a place called El Rancho with Joe E. Lewis and Ted Fio Rito's orchestra and that was *it*. The Strip was two lanes, and after four miles it was a dirt road."

The Mob was running things, but the names on leases were intentionally vague. Wilbur Clark started building the Desert Inn in 1947, but ran out of money. The Cleveland Mob came to the rescue and hired Clark as its front man. "Wilbur was strictly showcase dressing for the [mobster Moe] Dalitz group," said Vegas columnist Ralph Pearl. "He had absolutely no voice in the operation of the Desert Inn—even though the huge neon sign, the menus, the bedding, the gaming chips and the promotional matter all advertised it as Wilbur Clark's Desert Inn. He couldn't get his nephew a job at the Desert Inn even as a busboy unless he asked.

Stan Irwin had been doing impressions for a couple years when he accepted a gig at the Club Bingo. "I was playing [Los Angeles] at Billy Gray's Band Box around 1948. Some vocal group got booked and said I should be playing the Club Bingo in Las Vegas. I said, 'Where is Las Vegas?' There was Las Vegas, New Mexico, and Las Vegas, Nevada. At that time most mail addressed to Vegas ended up in New Mexico."

The manager of Club Bingo liked Irwin and asked him to stay permanently, not as house comic, but as the face of the operation. Irwin says, "In the years after the war there were restrictions and in order to get steel you could only do so if you were enlarging an already existing building. The Club Bingo was the existing building that was enlarged into the Sahara." Irwin became the entertainment director of the Sahara Hotel, producing stage shows for Abbott & Costello and Mae West. He was the first person to place performers in the lounge, furthering the legends of Louis Prima, Keely Smith and Don Rickles.

"In those days Jack Entratter was the head man of the Sands Hotel," says Irwin. "He had been the main man at the Copacabana. For me to compete with Jack was ludicrous. I was just a comic. I suggested we talk to a man named Bill Miller who had the Riviera in New Jersey. He brought in Marlene Dietrich with what was known as the peekaboo dress: skin-colored lining with rhinestones, so it looked as if she was nude."

By 1952 Joey Bishop was opening at El Rancho, Buddy Lester was headlining the Last Frontier and Joe E. Lewis toasted the Sands. Mid-decade marked the opening of new hotel-casinos: the

Riviera, the Dunes and the Royal Nevada. If you became a star on television, you now knew where to go. Comedian Danny Thomas, star of a hit sitcom, was paid ten thousand dollars for one week in the new Las Vegas.

Joe E. Lewis was essential to early Vegas. He was a regular at El Rancho, the oldest club of them all, dating back to 1941. His persona was that of the track-addicted boozer, "The Aristotle of the Bottle," and it made him a favorite of Nevada hedonists. Columnist Ralph Pearl wrote, "I'd watch Lewis come staggering out of the wings. He'd be clutching at a tall glass of his favorite mouthwash, Ambassador Scotch, and wobbling in a manner that threatened to drop him into the laps of the ringsiders." Lewis would raise his glass to the crowd and say, "Forgive me for drinking onstage, but it's something I like to do while getting drunk."

For several comedians the Vegas combination of high pay and high stakes was disastrous. Comedy team Norman & Dean was playing El Rancho in 1952. "We were making seventy-five hundred a week," says Stanley Dean. "Around the second week I went to withdraw some and they told me, 'Sorry. There's no money left.' We were booked there for a month! That's close to thirty grand! There wasn't a dime. Harvey Norman, the fucking idiot, went and blew the whole thing gambling. I wanted to kill him!"

Norman was an average straight man until he was introduced to the tables. "We did sensational for the first two or three years, did all the Sullivan shows, but he turned out to be one of the most voracious gamblers on earth. We worked with a trio: two sisters and a guy. Harvey went and forged this girl's signature on checks and took everything she had, cleaned her out. One day I got a call that he was in jail. The cops stopped him, searched his car and found a sawed-off shotgun in his golf bag. I went and bailed him out. I said, 'What were you doing with a sawed-off shotgun in your golf bag?' He said, 'I was thinking of holding up a bank.'"

While Vegas boomed, the bomb was doing the same a few miles away. A 1952 wire story asked, "What would you do if you were in the middle of telling a joke and the atomic bomb went off? Comedian Jack Carter, who faced such an awesome interruption, conceded today that it's just about impossible to ad-lib your way past that."

The U.S. government was conducting experiments with atomic and hydrogen bombs in the desert and the detonations were felt in Vegas. It disrupted shows, paralyzed comics and turned the town on its head. According to United Press International: "When the first two blasts went off, Carter and a roomful of impressed clients just froze, while the tables danced in the after-blast. The veteran comic didn't have a crack to deliver until a third test misfired. Everyone got deathly quiet as the clock ticked off the last few seconds, then something went wrong and there wasn't a sound. He stood on the stage quivering for ten seconds, then brought down the house by suddenly asking, 'What was that?'" Carter recalls, "Customers used to stay up all night before a test explosion, so the clubs just ran continuous shows. It started a locust plague. The atomic blast loosened them and they headed into Vegas. They crawled all over the stage and were on the highway. They were everywhere. You went into a dining room and they were on your table, they were in your food; there were bugs all over. I was working the Desert Inn and one crawled onstage. A guy stood up, 'God-day-yam,' pulled his gun out, sent a bullet right beneath me and blew a hole in the floor."

One of the brightest new Vegas stars was Buddy Hackett. The rotund comedian was considered one of the great stand-up comics of his time. Years in the business would make him a dominant force onstage, but his beginnings were as just another Hanson's Drugstore straggler. Jack Carter grew up near Hackett. "He and I were from the same neighborhood in Bensonhurst. My father had a candy store and his father had an upholstery store. He used to hold the nails when they upholstered, and that's how he got his 'side mouth' like that."

Hackett's father invented the day bed. "He never made a quarter on it," said Hackett. "He wouldn't take out patents. He kept saying, 'I can make a better one.' He was up at four every morning, but just made enough to get by."

Hackett entered show business in 1945. He observed comedians at the Concord in the Catskills, eventually gaining the gumption to try it himself. He did impressions in Brooklyn beer parlors and eventually secured a role in the road company of the musical *Call Me Mister* with an unknown Carl Reiner. Dealing with Broadwayites brought him to the Hanson's scene. He befriended fellow bums Lenny Bruce, Frank Man and comedy writer Marvin Worth. "According to Lenny, it was possible that pound for pound, Buddy Hackett was the greatest comic talent in the world," said Honey Bruce. "Lenny couldn't wait to get backstage after the show to see Buddy. When they met, it was clear that the regard was mutual. Their minds meshed at the same RPM; they played off each other fast and funny." Frank Man says, "It was me, Lenny Bruce, Buddy Hackett, Marvin Worth and [comedian] Bob Leslie in that clique. We'd all hang around and get high. At that time Hackett had a lot of money. The owner of Montrose Motors in Brooklyn, Frank Faske, was acting as his manager. He'd give Buddy as much money as he ever needed. He had a Cadillac and the finest tuxedos. We'd all go back to my apartment and get high."

Hackett went to Los Angeles and played a highly successful engagement at Billy Gray's Band Box, a room at Beverly and Fairfax that featured and played to many the comedian's comedian. Seen by a showbiz crowd, he was signed by Universal-International to replace an ailing Lou Costello in the movie *Fireman, Save My Child*. When Lenny Bruce landed in Los Angeles, Hackett brought him to Universal and they punched up the Donald O'Connor musical *Walking My Baby Back Home*. Eventually the studio cut him loose, telling Hackett, "You're a fine comedian, but we don't know what to do with you."

Marvin Worth teamed with Arne Sultan and they wrote for *The Steve Allen Show*. Worth and Sultan wrote a comedy record for Hackett called *Seven Lively Highs*. It dealt "with the different humorous aspects of getting high under the influence of alcohol, marijuana, heroin and sordid other drugs." They had a deal with United Artists, but the record was canceled when Hackett abandoned such associations. "One day Buddy came to us," says Man. "He said, 'I can't hang out with you guys anymore. I get too paranoid. My eyes get too red. I'm afraid they're going to arrest me. I'm going to start hanging out on the golf course with Alan King and people like that.'"

Hackett started spending time at the Englewood Golf Club, owned by comedians Joey Bishop and Phil Foster. He bought a ranch house in Leonia, New Jersey. He befriended playwright Sidney Kingsley, who cast Hackett in the Broadway drama *Lunatics and Lovers*, for which Hackett would win a Donaldson Award for Male Debut. Max Liebman cast Hackett in the sitcom *Stanley*. Comedy writers William Friedberg and Neil Simon wrote the pilot, but were fired when they asked Liebman for a piece of the show. NBC replaced them with a kid from its Writers Development Program—Woody Allen.

Critics hailed Liebman as a genius during the days of *Your Show of Shows*, but he was a paradox of knowledge and ignorance, unable to achieve another success. He knew how to create grand-scale entertainment, but also considered Neil Simon disposable, told Carol Channing she was talentless and told Mel Brooks he wasn't funny. *Stanley* premiered September 24, 1956, and critics were miffed: "Hackett is a good comic; has ample know-how and a likeable quality, but the material handed him in the opener of this new NBC show isn't the kind which is apt to give him much of an audience." The sitcom had no sense of focus, a rotation of writers working on spec and an arrogant producer who felt he knew best. Woody Allen said, "Liebman was too strong a personality and too wrongheaded about what was going on." The show was canceled, despite having as its costars Carol Burnett and Paul Lynde. Hackett returned to clubs.

Hackett's first post-*Stanley* engagement was at the Copacabana with Ella Fitzgerald. He spent the next ten years turning his act into a potent force, but his best-known routine—speaking in pidgin English and taping his eyes back to play a Chinese waiter—was one of his worst. He was best when working free-form. "Hackett is a strange character," wrote *Variety* after he returned to Billy Gray's Band Box. "To the Band Box partisans he's the apple in their strudel. In any other spot he'd click as vigorously as a cricket scraping his hips. Material schmaterial." But it was precisely Hackett's ability to veer from a set act that made him exciting to watch. He was one of those rare acts that comedians found as funny as the general public did. Woody Woodbury says, "Hackett was *the* comic. Rickles and all those guys would be on their knees to Buddy."

As his status heightened, he grew nasty for no discernible reason. Actor Marvin Kaplan was with Hackett on the set of *It's a Mad, Mad, Mad, Mad World*. "I was leaning on a couch, and he threw a knife at me. Threw a knife at me!" Hackett's violent side frequently involved weapons. His friend and fellow comic Pete Barbutti says, "If Buddy Hackett wasn't *Buddy Hackett*—he would have been certifiable." Barbutti was once with Hackett in the greenroom of the Sands Hotel when Hackett started firing a gun. "Jack [Entratter] was sitting there saying how Totie [Fields] always did good business. Buddy was saying, 'That fat Jew broad! I hate her!' He was going on and on. Her picture was on the wall above Jack's head. Buddy reached under the couch, grabbed his gun and shot the picture off the wall."

One day Hackett shot up a car in the hotel parking lot. "He showed up for work at the Sahara and someone took his space," says Barbutti. "If that happened to you or me we'd put a note on his window. Not Buddy. He pulled out his gun and shot out all the windows, the headlights, the tires, *reloaded*—and shot it up *again* . . . then went in and did his show like nothing happened."

After Lenny Bruce died, Hackett assumed the title as dirtiest comedian in the business. Vegas tourists used to his impish television persona were shocked when Hackett opened his mouth. "He got very X-rated," says Freddie Roman. "I once asked him why. He said, 'Because there's no more challenge. I know I'm going to get laughs when I do my regular act, but I want to get the audience to *hate* me—and then see how long it takes to win them back.'"

Buddy Hackett and comedian Shecky Greene were Vegas superstars and close friends. Hackett's gun-toting and Greene's drinking coalesced one night in a violent desert struggle. "Buddy found me in a bar and came in with a portfolio under his arm, a gun in the portfolio," says Greene. "I fired a guy that worked for him who was also my gardener. Buddy came in and said, 'That man needs new teeth.' I said, 'Well, go buy him some new teeth!' He said, 'No, you should buy him some new teeth because you fired him.' We went across the street and started gambling. And drinking."

"They walked over and Shecky put down something like three hundred dollars and rolled a seven," says Barbutti. "He had six hundred and said, 'Let it ride.' He rolled eleven and he had twelve hundred and stuffed it in Buddy's pocket."

It was enough to help out the fired gardener, but by that point both Greene and Hackett were blotto. "We made a lot of money," says Greene. "We're walking across the street. As I'm walking, Buddy stands in the middle of the street and says, 'You know something? You're a Waldo!' I said, 'What?' He's in the middle of the fucking street! I said, 'I'm a *what?*' He said, 'Not only that . . . you're a *double* Waldo!'"

Greene says he had no idea what that was supposed to mean, "but it's something you should never call me when I'm drinking." Greene continues: "So now I walk back. I said, 'I'm a fuckin' double Waldo?' He's got the gun out. I punch him in the fucking stomach! As I'm walking away he comes running and jumps on my back! I flip him over my back. I put my foot on his throat. I said, 'If you get up, Buddy—I'm going to *kill* you.' I reached down, took his gun and car keys and threw them into the desert. I said, 'Now don't get up.' About three hours later my phone rings. 'Hi, Shecky. It's Buddy. You know, if someone was with us this morning they would think we didn't like each other.'"

Hackett's violent side never affected his standing as a regular in Walt Disney films or his frequent appearances on *The Tonight Show*. He was considered a fearless comic, but many of his relationships were strained. "Buddy did some terrible fucking things," says Greene. "He was like the devil. You never knew what was going to happen with Buddy. But he was a brilliant comedian."

Shecky Greene was a star comedian in Vegas during the 1950s and 1960s. To this day the name "Shecky" is used in parodies of old-fashioned comedy. Jack Carter says, "After a while people were saying, 'What are you—*Shecky Greene*?' They use his name like a phrase. Shecky's name is used as a symbol for comedy."

While the name is meant to symbolize those comedians who are out of touch, the truth is that Shecky Greene was one of comedy's great nonconformists and a far cry from an uncreative hack. When other comedians finished their final performance of the night they'd rush to where Greene was playing to soak up his brilliant madness. "One of the greatest I ever saw in a nightclub!" says comedian Pat Cooper. "I saw him climb the curtain and do twenty minutes from *on top* of the curtain! He *destroyed* an audience."

There being little modern memory of what Greene's act consisted of, the symbolic nature of his name is distorted. His contemporaries say he was irreverent and unforgettable—yet ask them what he said onstage and nobody has a clue. He was a creature of the nightclub—flying off on wild tangents, climbing walls and fighting owners. It was a free-form approach to comedy that a five-minute television spot could not convey. He was praised by legend Jack Benny, idolized by subversive Lenny Bruce and saluted by genre-expanding Ernie Kovacs. Greene was a genuine comedian's comedian.

Greene started in a comedy team with the future founder of the Comedy Store, Sammy Shore. Shore says Greene was difficult. "He was always putting down show business: 'I hate this fuckin' thing. Fuck show business!' And then he'd do another twenty minutes."

"I really didn't want the fucking business," says Greene. "Every job that came saved me from quitting. A job started at fifty, next one was seventy-five, then it went to one-fifty, then it went to five hundred . . . I kept on going like that and couldn't quit. I kept on lying to myself: 'I'm going to go back to college.' I saw people like Joan Rivers [with] that *drive*. I never had that shit. I just went and had my little nervous breakdowns with my depression."

He suffered from anxiety, depression and bipolar disorder in an era when such things weren't diagnosed. Comedian Don Sherman says, "Only in show business can a man look that uninhibited [onstage] and be experiencing such fear. The last thing he looked was frightened to the audience." Greene was not a drinker until he landed in Vegas, where he discovered that booze quelled his anxiety. Soon he was Dr. Shecky and Mr. Hyde. "When Shecky drinks he turns Las Vegas into Dodge City of a hundred years ago," wrote columnist Jim Bacon. "One explosive night, he rambled through Caesars Palace, knocking statues right and left off their pedestals."

"He'd come offstage and he'd be crying like a baby and shaking," says Pete Barbutti. "So he'd drink. It became a mood-altering drug for him and he would do these terrible things. He'd hit people. He drove his Cadillac into the fountains at Caesars Palace."

"I was completely drunk," says Greene. "I was completely *insane*. I forget what time it was in the morning. They gave me my car. They always gave me my car when I was drunk because they loved to see what was going to happen. I was driving about one hundred miles an hour. I hit a post. The post broke in two, went across my car, I swerved across the street, hit two signs and went right into the fountain."

No charges were pressed. Woody Woodbury explains, "In the old days if you got drunk and the cops stopped you, one cop would get out of the police car and he'd drive you home." Greene says, "In those days we had a different situation in Vegas. They would just talk to the sheriff's office and that was the end of it. I never even got a ticket."

Greene's success in Las Vegas brought television offers, but his offbeat style was not easily translated to the small screen. "I was signed by NBC and they offered me different kinds of pilots which I turned down. I got terrible depressions, so I never really worked on anything. The Las Vegas lounge was perfect for me. Every night was a different show. Every night was improv. When I finally got back into main rooms, you more or less had to have an *act*, and that wasn't who I was. I wasn't an A-B-C-D comic."

Barbutti was influenced by his style. "Comics would say to me, 'You need to organize your routines! You need a beginning, a middle and an end!' Growing up in jazz, I would say, 'Can't you go free-form?' They'd say, 'No, you can't do that.' When I came to Vegas I went to see Shecky and he had no routine at all. An hour and a half later I was laughing so hard I couldn't catch my breath. He didn't have a beginning, he didn't have an ending, he was just the funniest guy in the world for ninety minutes."

Greene's nonconformity infuriated Frank Sinatra. He wanted Greene for the Rat Pack, but Shecky had no interest. Sinatra didn't take rejection well. One night a real-life incident became Greene's most famous joke: "Frank Sinatra saved my life once. I was jumped by a bunch of guys in a parking lot. They were beating me with blackjacks. Sinatra said, 'Okay, boys—that's enough.'"

Sinatra did indeed have Greene beat up. It happened while they were in Miami Beach filming the movie *Tony Rome*. "We were going to the bar. Frank and I were on the second tier and this guy Terry, one of The Boys, goes to put a chair there. Sinatra throws the chair down. Terry says, 'Whadja do that for, Cheech?' Sinatra says, 'What are you gonna do about it?' Sinatra leaves and he's walking right down the middle of the street. We followed him back to the hotel and all hell broke loose. He was going to cancel the movie because this thing happened.

"He used to say, 'You're gonna get it, Shecky.' I used to say, 'Frank, what am I gonna get?' He loved me. I didn't love him. He said to me one day, 'Without a doubt, you're the sickest fucking human being I've ever met.' So I took him by the head and put him in front of the mirror. I said, 'There's one *sicker*.' He didn't say a fuckin' word . . .

"One day I come in drunk out of my mind about three o'clock in the morning. In the hotel five guys jump on me. The one guy was Fischetti who comes from a very noted family in Chicago. He always went to hit people with blackjacks. He kept on hitting me and the blood kept pouring down."

Greene sobered in later years, but his insistence on the free-form style meant his act would never find posterity. He was the first Las Vegas lounge comedian—a historical distinction—but the improvised material that so impressed other comedians is now lost to the ether. For those who only know the name as a symbol of the old-fashioned, it's surprising to hear the opinion of his contemporaries, like comic actor Marty Ingels: "For the most part he is considered the underground—and the underground's *number one guy*."

*   *   *

After Greene Don Rickles was the next Las Vegas lounge comedian. Rickles graduated from the American Academy of Dramatic Arts in 1946. His prestigious schooling equipped him for dramatics, but his secret ambition was comedy. He quietly admired the comedians at Hanson's and would stand in awe as Milton Berle walked past him, en route to his office upstairs. He said Berle "represented what I thought comedy was all about." Rickles was shy in the presence of the loud, established drugstore kibitzers. "The first time I met Rickles was at the stage door of the Roxy when I was appearing with Tommy Noonan," says Peter Marshall. "He was like a little fan. He wasn't going to be a comic—he was going to be an actor. He started hanging around Hanson's—and then he started doing Jack E. Leonard's act."

Jack E. Leonard was the primary insult comedian from the late 1940s through the 1950s. Initially he did the Chicago presentation house circuit with comic actor Billy House. Jack Waldron, a substitute insult comic from Club 18, took Leonard under his wing and asked Berle to get him gigs in New York. He moved up the ranks quickly and was hosting NBC's *Broadway Open House* in its final days. Leonard and Rickles had little in common. Their styles were dissimilar and their careers at different levels. Rickles was in Long Lake, New York, in the summer of 1949, working as a low-level social director at the Sagamore Hotel, while Leonard was a burgeoning star.

That autumn Rickles walked into the office of Phil-Web Attractions across from Rockefeller Plaza. It was known that agent Willie Weber gave inexperienced comedians a chance. Columnist Ralph Pearl wrote, "Weber is a man who spent his life peddling second rate acts." Weber's portfolio included forgotten comedians Pat Henry, Mickey Shaughnessy and Eddie White. He represented Jackie Gleason when he was a nobody and booked Gleason at Club 18. Weber was small-time, but he mentored those rejected by everyone else. His son Stu was a Catskill booker and his grandson Steven Weber became a television star. Comic Don Sherman says, "I was raised by Willie Weber. He had all the little clubs owned by Mafia guys tied up."

Weber sent Rickles on runs through Baltimore, Detroit, Montreal and Philadelphia. When they weren't interested in a comic, Weber lied and told bookers that Rickles was a harmonica virtuoso. "Rickles did hundreds of shows for this guy Willie Weber before anybody ever heard of him," says Will Jordan. "Hundreds of nightclubs all over the country, hundreds of shows. His act had *nothing* to do with insults. We're talking 1949–1950. Rickles would do a bit about a guy in a movie theater sneaking a smoke."

Nothing to do with insults—and just as little to do with comedy. Rickles was equipped mostly with the dramatic pieces he'd learned in school. "He had very little of an act," says comic Leo DeLyon. "He would imitate Peter Lorre doing an Edgar Allan Poe piece." It was the cornerstone of his early days, the dramatic soliloquy. "The Man with the Glass Head" was based on an Edgar Allan Poe story, one which Peter Lorre had been doing on the presentation house circuit. Rickles decided to do it himself. "He had glass over his head," says Sammy Shore. "I don't know what the hell it was."

Dramatic soliloquies did not sit well with drunken nightclub crowds. Heckling was inevitable. When it happened Rickles responded—and the insult shtick was born. "From that he would go off on millions of tangents with the audience," says DeLyon. "That became his whole persona, insulting and handling them."

Rickles crisscrossed the country. He became a regular at Murray Franklin's bar in Miami Beach. Woody Woodbury says, "We'd go see him at Murray Franklin's. When he was first starting out he was making anti-Semitic remarks. My friend Al Schwartz would say, 'I don't wanna go in there because the Jews hate him.' I said, 'He's Jewish.' It was before he was accepted for what he was. Those young Jewish kids didn't understand what the hell he was doing. They wanted to come over the goddamn bar and kill him."

"I met him in Philadelphia," says Jack Carter. "He used to work at a place called the Celebrity Room, which was in a back alley. I used to get him dates and we'd go out. He was a nebbish. He was scared to death of women and had no social life at all."

"We were working bad joints in Washington and Baltimore and there was this after-hours club called the Alibi Room," says comic Dick Curtis. "In those days you couldn't sell booze after midnight. This was a private after-hours club and Rickles was the emcee. He was working *so* blue, just for strippers and dirty comics." In 1958 a new manager entered his sphere and told him to keep it clean. "The guy who took over his career was a Mob guy named Joe Scandore," says Curtis. "He straightened him out. Scandore was an Outfit guy."

Scandore and his brother ran a large nightclub in Brooklyn called the Elegante. They opened it with money from their father, the owner of a massive cardboard box factory. Comic Art Metrano says, "I was told right off the bat, 'Don't fuck around with Joe Scandore.' He was pretty well *connected*. I performed at the Elegante on Ocean Parkway and he was very kind to me, but people also said, 'Don't do anything wrong.'" Willie Weber's client Lou Marsh says, "You didn't fool around with Scandore. Scandore . . . I mean, I'm not saying anything but . . . Joe . . . had a way of doing things."

It was rumored that the Elegante was a front for Johnny Biello, a mobster who worked for the Vito Genovese crime family. "I clicked at the Elegante," Rickles wrote in his memoir. "That's where my style came together. And Joe was there to witness the whole thing. Joe liked me so much he bought my contract from Willie Weber and decided to manage me. Leaving Willie wasn't easy, but he understood. No hard feelings."

Court documents indicate the feelings were harder than Rickles lets on. In February 1959, Weber filed suit against Rickles in New York Supreme Court for breach of contract. Rickles appealed to have the motion dismissed, but failed. Scandore's people then paid Weber a private visit—and suddenly the suit was dropped. "Weber never got a chance to revel in the glory of Rickles' enormous success because he was replaced," wrote columnist Ralph Pearl. "He died heartbroken and disillusioned."

"Rickles and I had the same manager early on," says comedian Frank Man. "Scandore was with the Mob. They provided the money and they got you the right jobs. I didn't want to get involved with anything like that, but they were all Mob-connected. He seemed like a nice guy."

Scandore made Rickles his primary focus and used his extensive connections to build his career. "Scandore was a devoted manager of Don Rickles," says producer George Schlatter. "He devoted his life to Rickles and did a helluva job. Nobody fucked around with Rickles *or* Scandore."

Scandore sent a relative, Peter Danizlo, to Miami Beach to secure a venue that could showcase Rickles on a nightly basis. They took charge of a bar at the Admiral Vee Motel and named it the Riot Room. "If you can fight your way in and don't mind being insulted— you might take a flier at the Riot Room and Don Rickles," reported columnist Herb Kelly opening night. "The dolt and the dullard won't dig it. Only the hip will get a kick out of it."

The insult thing clicked, although Rickles was terrified of actually hurting feelings. He was known as a kind and charitable man. "Jackson Heights—there was a newsstand there," says Will Jordan. "One day, I was going into the city and there was Rickles [working] at the newsstand. He wasn't broke. He was doing it as a favor. That's what Rickles is really like."

When Rickles went to California, the Hollywood mobster Mickey Cohen got a phone call. "Frank Costello called me and said, 'Hey, you're gonna get a kick out of this guy, he's a good kid. Go in and see if ya can give him a hand. The people back here like him.' So I went in and I caught Rickles and Jesus Christ, I never heard anybody like this guy."

Rickles got his West Coast break at the Slate Brothers in Los Angeles. Located on La Cienega Boulevard's Restaurant Row, it was a small room run by the former presentation house dance act of Henry, Jack and Syd Slate. Rickles was an emergency replacement after the Slate Brothers fired Lenny Bruce for swearing onstage.

Rickles was booked next at Gene Norman's Crescendo on the Sunset Strip. Norman remembered Rickles as "a very sweet man, but very insecure. After every show he'd come up to me and say, 'How'd I do? How'd I do?' Looking for approval."

Rickles was the opening act for singer Frances Faye, but Joe Scandore presented him as if he were the star. "His manager tried to stop the [lighting] man from turning off the spotlight on him," says

Gene Norman. "Faye's manager nearly had a fistfight with Don's manager."

Stan Irwin phoned Scandore and asked if Rickles would perform in the lounge at the Sahara Hotel in Las Vegas. Irwin was enjoying success with Louis Prima and Keely Smith. Prima and Smith, the first and only lounge act at the Sahara, were outdrawing the headliners in the main room. Irwin wondered if a comedian could do the same. Don Rickles was an experiment.

The Sahara lounge shows ran late. The last Rickles show of the evening started at 5 A.M. Many celebrities wandered through the lounge and were perfect targets. Show people loved it and started to hire Rickles on their programs as a result. Johnny Carson adored him and used him often. Meanwhile, Jack E. Leonard was losing out.

Leonard was pridefully dismissive as Rickles made a name for himself. "He got everything from me," said Leonard. "He's big, real big, but I'll tell you—I can still *destroy* Don Rickles." Earl Wilson wrote, "Jack E. Leonard still considers himself too big a star to worry about competition." But in private, he brooded. "Jack E. Leonard said Don Rickles stole his act," says Stan Irwin. "He truly believed that."

Most of Rickles' contemporaries also believe it. "Rickles denies he copied Jack E. Leonard—but of course he did," says Will Jordan. Peter Marshall says, "It was Jack's act. Don took it and expanded on it." And Sammy Shore concludes, "Rickles was very funny and became what he became—but it was all from Jack E. Leonard."

"There just weren't enough places for them to both work," says Shecky Greene. "Consequently, Rickles was getting popular, and that bothered Jack. He'd say, 'Shecky, he's doing me! He's doing me!' I'd say, 'Jack, he's *not* doing you. You are doing you and he's doing him.' But I watched the demise of Jack E. Leonard."

Rickles contested the accusation and said that he never ever emulated Leonard. "He was so wrong, and so were a lot of other people. They compared me to him. Jack was a funny guy but Jack was the kind of guy that did put-down things in a set routine. Whereas mine, I don't tell jokes. He was more of a jokester. I do situation things that become a joke. So we were so different but he insisted on saying, in a kind way, he said, 'You know, kid, you're doing me.' Which was not the case."

When the Friars Club roasted Rickles for the first time, it got Jack E. Leonard to host the show. He opened, "Friends . . . welcome once more to the Eichmann trial. I want to tell you what a thrill it is to be here in honor of one of America's great Americans . . . who has been doing my act for about twelve years now. I am here to make a citizen's arrest. I don't mind the guy doing my act, but the son of a bitch stole my [bald] head too. I also want to thank Johnny Carson for creating a monster."

Soon enough Don Rickles was a star and Jack E. Leonard was forgotten. Robert Klein saw Leonard perform at a nightclub around that time and sensed a sadness in the man. "After the show Jack went to a restaurant a couple doors down and I followed him. I thought there would be people and pretty girls and this and that—but nothing. There he was—eating by himself. He looked so lonely."

Rickles was simply the more talented of the two—and worked much harder. Rickles paid his dues, got some powerful help along the way and surpassed his detractors. He was criticized by Groucho Marx, who said, "A comedian will never be a star unless he is loved. It may be therapeutic to let out venom and hostility, but it's not the type of material that will make his name live through the ages. That is why Don Rickles will never be a star." Contrary to Groucho's prediction, Rickles is indeed loved, he is a star, and his name has lived through the ages.

CHAPTER SEVEN

STAND-UP'S GREAT CHANGE

Stand-up was about to get personal. For the first half of the twentieth century comedians performed without referencing their personal lives onstage. When Frank Fay changed the game in vaudeville he changed it only so much. Fay spoke not of himself but of others. The comedy was always about some elusive guy:

"Did you hear about the guy who . . ."

"A fella was walking down the street when . . ."

In the mid-1950s no longer was it "a fella" walking down the street. For the first time comedians told the audience: "*I* was walking down the street."

Old comedians joked about their mother-in-law even if they weren't married. An abstract, nonexistent mother-in-law suffered the brunt of their ridicule. Seldom was a comedian's material moored in reality. Seldom did a comic expose his real side. Jack Benny may have played on being cheap and Milton Berle may have talked of joke thievery, but they were fictional characteristics. What they sold to their audience was an illusion.

Stand-up was impersonal because few comedians wrote what they said. With the references generic, a comedy writer could sell the same routine to multiple people. A handful of comics like Morey Amsterdam and Nipsey Russell devised their own material, but even that conformed to a generic point of view. Without a personal stamp it was easily pillaged. Stand-up comedians copped from the popular joke books of Billy Glason, James Madison, Joe Miller and Robert Orben. They offered "1001 sure-fire gags for any occasion." Other comedy writers transcribed jokes right off the radio and sold them. It created a landscape of homogeneity.

James Madison was founding father of these jokebooks, according to comedian Fred Allen. "For twenty years—from 1898 to 1918—a man named James Madison published an annual collection of monologues, cross-fire jokes, sketches, minstrel-show afterpieces and parodies. This assortment of humorous matter sold for one dollar and was known as *Madison's Budget*. If a comedian found six or eight jokes in the *Budget* that he could adapt to his act, his dollar investment had returned a hearty dividend."

Journalist Bill Treadwell complained about joke recycling in 1950 and blamed Joe Miller. "Every joke ever written eventually gets back to a guy called Joe Miller. His old joke book has been a comedy bible to vaudeville clowns and radio comics, not to mention nightclub emcees. The first edition contained some 247 original anecdotes and sayings. In later editions the number increased to over 1,500."

Madison and Miller cornered the market during the vaudeville years. They were displaced by Robert Orben in the nightclub age. "I ran into the famous Robert Orben books," says comic Don Sherman. "He would break down a monologue. He'd talk about driving to a nightclub and then he'd have fifteen different driving jokes. Through that you would construct an act." Orben later became a speechwriter for Gerald Ford.

Some comedians invested in topical jokes, failing to acknowledge their expiry date. According to Joe Laurie Jr., "The end of World War II found comics holding the bag for about $150,000 in unused and usable war gags." God forbid they write something.

Norm Crosby pieced together his first nightclub act using material he'd seen on *The Ed Sullivan Show*. "I was doing everybody's material. I would watch Ed Sullivan on a Sunday and I would take a joke or a gag or a line from all the comics. I took from Buddy Hackett, Jan Murray and Red Buttons. I took just a thought, an idea, a gag, a line, just something—*not stealing really*. Because when you have no writers, no knowledge of writers, and no material of your own, you know, it was okay to do that." That attitude would change. The 1950s bred new hostility to joke thieves.

Material was not the only thing that was derivative in the life of a tuxedo comedian. Even the names of the comedians were the same. There were guys like Buddy Lester, Buddy Lewis and Buddy Hackett; Joe E. Brown, Joe E. Lewis and Joe E. Ross; Joey Adams, Joey Bishop and Joey Forman. An inexplicable number of them were named Jackie—Jackie Clark, Jackie Curtiss, Jackie Gayle, Jackie Gleason, Jackie Heller, Jackie Kahane, Jackie Kannon, Jackie Mason, Jackie Miles, Jackie Wakefield, Jackie Whalen, Jackie Winston, Jackie Vernon, Jack E. Leonard . . .

"It was a street thing," says Don Sherman. "Jackie! Lenny! Billy! 'Get Jerry to run to the store!' It was a term of affection. Although the name Jackie doesn't work after the age of thirty."

"I used various names when I was starting out," says character comic Chuck McCann. "I used the name Jack Frost. I came onstage and the people shouted, 'Jack Frost—get *lost!*' So I dropped that. Every comic in the world was named Jackie. I used Jackie McCann at one point. That didn't work either."

Comedy conformity was attacked in the mid-1950s, as coffee-house comedians Lenny Bruce, Mort Sahl and Jonathan Winters instigated a paradigm shift and revolutionized stand-up for a new generation. Together they killed off the Jackies and inspired those with an artistic sensibility.

"I didn't know anything about Lenny Bruce when I got his album," said George Carlin. "What it did for me was this. It let me know there was a place to go—to reach for—in terms of honesty of self-expression. The 1950s was when comedy changed forever for the better. Lenny Bruce, Mort Sahl, Dick Gregory, Nichols & May, Jonathan Winters was a departure from what had gone before. Thus, the old order, the Catskills way of playing it safe and avoiding controversial subjects, disappeared. I heard my first Lenny Bruce and my *life* changed."

In 1953 Lenny Bruce left Hanson's Drugstore and moved to the West Coast. He brought along his old-fashioned act, but in time he would shed that skin and emerge an artistic revolutionary. He got stoned among the Beats and distanced himself from his old persona. In a reversal of the trajectory of most comics, he first played big-time presentation houses and became a strip club emcee after. Comedian Slick Slavin was one of the first to encounter him in Los Angeles. "I got a booking at a place called the York Club in South Central. I wanted to get a feel for the place so I went in on a Sunday. Lenny Bruce was the act. He was wearing a tuxedo and doing impersonations of Al Jolson. I figured he was the squarest guy I had ever seen."

The impressions bided time until Bruce invented something new. He paid the bills writing material for impressionist Al Bernie. It was Bernie who connected Bruce with Frankie Ray Perilli, the comic who became Lenny's manager. Perilli says, "When I got to Los Angeles, I went to this club called Duffy's. That's where this owner let Lenny do anything he wanted." Duffy's was a Franklin Avenue strip club where the stakes were low and the crowds apathetic. It was where Bruce met jazz saxophonist Joe Maini, the man who taught him how to handle a syringe. "Joe was extremely influential on us in those days," said Honey Bruce. "It blew my mind the first time I discovered him in the bathroom with a belt around his arm, inserting a needle in his vein. That's when Lenny and I started getting the desire to use."

The venue and the drug use gave Bruce a feeling of freedom. He improvised, and his act entered new realms. "He'd take off on the bosses," says Perilli. "'These two guys, man. There's a girl singer on the show and the boss is in love with her, dig? She can't get a job and this asshole bought her a nightclub so he could get *laid*.'" This material was wild for 1953. "None of the stuff I saw Lenny Bruce do in strip joints did he ever do on his albums," says Will Jordan. "His talent came from ad-libbing, being on every night in a strip joint where you could be as dirty as you want and making the musicians laugh. We were always told, 'Do *not* make the band laugh.' He did exactly the opposite and that worked for him, because the band sense of humor, the musician's slang, began to dominate in the 1950s. Every time I saw him he was doing something very different, very dirty and very original. He would do an abortion doctor and use the microphone as some sort of instrument. He would talk about jerking off the Frankenstein monster."

"What he did was so shocking," says comic Dick Curtis. "He stood onstage naked, no clothes. 'Ladies and gentlemen, I'd like to introduce our next dancer . . . I've been following naked girls onstage all my life—for once I want them to have to follow *me*.'" He emceed at every strip joint that would have him: Club Mandalay on the Pacific Coast Highway, Club Cobblestone on San Fernando Road, the Colony Club in Gardenia, the Cup and Saucer in Downey. Most seminal was Strip City in the middle of Los Angeles. "Strip City was on the corner of Western and Pico," says proprietor Maynard Sloate. "There were always comedians, none of them famous: Jerry Moore, Dick Kimble, Joey Carter, Slick Slavin and Lord Buckley. Redd Foxx played Strip City. And our drummer, Bill Richmond, wrote all the movies with Jerry Lewis."

Agent Lou Dorn introduced Bruce to him, Sloate remembers. "Dorn booked all kinds of people in strip joints. All the comics were doing pretty much the same act; the 'army routine' was the number one piece of material. Lou took me to the Cup and Saucer. Lenny was different from the local comics, so I hired him. He played Strip City six nights a week."

Bruce derived subject matter from the depths of his personality. Jonathan Winters in New York and Mort Sahl in San Francisco were doing likewise at the same time. These three comedians—Bruce, Sahl and Winters—performed material that was by its very nature theft-proof. To take a Jonathan Winters improvisation, transcribe it and put it in the mouth of another man would have been futile. For Norm Crosby to recite the lines of Mort Sahl would have been pointless. For a guy named Jackie to improvise in a strip club in the style of Bruce would have been an embarrassment. "You could learn *nothing* from these [new] guys," says comedy writer Marshall Brickman. "It could not be learned and could not be taught."

The comedy came from honesty and original thought. Old comedians continued in major supper clubs, but there was now a new scene in Greenwich Village venues, which attracted a different kind of crowd. "As the nightclubs go out of business, so go into business the coffeehouses," wrote a *Variety* editorial. "There's every indication this newly created atmosphere will become an important spawning ground for new show business entities. It already has happened in San Francisco where a young comedian-satirist named Mort Sahl first found an audience."

Sahl took credit for the circuit. "I constructed a network of theaters where people can speak—they happen to be saloons, and people said it could not be done—in complete freedom . . . The whole climate has been changed."

Two beatniks in berets—Enrico Banducci and Big Daddy Nord—moderated the brick cavern in San Francisco called the hungry i. Nord used the lowercase name long before minimalist signage was a hipster staple. He said the letter *i* stood for "id." Spelling the venue's name in lowercase was "to show we weren't white bread."

The hungry i opened in 1950, but it wasn't until Sahl emerged in 1953 that it made its mark. Sahl had been indulging in experimental theater at the University of Southern California. He took the school name and did his first stand-up gigs under the name Cal Southern. He did impressions. He developed material around current events, but it bombed in traditional clubs. His act seemed to work only when he played to college crowds around Berkeley. Hoping to find educated audiences in a larger market, Sahl went to San Francisco. Comedy writer Larry Tucker told Banducci about him, but he resisted, telling Tucker, "I don't do comics." Eventually Tucker wore Banducci down. Sahl's first show went well, as the crowd was full of his friends. His second show was a disaster. "I thought I was really home free," said Sahl. "Then I got up onstage without my audience. People started throwing pennies and peanuts onstage. I was shaken."

Sahl spoke nervously, at a clipped pace. His fast patter was bred out of fear. "I was afraid no one would laugh and I wanted to pretend I wasn't noticing the audience. I was afraid to pause, afraid of silences. I didn't take that risk. I kept talking through it, kept filling up the gaps—that's where the verbosity comes from." His style was different from that of comedians of yore. "In my case it took about three months to get a laugh because I was speaking in a strange language. The audience didn't know what to make of it." It was a transitional period in which the crowd had to adapt as much as the comic. Banducci kept Sahl for a year and allowed him to grow. Little by little people got used to him. There were jokes buried in his delivery, but they didn't follow the traditional rhythm. In the words of San Francisco's *Examiner*, he was "funny without being much fun."

Sahl was one of the first to break away from the tuxedo uniform. He wore a red sweater vest that became a trademark, but when he was booked on television he was forced to wear a suit provided by a wardrobe department. Eddie Cantor told Sahl to ditch his red sweater because it gave off "the wrong associations."

He was influential for a new generation of fans turned performers. "Sahl was our god," says Marshall Brickman. "He was sensational, knocked everybody out. He found a whole new area of life that could be funny."

"He was the best thing I ever saw," said Woody Allen. "There was a need for revolution, everybody was ready for revolution, but some guy had to come along who could perform the revolution and be great. Mort was the one. He was the tip of the iceberg. Underneath were all the other people who came along: Lenny Bruce, Nichols & May, all the Second City. Mort was the vanguard of the group."

To less refined old-time comedians like Buddy Lester, he was a pariah: "Who wants a comic you gotta have a dictionary on your lap so you can figure out what he's saying, and even then he ain't funny."

He gained a cult following. Thanks to Sahl the hungry i was a moneymaker by 1954. Banducci invested and expanded. He bought the space next door, signed the Vince Guaraldi Trio, and called it The Other Room. After nearly a year with Sahl, Banducci booked other comedians for the first time. It became a contentious issue. Sahl wanted to be the only one. He and Banducci quarreled, and Sahl fled to New York.

Sahl had made the hungry i chic and in the years to come it featured comedians Shelley Berman, Dick Cavett, Irwin Corey, Phyllis Diller, Dick Gautier, Charlie Manna, Bob Newhart and Ronnie Schell. By the end of the 1950s jazz critic Ralph J. Gleason said it was "as important in the history of American entertainment as the

Palace was during vaudeville." It was profitable, but Banducci was bad with finances. Cavett says, "He was wonderful, but your check would always bounce."

The Los Angeles equivalent was Gene Norman's Crescendo at 8572 Sunset Boulevard. It booked comedians with jazz musicians and the manager of Strip City had a piece of it. "Gene Norman was a radio announcer who owned the Crescendo with Maynard Sloate," says comic Dick Curtis. "Maynard insisted on putting Lenny in, and that was the beginning of his great meteoric rise." The Crescendo presented two simultaneous shows, one on the ground floor and one upstairs in a room called The Interlude. Sometimes Bruce would be on the ground floor while Sahl worked upstairs or vice versa. "The days of Lenny Bruce and me at the Crescendo were pretty great days," said Sahl. "One night through the ventilator I heard him playing a prom—three or four hundred high school kids—and he had them chanting, 'Lynch Mort Sahl!'"

"When Lenny worked for me at the Crescendo, it was his most creative period," says Sloate. "That is when he was *writing*. Between Strip City and the Crescendo he was unbelievably brilliant." Gene Norman says, "Maynard told me about Lenny and brought him into the Crescendo. It was his idea, and I wasn't too happy about it. It was a little bit raw for me." Sloate says, "Gene had no sense of humor. He'd watch Lenny and then ask me if he was funny."

During the spring of 1957 Bruce's jazz cred was solidified during a four-month Crescendo run. He shared the bill with singers June Christy, Herb Jeffries, Mel Torme and the Hi-Lo's. The Dave Pell Octet backed him each night, providing saxophone-induced bubble sounds for his closing bit about Lawrence Welk. The premise had Welk conducting a job interview with a pot-smoking jazz hipster. Welk threatened Bruce with a lawsuit.

Future filmmaker Paul Mazursky followed Bruce into The Interlude. At the time Mazursky was part of a comedy team with playwright Herb Hartig called Igor & H. "He was brilliant," said Mazursky. "His act was a mixture of showbiz humor, great imitations, and strong social comment. He talked about jerking off. I didn't know if I was square or yesterday's news, but it shocked me."

The year 1957 was a fertile one for Bruce. He hosted a game show pilot with Carol Channing, sold a treatment to *Alfred Hitchcock Presents* and appeared on *The Steve Allen Show* for the first time, defying skeptics with a clean set. His television shots suffered a problem similar to the one his LPs did: Mainstream media required censorship— Lenny diluted. Turning a modern audience onto his so-called genius is difficult for this reason. "Seeing him live, he was incandescent," says writer Carl Gottlieb. "The records are only snapshots."

On Thursday, July 18, 1957, Bruce became the first act to play the new Slate Brothers nightclub on La Cienega Boulevard. The engagement was a highly anticipated affair. Opening night was crammed with celebrities. "At that time Lenny and I were living together," says Frankie Ray Perilli. "Opening night in the audience were the Ritz Brothers, the Marx Brothers and all these hookers with George Raft. But that night it was too noisy. They wouldn't stop talking. Anyone would have bombed that night, because you couldn't get anyone's attention." Bruce struggled through the first of two shows. Despite his reputation, he delivered a clean set for an apathetic crowd. By the time he got onstage for the second show, he was fuming. "Lenny went onstage *angry*—because the audience wouldn't be quiet," says Perilli. In rebellion, he opened with a street joke. "Kid says, 'Daddy, what's a degenerate?' Father says, 'Shut up and keep sucking.'"

The Slate Brothers pulled the plug. "He insulted everybody from the stage and swore and everything else," says Perilli. "We *ran*, because they said the Slate Brothers wanted to beat the shit out of him." At the exact same time Don Rickles was playing Zardi's at Hollywood and Vine. Maynard Sloate says, "I went to Zardi's to see Don Rickles. I had made arrangements to see Lenny [perform] the next night. I got a call in the morning and Lenny told me the story of telling the audience to go fuck themselves. Who did they get to replace him? Don Rickles."

"The Slate Brothers was full of celebrities," says comic Jackie Curtiss. "Don Rickles came over and he knew a little bit about every star and nailed them. Insulted them. They loved it. It *made* him."

Bruce went back to the Crescendo, where news of the incident made him more popular. He found a niche as the so-called dirty comic and it made other comics jealous. "Lenny became the envy of everyone," says comedian Van Harris. "He became a star with his nebulous reputation, and you'd hear comics in Hanson's Drugstore grumbling, 'How do you like that son of a bitch? He made it and I didn't! With his dirt! His filthy jokes!'"

Bruce and Sahl were the hottest comics of the 1950s and were hated for it. "Those guys tried their hardest to make it our way," complained Joey Bishop. "When they couldn't—they switched." Bruce responded, "As opposed to Mr. Bishop, who has been doing the same thirty minutes of café comedy for the last ten years. I've done thirty minutes on *The Steve Allen Show* that I'll *never* do again . . . Anyone who is still doing [the same] jokes . . . will make a good Lodge Commander in the American Legion."

Much of the press was on Bishop's side. *Time* magazine complained in its July 13, 1959, issue that Bruce "merely shouts angrily and tastelessly at the world." Sahl was dismissed because he "rambled." *Time*, taking its cue from the established appellations "beatnik" and "Sputnik," dubbed coffeehouse comedians "sickniks." The magazine said they were purveyors of "sick comedy," and "sick comedian" became a description without definition.

Progressive cartoonist Jules Feiffer thinks his *Village Voice* comic strip was partially responsible. "Through the title of my *Voice* strip—*Sick, Sick, Sick*—I had helped make current the media phrase 'sick humor,' which referred, misleadingly, to what was now a rising generation of young writers and comedians, from Terry Southern, Joseph Heller and Bruce Jay Friedman in fiction to Mike Nichols and Elaine May, Shelley Berman and Lenny Bruce in clubs."

Variety put down Bruce with regularity. As part of the old showbiz establishment, the trade paper was hostile to his approach. It reviewed him at the Blue Angel in March 1960. "Opening night witnessed . . . open protestations at his unfunny technique. A comic's shortcomings are more to be pitied than scorned. But an ineffectual comic's would-be attempts at humor, which is downright gutter conversation, deserves little sympathy. His lingo makes B. S. Pully sound like a tomboy. He is undisciplined and unfunny." *Billboard* was more sympathetic when jazz chronicler Jack Maher caught him at the Village Vanguard: "He continues to preach against suppression of the individual liberties in its many forms. Through it all Bruce remains in a league by himself, a man with lightning wit, graphic imagination, and a deep sensitivity for humanity."

Lenny Bruce was able to capitalize on his reputation, but Jonathan Winters had no such luxury. Winters was the final piece of the new comedy trifecta. Sahl spoke politically. Bruce broke down boundaries of language and subject matter. Winters was the comedian as a free-form artist.

Television executives objected to him improvising on the air and insisted he perform material provided by writers. It crippled the very thing that made him notable. "Everybody has to have some gimmick and our gimmick—at least mine—was to get away from jokes," said Winters. It was something the television industry couldn't understand.

The most successful Jonathan Winters television spots were his talk show appearances, in which he free-associated with hosts like Jack Paar. He was the earliest of the improv comics. "Not that I invented it," said Winters. "But I was in the race so to speak." The *Los Angeles Times* wrote, "He was a revolutionary who, with a can opener, opened up the 1950s. He was best when he was live. The joy was in the moment."

But the lifestyle of performing live—late nights, lousy hotels, access to booze—caused trouble. Winters had a family, but in order to support them he had to be far away. Gene Norman remembers his May 1959 Crescendo engagement: "Every night he became more disconnected. He was kind of unraveling onstage. He'd start talking to himself." Columnist James Bacon wrote, "He came out and was hilariously funny for five minutes and then abruptly left the stage. As we left the club we viewed an astonishing sight. There was Jonnie out in the middle of Sunset Boulevard, directing traffic."

A week later Winters was at the hungry i. He mentioned President Truman and was berated by hecklers. Banducci had to call the police. The next night Paul Mazursky was in the audience. "He began the show by telling the audience that he missed his wife and kids. It wasn't funny, but the audience figured it to be the prelude of a new bit. Winters seemed more and more depressed as the minutes ticked by. Then he took out his wallet and showed the audience photos of his family. There were real tears in his eyes. We all knew that Jonathan Winters was having a nervous breakdown."

A waiter escorted Winters to his hotel room. He didn't stay long. He wandered to the wharf and reportedly climbed the mast of a moored ship. Frightened locals called the cops. When police arrived Winters insisted he was "the man in the moon." Winters' manager assured the press he was only joking, but Winters said otherwise. "It was a mental breakdown. Actually put me in the psycho ward. I was drinking twenty-five to forty cups of coffee a day and wondering why I never slept. I couldn't even get my best friends to believe that it was a mental breakdown. They all thought it was the booze. They didn't know what working in nightclubs did to me. It just got to me." Sick comedy had no real definition, but Winters was literally a sick comedian.

Two years later it happened again, and he spent eight months in psychiatric care. James Cagney came to visit and joined Winters for meditative painting sessions. Doctors suggested Winters accept electroshock therapy, which he refused.

Winters never returned to live stand-up. His comedy records were done in a studio with an invite-only audience. He did talk shows and variety television, but never again faced drunks in the darkness. "You gotta say goodbye to some cash, but I didn't want to say goodbye to my kids."

The generation that followed would cite Bruce, Sahl and Winters as their primary inspiration. Lenny Bruce led to George Carlin. Mort Sahl led to Woody Allen. Jonathan Winters led to Robin Williams. The influence of Bruce, Sahl and Winters cannot be overstated. They created a new approach to stand-up. They were the New Wave.

Meanwhile network radio plodded along in a way reminiscent of the dying days of vaudeville. Scripted programming still existed, but listenership had plummeted and sponsors fled as television grew in popularity. By the end of the 1950s the disc jockeys and their rock 'n' roll records had ultimately replaced radio's big-budget comedy shows. In this climate, a satiric and acerbic program made its way onto CBS Radio while few were paying attention.

Stan Freberg had a series of hit parodies in the early 1950s. The most successful was a takeoff on the Jack Webb program *Dragnet*. Freberg's recordings for Capitol Records sold big. Having his own radio program was a natural extension of that. CBS Radio green-lit *The Stan Freberg Show* in 1957. It featured sketches biting, bizarre and bleak. It was the very last of the network radio comedy shows, debuting at a time when the others were already dead.

The first episode of *The Stan Freberg Show* satirized the way Las Vegas cashed in on personalities in the news. The premise of the sketch "Incident at Los Voraces" had the Gaza Strip being imported to a Vegas showroom. Showgirls sang:

> *Gaza Strip!*
> *[machine gunfire]*
> *Gaza Strip!*
> *[machine gunfire]*
> *Everybody's doing the gah-gah Gaza Strip!*
> *Man get hip!*
> *Then you'll flip!*
> *You'll go gah-gah when you do the gah-gah Gaza Strip!*

Freberg then addressed a pressing American anxiety—The Bomb.

> *The Rancho Gommorah*
> *Proudly Presents . . .*
> *For One Time Only . . .*
> *Onstage . . .*
> *. . . the Hydrogen Bomb!*
> *Yes, everybody who thought he was anybody was there that night. In*
> *fact, there were a million people in the room . . . until it came to rest on*

that grim, specter object. I wonder if the boys were still counting their
profits when time ran out. And the man . . . pushed . . . the button.

[sound of desolate wind]

This was the time slot during which listeners had previously heard Jack Benny. To hear a radio comedy end with the annihilation of mankind was pretty wild. "CBS went into shock," said Freberg. "What kind of a comedian was *this*? They seemed to forget they had hired a satirist, if indeed they had ever known it. It was like they were expecting maybe Henny Youngman." There was no reason for them not to have. *The Stan Freberg Show* was formatted in a way comparable to the way radio comedies of yore were. The parameters were similar to those of the old-time comedy shows, but its content was closer to the New Wave tone of Mort Sahl and Lenny Bruce.

Not surprisingly, the program aired without a commercial sponsor. The reason was not so much corporate disgust as Freberg's refusal to allow sponsors he considered immoral. "As a result, CBS had to turn down two different cigarette companies that wanted to sponsor me. That did not put them in the best frame of mind, considering that in 1957 radio was fading fast on the network level and most sponsors were putting the big bucks in television."

Freberg's program lasted fifteen episodes. He walked away from satire and joined the ranks of those he ridiculed—Madison Avenue. He became a profitable purveyor of humorous commercials. He printed business cards celebrating his shift. They read, "*Ars gratia pecuniae.*" Translated, it meant "Art for money's sake."

Radio comedy was dead and stand-up comedy was transformed. At the same time, sketch comedy left the domain of innocuous Broadway revues and entered a new world of subversion with Chicago's Compass Players. Formed in 1955, it was the group with which a number of significant names like Shelley Berman, Mike Nichols and Elaine May got their start. Frustrated thespians from the University of Chicago took their McCarthy-age anxiety and applied it to sketch comedy. The Compass was a seed from which all improvisation-based theater collectives sprouted. Former members seminated show business commercially, culturally and politically for the next forty years.

Cofounder David Shepherd helped shape the Compass's progressive point of view. Initial members Roger Bowen, Severn Darden, Barbara Harris and Paul Sills were all progressive actors, and early cast member Mark Gordon joined the group after he was blacklisted in Hollywood. Shelley Berman, Andrew Duncan, Ted Flicker, Elaine May and Mike Nichols joined shortly thereafter. As the first pangs of social relevance were appearing in stand-up coffeehouses, the Compass brought social commentary to sketch comedy. Duncan remembered, "Suddenly there was this place called The Compass. My God, what an incredible opportunity! To get up and start expressing the things we were thinking about and feeling at that time, with all those repressed political, social, psychological feelings. We were doing some very outspoken things on sex and politics, saying 'shit' onstage. We struck a responsive chord in our audience."

Shelley Berman developed material at the Compass before taking it to stand-up stardom. Andrew Duncan said, "He had a tremendous sense of an audience, but he didn't work our way. He wouldn't give an inch. You really had to fight him. I was one of the few who could get along with him." With a devoted sense of self and an insecurity typical of comedians, Berman was a natural for stand-up. Duncan said the Compass fell apart because of Berman. "The wedge was Shelley. We did scenarios that put us all together, obviously, but in the free-form time we broke up into little groups. There was some strife between Mike [Nichols] and Shelley over Elaine [May]. The Compass didn't last long after that. It ran downhill."

Ted Flicker opened a new Compass in St. Louis, and many notables came through the unlikely bohemian hub in Missouri. Improvisation guru Del Close was one. "I taught Del to improvise and I brought him out," says Flicker. "Elaine May came. She was sitting on the floor and said, 'Where does a girl get laid around here?' I thought, 'Oh no, not me.' She was a *very* strong, fascinating, brilliant woman, but I would just as soon stick my dick in a garbage disposal. I said, 'You can have Del!' And the next day Del was skipping around."

The Compass Players of St. Louis included, at various times, Close, Darden, May, Alan Arkin, Anne Meara and Jerry Stiller. Berman was absent. "I didn't bring him from Chicago because he was a greedy, selfish performer," says Flicker. "Severn would come onstage, 'Look at my rabbit.' Shelley would commit the cardinal sin of improvisation and make a fool of Severn because there was no rabbit. I said, 'When it's my company, he ain't going to be with it.' He was talented and he was funny, but I didn't like him. He was a mean man."

"It was not a very happy time," said Alan Arkin. "It wasn't a well-matched group." Personality conflicts were a daily detriment. "We had an unfortunate event take place," says Flicker. "I was out of town trying to raise money to bring us to New York. Elaine May called and said if I didn't fire Mike Nichols she was going to quit because Mike was trying to take the theater away from me. So I called him up and I fired him." Within months Nichols was reworking his Compass material for a nightclub act that would become the rage of Broadway.

Nichols & May and Shelley Berman found solo success, and it made the others crave similar stardom. David Shepherd went solo, and failed. He explained, "I wanted to make as much money out of it as other people had done." Del Close was next. "I thought I might as well get a nightclub act too. So I took some material from the Compass days, put together some new stuff, and I had an act. It took me two years to get a single going. Two years of absolutely humiliating defeat."

St. Louis seemed like an unlikely city for progressive comedy, but it had a venue called the Crystal Palace that was the equivalent of the hungry i. The Compass called it home. "St. Louis was where we learned 'pad' meant where you lived," said Jerry Stiller. "St. Louis was a very hip town." The hipness was strictly because of brothers Fred and Jay Landesman and Jay's wife, Fran. They published the beat journal *Neurotica* and became the nexus of a bohemian scene. "Fred Landesman had this mansion and he put us on the top floor," says Flicker. "I had one bedroom and Elaine May had the other. Below was a guesthouse for the rest of the cast. Fred was incredibly charming, very capable in terms of business and had barrels of Czechoslovakian crystal with which he built chandeliers." Fran Landesman made excellent royalties as the lyricist for the song "Spring Can Really Hang You Up the Most," which was written for the Beat Generation musical *The Nervous Set.* Those royalties sustained the club. "That broke her into the ranks," says writer Carl Gottlieb. "They conducted the only salon in St. Louis. It was a very conservative town, and this was the bohemian enclave. My very first high was in St. Louis—morning glory seeds, hanging out in this oasis."

When the Compass went under, the Crystal Palace became a full-time nightclub. It was a smart but difficult room. Paul Mazursky played it with his comedy team. "We performed for fifty hipsters standing up drinking martinis and talking, talking, talking. Many of them were destined for greatness, but it hadn't yet happened. Among the throng were Norman Mailer, Buckminster Fuller, Jack Kerouac, Gershon Legman, Allen Ginsberg and John Clellon Holmes."

One of the more interesting future stars to come through the Crystal Palace was Fred Willard. He played it in 1960 as part of a two-man comedy team. In the early 1960s Steve Allen called Willard "brilliantly clever" and "one of the funniest young comics around." Jazz critic Ralph J. Gleason called Willard and his partner "lineal descendants of the Marx Brothers."

Willard left his native Ohio for New York in the late 1950s. He enlisted in a course that gave amateur actors experience in front of a live audience. His class mounted a production of *Desperate Hours* at a local YMCA and he befriended fellow cast member Gus Mocerino. "He had a very good sense of humor," said Willard. "We joked around and had a lot of fun." They formed a team and soon stumbled across a trade advertisement for George Q. Lewis, an old joke book hack who preyed on amateurs looking for a break. He moderated workshops on how to be funny and ran a makeshift organization called the "Gagwriters Institute." He hosted meetings at a local restaurant and handed out copies of his book—*The Dictionary of Bloopers & Boners*.

Lewis charged inexperienced comics for his advice. Mocerino and Willard enrolled. "There were fifteen or twenty guys in it," says Mocerino. "One of them was Vaughn Meader and another was Ron Carey." Willard recalled, "Every week we would write a sketch and come back and perform it. After about eight or nine weeks the guy loved our material so much he said, 'We're going to do away with our sketches and just do a show of *your* material.' We did our show and eventually we started getting jobs in the Village." Mocerino changed his name to Vic Grecco and they hit the circuit as Willard & Grecco.

Cue magazine attempted to describe Willard & Grecco's "innate sense of the absurdity that passes for normality—superbly funny. Like the skit on a nearsighted baseball player. On a comic who does not wish to be funny . . . unique and ultimately indescribable."

They played the typical Village spots like the Bitter End and the Gaslight. They opened for Carmen McRae at the Village Gate. They mostly did characters in short sketches, although for the finale Willard addressed the audience. "We had an ending piece where I came out very seriously and said, 'I have this very valuable letter. It's called the Lincoln letter. My grandfather had written to Abraham Lincoln and Abraham Lincoln replied. It's very valuable—but for this audience—I want to read what Mr. Lincoln said from his heart . . .' I'd start to read and my partner in the background you could hear, '*cough cough*.' He was a little short guy. He had a cigar. He came up, looked at me, grabbed the Lincoln letter, spit into it, threw it on the floor and walked off. The audience would laugh for three or four minutes. I would stand there and say, 'Goodnight, everyone.'"

"Willard & Grecco were *hilarious*," says screenwriter Buck Henry. "They did a truly surrealistic act. I knew them from *The Garry Moore Show*." Variety television made many familiar with Willard & Grecco. They were semiregulars with Steve Allen and appeared on *The Ed Sullivan Show* four times. "Ed Sullivan was tough," said Willard. "One time we were on and Billy J. Kramer was a big pop star. Sullivan would come out of commercial and say, 'Are you ready for

Billy J. Kramer?' And the audience would *scream*. 'First—Grecco and Willard.'"

The Dean Martin Show, *The Mike Douglas Show* and *The Woody Woodbury Show* all welcomed them. "We did several *Tonight Show*s and did a tour of different coffeehouses around the country," said Willard. The gigs included the Inquisition in Vancouver, the King's Club in Dallas, the Ash Grove in Los Angeles, the Blue Angel in New York, the Shadows in Washington, D.C., and the hungry i in San Francisco, where they shared the bill with Barbra Streisand. *Variety* reviewed them at the Gate of Horn in Chicago: "A wildly funny comedy duo . . . off to an advantage because they look funny. Vic Grecco, the shorter of the two, looks like a dark visage used car salesman with a troubled conscience. Husky Fred Willard could be a young matinee idol. Done in blackout style, their material is hip. Among their many risible skits are a takeoff on a beauty school with Willard lecturing cheerfully on pimples and hairy legs and a radio interview on a comic who is violently serious about his comedy. Pair had the auditors howling and would seem to have a great potential for TV."

They were gaining momentum, but when Willard had the chance to join Second City he took it and the team temporarily broke up. Willard had more stage experience than his fellow Second City members Robert Klein and David Steinberg, and as a result was more focused. "I was kind of the weird guy. The original Second City guys all had beards and sat around smoking dope, and I heard stories of when the thaw came in the spring, you'd go out in this garden next door, and there were all these hypodermic needles and drug paraphernalia, but I was never into drugs."

Willard & Grecco reconvened after Willard's yearlong spell of Second City training. They landed a guest role on *Get Smart* in which the entire plot was to revolve around them. It was meant as a pilot for a Willard & Grecco series. However, their agent held out for more money and the production company said forget it and the opportunity was lost.

Willard & Grecco were offered another major television gig as supporting players on a new sketch comedy series, but Grecco didn't want Willard along for the ride. "My partner decided he wanted to go out on his own," said Willard. "This kind of threw me." The series turned into one of the longest-running sketch series of all time—*The Carol Burnett Show.*

Willard recalled, "My manager called and said, 'Vic has decided he'd like to get another partner and do this Carol Burnett show. Would you have any objection to that?' I said, 'Yeah! I would! I wrote all this material!' 'Well, if you want to, why don't you get another partner and audition and they'll choose?'" They each got new partners and auditioned separately. Neither got the gig. "We broke up a couple times," says Grecco. "The problem was, I wanted to promote the hell out us, and that was resisted by Fred. My wife was a graphic artist, and we sent out promotional cards. Fred resisted that, and we had some knockdown arguments."

They broke up in 1968. Carl Gottlieb operated lights for the boys at the Gaslight in the early 1960s. He says, "Vic Grecco was a very odd duck. Vic sat down with six different pens and wrote pretend fan mail. They did a *Smothers Brothers* [*Comedy Hour*] and Vic wrote, 'Have these guys back again. They're so funny.' The girls who read the fan mail—they could *tell* it was all written by the same person. Whatever chance they had, he blew it."

Another cerebral comedy team making waves in many of the same venues was Burns & Carlin. Jack Burns would enjoy a long career as an actor, writer and director, but it was his coffeehouse partner who became the enduring star. George Carlin may have been the only comedian who could count both Doris Day and Lenny Bruce as fans. For forty years he reveled in great creative bursts and suffered long, self-frustrated famines. Inspired by LSD and stunted by cocaine, he mastered multiple styles while contemporaries struggled to master just one. He was capable of crowd-pleasing impressions at one show and subversive routines that would have alarmed the FBI at another. Carlin delivered innocuous observations about refrigerator contents one decade and ranted about the futility of America's two-party system the next. His trajectory, perhaps more than any other comedian's, demonstrated the evolution of an artist.

When Carlin enrolled in the air force in 1954, it wasn't out of patriotic fervor. He enlisted to capitalize on the G.I. Bill and cover the cost of broadcasting school. While he was stationed in Louisiana, his air force record was pockmarked with multiple arrests and reprimands. He charmed a local radio station manager at an off-base party. When a newsreader got sick, Carlin filled in and eventually earned his own KJOE drive-time program with a Brill Building pop music playlist. The program, *Carlin's Corner*, gave him his first taste of fame. KJOE advertised his show on bus stop benches and Carlin was a local star, even if his face was frequently obscured by Shreveport's not-so-wonderful winos. "I was eighteen and I had the advantage of having a car," said Carlin. "I could go out at night and tell a chick, 'Hey, you wanna hear a song tomorrow? I'll dedicate it to you.' It was magic!"

Carlin was interested in a larger market and accepted a job at WEZE Boston in 1959. The news reporter at the station was Jack Burns, who influenced Carlin's way of thinking. "At that time George was fairly conservative," said Burns. "I always had a progressive agenda. I thought it was the duty of an artist to fight bigotry and intolerance. We had long, interesting conversations, good political discussions." Carlin said, "I kind of learned my politics and liberalism from him." They became roommates and considered doing a comedy act, but Carlin's stay in Boston was short-lived. WEZE fired him after he took the station's van on an unauthorized drive to New York to buy a bag of pot.

He found a vacancy at KXOL in Fort Worth, Texas. It was good practice—seven to midnight, nightly. Burns came for a visit and for the next several weeks they improvised on air. They decided to go onstage at a local coffeehouse. "It wasn't a very good act, but people laughed," said Carlin. "We probably had fifteen minutes. We felt secure enough to quit, and the guy said, 'Oh, you'll be back. Others have quit this station and thought they were going to Hollywood. You guys will be back.'" Eight months later they were on *The Tonight Show*.

Burns & Carlin arrived in Los Angeles in February 1960. They got jobs at radio KDAY and one of their coworkers, Murray Becker, got them a gig at a small venue called Cosmo Alley that Lenny Bruce, Herb Cohen and Theodore Bikel all had a piece of. Bruce used the spot at 1608 North Cosmo as a workout room. A caged mynah bird was part of the club's decor, and Bruce supposedly taught it to say "The pope sucks."

Cosmo Alley introduced Carlin to major players. "Mort [Sahl] came to see us," said Carlin. "He called us 'a cerebral duo' and later recommended us to Hugh Hefner for the Playboy Clubs." Becker recorded Burns & Carlin at Cosmo Alley. Hefner let them use the Playboy name, and the performance was deceptively released as *Burns & Carlin at the Playboy Club Tonight*, with a pair of Playboy bunnies flanking them on the cover.

Lenny Bruce was their biggest influence. "Lenny was incredibly important to me," said Carlin. "The defiance inherent in that material, the brilliance of the mimicry, the intellect at work, the freedom he had. I wanted to emulate it in any way I could. Jack and I, for its time, were very topical. We took stands. We took positions. We did jokes about racism, about the Ku Klux Klan, about the John Birch Society, about religions. We had a routine about giving kids heroin kits."

On October 10, 1960, Burns & Carlin did *The Tonight Show* with guest host Arlene Francis. It gave them a bump on the nightclub circuit. They got a bigger boost shortly thereafter when Bruce finally caught their act. "Murray Becker knew Lenny from the navy, and I used to do an impression of Lenny in the act," said Carlin. "So he brought Lenny in to see the impression, hoping Lenny would like us. Lenny called [talent agency] GAC the next day. We got a telegram. They want to sign us, all fields, based on Lenny Bruce's reaction." Bruce predicted, "George Carlin will one day assume the throne as king of the social comics."

GAC sent Burns & Carlin on tour. The first stop was the Tidelands in Houston, a club used to test new acts. A few months earlier Bob Newhart had been booked there and emerged a star. Burns & Carlin were too subversive to explode in the same way, but they were a hit nonetheless. *Variety* warned they were "too hip for general run of nitery patrons who don't have the marijuana habit."

Carlin went solo for the first time in February 1961. They were booked at the hungry i when Burns suffered a "kidney attack" and Carlin had to do the act on his own. A few months later Carlin laid over at the Racquet Club in Dayton, Ohio, where his future wife, Brenda, was a waitress. "Peter, Paul and Mary were scheduled to come in where she [Brenda] worked. Peter had some illness and they couldn't make it and they had two nights open and I was pressed into service. I took material of Jack's and mine and managed to get through two nights of it [as a solo]. That's how I knew I was ready."

Burns & Carlin broke up. Jack Burns joined Second City in Chicago, met future partner Avery Schreiber and briefly became Mayberry's deputy sheriff when Don Knotts left *The Andy Griffith Show*. Carlin became a regular on the Playboy Club circuit and at Howie Solomon's Café Au Go Go in the Village. "When Jack and I broke up, I took over these Playboy dates. Then I hit kind of a dip. 1963–64. The Café Au Go Go on Bleecker Street, I stayed there for two years on and off, just trying to work, work, work, work."

Much has been made of Carlin's transformation from mainstream TV act to underground scion, but his political viewpoint was evident from the start. A review from September 1962 said, "His texts are generally from the newspapers from which he has formed a viewpoint, which he readily expresses. He doesn't mind being political, which may be a handicap in some places. The conservative side loses out on this exchange. However, the total effect of his efforts is exceedingly strong."

There was an undercurrent of subversive things to come in the new comedians, but many of them also accepted gigs that would seem out of character for them today. In the early 1960s Woody Allen was working on Allen Funt's practical joke show *Candid Camera*, as were Marshall Brickman and Joan Rivers. Allen was on-screen posing as a bookseller who spoils endings for his customers and as an executive who dictated inappropriate letters to unwitting stenographers. Allen called it one of "the degrading things I had to do when I started. I did the show for career advancement. Now I'm trying to do Dostoyevsky trying to live down this shit."

It was at the behest of his managers, Jack Rollins and Charles Joffe, that he entered nightclubs. Allen had already won an Emmy for writing a Sid Caesar special. He wanted to make movies. Rollins said stand-up success would be the bargaining chip to help him achieve this dream. Allen reluctantly took his advice and entered three torturous years of nightclub gigging before seeing results.

Allen observed one of the hottest new comedians in the country— Bob Newhart—and appropriated his style. "When he first started at the Bitter End he was the opening act for my group The Tarriers," says Marshall Brickman. "He did premise stuff. 'What if Russia launched a missile and it was coming toward New York and Khrushchev had to call Mayor Lindsay?' He then did a phone bit like Bob Newhart."

When he seemed structured enough, Rollins booked him at the Blue Angel as an afterthought to Shelley Berman. Rather than have the amateur go first, which was standard procedure, Berman went first and handed Allen a hot crowd. Larry Gelbart was in the audience and said Allen emulated Nichols & May, calling it "Elaine May in drag." It continued to be hit and miss. "He knew zero about the art of performing," said Rollins. Charles Joffe said, "He was arrogant and hostile. If the audience didn't get it, he had no patience . . . The pain in those first years was terrible. Woody was just awful."

At the end of 1960 Allen told his management, "This is crazy. It's killing me. I'm throwing up. I'm sick. I shouldn't be doing this. I know I can make a big career as a writer. We've tried it with me as a stand-up and I'm not good. I can't handle this anymore." Despite the anxiety, he conceded to his managers and continued. Jay Landesman booked Allen at the Crystal Palace. "Woody was terrified of an audience. He used to pace the dressing room floor muttering, 'I hope they like me. I hope they like me.' They didn't."

His first year was the toughest. "It was the worst year of my life," said Allen. "I'd feel this fear in my stomach every morning, the minute I woke up, and it'd be there until eleven o'clock at night. I thought of myself as a writer and when I was onstage all I could think about was wanting to get through the performance and go home. I wasn't liking the audience. I was petrified."

After the Bob Newhart and Elaine May approaches, Allen tried emulating Mort Sahl. "When I first started out, I was such a great fan of Mort Sahl's that his delivery crept into me." But despite the influence of May, Newhart and Sahl, he felt the strongest kinship with the previous generation of comics. "People have always thought of me as an intellectual comedian, and I'm not. I'm a one-liner comic like Bob Hope and Henny Youngman. I do the wife jokes. I make faces. I'm a comedian in the classic style."

By 1962 he hit his stride. Lines formed where he played. Columnist Dorothy Kilgallen wrote, "Woody Allen is such a hit at the Bitter End that he had to do four shows on Friday and Saturday to keep his admirers satisfied, and over the weekend more than 400 customers had to be turned away." One of Jack Paar's writers came to see him. "I was sent to check out this comedian," said Dick Cavett. "I recognized immediately that there was no young comedian in the country in the same class as him for sheer brilliance of jokes."

Cavett booked Allen for the Paar show and Allen did it several times—even though he infuriated the host. "Jack was very upset with a piece I did about an island that didn't think sex was dirty but they thought food was," remembered Allen. "He was quite outraged. When they went through the piece to cut something, they couldn't find anything to censor. So they took *one* word out—'God'—just to pacify Jack."

Allen next got into a dustup with Ed Sullivan. During the afternoon run-through Allen used the phrase "orgasmic insurance." Sullivan stopped the rehearsal. "He apologized to the audience for me," said Allen. "He got me into his office afterward. He hit the ceiling. He was just enraged. It was humiliating." Sullivan pointed a stern finger and yelled, "It is because of you this whole Vietnam thing is happening. It's an attitude like yours that is responsible for young men burning their draft cards."

Marshall Brickman, along with Allen's childhood friend Mickey Rose, helped craft Allen's stand-up. Brickman cowrote Allen's vodka ad routine, and they became longtime collaborators. "The plan was to give him maximum exposure on television as soon as possible, so Charlie Joffe suggested we collaborate," says Brickman. "Together we wrote a lot of his early stand-up act, which he ultimately recorded." Brickman and Allen walked through Manhattan and found that conversation led to material.

Brickman says, "I would back into premises and ideas logically and he had a way, an instinct, of jumping to some absurd place. One day we were walking down the street and there was a guy coming toward us, a fashion designer. I said, 'Isn't that Roland Meledandri? He looks terrible.' Woody said, 'He's just gone through a very bad divorce.' I said, 'Didn't he used to have a mustache?' Woody said, 'His wife sued for the whole face, but settled for the mustache.' It just came out of him. That would happen a lot."

He was enjoying stand-up success, but when he performed outside his Manhattan comfort zone, he had trouble. He went to San Francisco and bombed at the hungry i. Some claim he used material belonging to more crowd-pleasing comedians in order to get by. A Playboy Club comic speaking under condition of anonymity says, "Woody generated his own material *but*—when he went out to do certain gigs, if he really wanted to be a hit, he would steal. His stuff was low-key and over some heads and a lot of audiences just didn't get it. I opened at the London Playboy Club when Woody was over there. I got him to go up because Hugh Hefner asked me. The son of a bitch got up and did half of Will Jordan's act." In hearing this anecdote, Brickman says, "I believe it—but I can't verify it. I can believe that he might have done that, sure."

Later the same evening the anonymous comic got into a fight with Allen. "In between shows I am standing in the foyer—unseen by Woody, who was around the corner talking to the press. They asked him why he was in England. He said, 'Oh, Hefner flew me over because the comedian here is so bad he had to have me as backup.' I walked around the corner, grabbed him by the throat and held him over the balcony. I said, 'Schmuck, take it back!' The press was taking pictures and Hefner stood there and forced them to empty the film."

By the end of 1962 Allen had come into his own and was anointed by comic legends. "He's one of the most amazing men

I've ever known," said Jack Benny. "It's very tough to use the word 'genius,' but I don't know anyone who is as clever and funny and has the knowledge of what to do in his writing. No one compares with him."

Dick Cavett had a respectable job at *The Tonight Show*, but the Rollins-Joffe management firm applied the same philosophy to him as they had to Allen: Establish yourself as a strong stand-up and you'll have a jockeying position for television and film. Cavett wrote an act and tried it out at the Bitter End. "The Bitter End was pretty good usually—a hip crowd and a young audience," says Cavett. "I bombed the first night, but I didn't really bomb after that." Bitter End manager Paul Colby gave a contradictory assessment: "Dick Cavett came in 1964. Stayed for six months and bombed for six months. Audiences hated him with a passion. I mean with a passion. It wasn't even neutral hatred. It was like they wanted to kill him. He was very offensive onstage and he just couldn't help coming off snotty. He did six months of dead silence in the middle spot." Cavett responds, "I have no recollection of Paul Colby. He sounds like a distorted and witless creep. He's full of shit."

Jack Rollins booked Cavett at the standard New Wave venues, but he never really made it as a stand-up. As a writer for *The Tonight Show*, however, Cavett was considered one of the best. "The monologue writers were responsible for a four-page monologue, about twelve jokes, every day," says Brickman. "You had to deliver the monologue by three-fifteen. Dick used to come in at two forty-five and knock out his monologue. It would be submitted with the work of three or four other guys. Eighty percent of the monologue that night would be Dick's. He was phenomenal."

Rollins-Joffe handled Allen and Cavett, but when Joan Rivers tried to sign with them, they refused. Rivers started at the same time as Allen and suffered the same humiliations. Initially she performed under her birth name, Joan Molinsky, and the moniker Pepper January. In the summer of 1960 she used the surname Rivers for the first time, in a one-woman show called *The Diary of Joan Rivers*. She was looking for something—*anything*—to click. She tried out for Second City. "They auditioned sixty ladies and I was sixty-first. I waited five and a half hours at William Morris, where they were holding the auditions, and when I went in I was angry and aggravated and upset by the whole thing. Paul [Sills] was there and he said, 'Describe what happens in this room.' And I said something like, 'A lot of fat, middle-aged men won't give people a chance in this room.' And I got the job right away."

Rivers was with Second City for one year. "I was never truly happy at Second City, but it made my whole career. By working with those people, I found out for the first time in my life that what I thought was funny, other people thought was funny also. I suddenly found out I didn't have to talk down in my humor, that there were a lot of people who could understand what I meant."

During the summer of 1964, Rivers formed a comedy team with Jim Connell and Jake Holmes. They had all played the Bitter End individually when co-owner Fred Weintraub put them together as Jim, Jake and Joan. He envisioned them as a modern-day version of Adolph Green, Judy Holliday and Betty Comden, who—as the Revuers—were the Village Vanguard's sophisticated parlor room act of the 1940s. "We definitely didn't get along, but it was a good formula," says Holmes. "Joan couldn't sing. If we had another person as funny as Joan that *could* sing—which we never would have found—we would have done better. I was the straight man with the guitar. Joan didn't like Jim because they were competing for the comedy. They were at each other's throats."

Jim, Jake and Joan played the Playboy Club in Miami Beach on a practice run. When the act seemed passable, Weintraub booked them in Chicago to open for Trini Lopez at Mister Kelly's. "The topical comedy trio of Jim, Jake and Joan not only overcame the restlessness of the Lopez-anticipating patrons, but soon had the crowd in their palm," wrote *Variety*. "Visibly nervous at the start, they rapidly caught their comedic stride and kept the house in an uproar with their refreshing humor. Their act is one of the more cleverly written and artfully presented turns to come along in some time. It moves with expresso [*sic*] speed and never misses a comedic trick. Their satire on such subjects as toothpaste commercials, a Nazi rocketeer at Cape Kennedy, and *Playboy* mag has bite, but doesn't leave a permanent wound."

Joan came offstage and accused Jim of jingling change in his pocket while she was on. Jim would make misogynistic comments under his breath. They did things to intentionally anger each other. "We were playing a '[Robert] Kennedy for Senator' rally when it went real bad," says Holmes. "She showed up wearing a [U.S. senator Kenneth] Keating button. Jim said, 'Take that Keating button off.' She said, 'Go fuck yourself.' He said, 'Well, who needs you anyway!' She never spoke to us again." Jim, Jake and Joan broke up, but the pressure taught Rivers how to write. Holmes says, "When you got down to the writing—she was great." Connell became a character actor. Holmes made folk-rock records and successfully sued Led Zeppelin for plagiarism. Rivers went solo and worked twice as hard.

One night while Rivers was bombing at the Duplex in the Village, Lenny Bruce walked in and caught her act. He sent a note backstage: "You're right and they're wrong." From then on whenever she doubted herself she looked at Bruce's note. "That kept me going for a year a half."

Rivers came of age during a time when there were few female comics. Vegas comedienne Totie Fields did not believe there was enough work to go around. She treated Rivers with contempt. "I could not understand why major clubs around the country refused to book me," said Rivers. "I learned later that Totie Fields was spreading the word that I was dirty and vicious, and not funny."

Gender was a stand-up obstacle. Because of it she fought harder than her male counterparts. "Joan was *determined* to win," says Dick Cavett. "You *knew* she was going to. She was so damn smart and could assemble an act of rapid jokes. Her smarts and her ambition to make it were awesome."

Sometimes her ambition overrode ethics. "I was signed with [manager] Irvin Arthur," says comic-turned-actor Dick Gautier. "Irvin said, 'Come up to the rehearsal studio. I'm looking at a bunch of young comics and I want your input.' I'm sitting in the back and Joan Rivers walks in. She goes on and she does *my* act. Really—my act, word for word. She said, 'Well? What do you think?' Irvin said, 'It's funnier when Dick does it.' He pointed to me in the back of the room and she went, 'Ah, shit.'"

Arthur signed Rivers despite not having much confidence in her ability. "I never believed [she] would make it. But she had this perseverance that went beyond the limit. I would go see her at the Duplex. She'd use some of Woody Allen's material, some of Henny Youngman's, she didn't care." But like Jack Benny decades earlier, she hired writers to develop material. Marshall Brickman was one of them, and they worked on her act from his *Candid Camera* office.

She became the house comic at Upstairs at the Downstairs at 37 W. 56th Street. Impresario Julius Monk ran simultaneous shows on two floors and the club was alternately referred to as the "Upstairs at the Downstairs" or the "Downstairs at the Upstairs," depending on which room you were playing. Will Jordan watched Rivers evolve in the venue. "Joan Rivers was bad, just terrible, but she got writers and every single day she *worked*. She is an example of intense hard work."

Stand-up comedy was tough for women. It was even harder for those who were Black. During the supper club era, Black comedians played primarily to Black audiences, ignored by white show business even if they were major headliners along the Chitlin' Circuit. The phrase "Chitlin' Circuit" was a takeoff on the alliterative "Borscht Belt." But while the Borscht Belt referred to a predominantly Jewish *area*, the Chitlin' Circuit was a vague catchall referring to black theaters and clubs all across the country. Major white comedians had the luxury of playing elaborate hotels and upscale supper clubs, but Black comedians of equal ability endured a second-tier experience. "Some were theaters, but the Chitlin' Circuit was mostly Black nightclubs," says comic-ventriloquist Willie Tyler. "These were the places where Black acts could perform for Black crowds. B. B. King called them 'Buckets of Blood,' because there was always someone fighting."

Comedian Jimmie Walker played many of the venues when he first started. "I did the tail end of the Chitlin' Circuit. Blacks were not allowed to go to the same theaters as white people. Due to the fact they couldn't participate, they decided to make their *own* entertainment. There were a series of big, majestic theaters, a whole circuit of them—in D.C., Detroit, Cleveland, Chicago—and the anchor was the Apollo in New York."

Black comedians aspired to the Apollo the way vaudevillians had once aspired to the Palace. The most famous Black theater in the world had once been a "whites only" establishment. From 1914 through 1928 the Apollo was a racist burlesque hall. After closing in disarray, it reopened in 1934 as "The New 125th Street Apollo." It turned into the preeminent showcase for African American show business and went on to present "America's Smartest Colored Shows."

The two biggest comedy stars in the early days of the Apollo were Jackie "Moms" Mabley and Dewey "Pigmeat" Markham. Mabley was the first female comedian to play the venue and one of the only female stand-ups in the country. In the 1930s, while still a young woman, she adopted the persona of a wisecracking, sex-crazed senior citizen, a hip, all-knowing matron with an incredibly gruff voice. "Jackie Mabley, always good for a laugh, delivers several, although some of the old standbys she tells should be buried," read a December 1934 review. "The slightly off-color gags she pulls hit the mark with her audience." Mabley's targets were interesting. She joked at the expense of bigots and "damned old men." With a benevolent voice she criticized the South and the empty promises of white liberals in Washington. From the 1930s through the 1950s Mabley was comedy's primary voice of the Civil Rights Movement.

Markham and Mabley were aligned in the public consciousness, but far apart in social consciousness. Like Mabley, Markham was already a bit of a legend when he first did the Apollo in 1934. He toured the Chitlin' Circuit performing sketches with various partners. Being Markham's straight man meant absorbing his physical abuse. His act closed with a bizarre climax in which he would assault his straight men with a cow's bladder, smacking them across the head with a loud splat again and again. Markham explained, "It's a real bladder. I can't tell you where I get them, but someone at a slaughterhouse picks them up for me. I tried many things, but this is the only thing that gives me that real good sound when it crashes on someone's head. Pig bladders don't get the effect of the beef bladders."

Markham was a controversial figure in the Black community for his use of blackface. The practice was inspired by Ziegfeld vaudevillian Bert Williams, who had applied burnt cork from the beginning of his career. It was an odd thing, an African American darkening his face as if he were a white minstrel, but it was standard procedure in the days of vaudeville. By the 1930s the use of blackface was increasingly considered distasteful and most Black performers stopped using it. Markham was the exception. He insisted that the use of blackface was an integral matter of "tradition" even as the NAACP objected and fellow Black comedians asked him to stop. The reality was he was insecure without it. As long as he was getting laughs, he wouldn't change his approach.

Timmie Rogers was one of the first African American comedians to forgo broad caricature after World War II, taking to the stage in a tuxedo without the use of props or gimmicks. Rogers was one of the young comedians who confronted Markham about his old-fashioned ways. He told him, "You don't need blackface to do the act, man! That's passé. You don't need to be in blackface to get a laugh."

Markham was forever defensive. "A lot of people have pointed out that my comedy is not exactly high-class . . . I won't argue with that. And a lot of others say my characters . . . do not represent the modern Negro; that they are caricatures. Well, I won't argue with that, either, [as] long as we admit they're funny . . . I was born and raised black. I learned my comedy from black comedians. The earliest skits and bits I did on stage or under a tent were invented by black men. The audiences I learned to please . . . they were mostly black, too."

Black comedy had changed, however, and Markham's stubbornness relegated him to the fringe. Show business evolved in the wake of tuxedo acts like Timmie Rogers and, several years later, progressive comics like Dick Gregory. "It wasn't a case of Pigmeat himself having faded out," says his manager, Dick Alen. "It was a case of Black sketch comedy [having] faded out. I guess that's what his problem was—he was at the end of that era. It was old-timey. His time just ended."

*   *   *

Bumming around the Apollo in the late 1940s were two street hustlers—John Sanford and Malcolm Little. Nicknamed Foxy and Detroit Red, they sold dime bags to musicians at the Savoy Ballroom. They were close friends, but drifted into separate worlds under their new chosen names—Redd Foxx and Malcolm X.

Together they ran a number of scams. "There was a girl who worked in a cleaners," said Foxx. "She liked me, so she left the store window open. Malcolm and I went in that night and took about a hundred suits off the racks and put them on the roof. We'd sell one or two of them a day. We never got caught."

Foxx played roughshod nightclubs around Baltimore and Newark in the late 1940s. He subsidized a nonexistent stand-up income recording rhythm and blues records for the Savoy label, but it was pot dealing that paid the bills. He was busted at a "Creole Burlesk" gig in Delair, New Jersey, in September 1949 when he sold reefers to an undercover cop. His car was searched and police found two pounds of high-quality dope in the trunk. A local paper reported, "Fellow entertainers often wondered how John Elroy Sanford, a small-time comedian, could afford to drive a Cadillac. Last week they got their answer. Sanford, better known as Redd Foxx, was growing marijuana in his Newark backyard. Federal agents found a quantity of reefers in his coat pocket and also in the Cadillac. Both he and his wife, Evelyn, are under five thousand dollars bail."

Foxx fled his criminal record and landed in Los Angeles, where he found a booster in Johnny Otis, an important rhythm and blues disc jockey and tastemaker. Otis introduced Foxx to fellow comedian Slappy White and brought them on air for late night rap sessions. The two became a team, and Foxx & White took to the Chitlin' Circuit. They got a break when Dinah Washington hired them as her opening act. She brought them to the Apollo in October 1951. *Variety* said of the engagement that they "display more care with their delivery than in their choice of material. Gags hinging on marijuana smoking and Harlem prostitution are in bad taste and don't score here."

Foxx & White booked themselves at the ailing Palace Theatre. The former vaudeville venue had seen better days and was mostly utilized for new Hollywood films and minor presentation shows. "We bombed so hard at the Palace," said White. "It was our first shot at a downtown white audience. It might have been the first shot for any black act. They just weren't ready for uptown comedy."

They broke up when they returned to Los Angeles. Foxx tried to get work at Maynard Sloate's Strip City. "I remember going over for an audition at Strip City. I couldn't even get in because it was all white." Sloate says racial factors had nothing to do with it. "The final thing I did before I left Strip City was turn it into an all-Negro burlesque, with Redd as the comic. He had no taste whatsoever. When he was dirty, it was obscene. He would do subjects that were just disgusting. When I talked to him about it he said, 'Man, that's my *integrity*.'"

The most successful of the new Black comedians in the 1950s was Nipsey Russell. He was a master of the ad-lib and a marathon talker. He held court on his WLIB radio program, on which he improvised nightly for several hours. He mastered stand-up at a small Harlem nightclub called the Baby Grand and was one of comedy's best-kept secrets throughout the decade.

Jack Krulik's Baby Grand was located at 125th Street and St. Nicholas Avenue. It offered a menu of high-end Chinese food, and its 180 seats were full more often than not. "Nipsey was the poet laureate of Harlem," says Hank Garrett, his neighbor and fellow comic. "He was at the Baby Grand for sixteen years as the house emcee." It was an integrated destination. *The New York Times* described the setup: "The walls are painted a dingy red, there is a mural of two huge, kissing fish overhead and on two of the walls are garish panels featuring peacocks. The floor show includes an organist, a jazz combo, a girl singer, a boy singer and an 'exotic' dancer who does a joyless striptease. But the chief attraction is Nipsey Russell."

Russell had his own record label, called Humorsonic, for which he cranked out low-budget comedy records with labored laugh tracks. He clocked thousands of hours of stage time, but still could not find work beyond Black venues. Although Steve Allen didn't hesitate to book Black musicians, he seldom used Black comedians. Allen claimed, "White audiences would not appreciate general interest jokes by Negroes." That attitude changed when Jack Paar took over *The Tonight Show*. Russell did two stand-up shots that were so successful Paar hired him as a regular in June 1961. A production company even packaged a spin-off for Russell—a late night talk show to be called *Point of View*—but it wasn't able to find a sponsor or network that would back an African American host.

Russell was outspoken about the disparity between white and Black comedians. He contended that the average salary of a white headliner in 1960 was $300,000 and the average salary for an African American comedian between $10,000 and $20,000. Show business employed more African Americans than other fields, but inequity was deep. "Why are Negro comedians left out?" asked Pigmeat Markham. "The Negro is an original performer. Whites have stolen much of his material. It is much easier for white comics to reach their people. Most club owners today would rather hire white comics, even if they are second-rate talents."

Basin Street East, located at 525 Lexington Avenue in New York, was the first white venue to consistently book African American comedians. Its impresario, Ralph Watkins, had a long history in nightclubs. He was leader of the house band at Bill Miller's Riviera in Fort Lee, New Jersey, during the 1940s and had managed a number of jazz clubs—Kelly's Stable, Bop City, the Onyx Club—all on 52nd Street. In 1959 he opened Basin Street East, taking over Xavier Cugat's failed Casa Cugat. He hired every African American comedian on the scene: Redd Foxx, Stu Gilliam, George Kirby, Moms Mabley, Timmie Rodgers and Nipsey Russell.

Redd Foxx played Basin Street East in 1959 and was terrified of its audience. "I went in with Maynard Ferguson's orchestra and [rhythm and blues group] the Treniers. I was scared shitless because I didn't know how far I could go with that crowd. I felt I couldn't say things like, 'This is a great band. Look at those initials on the music stands—MF!' My timing was off. On the third night, one of the Treniers said, 'Man, why don't you just do your thing, like you do?' So it just happened that night Ethel Merman was in the crowd and she was loud. So I really read [ridiculed] her, and I read somebody else that bugged me. I came on strong, just opened up and let myself be Redd Foxx. I was in the men's room after the show and heard some cat on the phone saying, 'You get down here and catch this guy; he's the dirtiest son of a bitch I ever heard!'"

Just being yourself was easier said than done. There were issues when a Black comic landed in front of a white crowd. Timmie Rogers spoke of the logistical problems. "White comics can insult their audiences freely. But Negroes can't insult white people. The Negro comic works with wraps on, always behind the cultural ghetto."

The civil rights era brought opportunity for a new generation of Black comics like Godfrey Cambridge, Bill Cosby and Flip Wilson, but veterans like Mabley and Markham were essentially too old to capitalize on the new world. "Mabley was too strong for society at the time," says comedian Pat Cooper. "Her era was too early. When it happened, it was too late for her." By the late 1960s Markham and Mabley were welcome on mainstream television shows like *Music Scene* and *Laugh-In*. But age had slowed their careers and their bodies—and they had time enough only to take a bow.

Redd Foxx was one of the most influential comedians of the twentieth century. He was responsible for what became one of the biggest trends in the early 1960s—comedy records. *Billboard* reported in November 1961 that comedy on vinyl was "the brightest aspect of the album business." Comedy records furthered the careers of Shelley Berman, Lenny Bruce, Nichols & May, Bob Newhart, Mort Sahl, the Smothers Brothers and Jonathan Winters. Hundreds of comedy records were released during the height of the craze—1959 through 1966. It was abnormal if a comedian didn't have a record. In the first half of the twentieth century there were occasional comedy recordings like *Cohen on the Telephone*—a novelty record with a Yiddish inflection—and the best-selling sketches of *Sam 'n' Henry*, an

Amos 'n' Andy precursor. The early 1950s had novelty recordings by Stan Freberg, Homer & Jethro and Spike Jones & His City Slickers, but it wasn't until Foxx came along in 1956 that comedy recordings featured straight up stand-up. Foxx released the first authentic recordings taken from the nightclub stage.

Dootsie Williams was the African American record executive in charge of Dooto Records. Located at 9512 South Central in Los Angeles, the label had one of the biggest hits of the doo-wop genre—"Earth Angel" by the Penguins. The money it made turned Williams into a successful businessman and gave him the freedom to sign new acts. He saw Foxx perform at the Oasis at 38th and Western and thought, "This guy can *sell*." Foxx was resistant. He told Williams, "If I record it they won't want to see me live." The next day Foxx realized he had no money. He went over to Dooto Records and said, "Hey, what was that you were saying last night about recording?"

Williams signed Foxx as the first stand-up comedian on vinyl. There was little promotion, but word of mouth propelled it. "I had no idea that the first album would sell like it did," said Foxx. "I had some pretty bad material, but the sales were fantastic."

Laff of the Party was released in mid-1956, and after a year and a half it had sold one million copies. Riding the wave, Dooto released fourteen full-length Redd Foxx comedy records and another ten EPs before decade's end. However, due to their suggestive material they seldom got mention in the mainstream record biz periodicals. Dootsie Williams and Redd Foxx invented comedy records as we know it—but like so many groundbreaking Black talents of the recording industry, they never got the credit.

Dooto signed Chitlin' Circuit comics Don Bexley, Allen Drew and Dave Turner after Foxx's initial success. Comedians Billy Allyn, Sloppy Daniels and George Kirby followed. Rudy Moore, later known as Rudy "Ray" Moore of the Dolemite movies, was emceeing at the California Club in South Central when Williams signed him to do the record *Below the Belt*. The contracts Williams offered these desperate comedians were always skewed. He paid each comedian a total of one hundred dollars regardless of sales. "I should have never signed," said Dooto comic Richard Stanfield. "It was the most horrible contract."

The records were also influential. Tommy Chong of Cheech & Chong credited the albums for his own trek into comedy: "Redd had a big influence on me right out of the gate. It was the first comedy record I had ever heard."

Dooto pressings became so profitable that bootleg versions flooded the market. Williams offered a reward for any information leading to the apprehension of Redd Foxx bootleggers. Dooto's profit margin inspired the industry. Decca, Capitol, Verve and Warner Bros. all signed comics, and by the early 1960s everyone was in the game. Comedy records were a national phenomenon.

Mort Sahl at Sunset was a comedy record released by Fantasy Records in October 1958. It had been recorded in 1955, but it was believed there was no market for it, and it was shelved. Dooto's sales changed minds at the company. Although the album sold poorly, Sahl has the distinction of being the first white stand-up comic to appear on vinyl.

Woody Woodbury was one of the next. The lounge comedian had been telling risqué jokes in Fort Lauderdale obscurity when Fletcher Smith, a former Hollywood effects wizard, came backstage. "After the show he approached me," says Woodbury. "He asked if I would like to put my act on a record. I said, 'You mean just record jokes? That's ridiculous. They've *heard* my jokes. They won't want to hear them again.' Fletcher said, 'If you just record them I'll pay for everything. I'll bring the technicians in from New York. I'll take care of all the distribution.' I thought he was nuts. I said, 'People aren't gonna buy comedy records!' " Recorded in 1959, *Laughing Room* was released in February 1960 and charted immediately.

Rusty Warren was a Jewish lounge comedian specializing in double entendre. Referencing the female bustline was her trademark. Too ribald for television, she found an audience on vinyl. The record label that signed her, Jubilee, was following the same doo-wop-to-comedy path as Dooto. Jubilee's president, Jerry Blaine, was essentially forced out of rock 'n' roll when he was implicated in the payola scandal that destroyed disc jockey Alan Freed. It hurt

Blaine's reputation in the rock scene, but payola didn't mean a thing in comedy.

"I was on a tour of the Midwest," recalls Rusty Warren. "The Pomp Room, a little piano bar. We went in the liquor room and plugged into the sound system with an Ampex tape machine. I told these women [in the audience] to stand up and get their boobies up and I came up with the 'Knockers Up March.' Jerry decided to name the album *Knockers Up!* And people said to him, 'You wouldn't dare call it that! How are you going to sell it? Where are you going to put it? No one is going to take it!' He did—and it blew me out of the world. *Knockers Up!* was on the charts for a full year."

Blaine used payola to get the records distribution. While competing recordings of sexual double entendre by Belle Barth were under the counter, Warren's recordings were on prominent display. "Jerry Blaine was a great businessman," says Warren. "Where did they find me? They went in the store and I was in the comedy section. It wasn't under the counter. I had sales you wouldn't believe. Payola? Listen, those were the times."

Sexual subject matter caused problems. The Los Angeles Sheriff's Department raided a Pico Boulevard warehouse in January 1961, arresting three employees for "distribution of obscene records" and seizing four thousand LPs by Belle Barth, B. S. Pully, Pearl Williams and Rusty Warren. They are so innocuous by today's standards that the clampdown seems insane. "The albums were innuendo," says Woody Woodbury. "They were called risqué, but today you could play them in their entirety during high mass."

Belle Barth had her comedy albums distributed by Roulette Records. The president of Roulette was Morris Levy, one of the top mobsters in the recording industry. He was notorious for securing publishing rights to songs written by others. When he released a series of Christmas music, he credited himself as the cowriter of "Silent Night." He seldom paid out royalties and had no qualms about threatening those who complained. Barth's Roulette releases were on Levy's After Hours subsidiary. Sales were enormous, but she never saw a cent. "Terrible things happened to her," says Rusty Warren. "They screwed Belle over terribly."

Roulette also screwed over comedy writer Bill Dana. Kapp Records released LPs based on Dana's comic character Jose Jimenez, which he'd been doing on *The Steve Allen Show*. When they proved profitable, Roulette decided to get in on the action, releasing a Bill Dana record without his knowledge or approval. The unauthorized release made a hefty profit and Dana filed a lawsuit seeking $200,000. "They did that record without my permission. It was a bone of contention and it got a little heavy. These voices called me saying it would be good for me to cooperate with them. It was like a scene from *The Sopranos*. They just compiled air checks of [my act from] *The Steve Allen Show* and released it as a record." Roulette promised to destroy the masters if Dana dropped his claim. There was no financial settlement, but with Levy's reputation it was the safest solution.

Fax Records also had ties to organized crime. Named for its Fairfax Avenue location, the Los Angeles label cranked out several risqué records by small-time comedian Bert Henry. Henry's LPs had titles like *Position Is Everything* and *At the Hungry Thigh*. A San Francisco postmaster seized three hundred copies of the Fax Records catalog in May 1960 because "they gave information on where obscene material could be obtained." While the albums were hardly profane, the owner of Fax Records, William H. Door, was a convicted pornographer with a "lewd picture syndicate" and suspected Mafia ties. In November 1963, at the height of his label's success, he was found hog-tied in his home with a bullet hole in the back of his head.

Shelley Berman and Bob Newhart owed their fame to the comedy record boom. Verve Records pressed *Inside Shelley Berman* in January 1959, and it was awarded certification as the first gold comedy record. Foxx actually beat Berman to the distinction, but his underground status kept the organization that governed gold record status from acknowledging him. Verve quickly pressed the follow-ups *Outside Shelley Berman* and *The Edge of Shelley Berman*; Don Rickles joked that the next LP would be called *Up Shelley Berman*.

Warner Bros. released Newhart's first record—*The Button-Down Mind of Bob Newhart*—in April 1960. Berman and Newhart were oddly similar—both from Chicago, performing while seated on stools, delivering monologues into imaginary telephones. Berman was convinced Newhart stole his shtick. "I was coming to work one night and a guy stopped his car when he passed me, 'Hey, Shelley! There's a guy stole your act!' When I finally saw Newhart—I was devastated."

Newhart's success was unforeseen. He was writing routines for Chicago radio, but had never been onstage when he got a recording contract. "A disc jockey friend of mine, Dan Sorkin, in Chicago, said that the Warner Brother record executives were coming through town. 'Put what you have on tape and I'll play it for them.' So I put them on tape, brought it down there, they listened to it. And they said, 'Okay . . . we'll record your next nightclub.' I said, 'Well, we have kind of [a] problem there. I've never played a nightclub.'"

Warner Bros. taped Newhart's first-ever stand-up performances —three of them, done the same evening at the Tidelands nightclub in Houston. The first recording was rendered useless when Newhart's voice quivered with fear. The second was a write-off as a drunk woman yelled throughout the show, "That's a bunch of crap!" The third show clicked. The recording sold two hundred thousand copies upon release and after twelve weeks it was the number one record in America. Lenny Bruce predicted Newhart would "make more money than me, Sahl and Berman because Paar, Sullivan and [Garry] Moore need a goy comic so bad their teeth ache." (Dan Sorkin, the man who helped Newhart get his recording contract, was fired over a comedy record dispute in 1963 when he played a Lenny Bruce LP on the air.)

In 1959 playwright Moss Hart threw a party to celebrate the publication of his memoir, *Act One*, at Mamma Leone's restaurant. The event featured Manhattan's glitterati. Among the guests were comedy writers Mel Tolkin and Mel Brooks. The two entertained the crowd with a routine soon dubbed the "2000 Year Old Man." Theater critic Kenneth Tynan had never heard of Mel Brooks before. "All I knew as I left Mamma Leone's that night was that [the] pseudo-Freudian partner was the most original comic improviser I had ever seen."

At the prompting of Steve Allen, the 2000 Year Old Man rou-
tine was pressed to vinyl, with Carl Reiner in the straight man role.
Released in November 1960, it gathered a cult following and marked
the first time Brooks was considered a performer. As with Berman,
Newhart and so many others, comedy records helped make Mel
Brooks a star.

The *Billboard* record charts for June 1961 had Frank Sinatra
and Elvis Presley sharing top honors with Berman, Newhart, Warren, Freberg, Dick Gregory and Jonathan Winters. Music writer
Joe X. Price marveled at the comedy record recipe. "Take a hundred
small round tables, a few hundred hard wooden chairs, set 'em up in
any recording studio available, order lotsa booze, send out as many
invites as you have chairs to the gigglingest people in town—and
you've got what it takes to make a comedy album. Oh, yes, you also
need a comedian."

By far the hottest comedy record of the early 1960s was *The
First Family*, starring Vaughn Meader, a piano player who did an
impression of President Kennedy. *The First Family* was a composite
of comedy sketches about White House life. It sold two and a half
million copies in four weeks and five million copies in less than a
year. It was the fastest-selling album, of any genre, in recording history up to that time.

Meader had been an unsuccessful barroom act playing country
and western. "Before I was a comedian, I had a country band," he said.
"But the music never seemed to get across." He added impressions of
Fats Domino and Nat King Cole, which got a much better response.
By the end of 1961 he was a regular at Phase II in the Village, and
in September 1962 he was booked at the Blue Angel for his first
substantial gig. He had been attempting stand-up for ten months,
but had yet to develop much of an act. He had one basic strength,
as *Variety* noted: "One of his assets is a resemblance to JFK; he even
has the same kind of haircut."

Comedy writers Earle Doud and George Foster conceived
The First Family with disc jockey Bob Booker. JFK was a national
phenomenon and ripe for satire. The script had been written, and
now they needed someone to play the lead role. Comic actor Chuck

McCann joined Earle Doud on the scouting mission. They went to the Village to catch Meader's act. "He was kind of a country hick from Maine, just another barrelhouse piano player, but his voice was very New England," says McCann. "He barely imitated Kennedy, because he *was* that voice."

Meader was hired to play JFK, but most record labels turned the idea down. They felt it was out of bounds to ridicule the president. A high-level executive at MGM Records called the subject matter "too sensitive." ABC-Paramount, Capitol and Mercury Records all turned it down for the same reason. It was left to the small-time Cadence label to take the chance. A recording date was set for October 22, 1962. "We made a little demo at Y&R Studios on 57th Street," says McCann. "Right before we recorded, the president made an announcement on television. It was the Cuban Missile Crisis speech . . . and then we went into the studio. The audience came to our studio, and they laughed out of nervousness; it became twice as funny to them. [Cadence Records president] Archie Bleyer was in the control room. He was livid after we finished. He said, 'We can never release this! There's too much laughter! They're laughing over the lines! We're going to have to do it again.' So the next week they did it again and it *bombed*. I mean, into the shit house. So they released the original right away."

The First Family was mailed to WNEW morning team Klavan & Finch and WINS disc jockey Stan Z. Burns. "It was an acetate copy that Earle laid on them," says McCann. "They played it and the people stormed the record stores to order it. They couldn't print the covers fast enough. People would buy the disc in a paper jacket and were entitled to come back and get the cover later on."

The First Family went platinum. The Jenkins Music Store chain in Manhattan remained open three extra hours each day to accommodate the lines. Eight separate pressing plants were hired to meet the overwhelming demand. *The First Family* created a craze within the craze, and countless new JFK-related comedy records hit the market. Bullwinkle writer George Atkins devised *Sing Along with JFK*, in which JFK speeches were comically set to music. Ron Clark, a frequent Mel Brooks collaborator, wrote the comedy LP *The President*

Strikes Back and an unknown Rich Little made a northern version called *My Fellow Canadians*. The Kennedys were surplanted in rip-off versions like *The Last Family*—a comic indictment of Castro's revolutionaries—and *The Other Family*, a Khrushchev-themed comedy record featuring Joan Rivers, George Segal and Buck Henry.

"No albums or singles that feature any takeoffs on the president of the United States or his family will be played now or any other time on WHK," announced a Cleveland program director. He said record companies "are deprecating the nation's leader at a critical time in our history." Radio WIND in Chicago said, "The *Sing Along with JFK* album is definitely in poor taste. We stopped playing *The First Family* here at WIND a week after we received it. The same holds true with all of this follow-up imitation material. The record people are running the gimmick into the ground."

Jack Paar said he and Richard Nixon listened to *The First Family* after eating Thanksgiving dinner together. "With cigars we retired to a room which had a record player. I had brought with me a recording written by one of my former writers, Earle Doud. Most of us laughed, and here is what may surprise you: Mr. Nixon walked over and lifted the playback head off the recording and said, 'That man is the President of our country. Neither he nor his family should be the butt of such jokes.'"

Vaughn Meader's new management wasted no time in capitalizing on the sensation. He was sent on a nationwide tour, but Meader was essentially still an amateur. He hadn't paid his dues, didn't have an act. One headline announced, "Meader Bombs." He was booked into Carnegie Hall, but his opener, Stanley Myron Handelman, got twice as many laughs.

Comedy about JFK was to the early 1960s what Monica Lewinsky jokes and Bill Clinton impressions were to the 1990s. It was everywhere. The president's father, Joseph P. Kennedy, was none too happy about it. Hugh Hefner invited Joe Kennedy to his Chicago Playboy Club to see Jack Burns and George Carlin. One report said Kennedy "sat stonily as George Carlin did his impresh of the Chief Executive," and muttered, "'I don't see anything funny in making fun of my son.'"

When Mort Sahl started ridiculing President Kennedy in his act, the hungry i was threatened. "Joseph Kennedy called Enrico Banducci and club owners with Mob ties who were part of the elder Kennedy's extended family," wrote Gerald Nachman. "He reportedly asked Bobby Kennedy to have the IRS close down the hungry i. Banducci was stunned to come to work one day and find the club's doors padlocked by the IRS for unpaid withholding taxes." The Crescendo stopped booking Sahl after a similar threat. Gene Norman said to him, "I've been told that the White House would be offended if I hired you and I'd be audited."

The JFK comedy craze was, of course, brought to an abrupt end on November 22, 1963, when the president was assassinated. It affected the mood of the country and it derailed nightclub comedy. Comedienne Marilyn Michaels was booked at a Long Island nightclub the following night. "It was the first job that I ever got fired from. I played it the day after President Kennedy got shot. It should have been canceled, but it was the stupidity of 'the show must go on.' Everyone was *very* drunk."

The hungry i reopened, and John Barbour was the comic. "I did it the first week of November 1963. That engagement was so successful they booked me again for the last week of November 1963. Unfortunately, President Kennedy was murdered on the twenty-second, so when I went back it was empty. The following week I was booked in Fresno—and there were a thousand people there every night *celebrating* the assassination. I became aware there were people in this country that were *glad* John F. Kennedy was killed. There was a pathological hatred of Kennedy the way there is a pathological hatred of Obama."

Producer George Schlatter says the assassination indirectly led to the editing style he later implemented on his program *Laugh-In*. Schlatter was prepping a Jonathan Winters television special that week. "We had Pat McCormick writing, Dwight Hemion directing, Art Carney as the guest. We came out of the reading and found out Kennedy had been shot. Jonathan went to one bar, Dwight went to another, and Art went to another. The next time we saw each other was the day of the show. We hadn't rehearsed anything and everybody was drunk. Nothing worked and I said, 'We're fucked, and I have to deliver this to the network.' I sent for the prop department to put props on a table. I said, 'Let Jonathan fuck around. Anything that looks funny, just shoot it.' So we taped an hour of Carney and Winters fucking with props. We sat down in the tape room and edited it together. Dwight said, 'But it's not a television show, it's just a bunch of cuts and nothing makes sense. [Programming executive] Mike Dann said, 'So, what's the show?' I said, 'That *is* the show.' He said, 'That's *not* a television show.' I said, 'You mean, you don't know what this is? In Europe this is what they call "comedy vérité." It's the latest thing in Europe. I'm amazed you haven't heard of it.' [Account executive] Irwin Siegel went, 'Oh, yeah, yeah, comedy vérité! Sure, I know about that.' The thing won a *TV Guide* award, and that was the beginning of the *Laugh-In* style, with that free-form, fast editing."

George Schlatter may have saved face, but there was no saving Vaughn Meader after the assassination. His only career success had been imitating JFK. Now he was left in the lurch.

"Lenny Bruce went onstage a week after the assassination," says Bruce's friend and ghostwriter Paul Krassner. "Everybody knew he had to say something. He couldn't ignore it. Nobody knew what he would do. He stood there milking the tension. Finally he said, 'Vaughn Meader is screwed.'"

He sure was. Verve Records had been prepping a Vaughn Meader Christmas album. Not only was that project canceled, but most copies of *The First Family* were pulled from shelves. Meader had taped an appearance on the Joey Bishop sitcom, but it never aired. The television show *Hootenanny* tore up a contract with Meader, invoking the Act of God clause. The Grammy Awards had to cancel Meader's appearance, which was going to be a cornerstone of the show. Cadence Records officially issued a recall of *The First Family* in December.

Meader changed angles and attempted alternate characters, but with so little stand-up experience, nothing clicked for him. He drifted from show business into a life of drug use and self-doubt. "Nobody would hire him," says Krassner. "He moved to San Francisco and became an overaged flower child. He called me in 1968 and asked me for a tab of acid."

Ten years passed when *Life* magazine decided to do a "Whatever Became Of" profile: "He began drinking. In two years the bank account was zero. He dabbled in Eastern religions and witchcraft, experimented with LSD, became a Yippie, retreated to a Bronx apartment and finally to a tepee in the California redwoods. In Los Angeles he was so broke he scrounged food from back-alley garbage cans. He hit rock bottom one night in Chicago. He was mugged and, falling unconscious to the gutter, he had a horrible vision of his own death. He speaks of himself often in the third person now. 'Vaughn Meader had become totally empty, physically and spiritually. That night he was no more.'"

CHAPTER EIGHT

PERCOLATION IN THE MID-1960S

A new era of domestic upheaval followed the president's death. The cynicism of Bruce and Sahl expanded with the comedy of Dick Gregory, *Dr. Strangelove*, Second City and an improvisational sketch collective featuring Godfrey Cambridge, Buck Henry and George Segal called The Premise.

Ted Flicker founded The Premise after his Compass Players flunked in St. Louis. While other Compass members created Second City, Flicker went his own overtly political way. "I knew everybody at Second City. We just had a different philosophy." Flicker said The Premise would "declare war against the huge stage machines . . . war against the playwrights who are themselves 'establishments' with phalanxes of agents, managers, advisers, gag writers and play doctors."

At various times The Premise roster included Thomas Aldredge, Sandy Baron, Peter Bonerz, Godfrey Cambridge, Joan Darling, James Frawley, Gene Hackman, Buck Henry and George Segal. Dustin Hoffman was the dishwasher in their Bleecker Street venue. He auditioned for the group, but was turned down because he swore—Flicker was already having trouble with authorities and didn't want any more heat.

Buck Henry says, "We were shut down by the cops several times. There was this longtime cabaret license feud. If you told jokes in public you had to have a license and all that stuff." Flicker says it placed him in a moral dilemma. "I found a venue to lease, and it was the toughest dyke bar in the Village—they stationed eight cops there every Saturday night. I knew I better get a local Village lawyer. He gave me a mimeographed sheet of who got paid off and how much. I thought, 'I'm opening a theater of political satire . . . and I need to pay people off?' The first guy who came in was the health inspector. He said, 'Let's go take a look at the kitchen.' I took thirty-five dollars—as instructed on the sheet—and kept it in my sweating palm. I said, 'It's so nice of you to come early to make sure the kitchen is all right . . .' He looked at me and said, 'Son, just hand me the thirty-five dollars.' Well, I *did*—and then I went crazy wondering how I could have done that. The next guy in was a police sergeant. He said, 'Let's go take a look at the kitchen.' That was the *code*."

The Premise was the first professional gig for many future stars. Flicker saw an amateur actor at Princeton named George Segal and hired him as a foil for Henry. "He and Buck turned out to be a perfect team," says Flicker. "George was always Buck's stooge."

Flicker put together a sister company called The Living Premise, consisting entirely of sketch comedy about race relations. The Living Premise starred African American actors Godfrey Cambridge, Al Freeman Jr. and Diana Sands. *The New York Times* called their satire "very disturbing." Flicker had two white actors play straight for his three African American leads. "When Godfrey Cambridge came to The Premise he showed what he could really do and his career started to happen," says Flicker. "We did a sketch about a Westchester couple in their big Westchester house with a white Jewish maid. We reversed all the clichés. It shook people up. *The New York Times* refused my first ad: 'The Premise—in Spades.' Then it was 'The Premise—In Living Color.' And they turned that down too. The Living Premise was the first integrated theater in New York."

The Premise had its swan song with *The Troublemaker*, a motion picture bankrolled by Janus Films. "Ted Flicker and I wrote it," says Buck Henry. "It had some funny moments and an interesting kazoo score written by Cy Coleman. It had local political references because Flicker felt there was an audience interested in his New York cabaret card troubles, but of course *no one* was interested in that. It was fun to make, but we bankrupted Janus Films. We put them out of the filmmaking business—cost them too much money, so they became a distribution arm."

Lenny Bruce hung out at The Premise from time to time, and Flicker was flattered by his presence—until he discovered *why* he was there. "Lenny hung out at The Premise. He was there a lot. I didn't know until later that our lobby was his drug drop."

Bruce influenced all the sketch collectives of the decade. "While I was in New York, I saw Lenny Bruce and he had a great effect on me," said Second City's Anthony Holland. Flicker says, "He influenced *all* of us." David Steinberg had his Lenny Bruce epiphany in Chicago. "Bill Alton was the head of the University [of Chicago] Theatre at that time. Bill did everything he could to get me to be a stand-up comedian before he would take me the Second City route. He insisted I go to the Gate of Horn with him. I thought, 'Who wants to go see a comic?' because at the time I thought comics were nowhere. But sure enough the comic he wanted me to see was Lenny Bruce. I went back to see him every single week for five weeks."

Bruce was an influence on Second City in other ways as well. John Brent was a Second City cast member whom Carl Gottlieb describes as "a hipster ladies' man, an early junkie-comic-poet-entrepreneur from the days when such a thing could coexist." Brent used heroin because he wanted to emulate Bruce. Likewise, legendary Second City member Del Close took his drug cues from Lenny. Premise member Peter Bonerz says, "He was really smart, had an immediate callback memory, could do Shakespeare, could do Gilbert & Sullivan, and was charismatic to the point he could talk you into trying heroin."

Second City was an underground sensation in the early 1960s. While not as overtly political as The Premise, it still had a socialist vibe. When it became wildly popular several producers wanted to package it for mainstream consumption. David Susskind and Max Liebman brought Second City to New York in 1961. It gave the Chicago outfit Broadway credibility, but compromised its underground credentials. Susskind promoted the cast—Howard Alk, Alan Arkin, Severn Darden, Andrew Duncan, Mina Kolb, Paul Sand and Eugene Troobnick—on his talk show *Open End*. "Immediately afterward we got a whole new kind of crowd," said Arkin. "We were getting the uptown crowd, the mink coat crowd, and I *hated them*. Because they would laugh at any kind of reference, whether they understood it or not. It had nothing to do with the content; it had to do with the reference. And I came offstage one night and I said, 'Damn these people to hell! I hate them. They're snobs.'"

Eugene Troobnick blamed Second City's Broadway failure on the man who previously gave so much trouble to Mel Brooks and Buddy Hackett. "The reason we didn't make it on Broadway was because our producer, Max Liebman, didn't have the courage to allow us to do what we were unique in doing. He was terrified to allow us to improvise in front of critics."

While stand-up and live sketch comedy evolved, television comedy was stagnant. Lenny Bruce, Mort Sahl and Second City seemed to have little effect on loosening the conservative restrictions of the small screen. Comedy programming like *Bewitched*, *My Favorite Martian*, *The Lucy Show* and *The Munsters* seemed to imply that the old Keith-Albee "blue rules" still applied.

The one exception—and even then it was very mild—was on the late night talk shows. Late night was one of the few places on television where subversive comedians were occasionally welcomed. Jack Paar left *The Tonight Show* in 1962 after negotiating for a once-a-week prime-time show called *The Jack Paar Program*. NBC did not have a replacement ready when he left. Johnny Carson was offered *The Tonight Show*—and accepted—but was contractually obligated to *Who Do You Trust?*, his five-day-a-week afternoon game show on ABC. In the meantime *The Tonight Show* was handled by a who's who of American popular culture. Art Linkletter, Joey Bishop, Bob Cummings, Merv Griffin, Jack Carter, Jan Murray, Peter Lind Hayes, Soupy Sales, Mort Sahl, Steve Lawrence, Jerry Lewis, Hugh Downs, Jimmy Dean, Arlene Francis, Jack E. Leonard, Groucho Marx, Hal March and Donald O'Connor—in that order—demonstrated their mostly inept talk show abilities for six months. It made one appreciate Jack Paar all the more.

Mort Sahl's attempt at hosting *The Tonight Show* was called "a dreary affair," but to his credit he booked George Carlin for his first solo stand-up performance and welcomed fellow comedy subversives Del Close and Henry Morgan on the same episode.

Dick Cavett was a writer on *The Tonight Show* during the six-month guest host spell. "It was great writing for Mort and Groucho. It was a joy if they thought anything you wrote was worth doing. And then there was Art Linkletter, where you just turned the whole job over to a Bennett Cerf joke book and went home. There was the week Donald O'Connor did it and no one could imagine *why*."

Of these interim hosts, only two truly succeeded. NBC hired each of them to do five nights, but Merv Griffin was such a natural he was held over for twenty. It made NBC wonder if it had made the right choice in Carson. Griffin was happy to instill network execs with doubt. "Merv was *dying* to get *The Tonight Show*," says Cavett. "It nearly killed him when he didn't." Instead NBC signed Griffin to do what was essentially a *Tonight Show* knockoff during the afternoon. It made his career.

Jerry Lewis was the other guest host who impressed viewers and executives alike. He shocked the industry with his numbers. He scored the highest ratings in the history of late night—surpassing all records set by Jerry Lester, Steve Allen and Jack Paar. All three networks were impressed and began wooing Lewis for his own talk show. In an expensive bidding war, ABC won the rights. The following year *The Jerry Lewis Show* debuted as the most expensive talk show in television history.

The Jerry Lewis Show was a two-hour talk show slated for Saturday nights, debuting autumn 1963. Lewis signed a contract for $8 million a season, forty-two episodes a year, with a five-season option including multimillion-dollar increases. The contract gave Lewis total creative control, a detail that turned costly. "I'll be in complete control," Lewis said at the ABC press conference. "I'll be doing something I've never done before. It'll be what people want. I'm going to play it loose. I'll be what I'm with. I suppose I'll have guests."

The vagaries of his vision were a concern. Lewis offered very few specifics other than some strange contractual demands—like an assurance there be no deodorant advertising during the time slot. "He wouldn't tell us what the show's format was," said ABC president Leonard Goldenson. "He kept giving us double-talk and double-talk and double-talk, insisting he would take the country by storm."

Lewis orchestrated a massive renovation of the El Capitan at 1735 Vine Street in Hollywood. He had performed on its stage years earlier during broadcasts of *The Colgate Comedy Hour*. His first point of business was changing the venue's name to the more modest-sounding Jerry Lewis Theater.

The walls were lined with gold vinyl wallpaper and the stairs with eighteen hundred yards of thick red carpet. New theater furniture was custom-made. An outdoor patio was built, with a fireplace that had a speaker system installed within the brick, playing music as embers flared. A 10x12 screen was installed to help the balcony sight lines. "About two thousand yards of drapes have gone into the stage area," wrote *Variety*. "Fifty new banks of dimmers have been added backstage. Up the circular staircase, to Lewis' private dressing room, there is a luxurious suite with a gold motif. Initials JL are ingrained in the tile of the shower."

"The very wiring and plumbing had been replaced," wrote Lewis biographer Shawn Levy. "The desk at which Jerry would sit when talking to guests was equipped with a control panel that allowed him to override the director and control shots while the show was in progress; at a cost of thirty thousand dollars, it was designed to be broken down and taken anywhere in the world on location."

"Oh my God, the money," says ABC producer Bill Harbach. "Oh, Jesus, there was a plaque of his profile in bronze in the cement. His dressing room was all brass fittings and mirrors." Phil Silvers told Lewis, "It's a little nauseating. The designer of this joint must have been smoking hashish."

On Saturday, September 21, 1963, at 9:30 P.M., *The Jerry Lewis Show* debuted. Scheduled guests were Mort Sahl, singer Kaye Stevens, crooner Jack Jones and author Clifton Fadiman. Larger stars like Steve Allen, Jimmy Durante and Robert Stack made surprise appearances. As the curtains parted, Jerry's hair glistened with Brylcreem. He mockingly berated his crew and sang "When You're Smiling."

When the song finished, Lewis said, "I'd like to say welcome to all you nice . . ." Shrieking feedback deafened the crowd. After a moment he continued: "I realize two hours is an unusual amount of time but . . . Have you ever heard anyone say, 'What can Liz [Elizabeth Taylor] and Dick [Richard Burton] do for two hours?'" Nobody laughed. Lewis tapped the boom mic and turned into a tragic Catskill act: "This is on, isn't it, sweetheart?"

Communication with the control room cut out. Headsets froze. The red light on each camera—indicating which camera the performer should look into—stopped working. The giant monitor installed in the balcony failed to turn on, and the upper section of the audience eventually walked out.

The morning reviews were vicious. *Variety* wrote, "It's truly amazing that so much could have gone awry. [The show] came off as disjointed, disorganized, tasteless. It was, in truth, an unimaginative, uninspired, unfunny show." *Time* said, "ABC has . . . the apparent illusion that several million people want to watch 120 minutes of the scriptless life of a semi-educated, egocentric boor."

ABC panicked. It blamed shortcomings on the host's "Jewishness" and asked him to "tone it down." ABC executive Thomas Moore said, "Lewis was agreeable to all our suggestions for the show's improvement. We have complete confidence that he'll make the changes we suggested and that the audience level will rise with each succeeding week. He's on his way."

Dick Cavett was lured from *The Tonight Show* to *The Jerry Lewis Show*. "He pissed away most nights," says Cavett. "He was deeply depressed on at least two, maybe three, shows. You could watch Jerry go down, down, down, the showbiz equivalent of the *Hindenburg*."

On November 18, 1963, after a mere eight weeks, ABC announced cancellation of the show. In order to erase it from the airwaves, the network had to buy out Lewis's contract. *The Jerry Lewis Show* finished with a total of thirteen episodes, but its star made off with an estimated $10 million (some claim the number was four times as much). Lewis purchased a full-page ad in the trades. The ad was surrounded by blankness and only a signature at the bottom, and Lewis had placed one word in small type at the center of the page: "Oops."

The Jerry Lewis Theater was sold back to ABC, which used it for Lewis's immediate replacement, a thrown-together variety show called *The Hollywood Palace*. Remarkably, the replacement program succeeded where Lewis did not, lasting a full five seasons. But over those years it had been hard to erase the memory of *The Jerry Lewis Show*: The entire theater remained covered in brass engravings that read "J.L."

Jerry Lewis had a reputation, but a new stand-up comedian rivaled it. Jackie Mason rose quickly in the mid-1960s. He was considered enormously clever onstage. Offstage he was widely loathed.

One of the brightest new acts of the period, Mason became a star comic with several appearances on the shows of Steve Allen, Garry Moore and Jack Paar. He made headlines after a set on *The Ed Sullivan Show* on October 18, 1964. Mason was in the middle of his act when he got a signal from the sidelines that he had a minute left. The stage cue distracted him and, in his opinion, distracted the audience. Mason was known for stabbing the air, punctuating his punch lines with an index finger. He gestured back at the stage manager and said, "Here's a finger for you." Sullivan was convinced he'd just seen Mason flip him the bird.

Former Sullivan director John Moffitt says, "He was going on and on. We put one finger up, 'One minute. Cut.' Jackie put up his forefinger and people thought it was the middle finger. He went to Ed's dressing room after and we heard Ed ranting for a half hour." Sullivan told Mason he was banned from the show. Sullivan's producer, Bob Precht, said Mason's contract with the show was terminated "as a result of Mason's on-camera obscene gestures and offensive conduct, insubordination and gross deviation from the material agreed upon." Mason fought back. He sued the program for $3 million, charging defamation of character and stating that Precht "maliciously and wickedly contrived to blacken and defame."

Mason seemed to have the better argument, but few sided with him. Columnist Herb Kelly reported, "Everyone who's discussed it with us had no sympathy for Mason. He can be an obnoxious fellow at times." Though Mason claimed it did the opposite, it seemed the publicity from the incident actually boosted his status. "It *made* his career," says George Schlatter. "Who knew who Jackie Mason was before that? Nobody. It established him."

Mason claimed he was blacklisted from show business as a result of the incident, but he was already burning his bridges. Fellow comedian Alan King said, "*The Ed Sullivan Show* really had nothing to do with his demise." Mason simply rubbed people the wrong way. "He's my least favorite person in the whole world," says Friars Club patriarch Freddie Roman. Lou Alexander says, "Jackie Mason was brilliant, but do I like him personally? Not one bit! I never liked him for one minute! None of us liked him." Shecky Greene says, "He's brilliant—but I think he's a piece of shit." And television director Alan Rafkin said, "Jackie Mason was one of the most unlikeable people I've ever met and a royal pain to work with."

Jack Carter was around Mason a lot in the 1960s and says, "Everybody wanted to hit him." In November 1966, someone wanted not only to hit him, but to kill him. Mason was in his bed at the Aladdin Hotel in Las Vegas when three shots were fired through the balcony. Mason was unscathed, but the gunfire peppered the headboard. The assassination attempt went unsolved.

Soon after, a woman phoned the entertainment director of the Concord Hotel in the Catskills, yelling, "Those bullets [that were] supposed to get Jackie in Las Vegas will kill you instead if you book him."

Two weeks later in Vegas, while Mason was sitting in the passenger seat of a friend's car, a vehicle accelerated toward the automobile and smashed into him. He was rushed to the hospital and treated for cuts and bruises. The attacking car fled the scene, and no one was ever arrested.

A year later another assault left him bloodied, battered and bruised. "Comedian Jackie Mason has a bandaged nose and blood-stained shirt at a Miami hospital . . ." reported a Florida paper. "He was hit 8 to 10 times in the face by an unknown assailant. Mason said he was parked in front of his apartment with his date about 5 a.m. when a man opened his car door, slugged him and ran."

Mason is aware of his reputation: "As soon as I walk into the Friars Club, you never saw such hostility. Alan King with venom, full of vicious hate, Freddie Roman, full of hate. They don't event try to hide it—it's right in their faces. I'm not close to too many comedians."

In a business where charm is often essential, it's amazing that Mason's career has endured. Another comedian was not so lucky. While Mason blamed Ed Sullivan for his career problems, Shelley Berman did the same regarding a remarkable 1963 cinema vérité documentary called *Comedian Backstage*. It was a compelling look at a comic at the height of his stardom, but Berman says it cost him hundreds of thousands of dollars in cancelled bookings and destroyed his career. However, as with Mason, there is a scapegoat at play. If anything hampered the career of Berman it was, according to contemporaries, Berman's own doing.

Maynard Sloate booked Berman for his first Los Angeles engagement in 1957. "Shelley was impossible and not easy to get along with. He was extremely temperamental. From the stage he'd yell, 'Maynard! Maynard! What's that noise?' This goes on for his entire act. 'Maynard! There it is again! Maynard! It's the refrigerator in the kitchen!' He was stopping his act to complain about the refrigerator. Putting up with him was difficult, and that temperament cost him his career."

Berman was riding high in 1963. *Time* said he was "the wealthiest of the new comics." He was one of the biggest stars in show business and a logical subject for a news profile. *Comedian Backstage* was inspired by the stunning black-and-white "direct cinema" that put documentarians Richard Leacock, Albert Maysles and D. A. Pennebaker on the map. (*Primary* and *Crisis* are among the best examples of the genre.) Working under director Robert Drew, they revolutionized the look of television news.

Cinematographer Doug Downs emulated the vérité style, following Berman around the Diplomat Hotel in Hollywood, Florida. The film opens with Berman in his hotel room, sitting in a silk robe, discussing performance specifications with his manager:

No service on the floor in the front. Not because I don't want the people to be served, but I don't want any part of the show to be hurt. They can serve delicately, cleanly, but I don't want to hear waiters in the back shouting their orders. I don't want them to hurt the show. You tell the maître d' down here . . . worry him. Please, Marty. Tell him I am the most temperamental human being you ever saw. Tell him this afternoon that I am a monster. Tell him that I walked off the stage at the Waldorf Astoria four times in the middle of the show. Tell him they had to refund money. Tell him that I am being sued! Tell him that I am terrible.

Berman saunters through the lobby, signing autographs, greeting the press, pensively worrying about the show. The camera closes in on his eyes as *Comedian Backstage* builds up to his nighttime performance. In the final minutes we see Berman onstage. He performs a monologue in which an elderly father addresses his son. It is constructed as a poignant moment, and Berman accentuates dramatics rather than laughs. And then in a moment that has since been mentioned many times in comedy lore—the loud ringing of a telephone offstage interrupts the flow of his routine. It rings and rings. The distraction is obvious to everyone, and the climax of Berman's performance has been ruined.

The frustration can be seen in Berman's brow. He rushes to the end of his piece and bows. The applause is sustained, but Berman is livid. He rushes backstage, screaming. He grabs the phone, jettisoning it from the wall, as he shouts at those around him. The camera freezes on Berman's angry face. The credits start to roll.

The next morning it was all rave reviews. The *Los Angeles Times* wrote, "Portrait of Shelley Berman really digs deeply. It was a brilliant piece of work." *The Washington Post* said, "Finest show biz biography ever to reach the TV screen. It was the most revealing, most realistic and most satisfying program of its kind ever produced." There was talk of a sequel. *The Hollywood Reporter* wrote, "So tremendous has the nationwide reaction been to the unvarnished profile, producer Fred Freed is already negotiating with Berman—whom he says 'has more guts and integrity than any performer I've ever met'—for a second documentary next season."

There were no complaints. But as Berman's career eroded in the coming years, he said *Comedian Backstage* was to blame. His career dipped substantially, and by the late 1960s he was making a fraction of the money he'd been enjoying in 1963. On the other hand, most of the coffeehouse comedians experienced a similar dip, as the coffeehouse style gave way to longhair psychedelia and live entertainment was replaced by discotheque dance floors. So the changing tides were partially to blame for Berman's career erosion. But the rest of the blame, according to fellow comedians, belongs to Berman's own arrogance. Phyllis Diller said, "If it happens too fast it goes to your head. He had a bodyguard, but nobody ever bothered him." His agent said, "He was temperamental and went out of his way, unknowingly, to make himself a bad guy. He destroyed himself."

Berman saw his bookings at major hotels vanish, but he could always play the Playboy Club. Any comic falling on hard times had a savior in the Hugh Hefner chain. The Playboy Club franchise was the most significant circuit for stand-up comics in the 1960s. It is best remembered for waitresses wearing bunny outfits, but the role it played in the history of stand-up should stand as its primary significance.

In cities across America, a struggling comedian could sign a Playboy contract and get a year's salary, accommodations, travel expenses and a steady crowd. It was the first such entity since vaudeville. Comedians like George Carlin, Jackie Vernon and Slappy White were under contract to Playboy during its height. Semi-names like Irwin Corey, Jackie Gayle and Sonny Mars were essentially kept alive by the work. Lifelines were handed to unknowns like Stu Allen, Albert T. Berry and Mart Rickey. "The notion originally was just to open a club where we could hang out," said Hugh Hefner. "There wasn't really a notion that it would become something beyond Chicago at the time." Initially Hefner wanted to sponsor a room within the established Black Orchid nightclub. "I actually suggested that they might turn the theme of the junior room into a Playboy Club.

The director said, 'Well, how much would you give me for that notion?' Of course, my notion was exactly the opposite."

Hefner decided to invest in a flagship Chicago club of his own. It was so successful that he soon branched out across America. The Playboy Clubs would feature anywhere from two to six shows a night, with simultaneous events happening on different floors. "They had two rooms—the Penthouse and the Playroom," says comedian Tom Dreesen. "A singer would do her act and then you'd do yours. Halfway through your act she went upstairs and started doing a show up there. So, when you finished, you'd walk upstairs and she'd be in her last song. Then they'd clear the room downstairs while you were upstairs. They would do that all night long."

Pat Morita was a Playboy Club comic, still a couple decades away from *Karate Kid* infamy. He was managed by Sally Marr, Lenny Bruce's mother, and billed himself as The Hip Nip. Booker Jackie Curtiss says, "Pat Morita was one of the comedians Sally pushed on the Playboy circuit. He was high all the time. He would come onstage smoking a joint."

Young comedians starting out relied on the Playboy Club. "At that time there were less than a hundred comics in the entire country getting paid," says comic Murray Langston. "There were very few [young] comics getting paid other than Playboy comics." Comedian Kelly Monteith says, "For me it was the first steady work I ever had. You'd go to New Orleans, Atlanta, Miami, Denver, Chicago, Kansas City—even Jamaica. They were all over the place. You'd get ten weeks in a row—or longer—and you'd work them all year long."

Dick Gregory's career was made at the Playboy Club, and he credited Hefner with opening the field for African American comics. "Never before until Hefner brought me in had a black comedian been committed to work white nightclubs. You could sing and you could dance, but you couldn't stand flat-footed and talk. So when Hefner brought me in, that broke the whole barrier."

Dick Gregory was jeered, cheered and jailed more than any other stand-up comedian in history. He was spat at, beaten up and shot in the leg. He was the first comedian to address the civil rights struggle directly. He managed to joke about segregation and its violent implementation. He was an antidote to liberal fear and a megaphone for black grievance. He hipped the white droves to the daily problems of African Americans, and because of him life was easier for every black comedian who followed.

Gregory started at a Chicago nightclub called the Esquire Show Lounge. It was lit with red lightbulbs, and rhythm and blues was the club's main attraction. Guitar Red was a mainstay at the Esquire in the late 1950s. According to Gregory, he was "an albino Negro who gets more out of an electric guitar than any man has a right to. He even plays with his feet. People come from all over Chicago to hear Guitar Red and on Saturday nights there were lines around the block."

Gregory said he "hit them hard and fast with jokes on processed hair and outer space and marijuana and integration and the numbers racket and long white Cadillacs and The Man downtown." He played the Esquire for two years until he got a big break.

Comedian Irwin Corey was working the Playboy Club in Chicago when he got into a dispute about working on a Sunday. He promised Hefner he'd find a suitable replacement if he was allowed to take Sundays off. A patron of black nightclubs, Corey was probably the only white comic aware of Gregory's existence. He pulled him from the Esquire and placed him in the Playboy Club on January 13, 1961. Gregory said, "They called my agent. He said, 'It pays fifty dollars for one night.' I couldn't believe there was that much money in the world. I had never been in downtown Chicago and I didn't have but a quarter. I got on the bus. I got off at the wrong stop. There was a blizzard that night. I'm supposed to be onstage at eight o'clock. I'm running and I'm slipping and I don't know where I'm going. The blizzard was so heavy you couldn't see—and I saw *Playboy* and that was like seeing heaven."

While he was scrambling in the snow, Gregory's phone was ringing at home. The Playboy Club was packed with a convention of white businessmen from the Deep South. Playboy decided to cancel the African American comic and pay him off rather than inflame a racial situation. Gregory never received the message and instead performed three consecutive shows—and killed. "Twelve o'clock I was still talking. Twelve-thirty Hugh Hefner came by. Two o'clock I finished. From that they hired me for two hundred and fifty a week, seven days a week."

Gregory talked about traveling through the South and the racism he encountered. It hadn't been particularly groundbreaking at the Esquire, but in front of a white crowd it was revolutionary. It hit the right nerve at the right time in American history. He had a succession of new bookings and soon he was in demand. The media picked up on it, and profiles in *Playboy*, *Time* and *Newsweek* made him the success story of the year. He became so hot so fast that he lost money honoring minor engagements scheduled before the fame. Freddie's supper club in Minneapolis had booked Gregory ahead of the momentum. When it came around, Gregory honored the gig, at four hundred dollars a week, in lieu of a much better New York offer for six thousand.

A few months earlier, a voice like Gregory's was considered one to avoid. Steve Allen said, "One reason that there is a shortage of Negro stand-up comedians or humorists is that comedy of this sort usually involves a certain amount of critical observation and our society is probably not civilized enough yet to permit or encourage the Negro comedian to make satirical commentary about . . . our bungled international relations, the Un-American Activities Committee or other things of that sort. Just imagine a Negro comic getting up on a stage and saying some of the things that Lenny Bruce or Mort Sahl are getting away with."

Imagine no more. "He brought down the house," reported *Playboy* magazine. "And with it, the tacit prohibition of race relations as a socially acceptable subject for humor in big-time nightclubs." In order to make his commentary easier for white consumption, Gregory hired joke book impresario Robert Orben to cloak his act in old jokes. "My wife can't cook. How do you burn Kool-Aid?" It was a line one would expect from Henny Youngman rather than Dick Gregory, but it was part of a greater strategy. "I needed eighty percent *white* material—you know, mother-in-law jokes and Khrushchev. I bought white man's joke books to figure out what whitey was laughing at."

Once the squares were laughing at his mother-in-law, Gregory hit them with jokes about the civil rights struggle.

Gregory's success was a victory for comedic equality. His next step was to use the power of celebrity to integrate the South. Civil rights leader Medgar Evers asked Gregory to speak at a voter registration rally in Jackson, Mississippi, in 1962. "For the first time, I was involved," said Gregory. "There was a battle going on, there was a war shaping up, and somehow writing checks and giving speeches didn't seem enough. Sure I could stay in the nightclubs and say clever things. But if America goes to war tomorrow would I stay at home and satirize it at the Blue Angel? I wanted a piece of the action now."

Civil rights advocate Clyde Kennard spent years trying to integrate Mississippi Southern College. When racist adversaries framed him for theft, Kennard was sentenced to seven years in prison. Kennard became Gregory's first banner cause, a metaphor for the greater struggle. Although Kennard was never pardoned, an aggressive campaign by Gregory won him parole.

As Gregory the comedian gave way to Gregory the activist, he canceled nightclub engagements on a whim. If a protest march and a stand-up gig landed on the same date—even if the stand-up gig was scheduled months in advance—Gregory chose the protest. Most of his venues were progressive coffeehouses, and people like Enrico Banducci did not usually hold a grudge. Still, Gregory's manager, Ralph Mann, said his client's activity amounted to "one million in travel expenses and canceled bookings, not to mention legal fees."

He was losing money and risking his life. At a rally in Clarksdale, Mississippi, a bomb came flying through the window of a church where Gregory was speaking. The bomb failed to detonate. "When the meeting was over, a man came in to tell me that I was going to be killed that night," said Gregory. "A roadblock had been set up for me on the highway back to Greenwood. Outside the church I could hear one of the police officers screaming, almost hysterical, 'If one of our men threw that bomb you'd better believe it would have gone off, we don't make mistakes like that, no, sir, we don't.'" Locals hid Gregory in the floorboards of a churchgoer's house that night.

Gregory was jailed for the first time in May 1963. He and approximately eight hundred demonstrators were arrested in Birmingham, Alabama, for parading without a permit. While Gregory was inside his cell, the notorious Bull Connor was outside, ordering officers to hose down black people in a famed moment seen around the world.

Bigot hatred was directed squarely at Gregory. "I'm scared, but I will stay as long as there's anything I can do to help," he said. The assassination of Dr. King was five years away, but Gregory anticipated such possibilities. While sitting in an Alabama jail cell, the thirty-one-year-old comedian made out his will.

The Crescendo in Los Angeles advertised a Dick Gregory engagement for August 17, 1963. Typically, when the date came around, Gregory was in jail. Such complications slowed his rising star, but Gregory was not concerned. He collaborated with the Student Nonviolent Coordinating Committee. Activist-historian Howard Zinn remembered Gregory's appearance at a SNCC rally in Selma, Alabama: "Never in the history of this area had a black man stood like this on a public platform, ridiculing and denouncing white officials to their faces. It was something of a miracle that Gregory was able to leave town alive."

It wasn't just the South. He was arrested in his native Chicago on charges of "participation in a racial demonstration." He refused to sign a paper acknowledging a court date, arguing he hadn't broken any law. He was thrown in jail. The Crescendo in Los Angeles lamented that it had spent a lot on advertising only to learn he couldn't make it, and the club used apolitical lounge comics Paul Gilbert, Buddy Lester and Corbett Monica in his place. "Any nightclub engagement I've missed, I've always made it up to them," said Gregory. "No nightclub owner has ever lost money on me because either I'll [perform] free for him or I'll give him a price he never could have gotten otherwise. My managers know that if a demonstration comes up—I'm gone."

Playboy magazine wondered about the cost. It asked, "Can you afford to keep up this outlay on the income from your irregular nightclub appearances?" Gregory answered, "Can't afford not to. If I'm willing to pay the price of dying for a cause, what do I care about a few bucks?"

On August 28, 1963, the legendary March on Washington for Jobs and Freedom featured a crowd of two hundred thousand people (among the throng was Woody Allen). Gregory opened his speech, "I never thought I'd be giving out more fingerprints than autographs." By the summer of 1964, he had been arrested eight times, spending a total of two months in prison. He had marched in Arkansas, Mississippi, Illinois and Massachusetts. Predictably, the press criticized him for abandoning stand-up. Syndicated newspaper columnist Drew Pearson called Gregory "a Negro extremist" and wrote in one column: "Recommended reading for Dick Gregory—*The South During Reconstruction* by E. M. Coulter." Coulter was a historian who believed in white supremacy.

Gregory was quick to defend himself. "I'm a Negro *before* I'm an entertainer. The white man's getting his due under the Constitution, but they got to give me a civil rights Bill to get mine. The Negro is going for the Constitution, for all the constitutional rights that are already rightfully his as a citizen—and he ain't going to stop until he gets them . . . The only way we can save America today is this great social revolution."

Comedians participating in the civil rights struggle were few and far between. Those who did, surprisingly, were not onstage progressives like Mort Sahl, but rather traditional comics like Alan King. Sahl said his politics would be more effective within the context of his act. He was dismissive of Gregory's choice to march. "It doesn't seem to be productive. He stood on the street corner, he was ignored, and he was finally jailed. I don't know. I don't think that's good."

At the invitation of Harry Belafonte, Alan King joined the march from Selma to Montgomery. "A bunch of us flew to Selma and were greeted there by Harry, [boxer] Floyd Patterson, James Baldwin and a bunch of other people," said King. "As we marched, we were spat on by the National Guard, which was there to protect us, and the only places that would give us shelter at night were Catholic monasteries."

The assassination of Dr. Martin Luther King Jr. on April 4, 1968, made some comedians feel that their vocation was irrelevant. Bill Cosby was playing Kansas City but walked off in the middle of

his act, overwhelmed with emotion. Richard Pryor was playing Mister
Kelly's in Chicago. "By the second show, the National Guard had surrounded the club and closed us down," said his manager, Jerry Wald.
Pryor and Wald drove through Chicago smoking a joint, observing
the anger in the streets. "There were troops and people shooting,
rioting, and he was crying. He was supposed to do *The Ed Sullivan
Show* the following week, and he didn't do it."

George Carlin said he was unaffected. "I didn't respond with
rage to any of what was happening in 1968. Dr. King's murder in
April was depressingly predictable. There was a sinking feeling: that
something good was ebbing away and being encouraged in that direction by its usual forces. The establishment was winning—its war,
its assassins, its secret government—and that fact overpowered and
debilitated me more than it enraged me."

The assassination hardened Dick Gregory's commitment. He
would never return to full-time stand-up, instead accepting speaking
engagements on the campus lecture circuit. Each appearance opened
with forty-five minutes of comedy followed by a tonal shift to activist
oration. He opened the second half shouting, "In case you don't know
it, America is the number one racist country in the world! Brother,
I'm going to tell you straight and true, this nation is insane!"

Other African American comedians benefited from the popularity
of Dick Gregory as white booking agents saw a new opportunity for
profit. Redd Foxx was one of the greatest beneficiaries. For years he
was considered too salacious to book in mainstream white nightclubs.
"I never really got in trouble with the sheriff for Lenny Bruce," said
Crescendo proprietor Gene Norman. "The one I always got heat
about was Redd Foxx. His stuff was kind of blue and the sheriff used
to object to his material." But after the success of Gregory, Foxx
was booked into white venues with regularity. In spring 1966 he
was booked at the Aladdin and became the first African American
comedian to headline a Vegas hotel. He made great money, and in
February 1967 he took his fortune and purchased the Slate Brothers
club on La Cienega. He renamed it the Redd Foxx Club and made

history as the first African American club owner on "Restaurant Row," along the border of Beverly Hills.

While Foxx was thrilled to have some of Gregory's residual prosperity, other old-timers resented Gregory's success. Stepin Fetchit, longtime scourge of the NAACP for his stereotyped portrayals in old movies, claimed Gregory wasn't doing anything he hadn't done years before. "[I was] doing social commentary at the Orpheum Theatre in Memphis as early as 1932 and I'm still doing it."

Slappy White carried the largest grudge. It was the success of Gregory that led to White's Playboy Club contract. Up to that point he had played only Black venues, but he resented anyone's pointing it out. "I was playing white audiences before Dick Gregory was colored," said White. He also circulated a rumor that Gregory was stealing his material. White appeared on *The Ed Sullivan Show* and opened with a dig: "I don't tell racial jokes because they don't solve anything." He then produced a white glove and a black glove from his pocket, put them on, clenched his hands and went into an "animated plea for racial brotherhood." Gregory saw the performance and called it "an insult to comedy."

Motown was the most successful Black-owned business in 1960s showbiz, and comedians were part of the operation. The Motortown Revue traveled the fading Chitlin' Circuit with acts like the Contours, the Four Tops, Little Stevie Wonder, the Marvelettes, Martha and the Vandellas, the Temptations and the Supremes. It also featured African American comedians Bill (not from *Ghostbusters*) Murry and Willie Tyler as the revue emcees. There was also the occasional appearance from Tommy Chong, who was a member of the Motown group Bobby Taylor & the Vancouvers.

Murry was fired from his job at a Chrysler plant in the mid-1950s. With no job prospects, he went onstage at a Detroit venue called the Vogue, homeroom of blues legend T-Bone Walker. Walker dug him and hired Murry for all his local gigs. Murry used Pigmeat Markham routines until he developed his own act. "I was doing slapstick comedy, with the baggy pants, the wine bottle and the big floppy hat. I was tagged Winehead Willie after the song 'Winehead Willie, Put That Bottle Down.' He [T-Bone] treated me like a son more or less and would look out for me if things threatened to get rough." Eventually Murry was hired as the emcee at the Fox Theater in Detroit, where the biggest Black names in show business appeared. Murry's stand-up act is lost to time, but his voice is immortalized on Stevie Wonder's "Fingertips Part I and II" as Murry shouts, "Let's hear it for him! Little Stevie Wonder!"

Tommy Chong, comedy's marijuana icon, had his first taste of big-time showbiz doing the shows. "I was in heaven, living my dream: touring America with a soul revue. Playing legendary places like the Fox Theater in Detroit, the Regal Theater in Chicago, the Uptown Theater in Philly and the Apollo Theater in New York City." Bobby Taylor & the Vancouvers charted with a hit song called "Does Your Mama Know About Me," cowritten by Chong.

Comedian Willie Tyler logged hundreds of hours of stage experience with Motown. Tyler was ubiquitous in 1970s television with his ventriloquist dummy Lester, but in the 1960s he battled tough crowds that wanted soul music, not ventriloquists. "I signed with Motown and was with them for eight years. I traveled the road with the Motortown Revue, one-nighters all over the place. Greenville, Knoxville, Nashville, Louisville—all the 'villes.' We'd drive through the night and get to the hotel in the morning, shower, go to the venue, check out and drive to the next one. Lester had a big Afro; you could smell that cigarette smoke in his hair. We worked a place called the Carter Barron in Washington, D.C., a Saturday night with the potential for a rowdy audience. There was something about the place . . . not a good feeling. The leader of the band for the Motortown Revue was Choker Campbell. Martha and the Vandellas were on and all of a sudden way up in the balcony—four shots. Campbell grabbed all his sheet music and walked off the stage—as did everyone else. I was the emcee."

Controversial urban renewal projects changed the look of Black communities throughout the 1960s. It led to the erosion of the Chitlin'

Circuit, and increasing integration made the Black-only venues irrelevant by decade's end.

Bill Cosby was the first African American comedian to emerge a star after Dick Gregory, a comic for the post–Chitlin' Circuit era. When he first tried stand-up his subject matter dealt with race, in an obvious attempt to emulate Dick Gregory. Cosby started in a small Philadelphia venue called the Cellar. It was an informal space, and there was no limit to the amount of time he had. Without time constraints, he developed his elaborate storytelling style.

Sam Levenson, a folksy storyteller who joked about childhood and child-rearing in the 1950s, influenced Cosby. Levenson had also inspired comedian Alan King, another Cosby favorite. Cosby wrote Alan King a letter, asking for show business advice. "This kid was writing to me and I wrote back and I developed a pen pal," said King. "He wanted to be a stand-up comedian. I said, if you're ever in New York, come see me, and all of a sudden one day my secretary says there's a black man outside."

Cosby went to Chicago in July 1962 and played the Gate of Horn. It was his first gig outside Philadelphia. He opened for Marshall Brickman's group The Tarriers. His confidence was at an irrational level for an amateur. "He stepped forward like Aphrodite—fully formed," says Brickman. "He was very confident and very funny—and even funnier then because it was new." *Variety* caught the show. "The Tarriers are a sparkling vocal trio and young Bill Cosby, a Negro newcomer, almost cops the show with his polished comedy. Bill Cosby is an astonishingly self-assured monologist."

Comedian Adam Keefe said, "It was like he'd already made it. Like he had an air of success about him. Of not only success, but social position." His confidence rubbed some the wrong way. "I thought he was arrogant," said manager-producer Jack Rollins. "I didn't want to be near an arrogant comedian. I had to at least start off liking people I was trying to manage. He was too slick, and a little corny. There was no substance."

Cosby moved easily into the Village scene, but the material was too Dick Gregory–esque for some. Fred Weintraub managed the Café Wha when Cosby became a regular. "He was a poor imitation of Dick Gregory. He was bitter but was trying desperately to be nice. Gregory was ahead of him and was much more brilliant than Cosby, and much more racial." Cosby agreed. "When I first began telling racial jokes, the Negroes looked at the whites, the whites looked at the Negroes, and nobody laughed."

Cosby and Woody Allen emerged as potent stand-up comics at the same time, coincidental in light of the sexual accusations against them decades later. Together they walked around the Village comparing notes between shows. "Woody Allen, a flesh-and-blood walk-on from the Jules Feiffer casebook, is holding forth at the Bitter End, while Bill Cosby, at the Gaslight, is riding in the back of Dick Gregory's bus, although pursuing a different route," reported the *Village Voice*. "Allen and Cosby are both in their mid-twenties, find their material in the all-too-real world, are sophisticates with broad appeal. Cosby is joining that wave of Negro wits with integrity who are burying the ghosts of Stepin Fetchit and *Amos 'n' Andy*."

On August 6, 1963, Bill Cosby did *The Tonight Show* for the first time, with guest host Allan Sherman behind the desk. His routine about karate was a hit and he was at home sharing the panel with columnist Art Buchwald, comedian Milt Kamen, singer Kaye Stevens and actor Jim Backus. It was a career-making moment. NBC signed Cosby for five more *Tonight Show* spots and an appearance on the premiere of *The Jack Paar Program*. Most important, he signed a recording contract with Warner Bros., and by 1967 had five simultaneous comedy albums in the Billboard Top 100.

Cosby was one of the last stars to emerge from the coffeehouse scene of Bruce, Sahl and Winters. During Cosby's first wave of success Lenny Bruce was still alive, but Bruce's life was falling apart. In the last six years of his life he was charged with obscenity on a regular basis. The charges were almost always thrown out, but his addiction to drugs complicated his legal status. Opiates constipated his career, and everything else. Friends were at a loss what to do when Bruce devolved from a charming hipster into an irrational tweaker.

Buddy Hackett abandoned Bruce after his first drug bust. "The first time that Lenny got busted in Philadelphia, I called Buddy," says comic Frank Man. "I said, 'You hear what happened to Lenny?' He said, 'Yeah, I heard.' I said, 'What can we do to help him?' He said, 'I'm not going to do anything to help him! He'll probably stick a needle in my kid's arm!' That was the end of the friendship between Buddy Hackett and Lenny Bruce."

Gene Norman stopped employing Lenny at his club. "He played the Crescendo for the last time around 1961. He was really unpleasant. He was mean and nasty. It was a tirade, just a vulgar tirade, [and] the sheriff's department was on the Sunset Strip." Angry cops busted him in the Crescendo parking lot, but found nothing incriminating on him. Not willing to let him go, they jailed him for the track marks on his arm.

Mort Sahl remained a supporter. "He'd take advantage of the one phone call under the law and he'd call *me*. And I'd do the show. And *I'd* get paid. Then I'd go to his lawyer, who'd get him out on a writ." The vice squad also harassed Sahl, simply because he was friends with Bruce. "I became associated in the popular mind with him. Then they started to record *me*, the police. They would sit in the front row and I was recorded eighty-four times. Never arrested."

Variety correctly predicted trouble the next time Bruce played Chicago. "Chicago is the largest Catholic archdiocese in the world and an attack on the church is considered an attack on the city. While a conviction might be considered highly unlikely, an onstage arrest would satisfy the bluenoses." As Paul Krassner explains, "There was no law against blasphemy, so they had to use obscenity as an excuse." Indeed, Bruce was arrested at Chicago's Gate of Horn. Captain McDermott of the Chicago Vice Squad told the owner, "If he ever speaks against religion, I'm going to pinch you and everyone in here. Do you understand? He mocks the pope—and I'm speaking to you as a Catholic—I'm here to tell you your license is in danger."

It was week two of Bruce's engagement when the cops came in. George Carlin and Marshall Brickman were both present. "He was taken offstage by the cops," says Brickman. "There was a drum set onstage and he picked up a drumstick and started to riff on one of the cymbals, 'Did you come good? Did you come good?' Two cops in raincoats escorted him offstage."

Patrons were asked to remain seated while police did an ID check of all in attendance. "Carlin refused, and they dragged him by the pants and threw him in the same paddy wagon as Lenny," says Krassner. The Gate of Horn's license was revoked. Hugh Hefner paid Bruce's legal expenses. Hefner said, "In the days that followed, I gave Lenny my lawyer to defend him and I gave him a necktie to wear. He didn't own any ties."

The trial started with no mention of obscenity. "You will hear the mockery of the church, not just any church, not just the Catholic Church, not just the Lutheran Church, but the church *per se*." The prosecution was immediately reminded that this was immaterial—but the point had been made. There was no hope for Lenny Bruce in this environment. He was sentenced to a year in jail. He challenged the conviction, but the Illinois Supreme Court upheld it. It took the Supreme Court of the United States to have it overturned. Old comedians who never counted themselves Lenny Bruce fans were outraged at the conviction. An angry Henny Youngman said, "Where do you stop with this kind of thing? I think Lenny is a brilliant performer and he advertises himself fairly when he says, 'Let the buyer beware.'"

Bruce was busted at Doug Weston's Troubadour on his return to Los Angeles. The crime was titillating Yiddish. The offending words noted in the police report were "fressing, schmuck, putz, schtup and tuchas." Bruce was busted so often that comedian Herkie Styles started traveling to his gigs as an emergency understudy.

At the end of 1962 Bruce was arrested for drug possession three times in four months. The third bust found him tweaking in a taxi cab, a pile of needles spread across the backseat and a gram of heroin knotted in a balloon.

Frank Laro of the *Los Angeles Times* foresaw Bruce's demise in March 1963. He observed the "signs of growing obesity, his face lined by traces of physical illness and perhaps past excesses . . . What is dismaying about the man is his façade of self-assurance: a soaring, if uncertain, egotism rooted in the eroded soil of unlettered knowledge, snippets of cliché liberalism, borrowed erudition, and a conviction he has a Messianic message."

Bruce turned paranoid, obsessed with his persecution, and according to friends he lost his chops as a funnyman. Paul Krassner was ghostwriting Bruce's autobiography when the dope-sick comic turned on him. "He got sick. He sent a telegram to one of his sources saying he needed Dilaudid. The telegram said something like, 'De Lawd is in de Sky.' I mentioned how he had to stop everything to have a fix and he said, 'Oh, you're going to write an article about how I'm in the gutter vomiting and you helped me? You're gonna tell the story at cocktail parties?' There was an unspoken agreement between us that I would not write about his drug use. He said, 'I want you to take a lie detector test.' I said, 'If you can't trust me, then there's no point.' I went back to New York and he sent a telegram, 'We're divorced.'"

Bruce trusted no one. When his screenwriter friend Terry Southern offered him a part in two seminal dark comedies—*Dr. Strangelove* and *The Loved One*—Bruce turned him down, certain he was being exploited.

Frankie Ray Perilli remained with him even as Sally Marr told him to keep his distance. "Sally told me not to go with Lenny. She said, 'You don't know junkies. They change their mind real fast.' I got on a plane with him. We went to St. Louis. He was with me nine weeks and never got loaded. He said, 'When I'm with you I don't think about it.' Finally we went to Chicago and some asshole gave him a pill. Lenny comes into the hotel and sees me. He says, 'Frank! What are you doing in Chicago!' I said, 'I'm packing my bags.'"

Friends watched as Bruce's world imploded. "Twelve days before Lenny died in 1966 Brenda and I went up to his house in Hollywood," said George Carlin. "He didn't appear in clubs anymore—the Irish cops and judges had indeed shut him the fuck up. He was just about bankrupt, having spent all his income and intellect trying to vindicate himself."

"He was pretty well out of his mind," says comedian Slick Slavin. "It looked like he didn't eat. And he was *very* paranoid. Shecky and I took him to a Chinese restaurant to get him a little food. His ankles were as big as his kneecaps. He couldn't take it. While Shecky was trying to get us a table, he hugged me and said, 'I can't stay. I'm sorry, I'm sorry, I'm sorry, I can't handle this.' Eight days later he was dead."

"We had a conversation two days before he died," said Sally Marr. "I'll never forget, he wore a gray and white shirt and he was in such pain. They'd taken away his cabaret license in New York and everyone knew he was losing the Hollywood house. He said, 'I really think I failed at what I tried.' I said, 'Don't say that; I think you're a big success because you stuck to what you believed in.' He said, 'I don't know, I don't know what the fuck I was thinking about. Only a handful of people would go along with me.' Lenny lived—so that old ladies today can talk like he talked."

On August 3, 1966, Lenny Bruce died of acute morphine poisoning. "Some people thought it was suicide because his house had just been foreclosed and he couldn't get work," says Paul Krassner. "He told his girlfriend, Lotus Weinstock, 'I think I'm going to die this year.' The tea was still boiling on the stove and his electric typewriter was still on—mid-word. The word was 'constitution,' only typed as far as *C-o-n-s-t*. The machine was still humming."

Lenny Bruce's death was the birth of his legend. He became myth more than man. His popularity surged as a counterculture martyr. Milton Berle, Jack Benny, George Burns and Phil Spector helped pay for his funeral and, before the casket was lowered, someone tossed a microphone into the grave.

Lenny Bruce inspired the two most important male comedians of the following decade. George Carlin and Richard Pryor were compared to Lenny Bruce in the coming years. Both men idolized Bruce, and like their idol they developed unpredictable personalities that were accelerated, aggravated and ultimately amputated by vast drug use.

Richard Pryor's television debut was in 1964 on a show called *On Broadway Tonight*, a low-budget summer replacement for *The Danny Kaye Show*. Produced by the husband of paperback superstar

Jacqueline Susann, the 1964 series presented semiprofessional "discoveries." The host was the man who had presented so many new comedians thirty years earlier—Rudy Vallee. Saul Turteltaub wrote the introductions for *On Broadway Tonight*. "Rudy Vallee was a strange guy. I wrote something like, 'And now here are the people who . . .' and Rudy said, 'It's not "people"—it's "persons"! You don't say "people"—you say "persons"!' So Marilyn Michaels came on. She was doing an impression of Barbra Streisand and I wrote as a joke, 'And now here is Marilyn Michaels to sing "Persons Who Need Persons."' The girls typed it up and it went to cue cards like that—and he read it like that! When the show was canceled, Rudy blamed *me*."

Vallee introduced Richard Pryor, and his spot was solid. Pryor did a routine about growing up in Peoria, Illinois, but a vocal detractor was on the phone. Bill Cosby hated the young Richie Pryor. He was convinced he was stealing his material.

The Merv Griffin Show signed Pryor to an exclusivity deal and Cosby would phone Griffin after each segment, asking Griffin to tell him what Pryor said. Cosby made similar calls to club managers around Manhattan: "What did that kid do tonight? Everyone is telling me he's stealing my stuff." An early Pryor piece, a hushed dialogue between the human heart and the human brain, certainly had a similar aural quality to Cosby's, but Cos seemed to forget that he had been roundly criticized as a Dick Gregory knockoff just eighteen months earlier. It didn't take long for Pryor to shed the influence. When he worked as Nina Simone's opening act at the Troubadour in Los Angeles in 1965, a reviewer described him as "a quiet, intense young man [with a] strange delivery, using a pattern of milking softly to force his audience to strain to hear, then belting it out in a booming transition."

Stories started to circulate about Pryor's unpredictable behavior. Opening for Trini Lopez at Basin Street East, Pryor walked onstage and lay on the floor. He stared at the ceiling and did a twenty-minute set without acknowledging the crowd. Manny Roth, manager of the Café Wha in the Village, said Pryor sprung from the stage and stabbed a heckler with a fork. *The Ed Sullivan Show* liked Pryor's boyish style, but by 1966 was having trouble with him. "There was always a danger, a subtext," Pryor's former agent Craig Kellem told Richard Zoglin. "Is he gonna get mad? Is he gonna show up on time? The big question was, who was going to get Richard Pryor out of bed to go to dress rehearsal? Usually, you'd try to get the most naïve guy in the office to do it. Nobody else wanted to face his wrath."

Las Vegas called and paid him three thousand dollars a week, but Jim Crow had barely dissipated in the desert and he hated appeasing white tourists. "I was doing material that was not funny to me," said Pryor. "It was Mickey Mouse material that I couldn't stomach anymore. In Vegas, my audience was mostly white and I had to cater to their tastes. I did a lot of that in those days. I wanted to do more black material, but I had people around me telling me to wait until I had really made it. I knew I had to get away from people who thought like that."

Pryor opened for Pat "the Hip Hypnotist" Collins at the Aladdin Hotel. "I told neat little inoffensive chickenshit stories. I thought that because it was safe, it would also be commercial. I was wrong. Couldn't have been wronger. What I was doing was phony. I was turning into plastic." In rebellion Pryor used forbidden cusswords like "damn" and "shit." The hotel complained about his material and told him to remove his routine about the wino who knew God personally. For seventeen consecutive shows Pryor fought with himself. Legend has it that he finally walked up to the microphone, asked the crowd, "What the fuck am I doing here?" and walked off.

"Comedian Richard Pryor was fired Sunday night by the Aladdin Hotel because of alleged obscenities he directed toward the audience several times during his seventeen day stand," *Variety* reported. "Entertainment director Dick Kanellis dismissed Pryor after taping his show, during which time Pryor uttered obscene language following four previous warnings during engagement."

This is often pegged as the moment of Richard Pryor's transformation from carbon Cosby to comedic artist, but his collaborator, fellow stand-up Paul Mooney, said it was a few more years before the new Richard Pryor emerged. Mooney and Pryor frequented the Redd Foxx Club on La Cienega, and it was there Pryor shed the old influence and found a new one. "I dropped out for a while to take a look into myself," said Pryor. "And I kept watching Redd. He was the epitome. He was doing it all—being himself on stage, pulling no punches, a totally no-bullshit act. Wherever he worked, he was always Redd Foxx. If it wasn't for him, I'd still be working clean. He has got to be the greatest fucking corrupter of youth since Socrates. I tell you, before I worked Redd's club, I didn't know shit. But he taught me how to say shit and piss and fuck and motherfuck and all of them God-forbid words."

CHAPTER NINE

HIPPIE MADNESS AT DECADE'S END

The 1960s were the last decade organized crime dominated night-clubs. Corporate governance in Las Vegas—and aggressive federal governance elsewhere—chipped away at its omnipotence. The relationship between comedians and organized crime eroded in the 1970s. Some who'd been chummy with the Mob for a generation started to change their track when Friars Club members were scammed out of hundreds of thousands of dollars.

Mobsters Johnny Roselli and Jimmy Fratianno called the Friars Club of Beverly Hills home for several years. They shared cigars with Milton Berle, Tony Martin and Phil Silvers. Nobody thought anything of it. Show people had long accepted the presence of the Mob in their lives. When the West Coast Friars Club moved into a new building in the 1960s, construction was overseen by Las Vegas contacts, and Roselli and Fratianno hired electronic surveillance experts to do an additional job: An electronic eye was clandestinely installed in the ceiling of the new game room. It would expose the hand of every gambling-addicted Friars member for the next five years, nearly bankrupting Zeppo Marx, Phil Silvers and businessman Harry Karl in the process.

A series of complicated hand codes was developed between Roselli, Fratianno and their spy in the sky. It was several years of bad luck for the Friars, as the Mob won hand after hand. Eventually the winning streak made Friars with Vegas experience—like Silver Slipper operator T. Warner Richardson—rather suspicious. Richardson started asking questions of Roselli and Fratianno. In order to silence him, they cut him in on the scam. Meanwhile, Phil Silvers continued to lose thousands of dollars every time he played a round.

After five profitable years, the cover was blown. A mobster held by the FBI tipped them off in exchange for amnesty. Johnny Roselli, T. Warner Richardson, Benjamin Teitelbaum, Manuel Jacobs and Maurice H. Friedman were arrested. Roselli was found guilty on forty-nine felony accounts and sentenced to five years in prison. He phoned another Vegas contact—billionaire Howard Hughes—and asked him to pay his legal expenses. The members of the Friars Club were embarrassed. They had been played for fools. Phil Silvers said, "I was terribly shocked to find all this out. It's despicable. It's sickening. It'll take the club years to recover."

Attorney General Robert Kennedy attacked the Mob in the 1960s, picking up where Senator Kefauver left off. Nevada's laxity regarding organized crime was starting to embarrass state officials. *Life* magazine ran a Mafiosi series painting Las Vegas as the Mob's favorite playground, humiliating Governor Paul Laxalt. After years of turning a blind eye, the Nevada Gaming Commission was denying licenses to those with suspected Mob ties. The Mob was furious with Robert Kennedy. It had a long-standing relationship with Bobby's father, Joseph P. Kennedy. The elder Kennedy's fortune was based on his investments in the liquor business during Prohibition. His associates were frequently members of the Mob, and he always got along with them. So it came as a shock when Bobby attacked them. Sam Giancana asked, "What the fuck is wrong with that Kennedy brat? Can you believe that little bastard Kennedy is gonna go for the throat? It doesn't make sense. Are they fucking nuts?"

Robert Kennedy's brother-in-law, Rat Packer Peter Lawford, received much of the Mob's invective. "They scared the shit out of Peter," wrote Rat Pack expert Shawn Levy. "He cowered in the corner of a Copacabana dressing room when a couple of thick-necked guys in fedoras walked in on him and wanted to know why Bobby Kennedy was being so hard on their friends."

Billionaire Howard Hughes took advantage of the situation. Hughes sold his Trans World Airlines for an enormous sum at the end of 1966, but the dough was subject to the undistributed profits tax. Hughes needed a massive investment to skirt taxes. Las Vegas was the answer. His move was a tax dodge, but he painted himself as an anti-Mob savior and promised to "chase out the hoods."

U.S. district attorney George Franklin and Nevada governor Paul Laxalt saw Hughes as a possible solution to Mob rule, so they were peeved when the Department of Justice investigated the acquisitions to see if they violated antitrust laws. Hughes was going to take over the Stardust Hotel when the feds revoked his application. Franklin said, "I wish the anti-racketeering division and the anti-trust division of the Department of Justice would get together so that they can make up their minds what they want to do with Vegas."

Hughes moved to Vegas and took over the Desert Inn. "Howard Hughes had the top floor of the Desert Inn," says former Vegas booker George Schlatter. "They wanted that suite back. Howard Hughes got pissed off so he *bought* the hotel. Then he brought in businessman Robert Maheu from Utah. Maheu brought in the Mormon Mafia. Hughes brought in all the corporate guys and started running it like a business. It changed Las Vegas forever."

Hughes purchased the Desert Inn, the Frontier and the Sands in 1967. Corporate powerhouses followed his lead. The Fujiya Corporation bought the Flamingo, and other corporations swallowed Hollywood next. In 1967 Transamerica Corporation took over United Artists, Gulf Western took over Paramount and Seagram became the primary stockholder of MGM. Showbiz was corporatized.

The mobsters and their corporate successors had plenty in common. The corporate element could be every bit as ruthless as the Mob in its pursuit of profit. If criticized for unethical business practices, it had the same defense of "operating a legitimate business." Corporate Vegas worked less crudely than the Mob, but its goals were the same. As the salient novelist Raymond Chandler had observed, there was a "spiritual kinship between the operations of big money business and the rackets. Same faces, same expressions, same manners. Same way of dressing and same exaggerated leisure of movement."

Hughes invested $300 million in Las Vegas over the next four years. Acquisitions included the Landmark Hotel, the Silver Slipper, the Castaways, an airport and a television station. He bought Harold's Club in Reno and invested in electronic technology. "The Sands and other hotels that Hughes acquired were computerized," said columnist Earl Wilson. "Gamblers' junkets, which hauled well known players to Las Vegas free and gave them complimentary rooms, were discontinued or greatly reduced. A more careful watch was kept on the credit of the stars who gambled."

"Everything changed," says comedienne Rusty Warren. "The counting was computerized. The waitresses no longer made the same kinds of tips. They bought the hotels and then leased out the gambling to people who knew what they were doing." It wasn't subtle. "Hughes changed the whole character of the town," wrote columnist James Bacon. "Banks and insurance companies started investing in hotels. Back in the old days it was run by the Mafia and run quite efficiently. You could see the greatest entertainment in the world at low cost. Now that the town is run by businessmen, the prices are outrageous. Every department must show a profit. In the old days, the Mafia let the casino carry the whole operation."

As Vegas changed, so too did American supper club culture. Mob entities fell around the country and the new hippie movement rejected traditional tuxedo showbiz. Supper club floor shows were replaced with deejays playing records. New York's top supper club faded away. "The Copacabana was ready to close and I get a call from Jules Podell," says Shecky Greene. "Jules Podell *pleaded* with me. 'Shecky, I *need* you.' I never went back. It was finished." Tom Dreesen saw the same thing at Mister Kelly's in Chicago. "If you played Mister Kelly's, you had made the big time—but now it was on its last legs. One night they didn't have any salad in the kitchen. The chef had to chip in to go to the store and get some."

Comedians did not like the changes. "When I was working Vegas, the Mob ran Vegas," says comedian Lou Alexander. "The Mob was great to us and they would give us everything: the shows, the rooms, the meals—whatever you want. They really knew how to treat performers. Vegas in the 1960s was real fun. Now it's corporate."

The late 1960s showed an incredible divide between a generation of young, stoned kids and their horrified parents. The gap is demonstrated by some end-of-decade statistics. While psychedelic longhairs dominated musical trends in 1967, Lawrence Welk, the king of squares, sold $4.5 million worth of albums. Bob Hope was polarizing fans with his unwavering support of the Vietnam War, but five of the ten highest-rated television programs in 1969 were Bob Hope specials. The unrest played out among comedians on the late night talk shows.

The late night talk show spread beyond NBC for the first time in 1964. ABC wanted to challenge Johnny Carson's *Tonight Show* and made three attempts—*The Les Crane Show, The Joey Bishop Show* and *The Dick Cavett Show*.

Les Crane was hired as ABC's first late night talk show host in November 1964. He had done a radio program for KGO San Francisco, sometimes interviewing comedians from the floor of the hungry i. Lured to WABC in New York, Crane welcomed controversial opinion, and became the first radio host to take calls from irate listeners. ABC, feeling his calculated outrage could lure viewers from Carson, put him under contract.

The Les Crane Show purposely booked guests who were unwelcome elsewhere. It blazed a television first when Randy Wicker, an openly gay man, came on the program to talk about the gay lifestyle. "It was the first time that an LGBT spokesperson faced an audience," said Wicker. "That was in 1965. [We] took call-in questions. I remember a technician followed me out to the car and, with tears streaming down his face, told me how much he appreciated what I had done."

ABC inserted the word "controversial" in its show publicity, but the labored approach rang false. "Les Crane was a real nice-looking guy, but I didn't think his show worked," says comedian-turned-talk-show-host John Barbour. "There was just something artificial about what Les did. Les was sort of *manufacturing* an image."

The Les Crane Show was canceled after a mere four months. ABC regretted Crane's "failure to cut in on Johnny Carson's *Tonight* audience." He was fired, and the format changed: Network suits saw no sense in giving cultural dissenters a platform if it didn't get ratings. "I'm quite shocked," said Crane. "I'd been on the network for fourteen weeks, but I suppose ABC wasn't satisfied with the speed of our growth. I'm also sorry and disappointed that ABC wasn't more patient."

ABC renamed the program *Nightlife* and producer Nick Vanoff tested a rotation of new hosts—Pat Boone, Dave Garroway, Allan Sherman, Jack Carter and Shelley Berman. Nobody watched, so Les Crane returned. ABC added Nipsey Russell as his sidekick and gave Crane new gimmicks. "He had a microphone that was hidden in a rifle, and he would point it at people," says Marty Ingels, a regular guest on the show. "He'd press a button on the rifle and then they spoke." In the words of television critic Jack Gould, "Mr. Crane is something of a fascinating product of gimmickry." Each episode of *Nightlife* had a different theme—censorship, drugs, draft dodging—but again, compared with the freewheeling fun of Johnny Carson's *Tonight Show*, *Nightlife* was a serious drag. Crane was canceled again, and is barely a footnote in history.

Comedian Joey Bishop was the next competitor. He seemed like formidable competition, but when ABC gave the Rat Pack jester a late night talk show starting April 17, 1967, Carson was unconcerned. Many affiliates didn't even bother to air *The Joey Bishop Show* in its proper 11:30 time slot, running old horror movies in its place. Only after the Mummy and the Wolfman were done with their respective rampaging did Bishop appear.

The Joey Bishop Show was ninety minutes of innocuous talk with occasional themed episodes (one episode served as an infomercial for the Rowan & Martin movie *The Maltese Bippy*). But by virtue of its existing in the late 1960s, it could not avoid cultural unrest.

The Joey Bishop Show featured the type of controversies that *The Les Crane Show* tried to manufacture. "It was really touch and go, because there were a lot of political people around at that time," says the program's head writer, Slick Slavin. "We were the first ones to give Jesse Jackson a national forum. He told the A&P stores in Chicago they had twenty-four hours [until a boycott was implemented] and scared everyone to death."

There were other tense moments. Folk singers Delaney & Bonnie stormed off the show, claiming Bishop's people were censoring their songs. Tom Smothers appeared on an episode ranting about his CBS censorship battles. Marlon Brando came on waving a gun. "In the midst of his interview with Joey, he suddenly pulls out a gun and holds it to the side of Joey's head," said Slavin. "Brando doesn't say anything . . . The audience goes into a deep freeze and they stay there. He says, 'You see, Joey, how easy it would be for me to kill you. And that's because it's too easy for anyone to get a gun. Tonight, I'm asking everyone to turn in their guns.'" The same appearance had Brando criticizing the Oakland police force for assassinating Black Panther Fred Hampton. The police slapped him with a lawsuit.

The FCC's Section 315 caused further havoc for *The Joey Bishop Show* during the election year of 1968. Media scholar Erik Barnouw explained the statute, also known as the equal time provision: "If a station licensee let a legally qualified [political] candidate 'use' the station, other candidates for the same office had to be given 'equal opportunities' to use the station. This was assumed to mean that if one candidate got free time, rival candidates were entitled to free time; if one paid for time, the same rates and conditions had to apply to the rivals. Such programs made licensees uncertain about their obligations."

Richard Nixon was running for president and was interviewed on *The Joey Bishop Show* for thirty minutes. Democratic candidate Hubert Humphrey appeared the following week under the provision. But then other candidates demanded the same, and Bishop's program became a platform for Henning Blomen of the Socialist Labor Party, Fred Halstead of the Socialist Workers Party and the vice presidential candidates from those same organizations. By law *The Joey Bishop Show* had to comply, even as the host complained that Commies had overthrown his program.

Comedian Dick Gregory also ran for president in 1968. Gregory had become one of the most famous political activists in America, and he had a lot of clout in the progressive community. "Dick Gregory called me," says Paul Krassner. "He said, 'I'm going to run for president. Do you think Bob Dylan would be a good running mate?'" Dylan wasn't interested. Instead Gregory chose Mark Lane, a scholar on the JFK assassination. Gregory and Lane ran under the banner of the Peace and Freedom Party and made it onto a handful of state ballots. The only comedic gimmick Gregory employed was a mock dollar bill with his face in place of George Washington's. The U.S. Treasury quickly confiscated the play money, claiming it was a violation of federal law.

The Gregory-Lane ticket ran on an antiwar platform and received little news coverage in comparison to George Wallace of Alabama, who was also campaigning for the presidency. Gregory and Wallace were the antithesis of each other. Gregory spent the 1960s fighting for racial equality while Wallace fought to maintain segregation. The Peace and Freedom Party filed a $5 million lawsuit against ABC, CBS and NBC for denying Gregory airtime. Dick Gregory never appeared on *The Joey Bishop Show*. Governor Wallace did.

Gregory felt there was a conspiracy to silence him. The lengths his detractors would go were made clear in declassified FBI memoranda. J. Edgar Hoover authored a series of memos suggesting they "develop counter-intelligence measures to neutralize him [Gregory]. This should not be in the nature of an expose, since he already gets far too much publicity. Instead, sophisticated completely untraceable means of neutralizing Gregory should be developed." Gregory had made a comment in the press about the nefarious nature of organized crime. Hoover clipped the news item and wrote in his memo, "Consider the use of this statement in developing a counter-intelligence operation to alert La Cosa Nostra to Gregory's attack."

In the end Dick Gregory received a meager forty-seven thousand votes (writer Hunter S. Thompson cast one of them). Gregory survived all neutralization plots and his campaign symbolically challenged the two-party system. "We keep voting for the lesser of two evils, but the evil keeps getting worse and worse."

The Joey Bishop Show was canceled after three fairly successful seasons. Coffeehouse comic Dick Cavett was hosting a low-rated morning talk show on ABC when he was tapped as Bishop's replacement. "I learned about it while sitting in a London theater with the curtain about to rise," says Cavett. "An American woman slapped me on the shoulder from the row behind and said, 'Congratulations!' I said, 'For what?' She said, 'You're replacing Joey Bishop.' I thought the woman was drunk."

Cavett entered late night at the right time. The conflict in the country made for compelling late night drama, and today *The Dick Cavett Show* stands as a helluva time capsule. It had a loyal audience, but a brief run compared with Carson's.

Cavett was often portrayed as an intellectual, but Joan Rivers argued it was Carson who used smarts on the air. "I'm a very good friend of Dick Cavett. He's wonderful and he's brilliant, but Johnny Carson is brighter. Dick is very smart, but Dick talks to smart people. Dick has a much better program, but any one of us could talk to Orson Welles. Johnny talks to *morons*. That's tough."

Activists like Jane Fonda, Abbie Hoffman and Dave Meggyesy had a network platform on Cavett's show, to the consternation of the Nixon administration. Years later, when the Nixon Tapes were declassified, it was revealed that the president had asked White House aides Chuck Colson and H. R. Haldeman what could be done about *The Dick Cavett Show.*

> **President Nixon:** Is he just a left-winger? Is that the problem?
> **Haldeman:** I guess so.
> **President Nixon:** Is he Jewish?
> **Haldeman:** Don't know. Doesn't look it.

President Nixon: What the hell is Cavett?

Colson: Oh Christ, he's, God, he's . . .

President Nixon: He's terrible?

Colson: He's impossible. He loads every program.

President Nixon: Nothing you can do about it, is there?

Colson: We've complained bitterly about the Cavett shows.

President Nixon: Well, is there any way we can screw him? That's what I mean. There must be ways.

Haldeman: We've been trying to.

While the administration failed to get Cavett canceled, ABC did demote him. It went from a nightly program to one week per month, sharing the time slot with a rotation of late night specials. "ABC never figured out how to promote *The Dick Cavett Show*," wrote *TV Guide*. "Nor did they promote it enough; and too few—about 141 out of 175—of its affiliates carried the show. Of these, some 25 stations delayed telecasting it until the wee hours of the morning."

Antiwar sketch troupe The Committee appeared on an episode of *The Dick Cavett Show*, sharing the panel with Janis Joplin. In the years to come, the fingerprints of The Committee were found on *The Bob Newhart Show*, Cheech & Chong, *WKRP in Cincinnati* and the Steve Martin film *The Jerk*. It was a merging of traditional sketch comedy and the hippie underground.

Alan Myerson and Irene Riordan founded The Committee in San Francisco in 1963. They adopted the name as a salute to the reviled House Un-American Activities Committee. Featuring politically minded members of Second City, The Committee was aligned with the 1960s protest movement. Counterculture youth flocked to The Committee's San Francisco theater to see comedy that reinforced their point of view.

"The Committee had a political nature that was different from Second City," says troupe member Peter Bonerz. "Because it was in San Francisco, it reflected the changes in America culturally, musically, narcotically. Freedom of speech happened. All kinds of people were drawn to San Francisco. San Francisco had topless entertainment and jazz and it had The Committee. Columbia, the University of Wisconsin, Kent State, the Free Speech Movement of Berkeley, the antiwar protests—it was all inspired by what was happening in the Bay Area. There were all these Masonic ballrooms that had been collecting flies now opening every other week, and all of a sudden there's Bob Dylan onstage with the Grateful Dead, Joan Baez and the Jefferson Airplane. The Committee reflected that."

The Committee was embraced by the San Francisco counterculture. Poet Michael McClure was a big fan—although literary leader Kenneth Rexroth dismissed it as "charades in a Quaker work camp." Either way, it had people talking. "The Vietnam War was very much a part of our show," says Bonerz. "We wanted to reflect the divergence of opinions in the country. In our audience uniformed members of the military were sitting at nightclub tables next to hippies. Onstage we'd have a scene between a recently returned Vietnam vet and a hippie. It reflected what our audience *was*. And people would get up and scream and walk out. There would be fistfights, which was *exactly* what we wanted—bring it to the surface. We weren't just entertainers. If you came to our show—you were made aware."

Before Carl Gottlieb wrote the screenplays for *Jaws* and *The Jerk*, he was a member of the group. "The Committee was a huge hit," he says. "It was playing through the summer and they were drawing tourists, the Berkeley crowd, beatniks and hipsters." Larry Hankin, a future *Breaking Bad* actor, recruited Gottlieb. "Larry Hankin told me how great San Francisco and Los Angeles was. There were ten rock 'n' roll clubs on the Sunset Strip. The Byrds were playing at the Whisky a Go Go and there were clubs called It's Boss and The Trip. It was happening in Los Angeles. In San Francisco you had the Jefferson Airplane and Bill Graham's Fillmore Auditorium, and all this stuff happening at the same time."

As with The Premise and Second City, The Committee was very much influenced by Lenny Bruce in terms of language, subject matter and drug use. The Committee's first scripted show was to be the life story of Bruce, and the man had sanctioned it himself, before paranoia took over. He decided the hippies were trying to exploit him and threatened to sue if they went forward with the show. It did nothing to diminish their admiration. "We in The Committee all looked up to him tremendously," says Gottlieb. "He was influential in that he made it okay to riff onstage, to find material in performance, which is why improvisers related to him. Because Lenny was a junkie and some of the folks in The Committee were junkies, they would spend time together."

After its success in San Francisco, The Committee joined the influx of hippies crowding the Sunset Strip in Los Angeles. "We got the Tiffany Theater, which at that time was a three-hundred-fifty-seat movie theater," says Gottlieb. "We opened in 1968 to uniformly rave reviews. *Variety* and *The Hollywood Reporter* gave us raves. The *L.A. Examiner* and the *L.A. Herald* gave us a rave. *The Avatar* and the *Free Press*, the underground papers, gave us a rave. We were a success across the board, full houses and doing great business, so much so that the Hollywood establishment all came to the show." Among those in the audience were Tom Smothers, who loved them; Groucho Marx, who hated them; and Sandy Good of the Manson Family, who creeped them out. "Sandy Good had seen me perform with The Committee," says Paul Krassner. "When people used to ask Sandy Good about Charles Manson, she compared him to me. It was a bizarre compliment."

Tommy Chong was a big fan of The Committee. While still an unknown, he regularly checked out its shows. "I went down to Los Angeles and I caught The Committee's new show while I was there. They were even funnier and fresher than they were in San Francisco. They did a bit where the entire cast got down on their hands and knees and started acting like dogs, sniffing one another's butts. I thought it was hilarious. We came up with a variation for our next show . . . Even though we were using somebody else's material I didn't even think about it at the time." The sketch morphed into the ass-sniffing dogs Ralph and Herbie, one of the most famous Cheech & Chong routines.

*   *   *

Marijuana and LSD were huge influences on comedy at the end of the 1960s. It was not uncommon for talk show guests to show up high. George Carlin said he took "a perverse delight in knowing that I never did a television show without being stoned." Paul Krassner dropped acid before a *Tonight Show* appearance with guest host Orson Bean. Krassner was immersed in his trip when he walked through the curtain. "I kept staring at Ed McMahon because his face was melting into his chest. Orson asked me, 'Have you taken LSD?' He meant in a general sense, but I had this thought, 'Oh, no, he can *tell*!'"

Phyllis Diller encapsulated the older generation's ignorance of counterculture elements when a reporter asked her if she would remarry. She responded, "What kind of LSD have you been smoking?" Such cluelessness was common as Hollywood's gatekeepers struggled to relate to the new hippie demographic. Television shows like *Dragnet* and *My Three Sons* portrayed counterculture protestors as morons. Carl Reiner's son Rob was cast in several sitcoms playing such roles. "I did three *Gomer Pyle*s, played a hippie in a couple of them. Did a *Beverly Hillbillies*, played a hippie in *that*. I was like the resident Hollywood hippie at the time. I had long hair and they needed somebody. In one of the *Gomer Pyle* episodes I actually sang 'Blowin' in the Wind' with Gomer."

Veteran filmmaker Otto Preminger gave LSD the Hollywood treatment in 1968 with a motion picture called *Skidoo*. Preminger contacted Rob Reiner to help write dialogue for the hippie characters in his film. "Preminger was a very interesting, liberal guy and he took acid early on," says Carl Gottlieb. "He wanted to meet The Committee. So we all trooped down to his offices with Rob Reiner." Reiner said, "I went in and turned out some pages for hippies so that they would say 'groovy' in the right place."

Groucho Marx was cast in *Skidoo* as an LSD dealer named God. It was surprising he agreed to it, as he was contemptuous of the new social mores ("That *Midnight Cowboy*. It's about a stud and a pimp. I *hated* that movie"). Marx may have hated the counterculture, but he was hip to many of its elements. He subscribed to Paul Krassner's paper *The Realist*, which featured articles about the drug culture.

Krassner says, "Groucho was concerned about the script of *Skidoo* because it pretty much advocated LSD, which he had never tried but he was curious. Moreover, he felt a certain responsibility to his young audience not to steer them wrong, so could I possibly get him some pure stuff and would I care to accompany him on a trip."

Groucho Marx high on LSD? Some who knew Groucho question the story. "It's a fucking lie," says producer George Schlatter. "Groucho never took acid. He didn't *need* acid. Everyone *else* needed acid!" Carl Gottlieb agrees. "I doubt that story, because my contact with Groucho was around the same time. He was pretty infirm. The acid that was around in those days was the Owsley acid— Windowpane. It was brain-breaking."

"Well, that was the reason Groucho asked *me*," Krassner responds. "I have a letter from Lionel Olay, a popular magazine writer. He had interviewed Groucho and Groucho told him he was very curious about LSD. He read *The Realist* and about my taking trips. Bill Targ, my editor at Putnam, was a friend of Groucho. The writer of the movie *Skidoo*, Bill Cannon, introduced me to him. Groucho and I had lunch. He asked me if I could get him some LSD. Groucho was not going to go around boasting about this. It was just to prepare for the movie *Skidoo*. I accompanied him on his trip. We used the home of an actress in Beverly Hills. Phil Ochs drove me there. It was Owsley acid. Three hundred micrograms."

Skidoo entered production with a cast that seemed plucked from *Hollywood Squares*. It included Frankie Avalon, Carol Channing, Frank Gorshin, Peter Lawford, Cesar Romero, Mickey Rooney, Arnold Stang and Jackie Gleason. It had a sound track by Harry Nilsson and an unforgettable scene in which Gleason, high on psychedelics, is haunted by the disembodied head of Groucho Marx.

Robert Evans, the head of Paramount, was not happy with it. "It was a zero on every level," said Evans after the screening. "The guy [Preminger] cost us a fuckin' fortune. His new entry belongs in the sewer, not on the screen. He's such a prick; he gets his nuts off seeing us sink."

*   *   *

Several comedians considered their psychedelic trips important, life-changing experiences. "Pot fueled Cheech & Chong during our heyday," said Tommy Chong. "Pot and to some extent acid. It had changed our world and it put me on a path to artistic and financial success. The spiritual effects and the revelations never leave. The secrets that LSD revealed to me changed my life forever."

George Carlin felt the same. "I know exactly when I first did acid—it was in October 1969 while I was playing a major, now long-defunct jazz club in Chicago called Mister Kelly's. Next to my [note-book] record of that booking, which was otherwise uneventful, is written in a trembling hand the word 'acid.' Actually in the course of a two-week gig I did acid multiple times, maybe five, maybe ten. Fuck the drug war. Dropping acid was a profound turning point for me, a seminal experience. I make no apologies for it. More people should do acid."

Chris Rush was another comedian who came into being with the counterculture. Psychedelics informed his act. "When I took lysergic acid diethylamide I started rapping comedy: full, polished conceptual chunks. It just flowed through me, and I was a stream-of-consciousness comedian. I started doing it for fun in loft buildings and I started doing some clubs. This guy Mark Meyers from Atlantic Records came to see me. He said, 'This guy talks like George Carlin.' Bingo, I had a record deal." His album *First Rush* sold half a million copies in the early 1970s, mostly to pot-smoking college kids. "They'd get high with twenty of their friends and put the album on."

Comedy and the counterculture coupled with the new technology of FM radio. During the early 1960s FM radio was mostly used to simulcast aurally superior versions of AM sister stations. In 1967 the FCC passed an ordinance that ended such simulcasts. It forced FM to devise original programming. In order to fill mass spaces of airtime in a pinch, young disc jockeys turned to playing entire sides of LPs rather than just one song. Soon FM was a place where hippie rawkers and their long jams received maximum exposure. Likewise, comedians who aligned themselves with the counterculture found entire sides of their comedy records being played on FM. College-aged kids tuning in to hear their favorite hippie music were turned on to the comedians being played on the same stations—and those comics saw their ticket sales increase enormously.

Amid the FM scene emerged an audio comedy troupe called the Firesign Theatre. Phil Austin, David Ossman, Phil Proctor and Peter Bergman met at the newly minted Los Angeles FM station KPFK. They worked in various executive positions and eventually left for KRLA and improvised drug-influenced comedy on the show *Radio Free Oz*. Surf music producer and KRLA employee Gary Usher used his industry connections to secure the boys a deal with Columbia Records. "I'd see The Byrds at Columbia Studios when we were all recording," said Phil Proctor. "We didn't realize how much history we were observing or even making. There was very easy access. People were very friendly and the music brought everybody together. Pot brought everybody together. It was a very sociable scene, you know, hot and cold running girls all the time . . . We were using the Columbia studio where The Byrds recorded, [but] also the radio studio where Fred Allen had been."

The Firesign Theatre, George Carlin and Cheech & Chong owed their vast success to FM. The radio stations were listened to by thousands of impressionable college students. "FM radio helped expose the records, and that led to our ability to headline shows on college campuses," said Proctor. "We were asked to go on the road with the Maharishi."

Comedian Jimmie Walker says FM radio was a platform for comedians who never would have been accepted in traditional circles. "They would never have gotten on Carson or anything like that. Lou Adler from A&M Records came up with these guys from Vancouver—Cheech & Chong. There was a new thing called FM and Lou said, 'I'm going to make an album with these guys.' These guys started selling out colleges, and we were *stunned*. Nobody was doing that. FM changed *everything*. It changed the face of comedy."

Jack Margolis, a comedy writer who once wrote for Jay Ward cartoons, composed the seminal counterculture comedy record of the time. *A Child's Garden of Grass* was based on his satirical paperback of the same name, the first in-depth comedic look at the effects of marijuana. Released by Elektra, the same label that had Jim Morrison and the Doors, *A Child's Garden of Grass* had its advertising turned down by every major magazine, was denied a spot on the shelves of Wallichs Music City in Hollywood and was banned in Washington State. An FCC ruling that forbade "drug lyrics" kept program managers from playing it. Despite the kibosh, it sold four hundred thousand copies. Its only real advertising came from a large billboard on Sunset Boulevard across from the Whisky a Go Go. It is impossible to calculate the number of joints that were rolled on its gatefold surface.

The longhairs dominated radio. Cinema was maturing rapidly. Battles against censorship were being won on both literary and nightclub fronts. But television, beyond its odd spontaneous talk show moment, appeared unaffected by the times. "There was a real revolution happening in other media," said comedy writer Rosie Shuster. "There were all these Jack Nicholson movies coming out that reflected that sensibility of the sixties. In music there was Jimi Hendrix and Janis Joplin, the Stones and the Beatles. But television was still stuck in some time warp that was more like the fifties."

Comedians appearing on *The Tonight Show* still had to adhere to a traditional dress code. "For a long time the rule on Johnny Carson was tie and jacket," says Robert Klein. "I came on without one once and Johnny didn't say anything, but it came down through [*Tonight Show* producer] Freddy de Cordova: 'Tie and jacket!'"

The Smothers Brothers were tie-and-jacket men turned counterculture champions. Initially a common television sight with their baby faces and sharp haircuts, guesting on *The Jack Benny Program* and *The Jack Paar Show*, their impeccably timed act led to an insipid 1965 sitcom that was right in line with the *Mister Ed* genre. Tom Smothers played an angel who could only be seen by Dick Smothers, and the show embraced every cliché in the sitcom book. "It was just vacuous, silly shit," said Tom. "It went thirty-two shows and won all its time slots and whatever, but it put us off. I said, 'Man, if I ever had another show, I'm gonna have creative control. There's gotta be some substance.'"

The industry was certain the Smothers Brothers were harmless, that they deserved a piece of the showbiz pie. But after his sitcom experience Tom Smothers was ready to quit. In 1966 he was going through a divorce and suffering from a chronic ulcer. He was searching for something else, and the Summer of Love gave rise to new considerations.

The Smothers Brothers were booked at the Flamingo in Las Vegas when a CBS executive came backstage. He wanted the brothers to consider a variety show on his network. Tom was hesitant, but the money would be good and Dick needed to cover the cost of his growing race car collection. They signed on, and *The Smothers Brothers Comedy Hour* had three infamous seasons.

CBS assembled a coterie of *Jack Benny* veterans to shape the show. Assigned by the network as they were, Tom Smothers was suspicious of their motives. Marijuana influenced his thinking and fueled his skepticism of these older men. He respected the Jack Benny style, but didn't want to emulate it. Likewise, the writers didn't trust Tom, believing he was too inexperienced to make rational judgment calls.

Starting in 1967 an effective group of toilers wrote the program: Gene Farmer, Cecil Tuck, Ron Clark, Al Gordon, Hal Goldman and Sam Bobrick. Saul Illson and Ernie Chambers were producers. Illson says the legend of *The Smothers Brothers Comedy Hour* has been distorted, that the third season was not as controversial as some say—and that its early seasons weren't as tame. "They did a documentary on the Smothers, and for some reason they never mentioned myself or Ernie. When they did the documentary they talked about all the controversy, but they showed clips from *our* season. Even in those years Lyndon Johnson was just going crazy and we used to get letters from the Bible Belt saying, 'This show will not go unpunished by God.'"

Tom Smothers fought the network over every note, but according to Illson, Smothers never had the creative control he believed. "Tommy always went around and said the only reason he did the show was because he got creative control. It's not true. They had just come off a failed sitcom and CBS was not about to give Tommy Smothers creative control. They didn't even give that to Jackie Gleason."

The most subversive element of *The Smothers Brothers Comedy Hour* at that time was a deadpan comedian named Pat Paulsen. Paulsen was a stand-up comic who satirized folksingers. On the television series his persona was altered forever when he delivered editorials as a two-faced politician, a square doofus who took an ambiguous stand on every issue. His character was a cause célèbre for disenchanted voters. Paulsen ran a comedic campaign on the Straight Talking American Government Party (or STAG Party) ticket. "I want to be elected by the people, for the people and in spite of the people."

"Tommy told me he wanted to talk about things that were real in the world, but he wanted to do them seriously," says Illson. "Tommy wrote the first editorial, but it didn't belong on the show. I said, 'It's not funny. You're not a spokesperson. If we're going to do them, then do them with satire.' So we took the piece and gave it to the writers Hal Goldman and Al Gordon. They wrote the piece and shot it with Tommy. It still didn't work. So we said, 'Let Pat Paulsen take a crack at it.' And Pat was *hysterical* with the same piece of material. And that's how the Pat Paulsen editorials started on the show."

Paulsen spoke non sequitur wisdom in a monotone voice. A selection of lines from his many monologues during the run-up to the 1968 presidential election:

> *I will not run if nominated—and if elected I will not serve . . . I did not want this support. I have not desired it. As I have said, I would rather remain as I am today—a common, ordinary, simple savior of America's destiny . . . Issues have no place in politics. They only confuse matters . . . The current system is rigged so that only the majority can seize control . . . A good many people today feel the present draft laws are unjust. These people are called soldiers . . . What are the arguments against the draft? We hear it is unjust, immoral, discourages men from studying, ruins their careers and their lives. Picky, picky, picky . . . If you're old enough to be arrested, you're old enough to own a gun. Let's preserve our freedom to kill.*

Paulsen's campaign culminated with a clever television special, shot on film and narrated in all-American fashion by Henry

Fonda. Paulsen wanted to do more television appearances, but his comedy was plagued by FCC interference. His pseudo-presidential campaign was subject to the FCC equal time provision. He filed a complaint with AFTRA—the American Federation of Television and Radio Artists—which fought for the Paulsen side, calling the restriction "an obvious infringement on the right of an artist to pursue his art."

Paulsen never had another successful year like that of 1968. Despite the fame it brought him, he regretted the campaign in the years that followed. "The problem was that the 1968 election was so close that it took days before anyone could admit that Nixon actually won the thing," said the Bitter End's Paul Colby, who booked Paulsen. "Pat ran his campaign as a joke and actually wound up getting about one percent of the vote. Pat regretted it because he knew that those votes cast for him would have likely gone to [Democratic challenger] Hubert Humphrey."

The quiet subversion of the Paulsen segments spread to the general sketches during the program's third season in 1969. Tom Smothers hired a brand-new staff of untested writers for the program's summer replacement, starring Glen Campbell. The group included Steve Martin, Bob Einstein, Carl Gottlieb, Mason Williams, Lorenzo Music, Rob Reiner and Murray Roman. Steve Martin says the outgoing old men "were very nice. There was no real conflict. It was just kind of an undercurrent." Smothers says, "The guys were pretty young. There were a couple older guys, and the young guys thought they were CIA."

Bob Einstein was the son of Harry "Parkyakarkus" Einstein. Like his father, he started in advertising and entered show business as a sideline. In 1967 he made some amusing appearances on Bob Arbogast's regional Los Angeles talk show. Like his father, Einstein was a master of the deadpan put-on. He sat beside Arbogast posing as the man in charge of the Hollywood Walk of Fame, explaining his job in preposterous, convincing detail. Tom Smothers caught the segment and hired him. Einstein says, "We all started on Glen Campbell's *Summer Brothers Smothers Show* and then we moved en masse to the Smothers [program]."

Smothers liked hiring musicians for writing positions. He knew many of them from the Ice House in Pasadena and the Troubadour on Santa Monica Boulevard. New hires Hamilton Camp and Mason Williams were adept at playing folk songs. "The first thing we wanted to do was bring in people with fresh ideas and new approaches," said Smothers. "A musical background gives a person more freedom and depth than anything else. People in music are used to expressing themselves; they have more rhythm, better pacing. By the time we completed our staff, we only had two writers who weren't musicians."

Cy Howard was no musician. An unlikely straggler at *The Smothers Brothers Comedy Hour*, he was three times older than the rest. The former Martin & Lewis screenwriter just didn't fit in. "Cy Howard was one of the oldest people in the world," says Einstein. "Tommy went to his house to buy it. Cy said, 'I wrote *My Friend Irma*!' Tommy said, 'Do you want a job?'"

"Cy Howard was a concession to the network," says Carl Gottlieb. "The network was concerned that there were too many young writers and not enough old hands. I found him irritating, superfluous and nasty. Cy Howard would participate in the pitching with old radio jokes. When we'd pitch to the brothers and they rejected an idea, Cy would say to us in front of the Smothers, 'I told you it wouldn't work!'—when he hadn't told us anything of the sort. He was out of touch, but he tried to ingratiate himself by wearing a marijuana leaf belt buckle."

Smothers Brothers staff writer Murray Roman was a standup comic in love with Lenny Bruce and LSD. Initially he worked at MCA under his birth name, Murray Rosen, managing acts like the Righteous Brothers. He moved into stand-up after his agent's license was revoked. Television writer Ken Kolb was one of his clients, and said, "The D.A. came and got him. After he served time in Chino [prison], he became a nightclub comic. He [was] the prison librarian. He made a fairly decent living selling the key to the library restroom to various guys who wanted a place to meet their lover! The locked restroom in the library became Murray's whorehouse! When he went to jail he swindled all thirteen of his clients, for various sums."

By 1959 Roman was a free man and started playing San Francisco clubs like the hungry i. In the mid-1960s Elaine May was directing him at The Premise in a one-man show called *The Third Ear* and he was recording a comedy record that sounded almost like a Lenny Bruce impression. Comedy writer Marshall Brickman called Murray Roman "like Lenny Bruce without the genius." He was the primary counterculture figure in the hallways at CBS Television City, providing his coworkers with sativa and psilocybin.

"Murray turned the Smothers Brothers on to acid and was their dope guru," says Gottlieb. Bob Einstein says, "He was absolutely wild-looking with the hair and yellow glasses and the way he dressed. He was a *yidlock* from New York, but he lived as Lenny Bruce." His psychedelic comedy record, *You Can't Beat People Up and Have Them Say I Love You*, featured routines about police brutality and smoking banana peels. Psychedelic reverb echoed at the end of every punch line. "He was in the right place at the right time," says Gottlieb. "His performances are recorded, so you get a flavor of what the *trend* was in comedy. He found Lenny, idolized him and channeled him. He got a record deal and he worked as a writer with Steve Martin."

Martin says, "He wasn't really a writer. He was *very* patterned after Lenny. He just sort of stood up in the room and spoke. His ideas came from just being spontaneous, which kind of irritated us writers. He was always cheering for the right side and going against the establishment. He was a sweet guy at heart."

On a 1968 episode of *The Les Crane Show*, there was an on-air fight between Roman and television comedian Marty Ingels. Ingels said Roman's comedy LP was filthy and Roman yelled, "You will do anything to make yourself a star. I *haven't*. I was offered fifty thousand dollars if I would cut out two words and I refused because I felt they were social context. I had a chaplain say, 'Kill a gook for God, boys.' That was social comment."

The third season of *The Smothers Brothers Comedy Hour* was greeted with skepticism from the network. "The head of West Coast CBS sent a letter to Tommy Smothers after he saw the first show," says Einstein. "[He] blasted Tommy for hiring young kids who didn't know what the hell they were doing and he should be ashamed, all this stuff. And then the reviews came out and the ratings came out and he wrote a great letter back calling himself an asshole."

Enjoying the power of a hit television show, Tom Smothers became a mogul in the hippie scene. He oversaw a mini-empire that managed and bankrolled other artists. He, Ken Fritz and Ken Kragen founded a company that represented musicians Mason Williams, Kenny Rogers and the Hammond Organ–playing Detroit Tiger pitcher Denny McLain. They bankrolled the West Coast production of *Hair*, made a documentary called *My Brother, The Racer* about Dick Smothers' obsession with fast cars and invested in a primitive tech company called Computer Image. Tommy had a hand in everything, even introducing Otis Redding at the Monterey Pop Festival while high on acid. Smothers, now a counterculture tycoon, sat in the CBS office that once belonged to Danny Thomas. Where Thomas once sat gloating, beaming, smoking a big fat cigar, there was now Tommy—gloating, beaming, smoking a big fat joint.

The Smothers Brothers Comedy Hour was renewed for a fourth season in March 1969. So it came as a shock when just weeks after that announcement, it was canceled. Reasons for the cancellation vary depending on whom you ask. "It was *my* fault," said Tommy Smothers. "I was a head; I smoked, I was a weed dude. I'd come on and try to be so cool."

Gottlieb says, "In a strategy to avoid network censorship, Tommy would delay the delivery of the Sunday show tape until the last possible minute. Even then the network would preview our show for the affiliates and they would make notes on what was objectionable. Even though they couldn't physically edit the tape anymore, the red states would instruct the transmitter engineer to dump the sound at questionable moments."

Comedian David Steinberg contended that his appearances on the program led to the cancellation. Steinberg delivered satirical sermons in a church setting, which upset some religious viewers. Gottlieb says there were other factors. "Steinberg likes to say that his monologues were pivotal in the cancellation. They *weren't*. It makes him appear more important than he was. Tommy chose to portray it as a political disagreement, but it was also that we were pushing the envelope of general taste—tit jokes and erection jokes. CBS was the 'Tiffany Network' at that time, the favorite network of the older people in the country. It was as much about general censorship as politics."

Smothers was angry, but he still had his production company. He sold a series to ABC called *Music Scene* that showcased the top pop acts on the *Billboard* charts. It featured comedy interstitials with Lily Tomlin, David Steinberg and members of The Committee. Gottlieb wrote for that program as well. "Our producer was partially deaf—a nice guy, but completely out of touch and old-fashioned. We had Janis Joplin and Crosby, Stills, Nash and Young on the show, but he'd be pushing for Nino Tempo and April Stevens. It started at 7:30 and ran till 8:15 in an attempt to break the channel-switching habit. [Committee founder] Alan Myerson wanted casting control and to rotate members of The Committee. The network said no and insisted on a fixed cast. Steinberg's manager at that time was very aggressive. She had disproportionate influence. Halfway through the season she convinced the network that David should be the focal point of the show. They pushed everyone else aside. They fired Lily Tomlin, but *kept* David Steinberg."

Lily Tomlin had a repertoire of characters she honed at the Upstairs at the Downstairs in the mid-1960s. Inspired by the classy stand-up of Jean Carroll and the records of Nichols & May, Tomlin was essentially an actress with a comic bent. She performed on programs like *The Garry Moore Show* and *The Merv Griffin Show* as a smarmy telephone operator, a barefoot tap dancer and a rubber-eating maniac on programs. Joan Rivers was one of her earliest champions. When *Music Scene* let Tomlin go, producer George Schlatter immediately hired her to do the characters on *Laugh-In*. Her telephone operator Ernestine—a direct descendant of a bit done by 1930s actress Helen Troy—was the breakout character. It wasn't long before Tomlin had a best-selling comedy record and a pair of award-winning specials.

Laugh-In, more than any other program of its period, was a starmaker. It featured fast sketches, go-go dancers in psychedelic body paint and the Joke Wall, in which cast members poked their heads through cardboard doors doing one-liners. It was an effective combination of old-fashioned burlesque methods and 1960s hippie aesthetics. George Schlatter ran with his "comedy vérité" invention, working closely with editor Carolyn Raskin to develop their jump-cut technique. Schlatter says, "She was fucking brilliant. Carolyn started with me as a script girl and did all of the editing on *Laugh-In*. Those bright, fast cuts—all of that was Carolyn. When you watch shows now, everything is a two-second shot and the camera is always moving. *Laugh-In* helped create that."

It altered the pace of television comedy. The comedy itself was not particularly influential, but the speed at which it was presented was. Furthermore, much of its cast and crew, from writer Lorne Michaels to actress Goldie Hawn, became important industry players. Hawn was an unknown with only one sitcom on her résumé when she was cast. When Schlatter aired outtakes of Hawn stumbling over her lines and giggling, it charmed America and she became a sensation.

Laugh-In landed on the cover of *Time*. It was merchandised in the form of trading cards, lunch boxes, a magazine, linens based on the backdrops and even an ill-fated restaurant chain. It became so popular that it spawned a succession of spin-offs: *Turn-On*—a fast-edit comedy with an accent on sexual content; *Letters to Laugh-In*—a daytime game show based on viewer mail; *Arnold's Closet Revue*—a sketch vehicle for cast member Arte Johnson; *Soul*—an all-Black version of *Laugh-In* featuring Redd Foxx, Lou Rawls, Slappy White and Gregory Hines; and *Burlesque Is Alive and Living in Beautiful Downtown Burbank*, starring Goldie Hawn—which the network refused to broadcast because it showed too much skin.

Its success spawned imitators. Manager Bernie Brillstein implemented the *Laugh-In* concept for the country and western comedy *Hee Haw*. "I'd found a list of the week's top ten shows on my desk and I'd been staring at it, waiting for inspiration to strike. *Green Acres, The Andy Griffith Show, The Beverly Hillbillies, Laugh-In* . . . Suddenly it hit me: How about a country *Laugh-In*? We'll have a cornfield instead of a joke wall. Obviously, I'd liberally helped myself to everything I could from *Laugh-In*."

Hee Haw replaced psychedelia with hayseeds, marijuana with moonshine, but 1960s influences were unavoidable. *Hee Haw* cast member Lulu Roman was busted for amphetamine, marijuana, LSD and "some unknown capsules." Sentenced to four years in prison, she brokered a deal that allowed her to appear on *Hee Haw*, provided she return to jail after each taping.

The changing tides of late 1960s America were well exemplified by George Carlin. He went from being a mainstream darling on laugh-tracked variety shows to comedy's spokesman for the hippie generation. LSD was partially responsible for Carlin's change of direction, but he also knew that with the counterculture influencing fashion, music and political discourse, it was a sound business decision to gear things toward the hippies. "It seemed to me at the time that he was *emulating* hippies—not *being* a hippie," says Carl Gottlieb. To a degree, Carlin's transformation was a marketing choice.

Carlin's seven appearances on *The Merv Griffin Show* in 1965 widened his audience. "*The Merv Griffin Show* was my big breakthrough," he said. "All that happened afterward flowed from that." In 1966 he opened for crooner Jack Jones in Las Vegas and did a sitcom pilot for Fred de Cordova called *Manley and the Mob*. He was cast as a regular on the Marlo Thomas sitcom *That Girl* and wrote for *The Kraft Summer Music Hall*, along with fellow staff writer Richard Pryor. Singer John Davidson hosted *The Kraft Summer Music Hall*, and it featured comedian Flip Wilson in his first major television appearance. While most comedians in 1966 chose marijuana or psychedelics as their drug of choice, Wilson was already deeply into cocaine. Backstage he shared his wares with Pryor and Carlin, long before either developed their habits. The summer replacement was inconsequential, but it got Carlin and Pryor into the Writers Guild. "John Davidson himself was bland as hell but easy to please," said Carlin. "Nothing seemed to upset him. One reason could've been, as he told me years later, that he'd fucked every girl on the show."

Carlin appeared on *The Hollywood Palace* in October 1966. He had to follow Adam West dressed as Batman and singing "Orange Colored Sky." It was the kind of gig Carlin was tired of. "I was in the depth of this kind of discontent. I'd open for the singer and I'd do these cute little things and I just knew I wasn't being true to myself. I was a victim of my own success."

A couple weeks later, at the Roostertail supper club in Detroit, RCA engineers recorded a weekend's worth of shows. The result was the 1967 release *Take-Offs and Put-Ons*, Carlin's first solo comedy record. "*Take-Offs and Put-Ons* came out and went gold," said Carlin. "It was nominated for a Grammy and lost by a squeaker to Bill Cosby." The record took Carlin to the next echelon. "I was playing the biggest nightclubs in the country."

Hollywood called in 1968. *With Six You Get Eggroll*, starring Doris Day and directed by Sid Caesar's former stooge Howard Morris, was Carlin's film debut. It was again at odds with his new psychedelic perspective. "From when I was a kid, I wanted to be Danny Kaye. It had to do with being in the movies and being funny. But underneath there's this pot-smoker. Psychedelics helped me to have confidence in instincts and to act on them. All of that came to fruition after *With Six You Get Eggroll*. I found out I can't do this shit. Man, they want you to change a little bit here, get out of Doris Day's light . . . Fuck all that!"

Carlin was an emergency replacement for Sarah Vaughan at Mister Kelly's in Chicago in November 1969. He did three shows high on LSD. *Variety* noticed something was different, but had no idea he was tripping: "He looked to be a trifle under the weather, which affected his normally first rate timing and delivery and as a result came across as somewhat uneasy. It is to his credit that despite these difficulties he provided the type of solid 45-minute act that had the auditors palming for more."

Coming down from his psychedelic experience, Carlin played Washington, D.C., where he entertained Vice President Spiro Agnew and other enemies. From there he went to the Copacabana, opening for pop star Oliver. Jules Podell objected to Carlin's reference to a bordello and fired him.

Such conflict became more common, as Carlin sabotaged his mainstream standing. "All of my friends had been working their way through the folk movement and were going into the hippie movement . . . They were saying what they were thinking about, what they saw wrong with the country. And here I was doing silly things for audiences of older people who were the parents of my friends and I realized what assholes they were. I had a few incidents in nightclubs where I provoked the audience or they provoked me and it became a scene."

He emerged in Las Vegas in September 1970 with his first beard. He was booked at the Frontier as the opening act for the Supremes, their first time without Diana Ross. He was held over when Al Martino came in as the headliner. "I don't say shit," Carlin told the conservative Martino fan base. "Down the street Buddy Hackett says shit, Redd Foxx says shit. I don't say shit. I smoke a little of it, but I don't say it." The Frontier fired him for "offensive and abusive language toward the audience."

On November 28, 1970, Carlin and Bette Midler were performing at the Playboy Club in Lake Geneva, Wisconsin, a venue attached to a bourgeois ski resort. Carlin made mention of the Vietnam War. "Of course, we're leaving Vietnam. We're leaving through Laos, Cambodia and Thailand. It's an overland route! Gotta remember why we're there in the first place." Carlin adopted a confused look as he tried to recall why America was in Vietnam. The audience grew restless during his second show "and management feared for his personal safety."

Carlin next played an outdoor festival with folkie Arlo Guthrie along Lake Michigan. He was arrested by a police officer who "couldn't believe [his] ears." With a cop waiting in the wings, Carlin's wife walked onstage and removed his jacket, which contained a vial of cocaine. When Carlin walked off he was busted for language, but escaped further charges. The grievance was later thrown out of court.

Carlin used forbidden words and was fired at the Oakton Manor in Wisconsin, the Club Copa in Ohio and the Lake Club in Illinois. America was changing, and defiant figures like Carlin were helping erode the old obscenity laws. Newspaper columnist Jack O'Brian was aghast. He wrote that Carlin "seems lost on the Lenny Bruce path to notoriety and ultimately obscurity ... To Carlin's fans who adored his TV and record performances ... it was a blow to discover he'd gone over to the anti-everything side ... George seems now an artistic dropout ... long pony-tail hairdo ... a totally unwashed, shambling, savagely apologetic aspect as if speaking straight from a hobo jungle."

Vice squads were overwhelmed as community standards changed. Topless bars were springing up in urban areas, banned books were being published, marijuana use was flaunted; feminists burned their bras, Black Panthers made demands and protestors occupied the Pentagon. George Carlin's transition from a clean-cut crowd-pleaser to an underground rebel rouser mirrored the transformation of America in the late 1960s.

As Carlin became comedy's hippie spokesman, Bob Hope turned into the spokesman for Richard Nixon's America. Just like Jack O'Brian, Hope used the phrase "anti-everythings" to describe those who objected to the Vietnam War or marched on behalf of equal rights for minorities. It was a big change for the Hope persona. For many years, a mass audience had enjoyed his movies and radio shows. His programs and films were usually top ten moneymakers. If there was a Hope dissenter it was usually a disgruntled employee, but by the late 1960s he was a controversial figure. He had a distinctive political point of view that made him a hero to some and a pariah to others. If Carlin exemplified the change in America, Hope exemplified those who resisted that change.

Sherwood Schwartz, creator of *Gilligan's Island* and *The Brady Bunch*, had his first gig writing jokes for Hope and considered him a progressive guy in the 1940s. "He didn't care if you were Chinese or black or Jewish, you wrote a good joke and he would love you." Hope worked extremely hard to earn his $25,000 per episode. His radio show broadcast thirty-nine episodes per season and for a long time there were two different broadcasts each week, one for the East

Coast and another for the West Coast, totaling an insane seventy-eight live broadcasts per season.

Hope was the first comedian to invest in *volume writing*. In the old days, it was unusual for a show to have more than three writers. "Hope really invented a new way of writing comedy," said Schwartz. "Jack Benny had two writers originally—then all of a sudden, Bob had seven or eight guys. At that time, nobody was doing that."

By the mid-1960s Hope was one of the wealthiest men in America and one of the largest private landowners in California. Radio star, television star, movie star—he'd achieved every possible show business goal. There was nothing left. And without ambition driving him, the quality of his comedy plummeted. He was still doing up to six television specials each year, but he was phoning it in.

John Barbour, a stand-up comic turned commentator, became disenchanted with his hero. Working as an on-air critic for NBC in Los Angeles, he objected to Hope's television work. "I saw a Bob Hope special and it was absolutely dreadful. I said, 'At sixty-five I have to retire because, like those who work in factories, it's compulsory. Well, they should have the same law for comedians—or ex-comedians—like Bob Hope.' The phone started to ring. His lawyer called, his agent called and then the general manager came over. 'John, you're going to have to talk to these people.' The phone rings and this voice says, 'Hey, pal! What I ever do to you?' It was Bob Hope. I said, 'You bored me, that's what. Mr. Hope, you were one of my favorites when you were in radio and movies, but you were just god-awful on your special, and shame on you.'"

Woody Allen was quick to credit Hope as a major influence, but had to clarify that he was referring to his early work. "There is a tendency to confuse his television work and his politics with the best of his stuff—and that's *wrong*. His politics, in my opinion, have been atrocious. His television shows—he just walks through them and reads off cards. But I found him [to have been] a very, very gifted comedian. There are films that he did, that if you watched with a full audience, you would find them quite hilarious."

But in the late 1960s his movies, just like his television work, were shoddy. Despite supporting comic talent like Phyllis Diller,

Peter Leeds and Jonathan Winters, Hope's later films played like bad sitcoms with anti-hippie jokes and generic situations. His focus was elsewhere. The majority of his time was no longer devoted to film or television. Hope channeled most of his energy into a formulaic but effective stand-up act done for American soldiers stationed around the world.

When Hope first started with military tours, his film studio wasn't thrilled. Paramount suspended him in 1944 for abandoning a movie to entertain troops instead. "The studio says they've suspended me," said Hope. "They've got it all backwards. I've suspended *them*."

He cultivated his all-American image during the Korean War and was hailed as a selfless patriot. By 1963 the persona was so entrenched that kidnappers planning to snatch his son changed their minds. "Hope is a good American and has done so much in entertaining troops," decided one of the culprits. They kidnapped Frank Sinatra Jr. instead.

Hope had not articulated a political position prior to Vietnam. He golfed with politicians of either party and was a friend as long as you were powerful. If he addressed politics it was on a superficial level, making fun of the president's golf game. He didn't take a stance for fear of alienating world leaders. John Lahr of *The New Yorker* wrote, "All clowns in the American theater have been conservative men. Outsiders who crave to be insiders. They can't risk being offensive because they might be pushed out in the cold again. [Bob Hope] may use political humor but basically he preaches acceptance, satisfaction with what is."

It was a lesson Dick Gregory and Mort Sahl did not care to heed—and it was no coincidence that their careers faded out. Hope lamented that Sahl and Gregory "go a little too deep and people resent it, so they aren't invited anymore." But Hope lost sight of this very advice and would suffer a similar fate. His opinions bolstered supporters of the Vietnam War, but alienated moderate fans. Vietnam was polarizing, and Hope could not comprehend the dissent. On the lecture circuit, he insisted antiwar protestors were "on some kind of dope" and consisted of "fringe groups that are trying to louse it up, backed by certain people, subversive forces."

Vice President Spiro Agnew chastised protestors at the end of 1968, elevating his crotchety persona. In an effort to improve Agnew's image, Hope assigned his writers to punch up his speeches. "We're reluctant dragons," said an anonymous Hope employee. "We hate writing for a repressive reactionary like Agnew, but when you work for Hope these days, that's part of the job."

Hope had never publicly endorsed a politician in the past, but now he endorsed the actions of Mayor Daley in Chicago after the riot at the 1968 Democratic National Convention and stood behind Ohio governor Jim Rhodes when he called Kent State protestors "the worst type of people that we harbor in America." Hope told *Life* magazine that he "looked into the Kent State thing very carefully and I believe—I know it for sure—that that wasn't just students there. And if they were students, they were led. They get hooked up with subversive forces . . . I do believe in a Communist conspiracy in this country. Don't you? . . . You see kids up on the Sunset Strip . . . smoking this stuff, and 75% or 80% of them have social disease, see?"

Hope played Vietnam every year from 1964 through 1972. The stage shows consisted of a long Hope monologue, dancing girls, a popular singer of the day, a guest comic or current TV star and an orchestra. The television specials put together from these tours aired on NBC every Christmas and dominated the Nielsens. The stamina of Hope and his crew was rather remarkable. In 1969 he played to soldiers stationed in Guam, Italy, Taiwan, Thailand, Turkey and Vietnam. The Black cast member of *Laugh-In*, Teresa Graves, joined his tour and sang "The Weight."

Ron Kovic, the dissenting soldier immortalized in *Born on the Fourth of July*, remembered, "When they filmed us, they tried to make us feel that we might be seen by our families back home— Hope exploited every soldier who ever fought in that war. As a kid I had seen Hope's Korea shows on TV, but as I sat there in 'Nam, the romance I had felt about them was gone. Our [positive] response to him came out of fear and loneliness." At one base Hope assured his audience, "President Nixon asked me to tell you he has a solid plan for ending the war." A contingent of skeptical troops booed him.

As the counterculture dominated discourse and more soldiers began to smoke weed, Hope amended his material. During his seventh tour of Vietnam he joked onstage, "I hear you are interested in gardening here. Growing your own grass. Before the show I saw a sergeant standing in a corner with a lampshade on his head waiting to be turned on. Where else can you spend eight years on grass and not get busted? Instead of taking grass away from the GIs they should give it to the negotiators in Paris."

As the monotony of the war continued, some bases rejected Hope for the first time. The chief of the Special Services said he wasn't able to book Hope in some spots because of strong resistance from the contingent of "*now* generation GIs." He said, "Older pros such as Bob Hope, Art Linkletter, George Jessel and others are unacceptable to the troops of the 18–25 group."

Many who supported the Vietnam War in the mid-1960s were now joining the growing chorus calling for withdrawal in the early 1970s. Hope, however, continued to insist that those opposed to the war were a "lunatic fringe that gets mixed up with outsiders and subversive forces. I can't believe that American kids would [protest], they'd have to be doped up, or they have to have companions that are anti-everything. Ladies and gentlemen, when you hear politicians running on a peace platform, suspect them! History will record that [America] not only saved South Vietnam but all of Southeast Asia, and saved us from having a big fight on our shores."

Old men like George Jessel were among Hope's only political allies in comedy. Jerry Lewis became an unlikely critic of the Vietnam War when his son Gary returned from the fighting. "He came back totally devoid of any feelings or emotions," said Jerry. "He just doesn't give a damn about anything anymore." Lewis considered moving his family to Switzerland so no more of his children could be drafted.

Jack Benny sponsored a luncheon for Richard Nixon at the Hillcrest Country Club in Los Angeles and grew close with Spiro Agnew. Benny referenced Vietnam only once: "I am neither a Democrat nor a Republican. I'm a registered Whig. President Fillmore, after all, kept us out of Vietnam."

Stan Freberg turned antiwar sentiment into a bit of comedic activism. The former CBS Radio comedian was hired to write three commercials endorsing the McGovern-Hatfield Amendment, which called for withdrawal from Vietnam. One featured an exchange between a toy seller and a customer:

> *[gunfire]*
> *"And over here we have the 1971 Vietnam War toy."*
> *"Is that the same war that's on TV every night?"*
> *"That's right."*
> *"What do you do with it?"*
> *"You just wind it down. Watch."*
> *[slower gunfire]*
> *"It's still going."*
> *"Oh yes, I didn't say it stopped, it just winds down."*
> *"But . . ." [gunfire]*
> *"Let's step into the next room where it's a little quieter."*
> *"The implication in the term 'winding down' . . . [gunfire] Say, I can still hear the battle noise from the war toy."*
> *"You'll get used to it, the further away you are from it, you know."*
> *"Isn't there any way to stop it?"*
> *"There is."*
> *[narration] The United States Senate is about to vote on the withdrawal of American troops from Vietnam by the end of 1971 so that an end to the fighting and the return of all prisoners is allowed to become a reality. Send a telegram now in support of the McGovern-Hatfield Amendment or call your senator and congressman in Washington.*

President Richard Nixon was a common target for comedians, and that was no surprise. What *was* surprising was that the reverse was also true—comedians were a common target of the president. Any disparaging remark made him defensive and he used the tools of the presidency to fight back. Groucho Marx gave an interview to an underground newspaper called *Flash* and said, "I think the only hope this country has is Nixon's assassination." The FBI reopened its Groucho file, still full of filings from the blacklist years, and branded him a national security risk.

Groucho was a cantankerous elder statesman, appearing regularly on late night talk shows complaining about the president. "Townspeople said to hide their daughters when they knew actors were coming to town [during vaudeville]. Today actors are invited to the White House! But I don't want to be invited there! Nixon! I hate that son of a bitch. I've hated him for more than thirty years."

David Steinberg said undercover Nixon agents targeted his stand-up gigs in the early 1970s. Steinberg was at the Plaza Hotel in New York when two FBI agents told him they had information about a death threat and were assigned to protect him. Steinberg claimed his shows were sabotaged for several months after the visit. Whenever he did political material, pro-Nixon hecklers catcalled. A few months later Steinberg saw those same concerned agents on television during the Watergate hearings. They were not FBI agents at all, but employees of the administration.

Woody Allen made a PBS television special called *Men of Crisis: The Harvey Wallinger Story* in 1971, a half-hour satire of Henry Kissinger. The mockumentary was a natural follow-up to Allen's directorial debut, *Take the Money and Run*. It opened with a Kissinger-esque character played by Allen, complaining on the phone: "I want you to get an injunction against *The Times*. Yes, it's a New York, Jewish, Communist, left-wing, homosexual newspaper. And that's just the sports section."

President Nixon already believed PBS was against him and had sent word through Clay Whitehead of the White House Office of Telecommunications Policy that criticism of the administration would result in funding cuts. PBS screened the Woody Allen special for its legal department, which found nothing objectionable. Still, station president Ethan Hitchcock wrote a memo: "Under no account must it be shown."

"It was not terribly incisive, but there was a big to-do over it at the time," said Allen. "They would only put it on if I edited out certain remarks. Of course, by that time they had painted me into a corner where I couldn't take *anything* out of it—it would look terrible in my biography years later! What could I do? I wouldn't give an inch and finally they just dropped it. The stuff that's in that thing was very mild."

Tom Smothers produced a low-budget motion picture in 1972 called *Another Nice Mess*. Directed by Bob Einstein, the film starred Rich Little as President Nixon and Herb Voland as Spiro Agnew, portraying them as if they were Laurel & Hardy. Steve Martin played a hippie protestor in one sequence—his film debut. Word about the production reached the White House. Watergate henchmen Chuck Colson and H. R. Haldeman warned White House counsel John Dean of the "derogatory film about the president being produced by the Smothers Brothers." Dean sent undercover men to "assess its potential impact."

An insider who was sympathetic to the antiwar movement contacted Smothers to let him know "a drug bust was being set up." Smothers was advised never to travel alone. He mailed a letter to the attorney general of California outlining his suspicion that he was being framed. Smothers was in an editing session of *Another Nice Mess* in Los Angeles when his Bay Area home was raided and the furniture upended. Nothing was found.

Peter Lawford screened *Another Nice Mess* at a Democratic fund-raiser in Beverly Hills, Bob Einstein promoted it on *The Dick Cavett Show* and Rich Little plugged it on *The Tonight Show*, but the film was barely distributed. The Nixon administration had nothing to do with it. Tom Smothers buried it himself: "It was a terrible film."

Those considered underground or subversive would soon become the establishment—and there was no greater example of such an evolution than Lorne Michaels. Once a pot-smoking cokehead intent on destroying the old order, he became the most influential leader of the mainstream comedy establishment.

In 1965 Michaels was a University of Toronto graduate directing shows at the Bohemian Embassy, Canada's answer to Greenwich Village coffeehouses. It was a dark little room that hosted poetry readings and had one of the city's first espresso machines. Michaels directed a show starring Don Cullen, a character actor best known for his work with the comedy team Wayne & Shuster. It featured sketches about Cold War paranoia and the perils of cigarette smoking. Michaels wrote them under his birth name, Lorne Lipowitz, and staged the entire production. He was looking for a collaborator when he phoned his schoolmate Hart Pomerantz. "Lorne Lipowitz came to me when I had just graduated law," said Pomerantz. "He phoned me. 'Do you want to be in show business? I want to be in it fulltime.' I said, 'I have to be a lawyer—*and* be in show business.' The first thing I did [as a lawyer] was change his name to Lorne Michaels. He didn't like Lipowitz. In those days you had to go to court and give reasons to the judge [to prove] you weren't avoiding creditors. I went to the judge and said, 'Your honor, my client's name is Lipowitz and he wants to change it to Michaels and here are my reasons.' He said, 'I don't need any reason.' I said, 'Thank you, Judge Lipshitz.'"

They wrote sketches in their off-hours while Pomerantz practiced law and Michaels worked for Cinethon, an underground film festival that presented guests like Kenneth Anger and Shirley Clarke. In 1967 they made their first sale, to CBC Radio's *The Russ Thompson Show*, and were hired as regulars, doing phony man-in-the-street segments. Michaels played straight man to Pomerantz's different characters. Their routines were collected on an LP called *The Comedy of Hart and Lorne* and distributed to CBC Radio stations around the country.

"It was like *The Tonight Show*," said Michaels. "Done every day. Full orchestra. We were hired as the writers and performed once or twice a week. At a certain point, five or six months into it, the producer of the show met with us. He said, 'The show's not working. We're not sure if it's you guys or Russ. So, we thought we'd start with you guys.' We were let go."

They had garnered national exposure and made a comedy LP, but remained dead-broke amateurs. Phyllis Diller was known to accept solicitations of freelance jokes, so they devised some gags, shoved them in an envelope and sent them to her manager. Diller was in the process of prepping a new series called *The Beautiful*

Phyllis Diller Show. The producer was Saul Turteltaub: "When we were staffing the show, Phyllis gave us a pile of jokes different writers had sent her. We went through them and there was one written by Michaels and Pomerantz. 'I was driving through the Catskill Mountains. I knew I was in a small town when I saw a sign that said, "Sam's Hospital . . . and Grill." ' We hired them on that joke alone."

The Beautiful Phyllis Diller Show was an attempt to re-create the runaway success of *Laugh-In*. Michaels and Pomerantz were brought to Hollywood, and Michaels felt at home immediately. Future *SNL* contributor Tom Schiller said, "My father, Bob Schiller, was working on this show called *The Beautiful Phyllis Diller Show*. He said there was a junior writer on the show that he'd love me to meet. I said, 'Why?' And he said, 'Well, he knows all of the best restaurants in L.A.' So one day Lorne comes over. Lorne lit up a joint right there in the house."

The Beautiful Phyllis Diller Show lasted thirteen episodes, but Michaels made an impression. Backstage he chatted up Bernie Brillstein, who was managing one of the show's cast members, Norm Crosby. Their chat led to Brillstein's taking on Michaels as a client, and he managed his career for the next thirty-five years. Brillstein immediately got Michaels and Pomerantz their next job—a position as staff writers on *Laugh-In*.

Michaels was thrilled, but the thrill didn't last. "It wasn't at all the romantic idea of what I thought being in show business would be," he said. "The writers would write and then it would be edited by a head writer. We wouldn't go to the read-through, we were at a motel in Burbank. On one level it was the greatest credit you could have. It did wonders for self-image and career—but it wasn't fun." Still, it was a lucky break. An episode Michaels worked on was nominated for an Emmy. *Laugh-In* writers lost the Emmy to Steve Martin and the scribes from *The Smothers Brothers Comedy Hour*, but nonetheless, the nomination opened every door for Michaels.

The new Hollywood credits of Michaels and Pomerantz made them a commodity at the very network that had fired them. In 1968 the Canadian government implemented an official "broadcasting policy." It required, by law, that a high percentage of television programming be Canadian in origin. Suddenly there was a great need for seasoned professionals who could create original content in Toronto.

Variety said Canadian comedy was "a field which the Canadian Broadcasting Corp. has allowed to shipwreck and sag to abysmal depths," so the CBC began courting Canadians working in Hollywood. In order to lure them back from the glorious sunshine to the unbearable cold, Canadians in Hollywood were offered unprecedented creative control at the CBC. "I got a call from the head of the CBC asking what it would take," said Michaels. The boys were handed a series of comedy specials that they would write, produce and star in.

Their initial contract was for a quartet of hour-long specials during the 1969–1970 season. Barry Cranston, a producer for Wayne & Shuster, and Bob Finkel, another Canadian lured back from Hollywood, produced. The four Friday night specials—*That's Canada for You*; *Today Makes Me Nervous*; *The Students Are Coming, the Students Are Coming*; and *I Am Curious (Maple)*—were very much inspired by Michaels' and Pomerantz's previous gig. One critic described the duo as "*Laugh-In* North" and the CBC placed them in the very time slot in which it had been airing *Laugh-In*. Finkel said there was no choice but to emulate the American program because "the influence of *Laugh-In* has created an impatient audience." All four specials were successful, and the CBC green-lit a Sunday night series, to air the following season, called *The Hart and Lorne Terrific Hour*.

Toronto was going through a hippie renaissance. Its Yorkville district was a Canadian version of San Francisco's Haight-Ashbury, with musicians Joni Mitchell and Neil Young regulars in the neighborhood. Michaels plucked musical guests from its scene. Lighthouse, Melanie, The Sugar Shoppe and blues legends Sonny Terry & Brownie McGhee broke up the sketch comedy. It was the same theory later adopted for *Saturday Night Live*. "We would shoot in front of an audience," said Michaels. "It was an ensemble with a musical guest; James Taylor was on one. Cat Stevens was on one. There was a real form then called comedy-variety, but mostly it was built in the editing room the way *Laugh-In* was." Pomerantz said, "*Hart and Lorne* was the matrix for *Saturday Night Live*. If you look at *The Hart and*

Lorne Terrific Hour, he [Michaels] used that as a model to sell himself to NBC."

Under the tutelage of CBC editor Ron Meraska, Michaels learned how to cut and paste. "I spent a huge chunk of my twenties in an editing room. We came out of the first show with sixteen hours' worth of tape. I met with the editor. I had no experience. I was still thinking *script*. I wasn't in any way thinking visually. He actually *saw* it. He said, 'I can teach your eye to see.' He *did*. I learned how things are put together and what to look for in composition. What I learned then about myself is that I am much more interested in the production than in the performing."

The Hart and Lorne Terrific Hour was the bridge between the *Laugh-In* quick-edit style and the *Saturday Night Live* template. The specials and subsequent series featured Michaels and Pomerantz as the stars, supported by a recurring cast that included Paul Bradley of the classic Canadian film *Goin' Down the Road*, actor Paul Soles of animated *Spider-Man* fame, and Canadian perennial Alan Thicke (whom Bob Finkel eventually fired). The program also featured the genesis of "Weekend Update" with a fake news segment called "The Lorne Report."

Even with the success of Michaels and Pomerantz, the CBC needed far more Canadian content to adhere to the government's broadcasting policy. When *The Hart and Lorne Terrific Hour* became a success, the CBC hired the twenty-five-year-old Michaels to train Canadian comedy writers. "We've been pleased by the great concern Hart and Lorne have shown in encouraging new talent," said a CBC spokesman. "We want to continue to develop this balance between new and more experienced artists and at the same time, we want to [be] constantly trying new ideas and styles. Hart and Lorne will be available as consultants for this purpose."

At the end of the season, CBC waffled about renewing *The Hart and Lorne Terrific Hour*. Brillstein called Michaels asking him to return to Los Angeles and write on a summer replacement show starring the comedy team of Jack Burns and Avery Schreiber. "It was thirteen shows in ten weeks," said Michaels. "I went to the head of the department at the CBC and I said, 'I have this other offer, but I will stay here [if you renew].'" The CBC hemmed and hawed, while Michaels waited and waited. The decision never came, and Michaels left Canada, a twenty-seven-year-old comedy veteran.

The Burns and Schreiber Comedy Hour paid Michaels five hundred dollars a week, but his ambitions made him restless in the writers room. After contributing a sketch for a Perry Como Christmas special, he received two new offers. "I brought him the first," said Brillstein. "A TV special with Mama Cass, Jackie Gleason and Art Carney for ten thousand dollars. The other [offer] was to write on Lily Tomlin's second comedy special for CBS, *Lily*, for thirty-five hundred dollars."

The hour-long *Lily* was a vast departure from typical variety television. Its themes were urban poverty and substance abuse. It was the kind of social relevance Lily Tomlin would become known for and the type of subversion that appealed to Michaels. However, when Michaels and Tomlin first started working together, there was conflict. Producer Irene Pinn said, "About ten days into Lorne working on the show Lily came into my office and said, 'I want you to fire him.' I said, 'Okay, but what's the problem?' She said, 'Well, as you know, he comes in late every day and then he talks to everybody so none of the writers are writing, they're all talking.'" Pinn summoned Michaels and gave him an ultimatum: Work harder or leave. Michaels sat with her for three hours, talking and charming, arguing that his role was to broaden the audience, to gently subvert without alienating. His confidence was astounding.

"When Lorne worked with me on my specials he would spend too much time editing and be too fanatical about everything," said Lily Tomlin. "[Cowriter] Jane Wagner would say, 'You're going too far and you're spending too much money and the show needs to be rougher.' Lorne and I would get into the editing room and get too perfectionist, you know. I must say I think some illegal substances had something to do with it." Cocaine was rampant. Its use only accelerated when Richard Pryor was hired as the guest star.

The cocaine-induced fanaticism had Michaels scouting America during the casting process. Michaels went to Bleecker Street, North Wells Street and Melrose Avenue. He saw Laraine Newman for the first time in Los Angeles at a theater founded by her sister and The

Committee's Gary Austin. "He had come to see me when we had just formed the Groundlings," said Newman. "They really were looking for men for the Lily Tomlin special, they didn't need any more women. But they ended up hiring me."

The fanaticism paid off. *Lily* was an enormous success. It boosted Tomlin to a new echelon, impressed those skeptical of Richard Pryor's professionalism and turned Michaels into a celebrity producer. "It got nominated for an Emmy and it was a pilot special for a series," said Michaels. "I coproduced with Jane Wagner and we spent forever on it. In the end it didn't get picked up. But Dick Ebersol, who was the newly appointed head of late night, had this idea of doing many pilots in late night. Using late night as a testing ground for prime time. I agreed to do one for Dick."

Ebersol green-lit the idea he felt had the most potential, a sketch comedy program with musical guests. "I was excited by it," said Michaels. "[NBC executive] Herb Schlosser, who had a very romantic notion of production in New York, thought it should be live. For me live meant 'no pilot.' Somewhere in the process of doing a pilot all your most conservative instincts come out. It's what you *think* will get you on the air. So the idea that I could do a show in which the audience would see it at the same time as a network was thrilling."

Michaels again scouted underground comedy shows for a cast. Meanwhile, in order to sustain himself financially, he accepted two other writing gigs. One was the special *Flip Wilson . . . Of Course* in October 1974. Michaels said, "I'd been offered four Flip Wilson shows, four specials, for a little over a hundred thousand dollars. I said I would do *one*. It wasn't a show I was terribly proud of." His final gig before *Saturday Night Live* was writing a John Davidson special. Davidson's polished personality appealed to middle America, along with his bland renditions of pop songs like "Little Green Apples." For a man with such a toothy smile, his television personality was completely toothless. It was the antithesis of what Michaels wanted to do. Completely distracted by his *SNL* dreams, Michaels phoned it in, and reviewers could tell. *Variety* observed, "Writing was zilch and originality absent." Michaels was focused on more important things—like changing the face of American variety television.

CHAPTER TEN

THE FIRST COMEDY CLUBS
AND THE 1970S

What constitutes the first comedy club is a matter of definition. The earliest comedy clubs took their cues from supper club culture, where comedians shared the bill with a singer and a band. In the 1950s Billy Gray's Band Box in Los Angeles presented shows top-heavy with comics, as many as five stand-ups on the same bill, but crooners and orchestras still shared the show. New York gets credit for the first comedy club, and two venues in particular, but they too had a format initially no different from the rest.

Pips opened in Brooklyn at 2005 Emmons Avenue in 1962. The Improvisation opened at 358 West 44th Street in Manhattan in 1963. The clubs were run by George Schultz and Budd Friedman, respectively, and showcased singers along with comedians. But as the concept of dressing formally for a show withered away, the comedian would soon supersede the crooner. The supper club format was that of your parents' generation. Pips and the Improvisation were for the new generation. The tastes of nightclub patrons changed in the 1960s. The singers were phased out and the first stars of the coming comedy club era emerged.

George Schultz had done stand-up under the stage name Georgie Starr in the 1940s and 1950s. He was unsuccessful, but his experience gave him an inherent bond with the struggling comedians at Pips. "George Schultz was this crazy comic that didn't make it," says Richard Lewis. "But he *really* knew what great comedy was. He hung out with Lenny and Rodney. They called him 'The Ear.' He walked me across the street and said, 'You *got it*. And you have to eat, shit, suck and fuck this career if you want to be a star.' Pips was important because of George Schultz."

Pips was the first paying gig for a generation of comedians in the early 1970s. "It was a tough, hard room, but for many of us it was the first room," says comedian Paul Provenza. "A lot of people cut their teeth there, and it had a lot to do with the New York style of comedy that emerged. The place was pretty rough and it was a very tough neighborhood. By the time I got there George had let his sons, Seth and Marty, take over. Seth was kind of a cool guy, but Marty was fucking nuts. He would pull out a gun and point it at the comedians onstage."

David Brenner was an early Pips product. He was one of the first comedians to regularly start his jokes with "Did you ever notice," informing the style of the many observational comedians to come. Brenner rode a wave of success in 1970 and became the first of the comedy club generation to emerge a star because of Johnny Carson's *Tonight Show*. Flush with cash, Brenner sent money back to Pips and paid for its renovations.

Budd Friedman's Improv was initially a folk music venue in 1963. Friedman credits a forgotten comedian named Dave Astor for turning it into a comedy venue. "He was well respected by other comedians. They would all come to see him at the Blue Angel and he'd bring them over to the Improv."

Robert Klein remembers his first time at Friedman's joint. "The atmosphere was amazing. I did it and this guy came up to me, 'Hey, I tell ya! You were fucking brilliant—and I am a tough cocksucker!' I didn't know who this guy was and whether or not I should call the police. It was Rodney Dangerfield." What Brenner was to Pips, Klein was to the Improv: a new star who put the joint on the map. He had an observational perspective not unlike Brenner's and a free-form style not unlike Lenny Bruce's—a bridge between the two. An entire generation of comedians who came later, Jerry Seinfeld among them, cited Klein as their primary influence. His Grammy-nominated LP *Child of the 50's* was transcribed word for word by future comedian Bill Maher so he could study the anatomy of a stand-up act. Jay Leno said Klein was the first comedian he could relate to. "Robert Klein came along. Here was a guy [with] the same kind of upbringing. Here was a guy that was kind of talking to me."

By 1969 it was clear that the Improv and Pips had succeeded with a comedian-centric mandate, and the country's third comedy club was opened at 1118 1st Avenue by Rodney Dangerfield. "Rodney was getting hot, but he wasn't by any means a superstar," says Robert Klein. "It cost him $220,000 to open the club. He borrowed money from the Franklin National Bank, from an aunt and from me. I had eleven thousand dollars in the bank and I lent him five. He paid me back in a year, but he had to borrow it back one more time because they did so well that they owed money in taxes."

In Los Angeles most of the supper clubs were gone or at least seriously frayed by 1969. The cultural revolution eroded the tuxedo class, and hippies dictated the new showbiz. If you wanted old-time show business, you went to Las Vegas, not Hollywood, and the former coffeehouses of Shelley Berman and Mort Sahl were no longer hip. The primary comedy venue on the Sunset Strip, the Crescendo, had been replaced with a psychedelic venue called The Trip. The places for a new comedian to play were limited.

The new comedians played the stages of the hippie country-rock scene. The Byrds, Kris Kristofferson, Gram Parsons and Neil Young headlined the stages where new comedians like Albert Brooks, Steve Martin and Cheech & Chong appeared. The venues included Ledbetter's in Westwood, the Ice House in Pasadena, PJ's on Crescent Heights and, most important, the Troubadour on Santa Monica Boulevard. "The Troubadour was part of that David Geffen scene," says comedian Franklyn Ajaye. "You'd find Steve Martin, Albert Brooks and Robert Klein there. Richard Pryor did an album there."

The new comedians performed on what was known as Hoot Night. "Hoot Night was when the regular acts were off," says Robert Klein. "Today they call it an open mic, but back then it was called Hootenanny Night because it was almost exclusively folk singers." Tim Thomerson entered the stand-up scene on a Hoot Night.

"There were not many comics back then—1970. The first time I saw Cheech & Chong was at Hoot Night and the first time I saw Steve Martin was at Hoot Night."

The comedy records of Lenny Bruce, Nichols & May and Tom Lehrer inspired Steve Martin. While his act ridiculed traditional showbiz, he idolized elder statesmen like Steve Allen, Jerry Lewis, Don Rickles and Jackie Vernon. Martin was a regular at the Ice House and Ledbetter's. Comic-musician Gary Mule Deer was playing the same venues. "Steve Martin and I met at Ledbetter's when John Denver was hosting under the name John Deutschendorf. It was half comedy and half music, Steve Martin to Gordon Lightfoot."

Steve Martin was writing for Sonny & Cher's television series, but questioning the reason. "It was a lot of fun for a while, but I started to feel that what I was writing was very far away from me. I thought, 'I'm wasting my life.'" Martin performed onstage as a bad magician with a cocky attitude. It often confused the crowds, and only his fellow television writers lent moral support. "We'd go to see him at the Troubadour and sometimes it would just be me and four other people in the audience," said Sonny & Cher writer Chris Bearde. "He'd ask me afterward, 'Do you think I should keep doing this?'"

Old comedians told Martin to quit being so weird. Once, as he sat beside veteran comedian Morey Amsterdam during an appearance on *The Steve Allen Show*, Amsterdam told him he would never succeed with an arrow through his head.

Albert Brooks had early appearances on *The Steve Allen Show*, and he too mocked showbiz clichés. Brooks had encountered old-school showbiz types through his father, Harry "Parkyakarkus" Einstein. He befriended the children of Joey Bishop and Carl Reiner and discovered his comic instincts while in high school. "At Beverly High, there was a parent-student talent show. Beverly High—a lot of the parents were famous. You had Tony Curtis, you had Carl Reiner, Rod Serling. I was the host of the evening—and I was this kid. I wrote jokes and made comments. One of the kids, for their talent portion, did those batons—you twirl them around and around—and I still remember, because it was an ad-lib. 'Wasn't she wonderful? Do you know, in practice, a 707 accidentally landed on the football field.' People roared." Larry Bishop said Brooks "had the rhythms of a professional comedian in place at the age of fifteen."

Rob Reiner and Albert Brooks were neighbors, and they bonded. Brooks left California to perform at assorted summer theaters around the country, and Reiner joined him for a show in Plymouth, Massachusetts. Brooks enrolled in the Carnegie Mellon School of Drama in Pennsylvania and did a number of plays. When he appeared in a revue called *Is There Anyone We Haven't Offended?* the local paper wrote, "Al Einstein is still not experienced enough for this strong competition, but shows an excellent flair for comedy."

Brooks returned to Los Angeles. He and Reiner moved in together and Brooks got a job helping radio personality Gary Owens, the announcer from *Laugh-In*. Owens says, "I *created* Albert Brooks. He worked for me at KMPC in Hollywood. Albert, working in the sports department, would come in and hand me scores for my radio show in the afternoon. On the bottom of the scores he would always have some little one-liner. At that time [the sponsor slogan] was 'With a name like Smucker's, it's got to be good.' So Albert writes down, 'Gary, how about this? "With a name like Smucker's, it *better* be good."'"

Owens got Brooks his first television shot, wherein Brooks played an inept ventriloquist. "This guy Bill Keene had a little talk show at noon and Gary Owens took over for a week," said Brooks. "He knew about this dummy bit I used to do, this ventriloquist thing, and I was on *Keene at Noon*. From that I got an agent and I got three Steve Allen shows in 1968. Almost nobody laughed, but Steve Allen laughed so hard and that was the laugh you needed. From that I was offered a spot as a regular on a Dean Martin [summer replacement] show." Producer Greg Garrison cut and pasted Brooks into four Dean Martin summer shows between 1969 and 1971. One episode also featured comedy team Hart Pomerantz and Lorne Michaels.

Unlike most of his contemporaries, Brooks went on television without ever having tried his material in a nightclub. He got his first stand-up experience only after Neil Diamond's manager saw him on TV. Brooks started working as Diamond's opening act and was soon headlining on his own. He created something new for every appearance. At the Bitter End in November 1971 he told the audience his act was three-dimensional and handed out polarized glasses for them to wear. At an honorary dinner for Carol Burnett he played ignorant and delivered a tribute to Carroll O'Connor. ABC-Paramount signed him to a recording contract and he released an innovative comedy LP with material written specifically for the audio medium. The debut record, *Comedy Minus One*, developed a cult following and the label booked him at the Troubadour to promote it. Brooks started his act from backstage, reading a tragic Dear John letter over the amplification system. A critic who saw his show that evening wrote, "His best moments suggest he will be one of the great comedians."

Brooks was a success in comedy from the start. He was totally confident as a teenager. He mastered television appearances immediately. It was only when he was firmly established that he experienced the anxiety typical of new comedians. It all came to the surface at the Boston jazz club run by Paul Vallon called Paul's Mall. Richard Zoglin wrote about it in his book *Comedy at the Edge*: "When Brooks showed up for the first night of his weeklong engagement, he found a surreal scene: the audience was filled with people in clown suits, part of a promotion for his opening act, singer Leo Sayer." Brooks told Zoglin, "I had to come out to that. It was like, wait a minute. I got shit on as an opening act, and now I'm a headliner. How did this happen? And I just sort of reached the end of my rope . . . the most painful hour I've ever endured in my life. I never, ever got nervous, and it was really unnatural. I had to catch up with all those emotions. And then it was like I was examining everything. Who are these people and where am I going and what am I doing? I hit a brick wall." He never did stand-up again.

Hoot Nights accommodated the new comedians in Los Angeles, but there was still a vacuum. At Fairfax and Beverly the nightclub known as Billy Gray's Band Box—where three out of five acts were comedians—closed in 1966. Notably, the last comedian to ever play the Band Box was Sammy Shore.

Sammy Shore opened the first actual Los Angeles comedy club on real estate that had hosted many comedians over the decades. From 1941 until 1957, 8433 Sunset Boulevard was home to Ciro's, an enormously successful supper club featuring major acts. It is said that its managers—*Hollywood Reporter* publisher Billy Wilkerson and his point man Herman Hover—made monthly payments to mobster Mickey Cohen to keep things running smoothly. There were famous anecdotes about the night when stripper Lili St. Cyr was raided by the vice squad and the evening actress Paulette Goddard fellated director Anatole Litvak right at his table. Comedians Jerry Lester, Joe E. Lewis, Larry Storch, Danny Thomas and the team of Martin & Lewis headlined Ciro's in its prime.

In 1957 Ciro's was severely damaged by a fire while opposing fire departments argued about whose jurisdiction it was. "Part of the building is on city property and part on county," said Wilkerson. "While the two outfits were trying to decide who had jurisdiction, Ciro's practically burned down." The expense was too great for Wilkerson to rebuild, and he owed money to his creditors. The property was foreclosed, sold at public auction to a bank and turned over to Frank Sennes, a former Vegas booker and local impresario.

Sennes reopened it as The New Ciro's and showcased the female singers he was sleeping with. The incarnation didn't last, and Sennes became landlord to an endless succession of losers over the next fifteen years. It reopened in 1961 as Le Crazy Horse, with dance contests and "European showgirl types." Next was The Bed-Room, advertised as "Hollywood's most intimate lounge," featuring an assortment of singers and hypnotists. By 1964 it was called Le Disc and bragging about its new casual dress policy in which male patrons were no longer required to wear neckties. It was renamed and remodeled as Lou Young's Living Room, but closed after only two months. Rockers like the Bobby Fuller Five arrived in 1965 under new club name It's Boss, which succeeded by admitting teenagers as young as fifteen. City authorities shut it down, claiming the underage policy resulted in delinquency on the Sunset Strip.

In 1967 the old name was resurrected and it reopened as Ciro's, booking Black acts exclusively, including Count Basie, Marvin Gaye, Otis Redding and—at 8433 Sunset for the first time—Richard Pryor. By 1968 it was known as Spectrum 2000 and featured "Gary Berwin's Mad Mod Parties." In 1970 it was renamed Ciro's Jr. by singer Duke Mitchell, former member of forgotten comedy team Mitchell & Petrillo. It was an exhausting turnover of business models, and everyone was sure the space was cursed.

In 1972 comedian Sammy Shore leased the lot, and a new phase of stand-up history began. Shore was a journeyman comic with limited success in the 1950s and 1960s. Longevity introduced him to every comedian in the business, and he had a lot of contacts. Shore wanted to exploit those contacts by opening his own venue, one loosely based on the Billy Gray's Band Box model. For once, he wanted to see a venue where the roster consisted of comedians—and *only* comedians.

"I was with Sammy Shore when he decided to open it," says comedian Jeremy Vernon. "He said, 'We oughta get a storefront and make it a club. You and me and [comedians] Jack DeLeon and Howie Storm can all work there, at our own club, and we can alternate. When one guy is doing the road, the other three will be there. We can get *producers* to come and see us.' I remember how I laughed when he said '*producers*.' Lou Alexander said, 'We'll call it . . . we'll call it—the House of Comedy!' I thought to myself, 'Jesus, this is corny, wow.'"

It was the genesis of an idea. Among those who needed to be seen by "producers" were future actor Craig T. Nelson, future screenwriter Rudy De Luca and future film director Barry Levinson. They would be the first to stand on the Comedy Store stage.

De Luca, Levinson and Nelson performed at the Ice House in Pasadena as the Three Bananas, doing a series of short, fast sketches. Penny Marshall caught their act and told them about *Lohman and Barkley*, a sketch program starring a pair of disc jockeys on the regional NBC affiliate. De Luca, Levinson and Nelson got the gig and wrote on the program long enough to amass a body of work they could submit elsewhere. It wasn't long before they were staff writers on *The Tim Conway Comedy Hour*.

De Luca, Levinson and Nelson were influenced by the recent success of *Monty Python's Flying Circus* and wanted to make the *Conway* show an American equivalent. "We read some of their material, and it was wonderful," says *Conway* producer Sam Bobrick. "They were writing outrageous sketches—Hitler giving a football team a pep talk, a sketch with mountain climbers trying to climb a floor." Levinson says, "We opened the season with the Christmas episode. If we got canceled too soon, we may never do a Christmas show, so we did it right up front." It was perhaps a little too weird. *The Tim Conway Comedy Hour* was canceled after thirteen episodes. Staff writer Ron Clark says, "It had an interesting following of college kids—but there weren't enough of them. It was a little ahead of its time."

De Luca started writing for nightclub comics. "I was writing for Sammy Shore's act in 1972. Sammy wanted to take over Ciro's. He said, 'Gee, I'd like to call this the Sammy Shore Room.' I said, 'Sammy, who the hell is going to *go* to the Sammy Shore Room? No one even knows who you are.'"

Shore would not be deterred. He knew that by having his own room he could work with impunity. Comedy had changed, but Shore had not. Shore was rarely booked in Los Angeles, and some of his contemporaries were surprised he worked at all. "Sammy didn't have the best *taste* in the business," says comedian Dick Curtis. "I'd say to club owners, 'Do you actually *like* what Sammy does?' They would shrug." With a room of his own it wouldn't matter: Shore could be the star.

De Luca and Shore joined forces, and they implemented the Budd Friedman model. "I said to Sammy, 'There's a place in New York called the Improv and there's no club in Los Angeles for comics. Let's make it an Improv type place.' And that's what we did." April 12, 1972, marked the opening on the Sunset Strip, and Shore told the press, none too humbly, "It is my gift to the industry."

Murray Langston remembers coming by the first week. "I went over with [comedian] Jackie Gayle. He was pissed because Sammy hogged the stage most of the night." Gary Mule Deer was also there. He'd just finished his stint at Ledbetter's as part of his new comedy team Mule Deer and Moondog and intended to leave for Colorado that evening. "We were driving down Sunset and we see this sign—'Comedy Store.' There were four guys at the door—Craig T. Nelson, Barry Levinson, Rudy De Luca and Sammy Shore. They had nine people in the audience and no acts. So we went in, performed and walked to the parking lot to drive back to Denver. Two of the nine people in the audience were John Byner and his manager, Harry Colomby. They came up to us: 'We're replacing Carol Burnett for the summer on CBS. Would you like to be regulars on *The John Byner Comedy Hour*?' Then we got all of these shows—David Frost's *Madhouse 90*, *The Burns and Schreiber Comedy Hour*—all of this stuff out of the Comedy Store." It was the first of many times an act would go from the Comedy Store to television success. It was blind luck, but Sammy Shore had delivered on his promise.

The Comedy Store quickly established a reputation for gimmicky prop acts. Comedians from New York stuck their noses up at what became the Comedy Store style. "When Sammy Shore opened the Comedy Store he wouldn't call on standard acts," says Jeremy Vernon. "He preferred to call on young amateur people who were goofy. There was a girl who came onstage holding a bunch of celery for no reason. Somebody else came on with a carrot in their ear. There was this guy Charles Fleischer who came on swinging a rubber tube around his head that made a noise like '*Whrrrr, whrrrr, whrrrr.*' Someone else came out with a toilet seat around their neck. Sammy Shore, by doing this, attracted a crowd that made it impossible for him to break in his material. So when Sammy wanted to break in material he had to go to The Horn [nightclub] in Santa Monica!"

The idea of a venue that booked only comedians took some getting used to. Dick Curtis was invited to check out the new club. "I went over and after I'd seen three comics he said, 'What do you think?' I said, 'Well, it's all wrong. You need to have variety, not a bunch of comics all in a row.'"

It was precisely this new format that started attracting a crowd, although De Luca and Shore failed to turn a profit. Their strength was not as businessmen, and they failed to take note of the missing receipts. "There was always a big audience," says De Luca. "But we didn't make money because the bartender and the waitress robbed us blind." They devised new business schemes, and in 1973 they incorporated Four Star International with Barry Levinson and comedy writer Pat McCormick. The plan was to produce TV shows using Comedy Store talent, but just as Four Star International formed, De Luca and Shore had a falling-out. "As the months progressed, Rudy and I had our differences about running a nightclub," said Shore. "There were nights when we were literally at each other's throats. He told me to 'take the club and shove it' and left."

Shore was accepting gigs in Las Vegas at the time, and with De Luca gone there was no one to run the club. The keys were briefly handed to actor Jack Knight, but the club lost more money than before. When Knight left to join the sitcom *Lotsa Luck*, Sammy Shore's wife, Mitzi, took control. She immediately implemented changes and turned it into a proper business.

The Shores broke up, and John Gregory Dunne's novel *Vegas* played a part in it. Dunne based a character on Sammy Shore, portraying him as a pathetic old comedian addicted to prostitutes. "When Mitzi read the book, our marriage was already in trouble," said Sammy. "*Vegas* clinched it. She cried for two days and I have never forgiven John Gregory Dunne."

They brokered a deal in August 1974. In lieu of alimony, Mitzi Shore got the Comedy Store. Profits were maximized and presentation emphasized. "With Sammy, any comic could walk in and do forty-five minutes," says comedian Tom Dreesen. "Mitzi streamlined it. Each comic got eighteen minutes and she'd put on four or five." Comedian Paul Mooney went so far as to call Sammy's absence "the best thing that ever happened to comedy in Los Angeles."

Sammy Shore felt all washed up. Staving off irrelevance was increasingly difficult for older comedians during this time. Some of the biggest comedy figures of the early 1960s—Dick Van Dyke, Andy Griffith, Jack Paar and Danny Thomas—attempted comebacks. But most pretended the social revolution of the late 1960s hadn't happened—and suffered because of it. Comedy was unkind to those who refused to adjust to a new generation.

Danny Thomas could have retired a wealthy man, but instead grew a pair of long sideburns and starred in a new sitcom called *Make Room for Granddaddy*. It was a relic of another era that resembled an advertisement for Mennen hair coloring. Sitcom director John Rich was there on the first day. "Gathering for our first reading of the script, I had taken my normal position at the head of the table, with Danny sitting immediately to my left. To my surprise, he was chewing tobacco as we read, and had brought along an empty coffee can to use as a cuspidor, sitting just a few inches from my left leg. Some ten or fifteen expectorations later I asked Danny if he would mind moving the coffee can a little further away. In response, he reached into his briefcase and pulled out a revolver. 'I keep this handy so I don't have to move anything.'"

Milton Berle spent the 1970s fighting age with plumes of cake makeup. According to his son William, every day he painted over his wrinkles like a crazed embalmer. "It was a strange sight to see unnatural shades of thick paint applied to a sagging, tired face. Various coats of thick makeup, blackish gray spray paint over bare skin and old hair alike, crusty wax pencil streaks in front of a faded and thin hairline, all sort of poured and arranged over a wrinkled, sagging head. He didn't look younger, just a painted version of the same elderly man. The sight up close was almost frightening."

Jack Paar came out of retirement for a new program called *Jack Paar Tonite* on January 8, 1973. It was one of four rotating shows under the catchall of *ABC's Wide World of Entertainment*. Other programs under the banner included *Good Night America*, with Geraldo Rivera; *ABC Comedy News*, featuring members of Second City; and a scaled-down version of *The Dick Cavett Show*. *Jack Paar Tonite* was ninety minutes of opposition to a post-Woodstock America. Reviewing the first episode, *Variety* wrote, "He [Paar] was ensconced in his world of the past, but should understand what worked in that era does not necessarily work today." During its brief run it gave comedians Freddie Prinze and Jimmie Walker their television debuts. Comedian Kelly Monteith also had one of his first shots on the program. "It was his heralded return to television, but it was like he had been in a coma and didn't realize everything had changed," says Monteith.

"I went up to the Paar offices in the Plaza Hotel and he said, 'I carry a gun, you know.' He showed me his gun. Jesus, what do you even say to that?"

Paar always had a streak of paranoia. In his 1962 paperback *My Saber Is Bent*, he wrote a chapter about a homosexual conspiracy: "There used to be a time when it looked like the Communists were taking over show business. Now it's fairies. Just as there used to be no such thing as one Communist in a play or movie, now there is no such thing as one fairy . . . Wherever there is one you will find others. I just wish they would leave show business alone."

Eleven years later he picked up the rant on *Jack Paar Tonite*, and the new gay rights movement addressed letters to *The New York Times* in protest: "One word that Paar himself seems addicted to is 'fairy.' We guess that those of us in the Gay movement he calls 'amateur fairies' will have to go on battling until 'professionals' like Paar are forced to shut their bigoted yaps."

ABC vice president Tom Mackin said Paar was incapable of adjusting to the new America and "up to his old campaigns against marijuana, long hair and other manifestations of the sixties. He and his TV guests still used such terms as 'fairies,' 'dykes' and 'fags.' As the ratings plummeted, Paar called me several times to ask me what I thought of this program or that. I sensed that he did not want advice." Paar quit the show voluntarily after six months, rather than wait for the inevitable cancellation. He said, "One of the reasons I left television was that I could not understand or appreciate the vogue for rock music and the dope culture which goes with this trash."

The dyed sideburns of Danny Thomas, the pancake makeup of Milton Berle and the impending irrelevance of comedy's giants culminated in the hollow orange hues of *The Dean Martin Celebrity Roast*. While it was fun to see an assemblage of comic celebrities in a perfectly kitschy time capsule, production values were so low it did a disservice to all involved. Greg Garrison produced the roasts, which aired in their *Dean Martin Show* time slots quickly and cheaply. When Don Rickles tore through the room the show sparkled, but more often than not it was a laugh-tracked marathon of inept delivery from the likes of Grizzly Adams, Spiro Agnew or Wilt Chamberlain. Dean

Martin biographer Nick Tosches wrote, "Guests often delivered their lines to empty chairs or pretended spontaneous laughter at words that had been uttered in another state. As many as a thousand cut-and-paste edits were done to give each show the illusion that everyone was together in the same place at the same time."

"Garrison would edit the show and put two straight lines in a row," says Tom Dreesen, one of the youngest comedians to appear on the show. Footage of Jimmie Walker laughing randomly was edited into several episodes. Walker says, "He would have me sit there and laugh different laughs. I'd see the show later. Someone would do a terrible joke and he'd edit me in doing a *huge* laugh. That was Garrison. He said, 'I don't think you're funny. The network thinks you're funny so I'm putting you on, but I don't give a shit.'" Kelly Monteith concurs: "There were no bones about it—he was the worst editor in the world. But Greg Garrison always said, 'I can count on two fingers the number of letters I get about *editing*.'"

The Dean Martin Celebrity Roast did not resemble the Friars Club roasts on which it was based. The actual Friars roasts were closed affairs and far more profane than anything television allowed. *Tonight Show* writer Pat McCormick was a regular roaster. The language he used defies those that claim the old timers never used a four-letter word to get a laugh. At a roast of Red Buttons he joked, "Many of the people on this dais are great lovers. Red Buttons is not. For a good reason. His cock is so small his wife doesn't know he's fucking her except when she shrinks her cunt with Preparation H. Red is a weird, weird man. He's not like other people. When's the last time you attached four little boys' cocks to a milking machine? How many of you have gotten blown from someone in an iron lung?" Even a traditional guy like Henny Youngman unleashed vicious language at the roasts: "Milton Berle couldn't be here tonight," said Youngman. "He's at the dentist having an impacted cunt removed from his throat."

A common topic at these profane roasts was Milton Berle's large cock. "It was the ideal subject," says elderly comedian Will Jordan. "Not the ones on TV, of course, but the *real* Friars roasts." It was common gossip that Berle had the biggest schlong in showbiz.

References to his dick became so common that Freddie Roman of the Friars Club quipped, "Milton Berle's penis has become more popular than the rest of him."

There are several variants of the most famous of the Berle genital jokes. It took place at the Luxor bathhouse in New York, where a gent yelled, "Hey, Berle, I hear you got a big one! I'm willing to bet cash money that mine is bigger than yours!" The punch line supposedly came from Berle's friend, who witnessed this aggravation: "Go ahead, Milton. Just take out enough to win."

"I wrote jokes for a lot of the Friars Club roasts," said comedy writer Alan Zweibel. "I learned early on that he was the guy with the big dick, one of the biggest in show business. So I started writing big-dick jokes about him for these Friars roasts." Zweibel approached Berle backstage at NBC. "For years I was writing jokes about your dick," he told him. "I wrote all these jokes about your cock and now I'm talking to you—I feel like there's some violation or something here." Berle said, "You mean you've never seen it? Would you like to?" Zweibel remembered, "He parts his bathrobe and he just takes out this—this anaconda. He lays it on the table and I'm looking into this thing. I'm looking into the head of Milton Berle's dick. It was like a pepperoni."

You'd never know it from *The Dean Martin Celebrity Roast*, but television comedy matured significantly at the start of the bellbottom decade. *All in the Family* loosened restrictions, bringing social comment into the sitcom world for the first time. Had it not succeeded, the floodgate might not have been opened. When initially pitched, *All in the Family* was considered too salacious to air. Two separate pilots were shelved at the end of the 1960s, but two years later executives felt the time was right. The sitcom that pitted the bigoted, conservative father Archie Bunker (Carroll O'Connor) against his liberal, hippie son-in-law Michael "Meathead" Stivic (Rob Reiner) initially polarized critics. *Variety* couldn't even agree with *itself*. Its daily edition called *All in the Family* "a one-joke show and a sick joke at that." But its weekend edition raved, "This is the best TV comedy since the original *Honeymooners*, the best casting since *Sgt. Bilko*'s squad. Relative to the rest of primetime TV, the show [has] shocking bite."

African American comedians were prevalent on television for the first time in the early 1970s. Flip Wilson became the first African American comedian to star in his own network variety program when *The Flip Wilson Show* premiered on NBC in September 1970. Nat King Cole and Sammy Davis Jr. had attempted their own variety programs several years earlier, but were quickly canceled when neither was able to find a sponsor. By 1970 Black activism was having an effect, and white corporations made an attempt to appease the voices of protest.

Flip Wilson was considered a "nonthreatening" personality for white America to consume. Much of *The Flip Wilson Show*'s comedy would have been right at home on Milton Berle's old *Texaco* program, with its broad sketches and Wilson often dressed in drag. Members of Wilson's writing staff included veterans of *I Love Lucy* and *The Jack Benny Program*, giving the show a conservative grounding. It was probably necessary, as Wilson's offstage cocaine habit made him unpredictable, and the same could be said of the two youngest members of his writing staff—Richard Pryor and George Carlin. Pryor admired Wilson, but hated that the show was defanged to ensure broad success. According to Flip Wilson biographer Kevin Cook, "Pryor dismissed his boss as a token, hooting with derision when Flip played celebrity golf tournaments."

The Flip Wilson Show made its star a wealthy man. Wilson and his manager, Monte Kay, invested some of that dough in their own record label, Little David. Their first two releases were comedy records, by Franklyn Ajaye and George Carlin. Kay's daughter said Wilson "loved to help people who he thought were outside the mainstream. That's why he named the company Little David. It was always the little guys' rights he wanted to fight for." It also helped offset the conservative route of the television show. Little David released two of the most influential comedy records ever recorded, *Class Clown* and *FM & AM*, both featuring stark language by George Carlin. "It's an opportunity for George to feel freer as an artist," said Wilson.

Just before joining the *Wilson* program, Richard Pryor had been stewing in Berkeley, California, studying Black culture and reconsidering his act. Collaborator Paul Mooney called him "the new Richard. Born in Berkeley, midwifed by Malcolm X and Marvin Gaye." A film crew captured Pryor's new style during a late night session at the Improv. Gone was the aping of Bill Cosby, replaced with a degree of honesty that made the audience uncomfortable. Pryor told the brutal story of servicing an adult pervert when he was a child and acted out traumatic memories of winos, drug addicts and neighborhood prostitutes. He channeled a variety of bleak, true-to-life characters, revealing subconscious fears and obsessions, entering realms not previously explored by a stand-up comedian.

Previously verboten subject matter was acceptable to a new generation of comedy fans. Likewise, attitudes toward drug use had drastically changed. When Redd Foxx guested on *The Flip Wilson Show*, he joined Pryor and Wilson as they hotboxed the greenroom and snorted lines. Such behavior was out in the open at the television networks and rumored to have even been written into production budgets. "No talking about those times would be complete without talking about grass and coke," said sitcom writer Treva Silverman. "Pretty much every comedy writer I knew at that time was always smoking dope—always, always, always. And we would get complaints, 'Listen, guys, smoke your dope, but it shouldn't be in the corridors when guests come in.' I remember hearing that somebody only hired their assistant if they could really roll up a joint."

Norman Lear, riding the success of *All in the Family*, hired Redd Foxx for his new sitcom *Sanford and Son*. The show proved successful enough that Foxx felt secure flaunting his habits, snorting cocaine at the weekly table read. Contemporaries joked about Foxx's vice the way others joked about Dean Martin's drinking. Comedian Stu Gilliam cracked, "Redd was born with a silver spoon in his nose." Drug use did not harm his popularity. His gruff character Fred Sanford was charming, disarming and lovable. Movie legend James Cagney said, "That Redd Foxx on *Sanford and Son*—he's amazing.

I love him." Elvis Presley was a fan and showered Foxx with thousands of dollars' worth of gold medallions and rings. Tommy Chong said Redd Foxx was "in my opinion, the greatest comic of all time. I believe Redd was the role model who everyone in the business has to try to follow."

Foxx's behavior was accepted because he was beloved. But Demond Wilson, who played his son on *Sanford and Son*, was repulsed, and together they were a volatile combination. "He [Wilson] was one of the most evil actors I have ever worked with," said director Alan Rafkin, adding "Both men carried guns . . . they would get stoned and start to play with their guns. I was scared someone was going to get killed."

Foxx used his television power to land jobs for elderly Chitlin' Circuit comedians who'd never quite made it. Former members of the Dooto Records roster like Dave Turner and Billy Allyn received their first television credits on *Sanford and Son* after years in the business. "He looked after his old friends," said *Sanford and Son* producer Saul Turteltaub. "He would come into the studio with some guy and say, 'Put him in the show, Turtle.' And we would put him in the show. There were a lot of guys from the old days . . . and they were all good."

Many of the Black comedians Foxx used—Skillet & Leroy, Reynaldo Rey, the memorable LaWanda Page—recorded for the 1970s comedy label Laff Records, a small Los Angeles outfit specializing in African American comedians. No other company cranked out as many comedy LPs during the 1970s. While much of its content was undeniably amateurish, it documented a subculture most comedy fans were unaware existed.

Its founder, Lou Drozen, ran a jewelry store in downtown Los Angeles and frequently dealt with vinyl record rack jobbers—hustlers who placed merchandise on racks near store counters, cheap items meant for impulse buys and sold on consignment. "This guy kept coming in and pestering me, trying to convince me to display his product," said Drozen. "Finally I set up a consignment deal just to get rid of him. But it turned out that those records could *sell*. So I figured, here was a way a guy could make some money." Drozen read the fine print and visited the vinyl headquarters. He negotiated a percentage deal and was furnished with overstock. So profitable was the venture, Drozen abandoned the jewelry trade altogether and became a full-time rack jobber. The items that sold best were the risqué comedy records of Belle Barth. Drozen decided to go a step further and started his own record label, with Barth as his first client.

Drozen's second act was the African American comedy team Skillet & Leroy, regulars at the York Club at Florence and Western. To Drozen's surprise, they far outsold Barth. He returned to the York Club and signed all the Black comics who played there, unveiling Laff's new "soul comedy policy."

Legendary rhythm and blues disc jockey Johnny Otis acted as a Drozen scout, suggesting comedians south of Adams Boulevard. Laff went on a signing frenzy. For most comics the terms were unfavorable, but no other record label would hire these raunchy acts geared to an African American demographic.

As the business grew, Lou Drozen recruited his son David to help out. Together they documented an immense underground circuit of African American comedians who would otherwise have been forgotten. They made a point of securing distribution in cities with large Black populations. Laff product flooded Chicago, Philadelphia, Oakland and the District of Columbia. Obscure comedians who played South Los Angeles—Chester Calhoun, Tina Dixon, Booty Green, Jimmy "The Funky Tramp" Lynch, Potts & Panzy, Sonny & Pepper, Baby Seal, Wild Man Steve—became obscure stars in obscure neighborhoods. It was a fascinating, parallel world of stand-up that never made it to television or radio.

The cover art of Laff Records was unforgettable. Comic book talk bubbles crowded the space above comedians posing in sexually suggestive manners. A record by ventriloquist Richard Stanfield showed his Afro-headed dummy with eyes closed in ecstasy, a woman going down on him.

One Laff comedian whose material superseded the cover art was Richard Pryor. *Craps (After Hours)* was Richard Pryor's second album and his first for Lou Drozen. Pryor's contract didn't have the best of terms, and it became a contentious issue when the 1971 LP sold a million copies. "When we signed Richard Pryor we gave him an advance of five thousand dollars," said David Drozen. "He had to have it or otherwise he was going to get killed. He said, 'If I don't get this I'm going to die.' He owed his drug people."

Pryor's career was experiencing a breakthrough, and Lou Drozen took the credit. "We believe our album was instrumental in Pryor's success. The album *Craps (After Hours)* helped show the world Pryor's comic genius. Since that time, we have released six albums featuring Richard Pryor and additional material is in the can, although Pryor is no longer signed to Laff."

Pryor sought an injunction in August 1975 to halt all sales of Laff albums derived from his recordings. The label was cashing in on its surplus of Pryor outtakes, hocking it as new material. By then Pryor was signed to Warner Bros., and he was angered when one of the Laff releases was nominated for a Grammy.

Perhaps there had been chicanery, but Laff had the upper hand: Pryor had signed off on the deal years earlier, when he was either too high or too desperate to consider the implications of the contract. "I still had a lot of Richard Pryor tape and continued to buy tape," said David Drozen. "While he was working road gigs club owners would record those performances and, with his permission, for extra money they gave him to buy white powder, they sold me those tapes." Drozen sometimes bought recordings from Pryor's drug dealer directly. "In the middle of the coffee table was a pile of cocaine and a gun. After we'd negotiate an amount we would leave for the bank with his gun in a paper bag. That's how many of those albums came to be. Every time Warner Bros. would release a movie or a Richard Pryor album, I would release one and market it on the heels of their release."

Drugs-for-records explained the Pryor problem, but not the other unauthorized Laff releases. In 1978 Laff released one of its albums by a white comedian—*A Day at the Races* by Shecky Greene. "I went to sue them," says Greene. "It wasn't authorized at all. He was a guy who, for years and years, stole money from the Black performers. He made millions and millions from Black artists. I didn't win anything with the lawsuit, but I got back a lot of the records that he had. He *still* sold it."

"Lou Drozen was a real hustler," says comedian Steve Rossi, who did a Laff pressing with African American comedian Slappy White. "He offered us three hundred dollars and they made a fortune because he never gave an honest shake."

In Laff's defense, the majority of its roster was nowhere near the level of a Richard Pryor or Shecky Greene and never would have been signed by any other label. Most of the comedians on Laff Records were grateful to have the chance.

Eventually the legal hassles took their toll and Laff fell into receivership. David and Lou Drozen got into a fight and ended up suing each other. Laff Records documented countless African American comedians, and to dip into the discography is to be transported into a parallel comedy netherworld that is otherwise lost. "I liked Lou a lot," said Richard Stanfield, the Laff Records ventriloquist act. "They knew how to sell records. They knew how to run radio ads across the country. They got my records moving. He might have screwed me, but . . . he ran a good company."

Johnny Carson moved his *Tonight Show* from New York to Burbank on May 1, 1972, and it created a West Coast comedy boom. Comedians in New York realized that if they wanted their big network television break, geography was going to be an important consideration. Everyone started moving to California. Murray Langston says, "If Johnny Carson hadn't decided to move his show to L.A., the Comedy Store would not have survived more than a couple months."

David Letterman was watching *The Tonight Show* from Indiana: "In those days, if you wanted to go to California and become a comic or get involved in comedy writing, performing, whatever, the blueprint was laid out in front of you every night on *The Tonight Show*. They would have brand-new comedians. 'That was Steve Landesberg. You can see Steve Landesberg every night of the week at the Comedy Store on Sunset Boulevard here in Hollywood.' Pretty soon you realized that was an instant connection: the Comedy Store."

Letterman was doing sketch comedy as part of an Indiana trio that included Joyce DeWitt, best known today as Janet from *Three's Company*. Their biggest gig was a local bank's Christmas party, and Letterman warmed up the crowd. It was his first stab at stand-up, and it went poorly. Letterman worked in regional radio and television, hosting late night movies and doing the weather. His quiet ambition was vindicated when Betty White and her game show hosting husband, Allen Ludden, came through Indianapolis. They were promoting their syndicated radio program, which was carried on Letterman's station. They found him witty and charming and suggested he move to Hollywood.

Letterman arrived in Los Angeles in a beat-up old truck. He went onstage at a North Hollywood bar managed by Murray Langston. "Langston had a little place in the Valley called the Showbiz," says comic Bill Kirchenbauer. "It was nowhere *near* show business. It was at the corner of Lankershim and Victory and it was just a little hole-in-the-wall. There was never much of a crowd." Langston remembers Letterman being good from the start. "He lived one block away on Oxnard and was so damn good onstage, with a natural sarcastic ability."

As soon as Letterman went onstage at the Comedy Store, he was considered unique. "Usually when a new guy came into the Comedy Store, the guys stood in the back and wouldn't pay attention," says Gary Mule Deer. "David went onstage in 1975. He had just been a weatherman and the first thing he said was something like, 'The management of WNAS would like to take this time to state they are diametrically opposed to the use of orphans as yardage markers at driving ranges.' Boy, did that get me. I went and sat in the front row."

Letterman had written six spec scripts in hopes of landing a sitcom job, but without a proper agent it was impossible to sell them. He decided stand-up was the best way to get attention. "I started working at the Comedy Store because it seemed like a more direct means of showing my work than printing up six truckloads of scripts and driving them all over town trying to get somebody to read them."

Letterman was a master at working crowds and much preferred the grind of hosting to a ten-minute set. "He never wanted to be the middle act or the headliner," says Mule Deer. "David always wanted to be the emcee." Comic Denny Johnston says, "We were amazed that he wanted to emcee all the time. We always wondered, 'Why would he want to do *that*?'"

He did the road, opening for singers like Lola Falana and Tony Orlando. The latter said Letterman was the worst opening act he ever had. Letterman admitted, "I can't tell jokes very well. A good joke is such a well-constructed piece of writing, and writing a joke is just not natural for me." Tom Dreesen says it was apparent Letterman had a different calling. "He didn't enjoy stand-up, but he had an energy about him when he went onstage. David Letterman was a broadcaster *being* a stand-up comedian. He was destined to be a talk show host. I went with him the first time he hosted *The Tonight Show*. He walked out and I said to myself, 'This guy is home.'"

Jay Leno memorized George Carlin's *Class Clown* in 1972 and did early gigs in Boston strip clubs reciting the material. He eventually developed original material, opened for Linda Ronstadt and earned experience working for the Massachusetts state government. "I used to do these psychiatric homes. This is not to make fun of psychiatric patients, but you'd go out there, 'Hi, everyone, how you doing?' And in the middle of your act there'd be a guy in the corner going, 'Yeeeeee! Aiyeeeee!' Orderlies would come in."

In 1975 Leno made his way to Los Angeles, hitchhiking from the airport to the Comedy Store. He embodied the 1970s with his wide collars and large glasses, smoking a pipe. He bought a car, parked it behind the Comedy Store and lived in it.

It was no longer irrational to think one could go from vagrancy to stardom. The Improv and Comedy Store showed it was possible. Jimmie Walker was a regular at the Improv in New York when Norman Lear brought him west at the end of 1973 to star in the sitcom *Good Times*. Just like Leno, Walker did his first stand-up sets reciting material from comedy records, like those of Clay Tyson, an opening act for James Brown. *Good Times* made Walker an enormous star, and his path made comedy club regulars determined to emulate it.

Freddie Prinze started at the Improv in New York and became one of the Comedy Store's biggest acts. "He was so good-looking and so charming that you could not help but like him," said Jimmie Walker. "He had enough chutzpah to get on stage and do forty-five minutes despite having almost no act." David Brenner helped Prinze with the little material he had. Comic Billy Braver says, "He was special. He was twenty years old but it was as if he were Milton Berle. He acted like a guy with forty years' experience." Robert Klein agrees. "Prinze was virtuosic as a stand-up. He had command. This kid was *really* advanced for his age."

James Komack cast Prinze in the sitcom *Chico and the Man*. Komack had been a minor coffeehouse comedian at the Blue Angel twenty years earlier. He was accused of co-opting *Chico and the Man* from Cheech & Chong. "The show *Chico and the Man* was from a bit Cheech and I did called 'The Old Man in the Park' and from our record bit called 'Pedro and the Man,'" said Tommy Chong. "James combined these two bits into his show. I talked to him after the show came out and he acknowledged he took our bits."

Prinze was the youngest comedy star of his generation. He felt a kinship with Lenny Bruce and looked up to Richard Pryor. "Freddie Prinze's success was so big and so quick," says Franklyn Ajaye. "The moneymaking potential was huge. He idolized Pryor. He started hanging with Richard, who is a great influence on comedy, but if you're a candidate for self-destructive behavior, he's the worst person to hang out with. Once Freddie started hanging out with him, it meant there was going to be a lot of cocaine."

Prinze dated Lenny Bruce's daughter and supposedly had sex on his grave. Robert Klein says Prinze sometimes used Bruce's material verbatim. "I was resentful that he was doing Lenny Bruce's material without representing it as such. He said, 'Oh, I have permission from his daughter.' Whatever."

Prinze had a fetish for guns. When he stayed with Jay Leno in Boston he shot a wall full of holes. Soon he would do the same thing to himself. Prinze was with comedian Alan Bursky and a bottle of Quaaludes. Prinze was playing Russian roulette when he shot himself in the head. The warning signs of destructive behavior had been there. "I don't know why Komack didn't just shut down the show," says Ajaye. "This was a *kid*. I always thought it was very sad. No one interceded."

David Letterman got what seemed like a big break in late 1977 when former Comedy Store manager Rudy De Luca wrote a television pilot with Christopher Guest. They created a satire of *60 Minutes* called *Peeping Times*. Mel Brooks appeared in one segment and the program was the first directing job for Barry Levinson. De Luca explains how Letterman got cast. "This agent called me up and said, 'Would you hire this guy David Letterman? He's going to be very big.' I said, 'Bullshit. They all say that.'"

The famous Letterman tooth gap was a network concern. Letterman was told he would have to go get dental surgery and have his teeth fixed before things could proceed. Letterman fought for himself and won a compromise to wear fake inserts. "Which was fine," said Letterman, "except that when I wore them, I couldn't speak."

The network played *Peeping Times* for a test audience, and Letterman didn't do well. Levinson was told he would have to replace Letterman if the project were to move ahead as a series. Levinson recalls, "It didn't go forward, and that was the end of it. We had him under contract for five thousand an episode if it turned into a series. He went on Johnny Carson a few months later and NBC signed him to a million-dollar holding deal. We had him for five thousand dollars, and they didn't even want him in the show!"

The Comedy Store was a nightly casting session. It was hard to turn on a variety show without spotting a Store regular. Tom Dreesen rattles off a list: "Johnny Carson, Merv Griffin, Mike Douglas, Dinah Shore, *Midnight Special, Don Kirshner's Rock Concert, Soul Train, American Bandstand.* Every night—*every night*—the talent coordinators for those shows were in the Comedy Store."

Robin Williams got his first television gig because of it. George Schlatter sat at Mitzi Shore's table while planning a 1978 summer replacement, a six-episode reboot of *Laugh-In*. Robin Williams had just completed an acting course with former *Sgt. Bilko* cast member Harvey Lembeck when Schlatter hired him. "Robin Williams hung the microphone over the audience and said, 'I'm fishin' for assholes.' I said we're doing this show and whenever you stop saying 'fuck' and 'asshole,' you've got the job."

Williams unnerved fellow comedians with his fast style. "We were all accustomed to doing it one way, in which you stood at a microphone and told your jokes," Letterman told Richard Zoglin. "And he not only didn't stand at a microphone; he didn't stand on the stage. He made us all feel pretty insecure."

Williams improvised so quickly that his manager, Buddy Morra, hired a court stenographer to transcribe each performance. Williams was immensely likable, even as he gained a reputation as a joke thief. Robert Klein says, "Robin was very nice and talented, but he had a tendency to absorb a lot of people's material—and then apologize." Comic Johnny Witherspoon says, "He would do people's material on television and take their best lines. When he'd come back to the Comedy Store they'd be waiting for him."

While George Schlatter asked Williams to drop the cusswords, a new television venture would allow comedians to keep their profanity intact. On New Year's Eve 1975, Home Box Office broadcast a Robert Klein concert in what was the very first HBO stand-up special. "A call came in from a guy named Harlan Kleiman," says Klein. "He was programming Home Box Office; nobody called it HBO. He said, 'We want you to do a comedy thing and you can say anything you want.' This was going to be *something*—but I had no idea how big, had no idea what it was."

Klein's special was used as a pilot of sorts to gauge response to the new idea. "The ballpark [of viewership] was somewhere between four and six hundred thousand subscribers," says Klein. "It was a fledgling thing that people weren't sure about. You must understand the restrictive television climate [at the time], censoring this and that and what you can and cannot say." The subsequent HBO specials were dubbed *On Location*. A press release said, "Home Box Office is spending some six hundred thousand dollars to produce twelve separate comedy shows." The new genre—the televised stand-up special—was news.

The follow-up special used an anthology format with multiple comedians. *On Location: Freddie Prinze and Friends* was the first program to utilize the template adopted by most stand-up shows in the 1980s: that of several comedians doing short sets, bridged by an emcee. Hosted by Prinze, the lineup included Elayne Boosler, Gary Mule Deer, Tim Thomerson and the first significant television exposure for Jay Leno. HBO spent 1976 taping several more hour specials and aired them along with *Freddie Prinze and Friends* in an all-night marathon on December 31, 1976. Most Comedy Store comedians did not possess an hour of material, and as a result the majority of the *On Location* specials starred veterans like Myron Cohen, Rodney Dangerfield, Mort Sahl and Henny Youngman. The two youngest comedians starring in *On Location* for the marathon were David Brenner and Steve Martin. Martin said that his special, taped at the Troubadour, made him as a stand-up.

David Steinberg hosted the next *On Location* anthology, in September 1977, a sequel to *Freddie Prinze and Friends* featuring Ed Bluestone, Andy Kaufman, Bobby Kelton, Bill Saluga and Robin Williams. HBO's Michael Fuchs approached Bernie Brillstein to get Steinberg for the project. "He walked into my office and asked me to give him the comedian David Steinberg for a half-hour comedy special," said Brillstein. "So I did, without telling him that I'd been having big trouble getting Steinberg a job and that he really needed the twenty grand. Fuchs seduced me with his passion. He painted a compelling picture of HBO's potential. Uncensored comedy would be a major part of the equation."

George Carlin did his first HBO special in September 1977. He had done a pair of comedy specials for ABC four years earlier. ABC hired him to do a late night talk show pilot in January 1973. Sitting behind a desk in a tie-dyed shirt, Carlin interviewed Shelley Winters and writer Jimmy Breslin. The network followed it up with a stand-up special in August 1973 called *The Real George Carlin* featuring performance footage from the Bitter End, Columbia University, the Montreal Forum and a club called Grant's Tomb.

Carlin's *On Location* was done at the University of Southern California. It had more bite than previous *On Location* specials, and it made HBO nervous. "People in the company were afraid of it," said Michael Fuchs. "We sort of muscled it on the air." It contained an on-screen warning: "We respect your decision about whether you want to see it. It contains language you hear every day on the street, though rarely on TV."

Comedy Store comedians dominated variety TV in the late 1970s. They made up the cast on *The Richard Pryor Show*, an unlikely program for network television. Three years earlier NBC had put the kibosh on a potential Pryor series, considering him too risky, but since then he'd become bankable box office. With dollar signs in its eyes, the network changed its mind. Initially NBC suggested Sid Caesar and Imogene Coca as Pryor's recurring players. Pryor and writing partner Paul Mooney dismissed that suggestion and instead hired Sandra Bernhard, Vic Dunlop, Jimmy Martinez, Tim Reid, Marsha Warfield, Johnny Witherspoon and Robin Williams, all from the Comedy Store.

The Richard Pryor Show debuted at 8 P.M. Tuesday, September 13, 1977, and lasted only four episodes. There was some daring material, pieces about censorship and references to cocaine, but according to Mooney its quick cancellation had nothing to do with content. Pryor pulled out of the series in protest when NBC announced it wanted its Tuesday 8 P.M. time slot to be family-friendly. "Richard freaks," said Mooney. "*The Richard Pryor Show* is over before it ever gets started."

The Gong Show was another program loaded with comedy club kids. David Letterman was an occasional panelist and unknown sketch comic Paul Reubens was a regular contestant. The campy talent contest made Murray Langston one of the hottest comedy stars of the era. "I needed some money," says Langston. "My club the Showbiz went out of business and I was broke. I didn't want my friends to see me on *The Gong Show*, but I needed the money and they paid you whether you won or lost. I came up with this idea of putting a bag over my head."

"The Unknown Comic," delivering one-liners in disguise, was an immediate success that he was not prepared for. "I created the Unknown Comic, but I had no act. I was offered a job in Las Vegas for five thousand a week. Since I had no act I hired a band, put bags over their heads and called them the Brown Baggers. I hired a line of dancers and called them the Baggettes, and that filled out the show." The Unknown Comic was a large draw for the next four years, but as with most gimmicks the novelty wore off. Regardless, Louis C.K. cites him as an influence. "The Unknown Comic, I loved him. I was addicted to watching that. At that point, sixth grade, I was like, 'I want to be a comedian.'"

While stand-up comedians made appearances on a number of programs and HBO's *On Location* broadcast hour-long specials, there had yet to be an actual stand-up series until *Norm Crosby's Comedy Shop* came along in 1978. It was created by Joe Siegman, who was also known for cheap programming like *Celebrity Bowling* and *Celebrity Tennis*. Over four seasons *Norm Crosby's Comedy Shop* syndicated comedy unknowns like Brad Garrett, Michael Keaton, Nathan Lane and Kevin Nealon. It had typical 1970s aesthetics: a glittering gold curtain, a rotating stage and comedians in bellbottom pants. Host Norm Crosby stood on a phony living room set and introduced the acts. He'd be interrupted near the end of the show by a knock on the door. "Oh, what's that? It's time for our mystery surprise guest!" With the turn of a doorknob a television actor materialized. "Why, it's Vic Tayback! Vic, what in the world are you doing here?" Tayback squinted at a cue card. "Well, Norm, I'm here to introduce a real funny young kid who has done some writing for my *Alice* show. Here he is—Garry Shand-a-ling!"

"I did *Norm Crosby's Comedy Shop* for a lot of years," says Crosby. "There were hundreds of comics on that show. They would come in the morning, do five minutes, and we would tape them all day long, one after another. Then we would tape the mystery guest one after another. Then the editing people would go at it and take four comics and a mystery guest, snip it and put the show together. That's why I always wore the same jacket."

Comic Bill Kirchenbauer says, "It was just a marathon taping, just a conveyor belt. They probably recorded twenty comedians a day, and Norm would tape his little wraparound." The show came to an end when producer Siegman violated FCC law. "The people that owned the show were bartering it, making deals that were not legitimate," says Crosby. "I had a friend who ran a television station in Las Vegas and he said, 'I want Norm Crosby's show.' They said, 'Well, if you want Norm Crosby's show, you have to take our cooking show and our fishing show and our javelin-throwing show and whatever.' You're not allowed to do that, and that's what they did. We were all ready to go five days a week, and then we lost it."

It was great exposure while it lasted. Syndicated programming could boost comedians' standing in smaller markets, generating interest when they came through town for a stand-up gig. Such was the case with a syndicated comedy–game show called *Make Me Laugh*, essentially an infomercial for the gimmicky acts of the Comedy Store. Civilians were placed on a chair and subjected to an in-your-face comedy routine. The contestant's goal was to keep a straight face. If you cracked a smile you lost and if you stayed firm you won a prize.

"*Make Me Laugh* did more for me than any of my *Tonight Show* appearances," says Franklyn Ajaye. "*Make Me Laugh* was on five straight nights, and those five nights had far more impact on my career than talk show performances. Talk shows were always spaced out, and even if you had a really good one, you didn't return for another three months. You couldn't build momentum the same way. *Make Me Laugh* made more people aware of me, and I was able to get better bookings." Bill Kirchenbauer agrees. "It was in many ways better than a *Tonight Show* because you did a week of them. When it aired in syndication around the country you were on five nights a week and got huge exposure. You'd go into towns where the show aired, places like Cleveland, and people loved you."

Make Me Laugh performer Roger Behr believes the show brought about the Comedy Boom of the following decade. "It was a great boost for a lot of comedians' careers. It was nationally syndicated and very popular. The next thing you know a comedy club would open where the show was airing. *Make Me Laugh* was the reason for the comedy club explosion around the country."

The initial impetus for new comedy clubs was the success of Budd Friedman and Mitzi Shore. Businessman Rick Newman purchased a defunct New York dance club called Fiddlesticks in 1972, and it became Manhattan's hottest comedy club, under the name Catch a Rising Star. "Catch was on the East Side and it was trendy," says comedian Tim Thomerson. "Rick Newman was a *really* good guy. You could hang out there more than the Improv, and physically they just looked like two different places." David Brenner walked into Catch a Rising Star hot off *The Tonight Show* and made it a happening.

In 1974 a second branch of the Comedy Store opened in the space of the now-defunct Ledbetter's while Jimmie Walker invested his money in Budd Friedman's new Los Angeles branch of the Improv. It made Budd Friedman and Mitzi Shore immediate rivals. They had similar business models. Their shows were a rotation of young, unpaid comics with the occasional paid name like Shelley Berman or Jackie Mason. Two different clubs in the heart of Hollywood forced stand-up comics to choose sides, and Walker was put in a difficult position. "When Budd opened the Improv here in Los Angeles, I was working the Comedy Store. I went to work at the Improv because Budd asked me to, and Mitzi went berserk. She said, 'If you keep going to the Improv, then you cannot work here.' I was already established at the Store. It was nothing personal against Budd, but Mitzi made it tough."

The emerging Comedy Boom was helped along by the publication of *The Last Laugh*, a 1975 book by journalist Phil Berger. It was the first book about the art form of stand-up and the only book on the subject for many years. It chronicled the struggles of Rodney Dangerfield and beatnik comic Lord Buckley, and illustrated the rise of Robert Klein and Lily Tomlin. It inspired a generation of funny people to try comedy, serving as a blueprint for those who didn't have a clue. "It was the crucial book of my generation," says comedian Wayne Federman. "It was like, 'Oh! There's a road map for this.'" Comic Scott Blakeman gifted copies to fellow comedians. "I bought a whole bunch of *The Last Laugh* by Phil Berger and gave them out. To this day I recommend it." Jerry Seinfeld said, "It was a book about stand-up, which I had never seen before. And it was a serious book. It just lit me up. I read that book and I was gone. I became a comedian that day."

The Comedy Store and the Improv demonstrated the business model. *The Last Laugh* demonstrated the artistic model. HBO discovered an existing audience. Syndicated stand-up programming created a new audience. Together they caused the Comedy Boom.

CHAPTER ELEVEN

THE STAND-UP COMEDY BOOM

On October 19, 1976, Budd Friedman's Hollywood Improv cele-
brated its anniversary with a marathon show. Rob Reiner, entering
his seventh season on *All in the Family*, was the celebrity emcee. He
took to the stage and said, "This is a good way for Budd Friedman
to capitalize on people for cheap talent for nothing. Budd Friedman
has been able to exploit people on their way up to his own end."

Reiner was making a joke, but it was essentially true. The seats
were full at the Improv and the Comedy Store, but the performers
didn't get paid for their services. Tom Dreesen couldn't understand
why the wealth wasn't spread at the Comedy Store. "They paid the
waiters, they paid the waitresses, they paid the valet, they paid the
guy who cleaned toilets. They don't pay the comedians?"

Comedians knew they needed a united front in order to get paid.
The Comedy Store was targeted rather than the Improv, as it was
the most profitable. Meetings were hosted in the homes of Elayne
Boosler and Jimmie Walker, but it was tough to get the comedians
to engage in serious discussion. "Jay [Leno], bless his heart, couldn't
sit still," said David Letterman. "He was behaving like a hyperactive
child. Jumping up and down, being funny and distracting, to the point
where everybody sort of thought, well, maybe we shouldn't tell Jay
about the next meeting."

"Jay Leno was a loose cannon," says Dreesen. "I'd say, 'Jay,
Jay, Jay! Be quiet!' Gallagher was yelling, 'We'll burn the fucking
place down!' They were all in disarray. I began to take charge of the
meetings so they could get something done." Kelly Monteith says,

"It was hysterical—comedians at a union meeting. People were in the bathroom doing cocaine."

They drafted a proposal for the club to raise the cover charge one dollar and then split that amount among the comics. Mitzi Shore rejected the idea. She told Dreesen, "They don't deserve to be paid. This is a showcase. This is a college." Comedian Bill Kirchenbauer countered, "Tell me what college charges people to come in and watch students." The Comedy Store occasionally booked legends and they always got paid. Paul Mooney observed, "Shelley Berman works the main room and he draws half crowds, but he gets all the money from the door. Then Dave or Jay come in and pack the place and they get nothing? What kind of shit is that?"

Dreesen believes it was Shore's acrimony toward her ex-husband, Sammy, that kept her from paying comedians. "Mitzi had been married to a comedian that wanted to control her for years. Now she was controlling comedians. That's when I realized we're in deep shit now: The strike is going to last a long time." Fifty-nine comedians formed a picket line. The club closed until Shore assembled scab talent—Mike Binder, Argus Hamilton, Howie Mandel and Biff Maynard among them. Tensions heightened as comedians started crossing the picket line. "Eighteen guys and one girl crossed the picket line," says Dreesen. "If those kids had not crossed, that strike would have been over in twenty-four hours." After a couple of weeks Alan Bursky and Garry Shandling crossed.

It was a blow, but then David Letterman joined the picket line immediately after guest-hosting an episode of *The Tonight Show*. It gave the strike a new level of legitimacy. Media attention followed and everyone took a side. Bob Hope sent a letter of support. Buddy Hackett denounced it on television. Richard Pryor sent a letter of endorsement and David Brenner called it "the biggest joke to ever come out of the Comedy Store." George Carlin contributed money to the strike fund and Jackie Mason announced he would open his own club, operated by and for comics. Jerry Van Dyke, less famous brother of Dick, opened a restaurant in Encino and paid forty-eight striking comedians to perform. The Plaza Four restaurant in Century City quickly streamlined a comedy room to capitalize on the vacuum and Jamie Masada, a teenage dishwasher at the Comedy Store, got the idea to open a comedy club called The Laugh Factory.

Violence erupted around the Comedy Store. "Mitzi sent her thug punk comics to harass Elayne Boosler," says Dreesen. "They punched a gay comic in the face and gave him a black eye. A lot of ugly shit went down." Mitzi Shore met with her supporters. She was concerned that her contingent of star comics would abandon the Comedy Store and work the Improv. A picket-crossing comic said, "Well, what if there *was no* Improv?" A week later a Molotov cocktail hit the Improv's roof, and half the building burned to the ground.

On May 10, 1979, the two-month strike was resolved. After three days of negotiations with a federal mediator, a deal was hammered out. Comedians would be paid twenty-five dollars per show, with amateur nights exempted. Friedman put on a public front that he was noble compared with Mitzi Shore, but he held a quiet respect for Shore's methods and was just as reluctant to negotiate with comics. "I'm a little leery about the business now," he told the press. "Once the unions are involved they can kill everything. I have alternate plans. Maybe it's time for me to move on to something else." The National Association of Comedy Club Owners was formed to create a united front against collective bargaining with comics.

The Comedy Store reopened, but there was residual anger. It was an uncomfortable atmosphere for new stand-ups, and some say the Comedy Store has had bad vibes ever since. "Mitzi Shore was greedy, and I think it affected the quality of what goes on at the Comedy Store to this day," says Bill Kirchenbauer. "It's just greedy evil." Comedian Marc Maron spent his early career working the door at the Store. "It feeds on hate. You feel the walls wanting you to lose it." Jerry Seinfeld said the Comedy Store was "kind of a sick culture. Unless you were kind of a broken-wing bird, they had no interest in you. It wasn't a healthy environment. There's a darkness about the place."

Seinfeld was part of the New York scene in the late 1970s, emceeing at the Comic Strip, the final comedy club to open in New York that decade. Catch a Rising Star's nouveau chic made stand-up feel like rock 'n' roll. The Comic Strip felt suburban, as if your mom managed it. "Catch was the cool place," said Seinfeld. "The Comic Strip was lame."

Those who consider Jerry Seinfeld the epitome of clean comedy would probably find one account of his early act rather surprising. Comedian Paul Provenza remembers, "Jerry used the word 'fuck' so liberally in the early days. He would say, 'What's the *fucking* deal? What *the fuck* is up with that?' He used it all the time and then one day he just stopped. He said it was a challenge to stop using it." Cleaned up, his observational powers shone. Jackie Mason caught his act and told him, "You're gonna be so big it makes me sick."

Seinfeld's future collaborator was spending time at the original Improv. Larry David leaned on the bar and watched comedians like Richard Lewis bring down the house, thinking he could do the same.

David and Lewis had met years earlier, but didn't realize it. "Larry was born two weeks after me and we were in the same ward," says Lewis. "In 1961 I went to a sports camp in Upstate New York. Larry was at the same camp. He was the most obnoxious asshole. I really hated his guts. And he hated *my* guts. If we played baseball, I tried to bean him. I *despised* him. We got in fights. He was *so* obnoxious."

Camp ended and eleven years passed. Standing at the Improv bar, they befriended each other. "Larry lived a block from the Improv. I'd come to his place. He'd make halibut steak for us. He used to barter with a guy at the fish market on Ninth Avenue, and it was horrible to watch: 'How *dare* you charge me a dollar eight a pound for this fish! This fish looks demented!' One night at the bar I was a little drunk. We were already best friends. Inseparable. I was looking at him and said, 'There's something that's satanic about you, and I don't like it.' We traced our childhoods for some reason, and we got to the camp—and it hit us. 'You're *that* Richard Lewis!' 'You're *that* Larry David!' We almost came to blows."

Across the hall from David's bachelor pad was a pot smoker with big hair and a prominent mustache. His name was Kenny Kramer, and he was the basis for the Kramer character on *Seinfeld*.

Kenny Kramer did stand-up as a lark in the mid-1970s. One reviewer wrote, "Kenny Kraemer [*sic*], a gangling New Yorker who looks like he should be playing for the Knickerbockers, is a very funny rock comedian. Being a rock comedian means being selective about audiences and working on the bill with Lou Rawls doesn't guarantee all the right people for Kraemer. But he gets most of them, and given his material and delivery he should be a biggie on the rock concert scene, where young people won't have to discuss his lines to know they're funny." The premise of his closing bit was "What if Sly Stone was president of the United States?"

Larry David tried stand-up as a last resort. "I didn't know what I wanted to do," he said. "I had a series of jobs. Cab driver, paralegal, private chauffeur, stuff like that and I'm *lost*. I'm a lost soul. Parents beside themselves, I would overhear conversations that were heartbreaking, terrible. 'Oh, what are we going to do?' They sent me to a psychiatrist. Then, I don't know how or why I thought of this, I decided to take an acting class. This one time I had to speak in front of the class as myself and there were laughs. That was the moment for me. I knew somebody who was doing it [stand-up] and I had coffee with him. He said, 'Here's what you have to do. You have to write some material and you can go on here, you can go on here, you can go on there.' He gave me a list of places and I started."

He became a frequent sight at Catch a Rising Star, the Improv and a music venue called the Bottom Line. He did a bit about pickup lines, going to a bar and yelling, "My name is O'Banion—and I want a companion!" He rattled off a list of similarities between pancakes and Samoan people: "Round, flat, nice brown golden color, fit six to a plate. If you've ever been to the Polynesia Islands you see statues of Aunt Jemima everywhere." He had a routine about how he yearned to have plastic surgery so he could look like a famous star—Howdy Doody. Other subject matter included baldness, pornography and "Oriental yodeling."

Jerry Seinfeld said David was very fragile onstage and that any sign of disapproval could set him off. Comedian Kevin Nealon saw Larry David chase a heckler "right out into the street and slug it out with him." He was just as contemptuous of an audience that was *too* supportive. "One night he did his set and the audience was screaming and applauding," says comic Mike Rowe. "He was crossing into the bar and I said, 'Larry, they're still applauding!' He said, 'Yeah . . . but listen to *how* they're applauding.'"

"He would storm off the stage after only a *minute*," says Richard Lewis. "He would do that even if *The Tonight Show* people were there. He didn't care. He was a purist. If people were ordering, [he would yell] 'How dare you!'" The next comic always had to stand by, knowing that David could bail at any moment. "You'd hear *plunk-pluh-plunk-plunk-plunk*," says comedian Rick Overton. "That was him dropping the mic."

David did the occasional road gig, but remembers it as a nightmare. "Occasionally I would do some of those terrible Jersey clubs. *The Gong Show* was on at the time. So when people would come to comedy clubs they would *gong* you. They'd just yell it out, 'Gong!' I didn't quite have an act that was going to work on the road."

Despite the many stories, David killed quite often and became a cult favorite. In 1977 a makeshift organization called the Association of Comedy Artists named Richard Belzer the city's Best Emcee and awarded Larry David the title of Most Promising Comic.

Tom Dreesen was the opposite of Larry David, with a toothy smile and optimistic disposition. "I went to the Improv and watched Larry David. I said, 'You're very funny, I really enjoyed your set.' He just stared at me and walked away. Next night I went to Catch a Rising Star and he did another set, a different fifteen minutes. I said, 'God, you're really funny, I really enjoyed you again tonight!' He went, 'Uh-huh,' and walked by me. The next day I'm coming out of the Stage Delicatessen and I turn left and I walked into Larry David! I didn't know what to say. I said, 'Gee, I just want to tell you I really enjoyed you both nights.' He said, 'What's with all this nice guy shit?'"

After seven years in the stand-up trenches, David was hired for a late night sketch comedy program called *Fridays* and moved to Los Angeles. He ordered furniture for his new Hollywood apartment, and an amateur comedian happened to be his deliveryman. "I delivered a futon to Larry David," said Ray Romano. "He complained about it and we had to go exchange it."

Fridays was criticized as a shameless *Saturday Night Live* knock-off. The show lasted two seasons, 1980–1982, and was full of references to pot smoking and cocaine. Cast member Mark Blankfield had a recurring role as a drug-happy pharmacist who compulsively popped pills. Comedian Darrow Igus hosted a fake cooking show, "The Rasta Gourmet," where marijuana was the key to every recipe. Larry David was a utility actor, doing impressions of Gene Shalit and playing rebellious rabbis.

Fridays brought him into contact with future *Seinfeld* collaborators like Michael Richards, an Andy Kaufman–inspired stand-up who performed one-man sketches at the Improv. The conceptual pieces often confused audiences, who would laugh out of nervousness. On *Fridays* he and David appeared in several sketches together, some written by future *Seinfeld* writers like Larry Charles, Bruce Kirschbaum and Elaine Pope.

During the autumn of 1981 there was talk of using the *Fridays* name for a film franchise like *National Lampoon*. Jack Burns, the show's director, wrote a full screenplay, but by the time he was done *Fridays* was headed for cancellation. *Fridays* left the air in spring 1982 and the film was abandoned.

Larry David teamed with Elaine Pope and they pitched new projects around town. "Larry was always working on scripts," says Richard Lewis. "He was so embroiled in getting his footing out here [in Hollywood]." David and Pope created a television series called *Cable*, a satire about the emerging world of cable television, and sold it to producer Pierre Cossette, but like the *Fridays* film, it was shelved.

Fridays cast members returned to the clubs as the Comedy Boom exploded. There was a lot of work for a young comic at the start of the new decade. However, the Boom did not mean more work for the older demographic. Vegas comedians were considered too old-fashioned for the new comedy club era and many were displaced. "The last few times Dad played Vegas, he was billed as an opening act, not the headliner," said William Berle. "It never occurred to me that my father would ever be anyone except Milton Berle, the Star. I realized that something bad was happening to him in show business. My father wasn't the biggest star anymore. Without knowing any of the details, I still knew that Dad had fallen."

The comedy baton was passed to the new generation, but not willingly. Berle's television appearances exemplified it. When he was asked to host *Saturday Night Live* in 1979, he acted with arrogance and contempt. He told Lorne Michaels, "Yeah, I saw it once," and referred to the cast as "the stars of tomorrow." Lorne Michaels told *The Washington Post*, "What he didn't realize is that they're not the stars of tomorrow. They're the stars of today and *he's* the star of yesterday."

Likewise, members of the comedy club generation were occasionally booked in old-fashioned settings. "The Catskills had gone into decline in the early 1980s," says Paul Provenza. "There was a booker up there—Howie Rapp, an old-school guy. His son took over the business and wanted to liven things up and started booking some of us young comics. You'd do three nights in a row at three different hotels and they were *awful*. It was the same old Catskills audience, so we were out of place. The gigs were torturous, absolutely horrible."

A former joke writer named Mike Callie cast Comedy Store comedians Roger Behr, Joey Camen, Vic Dunlop, Murray Langston and Robin Williams in a sketch comedy film he produced called *Can I Do It . . . Til I Need Glasses?* It inspired Callie to open his own comedy club—the Laff Stop in Newport Beach. He was one of several people to open a club in 1978. The Comedy and Magic Club in Hermosa Beach, the Punch Line in San Francisco and the Comedy Workshop in Houston opened that year. The Cleveland Comedy Club, the Columbus Comedy Club and an Ohio chain called Giggles came next. The Comedy Corner opened in Long Beach and a small comedy club opened in the basement of Osko's, a disco venue in Los Angeles. Some local papers figured it was a regional phenomenon, not aware of the nationwide Boom afoot. *The Boston Globe* reported in January 1980, "Without much ado, Boston has become a mecca for the stand-up comedian. A few years ago, you could count them on one hand. Now there are about sixty of them who throw out the one-liners regularly while moving between the Comedy Connection or Ross Bickford's Comedy Cab in Boston or the Constant Comedy in Cambridge. These places are booming—sellouts are now the rule rather than the exception."

New clubs were identified with their emerging stars. The Comedy Workshop in Houston had Sam Kinison. The Comedy Works in Denver had Roseanne. The Cleveland Comedy Club had Drew Carey and the Pittsburgh Comedy Club had Dennis Miller. By mid-1982 there were new comedy clubs in Cincinnati, Fort Lauderdale, Kansas City, New Orleans, Philadelphia, San Antonio, Toledo and even Sandy Springs, Georgia, where Jeff Foxworthy got his start. Sweeps Comedy Club, the West Coast Comedy Club (the original Comedy Cellar) and the Manhattan Punch Line opened in New York. George Carlin shook his head and called the spread of comedy clubs "an infectious rash."

Joe E. Ross, onetime star of *Car 54, Where Are You?*, was another old comic unable to profit from the Boom. His career was at a standstill when he died dramatically in 1982. His fellow old comedians relay the story in a stand-up version of *Rashomon*:

> **Sammy Shore:** You know how he died? He was doing a show—I forget where.
> **Hank Garrett:** Joe E. was in some housing complex.
> **Bobby Ramsen:** In the building that he lived in they were putting on a show . . .
> **Ronnie Schell:** They hired him to do a show in an old folks' home.
> **Denny Johnston:** I heard it was for Budd Friedman's Improv.
> **Hank Garrett:** They were paying him a hundred dollars.
> **Will Jordan:** Fifty dollars.
> **Ronnie Schell:** He was offered two hundred dollars.
> **Steve Rossi:** Five hundred dollars . . .
> **Hank Garrett:** Joe E. was working . . .
> **Bobby Ramsen:** He got up to do a turn . . .
> **Sammy Shore:** He was doing old jokes . . .
> **Hank Garrett:** Suddenly felt ill . . .
> **Sammy Shore:** He fell backwards . . .

Hank Garrett: Keeled over.

Ronnie Schell: He died.

Bobby Ramsen: He expired onstage.

Hank Garrett: Joe E. Ross died performing.

Sammy Shore: And that was it.

Bobby Ramsen: His wife went to get his pay.

Steve Rossi: His agent went to get the money.

Hank Garrett: This hooker went to collect the hundred dollars.

Chuck McCann: I went and got his check.

Will Jordan: Chuck says he got the check.

Hank Garrett: It was supposed to be for a hundred, but they only gave her fifty.

Steve Rossi: They said, "Wait a minute. This is only half the amount!"

Hank Garrett: The booker said, "Yeah, well . . . he never finished the show."

New comedy clubs kept proliferating. Added to the comedian's itinerary between January 1982 and December 1983 were Cobb's in San Francisco, Charm City in Baltimore, Shirley's Comedy Club in Lexington, Comedy Cabana in St. Paul, Laugh Lounge in Philadelphia, Tickles in Pittsburgh, the Punch Line in Austin, the Laff Stop in Dallas, Mari's Comedy Club in D.C. and the East Side Comedy Club in Long Island. Caroline's Comedy Club opened in 1983 and became a favorite spot for New York headliners Carol Leifer, Larry Miller, Paul Reiser and Jerry Seinfeld. By August 1983 *The New York Times* was referring to "the nationwide comedy boom."

As the Comedy Boom expanded, comedians started to get to know the rock-star lifestyle. The clubs were packed, there were plenty of girls around, comics got preferential treatment and celebrities were making cameos.

More clubs, more comedians, more money—it also meant more cocaine. "It was everywhere," says Gary Mule Deer. "There were guys who used to take half their pay in cocaine. I bought cocaine in the basement of the Pittsburgh Comedy Club from two officers *in uniform.*"

Comedy stars with major cocaine habits included John Belushi, George Carlin, Chevy Chase, Rodney Dangerfield, Redd Foxx, Richard Pryor, Robin Williams and Flip Wilson. The new breed of stand-up comic took to cocaine the way old comedians once took to cigars. "The club owners in the 1980s would give us cocaine because they wanted the comedians to be crazy," said comic Kevin Rooney. "The drugs were free, but if you asked for a sandwich they charged you."

"We were all doing blow when we were young," says Rick Overton. "There was blow at the Improv, but luckily I was broke. Being broke probably saved my life. You trick yourself into thinking you can withstand it forever—but how many times can you *not* get an erection? You start to think, 'I'm no longer seeing the appeal of this. Give me a sign, God.' And then Belushi died. I didn't mean for it to be *that* big of a sign."

On March 4, 1982, John Belushi walked into the Melrose Improv with comedians Richard Belzer, Rick Overton and Robin Williams. Club manager Mark Lonow said, "He doesn't look too good." Belzer responded, "What do you mean? He's been like that for the last eight years." Bernie Brillstein naively gave Belushi a wad of cash a few hours before his death when the comic asked for a loan so he could buy a guitar. Belushi convinced Brillstein the store only took cash. A few hours later, he was dead from a combination of heroin and cocaine.

Overton accepted it as a sign, but for most people cocaine use remained routine. The new cast of *Saturday Night Live* kept the tradition going. "Whenever a new shipment arrived on the floor, I would come in and see everybody grinding their teeth," said *SNL* cast member Tim Kazurinsky. *SNL* capitalized on Flip Wilson's recent cocaine bust when it hired him to host the show in 1983.

"Cocaine was *huge* in the 1980s," says comedian Dana Gould. "The Punchline [comedy club chain] in the South was either a front for a cocaine business or the cocaine business underwrote the club. It was not uncommon to be asked if you wanted to be paid in cocaine. It had all been under the table. Then the IRS got a whiff that there was a lot of money going around. Once they started writing checks, people stopped offering you drugs instead of money."

*　*　*

While everyone else was high, David Letterman was dutifully work-ing toward his own television show. Letterman's style and cadence influenced hundreds of comedians during the Comedy Boom. He was one of the only things during the boom more influential than cocaine.

The modern Letterman was born on November 26, 1978, the night of his first *Tonight Show* appearance. Letterman said, "It was the most exciting thing in my career and it took me a week to get over it." He returned a few weeks later, and by his third appearance he was *hosting* the show. No other comedian in *Tonight Show* history had ever received such a quick vote of confidence. Letterman signed a holding deal with NBC in May 1979. By the time he got his own NBC morning show in February 1980 he had guest-hosted *The Tonight Show* twenty-four times.

Former *Tonight Show* host Jack Paar predicted big things: "Of the newest personalities, David Letterman will unquestionably be a big star. He has an original style and winning manner that is lasting. He will go the distance."

NBC president Fred Silverman devised potential projects, none of which suited Letterman's sensibility. One was called *Leave It to Dave*. "The whole project was just a disaster," said Letterman. "I was supposed to sit on a throne and the set was all pyramids. The walls were all covered in shag carpet." Letterman writing partner Merrill Markoe said, "The set was not even the worst idea to come down that particular pike. I remember that they wanted the guests to make their entrances by sliding down a chute."

Letterman resisted the network's many ideas, and when Silver-man finally suggested a ninety-minute daytime talk show, Letterman went along. "It may not be the high side of glory, but it sounds like fun."

The network made a twenty-six-week commitment. NBC presi-dent Brandon Tartikoff announced, "We think this program will upgrade and change the face of morning television." NBC ran an unironic, cross-country campaign with a photo of Letterman and the slogan: "A face *every* mother could love." *The David Letterman Show* replaced the game shows *Chain Reaction, High Rollers* and *Hollywood Squares*. It acted as the lead-in for *Wheel of Fortune*. NBC hired Bob Stewart to direct. Letterman didn't care for him. "The first director was a game-show director, and he could direct a game show in his sleep, but he couldn't direct a talk show," said Letterman. "Basic rules of television directing were being violated left and right. The guest would be saying something and the light would be on me. I'd be asking a question and the shot would be on who knows what. Finally he started to shoot everything with one wide shot. It looked like a security camera at a 7-Eleven. I mean, it just stunk."

Letterman forced Stewart to resign just days before the first episode. *The David Letterman Show* debuted at 10 A.M. on June 23, 1980, as a ninety-minute program. The management team of Rollins, Joffe, Morra & Brezner was named producer and worked under the aegis of Letterman's brand-new company, Space Age Meat Productions. There was an emphasis on conceptual comedy, improvised banter and offbeat comic guests like Steve Allen, Andy Kaufman and Steve Martin. Character actress Edie McClurg appeared as a sidekick of sorts, satirizing the daytime TV audience as "a disgustingly pert, cheery and bouffant-brained homemaker dispensing such valuable household hints as how to refreshen a room gone stale from air freshener."

It was evident after a few weeks that daytime viewers were not digging it. Fred Silverman cut the program down to an hour on August 4. Some affiliates, like KYW in Philadelphia, were so dissatisfied that they arbitrarily cut the show down to thirty minutes on their own. Forty-nine out of a possible two hundred and fifteen affiliates failed to carry the program. Four major markets—Boston, Baltimore, Detroit and San Francisco—decided to drop the show altogether. It was consistently the lowest-rated program on daytime TV.

Merrill Markoe said their refusal to pander meant doom from the start. "The morning show was a delusion in the sense that we felt you could just do whatever comedy you wanted, any time of day or night. And when the show started to fail, Dave was going crazy. It was not a happy time." Acknowledging his poor ratings, Letterman slapped a portable TV on his desk and invited the audience to join him in watching his competition. Flipping channels, he settled on Dinah Shore's daytime talk show. "Dinah's makin' an omelet. Unbelievable!" Remaining episodes of *The David Letterman Show* featured a sweepstakes in which viewers guessed the correct date of cancellation. October 24, 1980, was the winning answer, and Letterman was done with what he called "the best and worst experience of my life."

The show canceled, Letterman returned to guest-hosting, filling in for Johnny Carson for long stretches in December and January. NBC and Carson Productions signed Letterman to a new holding deal in February 1981 for $750,000 a year, while they tried to figure out what to do. They considered using Letterman as a replacement for *Saturday Night Live* reruns on the fourth Saturday of every month. They also proposed he follow Carson, but Tom Snyder, who held that time slot, was vehemently opposed. After the impasse was resolved, Snyder's contract was bought out and NBC announced that Letterman would get the time slot starting in 1982.

Letterman went back to stand-up. He played an anniversary show at the Los Angeles Improv in May 1981 on a lineup that included Billy Crystal, Larry David, Jay Leno, Fred Willard and Dr. Timothy Leary. That summer he played the Ice House in Pasadena and picked up a Daytime Emmy for the defunct morning program. He hosted a comic-travelogue for HBO called *David Letterman: Looking for Fun* and guest-hosted *The Tonight Show* for the rest of the year. *Late Night with David Letterman* premiered on Monday night, February 1, 1982, and he did his last-ever stand-up set on February 14, at Radio City Music Hall, as part of the ABC television special *Night of 100 Stars*.

Carson Productions dictated the procedure of Letterman's program. Nothing identifiable with *The Tonight Show* was allowed on *Late Night*: no guests like Buddy Hackett or Eydie Gorme, no brass instruments in the band and no reference to the monologue's being a monologue. For years Letterman's opening monologue was officially referred to as "opening remarks." Letterman's staff members were actually pleased by the restrictions—it gave them the freedom to be different. Since the new show was unable to acquire star power, *Late*

Night with David Letterman booked underground heroes like Captain Beefheart, Harvey Pekar, Brother Theodore, John Waters and the cast of *SCTV*. The marijuana smoke hovering above Paul Shaffer and the World's Most Dangerous Band added to the hipster cred. "You used to walk down that hallway on the sixth floor and you couldn't breathe," said producer Robert Morton. "It was the greatest fog ever."

Letterman's comedy was sometimes too weird for viewers and resulted in hostile reviews. "There are people running amok through the boardrooms of America's third place network these days, people who aren't playing with a full deck," wrote Bob Michaels in *The Palm Beach Post*. "The ludicrous quinella NBC is banking on to become their superstars of the 80s is David Letterman and [actress-singer] Susan Anton. If someone set out to find a more no-talent pair than those two, they'd probably find them clutching a bottle of Thunderbird in some alley. To even consider Letterman in the same breath as Milton Berle or Jerry Lewis is an insult to comedy."

James Wolcott wrote a brutal assessment in *New York* magazine in 1983: "*Late Night with David Letterman* has become a creaking, facetious contrivance—a choochoo forever wobbling off the tracks. If David Letterman is going to make it in the long haul, he's going to have to spend more time listening to grown-ups and less time staring at the shine on Paul Shaffer's head."

For seasoned comedy fans, however, and for the comedians on the club circuit in particular, *Late Night with David Letterman* was essential viewing. Exposure on the program boosted the ticket sales of established comedians like Robert Klein, Jay Leno, Richard Lewis and Jerry Seinfeld. It became a benchmark goal for comedy club comedians Bill Hicks, Jonathan Katz, Sam Kinison, Norm Macdonald, Dennis Miller and Drake Sather, all of whom got enormous boosts from the program.

Johnny Carson made David Letterman a star, but for the majority of comedians a *Tonight Show* appearance did *not* make them famous. Sure, there were major exceptions like Steven Wright, Roseanne and Louie Anderson, but they were not the norm. "There was a belief that one appearance on *The Tonight Show* made you a star," said Steve Martin. "But here are the facts. The first time you do the show, nothing. The second time you do the show, nothing ... The tenth time you do the show you could conceivably be remembered as being seen somewhere on television. The twelfth time you do the show, you might hear, 'Oh, I know you. You're that guy.'"

Jerry Seinfeld thought his Carson appearances would lift him out of comedy clubs, but it never did. "I had been on *The Tonight Show* with Johnny Carson for nine years," said Seinfeld. "Nobody at NBC— *nobody*—not one person after nine years of going on Carson three or four times a year and killing said, 'Why don't we talk to this kid?'"

"I did thirty *Tonight Show*s and nobody still knew who I was," said Bill Maher. "In the era that I came aboard, in the 1980s, it was no longer enough just to do *The Tonight Show* to become a star. The family thought you did one *Tonight Show*—you were a giant star, recognized everywhere. The truth was—no you weren't. Your life was just incrementally better and you could now headline at the Pittsburgh Comedy Club."

Mild-mannered *Tonight Show* booker Craig Tennis left the program in the late 1970s to produce *The Midnight Special*. A more vocal and ambitious man replaced him. Jim McCawley had previously been a Carson segment producer, but fled to Canada to accept a job as talent coordinator for *The Alan Hamel Show*. He flew comedians Billy Braver, Jay Leno, David Letterman and Kelly Monteith to Vancouver for the talk show and was eager to return to Hollywood with his newly acquired expertise. Monteith says, "I was on *The Alan Hamel Show* when McCawley heard Craig Tennis was leaving the Carson show. He jumped up and said, 'I've got to call! I've got to call!' He got the job." McCawley was hired to scout and book all stand-up comedians on Johnny Carson's behalf. He was hired just as the Comedy Boom was starting. It was perfect timing. He became one of the most powerful men in comedy.

Comedians would do anything to get on *The Tonight Show*. McCawley was hated, romanced and feared. When he walked into a stand-up show, the whole atmosphere changed backstage. Comedians cowered and shuddered. Jay Leno disliked him and didn't feel he deserved his position. "Jim didn't understand the comic sensibility. It was like he went to comedy school. He wasn't a natural. He always had a Willy Loman aspect to it."

McCawley scouted comedy clubs every night and enjoyed free drinks wherever he went. Sometimes it was a defeating combination. "It was my and every comedian's dream to do *The Tonight Show*," says comedian Wayne Federman. "Jim McCawley saw me once—*loved* me. He came back to see me again—got *drunk*. I had a great set, but he didn't remember it. That was it. I never did the show." Comedian Jeff Altman says, "It wasn't odd if Jim McCawley came to see your act at the Comedy Store and fell asleep on one of the back tables."

Comedians held grudges, but many of the complaints about McCawley were justified. McCawley booked the 1983 San Diego Comedy Festival and brought in Victoria Jackson, Bill Kirchenbauer, Bill Maher, Steven Wright and Maureen Murphy. An arts writer in the San Diego paper wrote, "McCawley's close personal interest in Maureen Murphy's career has sparked some controversy." It was common gossip that McCawley's relationship with Murphy got her on the show. "There were two comediennes up for *The Tonight Show*," says comic Roger Behr. "Elayne Boosler . . . and another McCawley was sleeping with. McCawley decided she deserved to be on *The Tonight Show* more than Elayne. That opinion was shared by no one."

The Tonight Show was aware of the situation, but ultimately ignored it. "There were a lot of complaints from the comics who said Jim mistreated them," said *Tonight Show* producer Peter Lassally. "He bullied people, allegedly. He was very good at his job. But the power he had maybe went to his head."

Drew Carey liked McCawley. "That's all you heard: Jim McCawley this and Jim McCawley that. McCawley was a really good taste-maker. He knew when people were ready and when they weren't. He knew Johnny's taste." Paul Provenza also defends him. "When we were working on my first *Tonight Show* set, he taught me things. I was doing two gigs a night every night for two weeks. I really wanted to be ready for it. After a couple weeks he calls, 'You ready?' I said, 'Jim, I've been doing it and it's not working anymore. It's not getting the laughs.' He said, 'That means it's ready for television.' He knew the show, he knew the audience, he knew Johnny—he knew the vibe."

Bill Kirchenbauer has a different assessment. "McCawley would make suggestions like, 'Maybe you should say blue instead of green.' That's the kind of shit he would come up with. Jim McCawley was a person in power who was totally unknowledgeable about comedy."

For the comedians who never landed on *The Tonight Show* or *Letterman*, there was always the proliferation of stand-up shows on cable TV. They were simple to shoot, cheap to produce, immensely popular—and there were a lot of them. "Cable didn't have any money," said comedian Rita Rudner. "So if they put a microphone in front of a wall and hired someone that they didn't have to pay any money to they had very cheap television."

An Evening at the Improv was one of the most successful stand-up programs. It came at the right time for Budd Friedman, who lost custody of his New York comedy club in 1981 during a bitter divorce. Silver Friedman took over and blacklisted comedians like Rita Rudner and Gilbert Gottfried because they had been favorites of her husband. "It didn't look good there for a while," said Budd Friedman. "In fact, by 1981 I was trying to sell the [Los Angeles] club and get out."

And then *An Evening at the Improv* changed his fortunes. "It was financed by Canadian money, a tax shelter for Canadians. The original fifty-two shows were sold to the A&E Network, which kept repeating them until 1987, when they commissioned me to do new shows." Both the initial 1981 series and its 1987 follow-up reran multiple times a day in different markets. Most professional stand-ups did more than one appearance and it was frequently compared to jury duty. "They used a *lot* of comedians on that show," says Kirchenbauer. "They used comedians that Budd wouldn't actually hire in his club."

Gary Mule Deer believes *An Evening at the Improv* screwed over the comics, denying them residuals. "We didn't get the money we were supposed to. No matter what they say, we got screwed on that—especially when it went into syndication. They were shown over and over and we never got a penny for any of it. It was good publicity for a while, but we never made a dime."

Carbon copies followed: Alex Bennett's *Comedy Tonight* in San Francisco, Bill Boggs's *Comedy Tonight* in New York, *The Big Laff-off*, *Comedy on the Road*, *Comic Strip Live*, *George Schlatter's Comedy Club*, *The Half-Hour Comedy Hour*, *Showtime Comedy Club Network*, *Stand-up America*, *Stand-up Spotlight* and *USA Comedy Cuts* clogged the airwaves. Brian Kiley was on one called *The Johnnie Walker National Comedy Search*. "They went around the country and gave everyone free whiskey. There were four or five hundred people in the audience and they were seriously hammered."

The popularity of the cable shows made the Comedy Boom even bigger. "A&E's *Evening at the Improv* and stuff like that created the clubs," says Robert Klein. "I was at the Just for Laughs festival when I heard them say 'comedy industry' for the first time. It became a thing." In 1985 four new comedy clubs opened in North Carolina alone. A franchise called Coconuts opened across Florida. Canadian stand-up chain Yuk Yuk's moved into the Northeastern United States. Fourteen new branches of the Funny Bone, the Punchline and Zanies opened between 1986 and 1988. New branches of the Improv opened in Dallas, Las Vegas and both San Diego and Irvine in California. Catch a Rising Star opened a location in Massachusetts and went public on the New York Stock Exchange. *The New York Times* reported, "One of the reasons for the nationwide popularity of stand-up comedy is that it is inexpensive . . . The average cost of turning a room into a 200-seat state-of-the-art comedy club [is] around $100,000. With any success, it can gross $20,000 to $25,000 a week."

VCRs were a common piece of living room furniture by the mid-1980s and VHS rentals sustained the Boom. Video stores stocked entire stand-up sections and fly-by-night companies released stand-up compilations. Wayne Federman appeared on a VHS tape called the *Dodge Comedy Showcase*. "If you went to test-drive a car, you got a VHS tape of young comedians. It was Comedy Boom insanity."

Film and television used the Boom as a backdrop. *The Funny Farm*, starring Howie Mandel, was a feature film set in the Boom.

Punchline, starring Tom Hanks and Sally Field, was another. Comedians started investing in the Boom. Rodney Dangerfield and Eddie Murphy both opened comedy clubs in Las Vegas. *Family Feud* host Ray Combs opened his own comedy club in Cincinnati. Al "Grandpa Munster" Lewis opened a comedy club on Staten Island. Mort Sahl briefly ran a comedy club in San Francisco. *The New York Times* reported in October 1987 that there were 260 comedy clubs in America and a total of 500 different comedy nights.

The estimate of working comedians was one thousand. How many of them were actually qualified was another matter. Questionable people capitalized on the Boom, teaching stand-up courses at community colleges, penning how-to books and encouraging suckers to give it a try, the talentless leading the talentless.

Some of the talentless were pitted against the talented in the Comedy Boom beauty pageant—*Star Search*. The talent contest, hosted by Ed McMahon from 1983 to 1995, hearkened back to the days of *Arthur Godfrey's Talent Scouts*, with a comedian's value determined by arbitrary votes. With only ninety seconds to prove themselves, shticky crowd-pleasers had an advantage over cerebral comics. Comedians willing to swallow their pride could get a career boost thanks to the exposure. However humiliating it may have been, the credit allowed a new comedian to tour and make decent money along the vast circuit. Among those who got early exposure on *Star Search* were Sinbad, Rosie O'Donnell and Dave Chappelle.

HBO presented future stars in a less humiliating setting on the annual *Young Comedians Special*. It was a five-year-old program when Rodney Dangerfield was asked to host it for the first time in 1984. What had been just another cable stand-up show took on new gravitas with Dangerfield, one of the hottest acts of the decade. "They were always decent specials and guys got exposure—but the ones hosted by Rodney were the first to *explode*," says comedian Harry Basil. "After it aired people would recognize you on the street and your money went up." Over the course of its history the *Young Comedians Special* presented Judd Apatow, Dennis Miller, Roseanne, Rita Rudner, Bob Saget, Adam Sandler, Rob Schneider, David Spade, Yakov Smirnoff and Sam Kinison long before the general public knew their names.

Kinison's spot in 1985 was his breakout moment. By 1986 he was a superstar, bolstered by appearances on *Letterman* and *The Tonight Show*. Dangerfield adored him and introduced him to all the right people. He became a magnet for drug addicts, floozies and rock musicians. He became comedy's cocaine spokesman and prolonged its popularity. For many drug-addicted comedians, Kinison was a vindication. "That period in Los Angeles with your whole Sam Kinison crowd was *all* fueled by cocaine," says Paul Provenza. And although Kinison's career functioned, his coke-induced mood swings were often directed at fellow comics. "Sam was jealous of Dice, Bobcat Goldthwait and Roseanne," says Harry Basil. "All these feuds were at the same time. Sam was jealous."

He was hostile yet likable, and comedians admired his guts. "Kinison was the first guy I ever saw go onstage and not ask the audience in any way, shape or form to like him," said comedian Bill Hicks. "I found that highly reassuring." Cassette tapes of his act were as popular as the comedy records of Shelley Berman twenty-five years earlier. Kinison was one of the Boom's biggest stars, and he influenced the younger comics starting out. "I try to be Sam Kinison comedically," said Chris Rock. "Sam Kinison was the only guy when I was coming up that sounded new. Everybody else was just kind of doing different versions of other guys. Kinison was totally new. I don't know anybody that sounded like Sam Kinison."

Kinison was one of the biggest stand-up draws in America come 1987. He had a natural rival in Andrew Dice Clay. Both had a following of angry young men, and both did stadium concerts, were the subject of tabloid controversies and had best-selling tapes. The similarities agitated Kinison. "I've known Dice since 1980 when he was doing impressions. In 1984, he did me. I haven't liked him since. He ripped me off."

Dice was known for his loud, obnoxious persona, but for years he toiled as a mild-mannered impressionist at Pips in Sheepshead Bay. During the 1970s he performed under his birth name, Andrew Silverstein, and impersonated the two Jerry Lewis characters from *The Nutty Professor*. Silverstein's interpretation of nerdy Professor Julius Kelp was a crowd-pleaser. His impression of the Lewis character

Buddy Love, a brooding narcissist who flicked a cigarette, evolved into his leather-jacketed tough guy Andrew Dice Clay.

Andrew Dice Clay was a fictional character turned into comedy's Frankenstein monster. He spoke in an explicit manner and directed his hostility at womankind. Male fans felt he articulated their own angry frustrations. They failed to realize Clay wasn't a real person, but an invention. As he reached superstar status, he himself stopped making the distinction—and became a poster child for misogyny. Jay Leno disliked the angry undercurrent. "I knew Andrew before, and I always thought he was an okay guy, but I hated his act because he came from the wrong point of view."

Some townships resurrected dormant obscenity laws to keep Clay away. He was booked for a major concert in Texas, but the gig was canceled when a county district attorney promised to file criminal charges. In 1990, while promoting his feature film *The Adventures of Ford Fairlane*, he was booked to host *Saturday Night Live*. *SNL* cast member Nora Dunn objected, and a media frenzy followed.

Silverstein said, "I was really going through it as far as controversy goes. It just turned into mania. Next thing you know, I'm getting calls from *Entertainment Tonight*. I'm getting calls from all these different tabloid shows. And what was supposed to be a fun, light week wound up the most stressful week I had in my entire career. It wasn't fun. What really bothered me about the whole thing is, these performers [who] are supposed to know what character comedy is didn't know I was playing a character. It was the only time that they threw people out of the audience. I got heckled during my opening monologue and they had to throw people out."

Andrew Dice Clay, Sam Kinison and cable stand-up programming embodied the 1980s. There was so much stand-up on television that some thought an entire comedy channel might be a good idea. Producer Tom Kay announced plans for The Comedy Television Co. in 1986, claiming he would "do for comedy what MTV did for music." But he was unable to find investors, and it never got off the ground.

In May 1989 HBO announced a new subsidiary called The Comedy Channel. Three recent transplants from the Midwest comedy club scene—brothers Dave and Steve Higgins and Dave "Gruber" Allen—introduced clips of old comedy shows in half-improvised interstitial segments. Viacom launched a competing network in April 1990 called Ha! that mostly showed reruns of old sitcoms. "I was head of operations at The Comedy Channel," says Vinnie Favale. "I worked out of HBO's broadcasting facilities and my job was to put the material together in a cohesive form. Mostly it was clips from all the comedy movies airing on HBO and Cinemax. It wasn't really programming so much as promo for what was on HBO that month."

When the two channels started competing, business analyst Dennis McAlpine concluded it was "very unlikely they can be successful." His reasoning was that comedy was now oversaturated. The Boom paid dividends for ten whole years, but it couldn't last forever. As in a stock market surge, a crash was inevitable. The struggle of the comedy channels was the first big sign of an impending comedy bust.

In October 1990 Viacom projected that its Ha! channel losses would reach $50 million. Andy Nulman of the Just for Laughs comedy festival said that both channels were "misled by the Comedy Boom and junk-bond euphoria of the late 1980s into actually thinking they could each make a go of it." In order to salvage some of the investment, the two channels merged on December 19, 1990. They became known as CTV (Comedy Television) and a month later emerged as Comedy Central.

The Boom was over. The years between 1991 and 1993 were a depressing time for those comedians who'd been convinced it would last forever. Gary Mule Deer noticed the downturn at the start of the new decade. "I was making as much money as you could make in a comedy club, but I could see the writing on the wall. I remember a club owner calling me: 'We want to have you back . . . but you know, we're not paying quite the same what we were before . . .'" Brian Kiley started losing money just as his career was advancing. "I was finally starting to do *The Tonight Show*—and my income went *down* from when I was middling. The clubs dried up. The Boom was over."

It was difficult to count the number of comedy clubs opening in the 1980s. Now, in the 1990s, it was difficult to count the number closing. The future of comedy looked bleak. Louis C.K. had been a stand-up for seven years. He was in New York at the time. "Every club in the city was closing. There was no work anymore, anywhere. It was 1992. The 1980s comedy surge—it was gone. At the Comedy Cellar there would literally be nobody in the audience and they'd make you do the show. You'd literally be on stage in an empty room and you had to do the jokes. I mean, it was fucking awful."

CHAPTER TWELVE

THE 1990S

The hack comedians of the Comedy Boom abandoned their Jack Nicholson impressions and returned to their former lives. Creative comedians who kept at it emerged as the top comedy stars of the new millennium. Mainstream comedy was in a slump, but two ancillary scenes—the Alternative Comedy world and a new genre of predominant African American comedy—created some giants.

Eddie Murphy's monumental success in the 1980s inspired a new generation of Black comics to enter the game. It created a parallel stand-up scene that flourished in the early 1990s while white comedy clubs were imploding. "Before I came out you had Richard [Pryor] and Bill Cosby and Flip Wilson and Redd Foxx and a handful of people," said Murphy. "After I came out it was just a fucking explosion of comics. Because I was so young it made the art form accessible to a lot of people."

Eddie Murphy was arguably the biggest comedy star of the 1980s. Stand-up, television, records and movies—he was dominant in every genre. His concert films *Raw* and *Delirious* inspired untold numbers of African American youth to try stand-up, and by the early 1990s they were seasoned professionals. While stand-up programming of the Boom era disappeared from television, new shows geared specifically to an African American demographic were successful. Eddie Murphy had created an entire movement.

"Eddie was the biggest star," said Chris Rock. "Anybody who says different is making a racist argument. Eddie Murphy has the biggest numbers in the history of movies. Grosses are people; it's not dollars marching in, those are people."

Murphy was Chris Rock's earliest champion, altering his life on a chance night at the Comic Strip in New York. "I just came in, like I always did, not on the schedule, just to hang out," said Rock. "I remember a bunch of Porsches and great cars out front. I come in and they say, 'Eddie Murphy's here.' Eddie wanted to see a black comic. I was the only one around so they put me up. And it was a Friday night, prime time, and the place was packed. I had never been onstage in front of more than like twelve people or whatever, and here the place was filled, and I went on in front of Eddie Murphy and I did great. Eddie liked it and I knew that because you could hear that distinctive laugh of his all through the room."

At the time Chris Rock's act sounded a lot like Henny Youngman:

My father is so cheap when we go to bed he unplugs the clocks.

Murphy loved him and told Rock to phone him on the weekend. Murphy invited Rock to join him for a screening of the Spike Lee film *She's Gotta Have It*. "This whole thing happened really, really quick. I met Eddie on a Friday, went to the movies that Sunday . . . after the movie Eddie says to me, 'We're going to L.A. tomorrow so if you wanna come, just come.' I had never been on a plane before, certainly never went to L.A. before, and never stayed at a hotel before. Eddie was doing re-shoots for *The Golden Child*. Eddie Murphy took me out to L.A. and was putting me in his movie."

Rock was part of *Saturday Night Live* by 1990. At the same time Fox, HBO and Showtime started using several Black comedians for sketch, sitcom and stand-up programming. Three shows in particular—*Showtime at the Apollo*, *Def Comedy Jam* and *In Living Color*—buoyed what was turning into a Black comedy boom.

Keenen Ivory Wayans and his brother Marlon had been stand-up mainstays at the Improv in New York when they sold their sketch series to Fox. *In Living Color* was the first Black-oriented sketch series in television history. Jim Carrey was its sole white cast member, Larry Wilmore was one of its writers and it got attention from important people. Jonathan Winters said, "To me one of the funniest shows that went way out was *In Living Color* with the Wayans Brothers and Jim Carrey."

Rock was frustrated watching Black performers with so much screen time while he was stuck with little to do on *SNL*. "The black comedy boom was happening and I wasn't part of it. *In Living Color* was a big show and *Def Comedy Jam* was on HBO and Martin Lawrence was on. So there was all this stuff happening and I was over here in this weird world, this weird, Waspy world." Rock left *SNL* in 1993 and joined *In Living Color*. Ironically, it was on the Black-centric program on which he was able to do comedy *not* about race. "On *SNL*, I either had to play a militant or a hip-hop guy. *Living Color* allowed me to talk about other shit."

Def Comedy Jam premiered on HBO July 1, 1992, and ran five years. It was by far HBO's most successful comedy program. The critical favorite on HBO was *The Larry Sanders Show*, starring Garry Shandling, Jeffrey Tambor and Rip Torn. And although Shandling's program gave early jobs to Judd Apatow, Todd Barry, Janeane Garofalo, Mary Lynn Rajskub, Bob Odenkirk, Jeremy Piven, Sarah Silverman and Jon Stewart, its ratings were below expectations. Brillstein-Grey producer Kevin Reilly said, "I used to get the numbers every week and *Def Comedy Jam* had like four times the ratings of *Larry Sanders*."

Def Comedy Jam was an offshoot of Russell Simmons's enormously successful Def Jam Recordings. "Russell always had a love of comedy and he would frequent comedy clubs," said the program's talent coordinator, Bob Sumner. "When it was mentioned that an African American comedy series might be cool everybody was in agreement to do it. I took some executives from HBO around to some comedy clubs and they could see black comedy was really popping. Then they allowed us to do a pilot. That pilot turned into eighty-two shows."

Def Jam had several hosts, but its first—Martin Lawrence—was the breakout star. On the heels of *In Living Color*'s success, the Fox network cranked out more African American talent than any other channel in television history, before or since. Martin Lawrence was the cornerstone from which Fox built its succession of Black sitcoms, and the network used *Def Comedy Jam* as its casting call.

Down the ladder in terms of quality, but almost as successful, was the BET channel's *Comic View*. This stand-up program, originally hosted by D. L. Hughley, endured despite its frequently amateurish approach. Hughley was a cut above the guests, but he had a reputation along the Black stand-up circuit as a joke thief and he bothered BET executives with his on-air cussing. BET replaced him with Cedric the Entertainer, who accepted the gig despite being warned against it. "A lot of my contemporaries were telling me not to do BET," said Cedric. "They were telling me that doing *Comic View* for me would have been a step in the wrong direction. They wanted me to wait and do my material on the next season of *Def Comedy Jam*. *Comic View* was a nightly show back then. It came on five nights a week, so I knew it would give a lot of boost to my career. It was a great run. It put me on the map."

As with the shows *Make Me Laugh* and *Star Search* that came before, many comedians decided frequent exposure on *Comic View* was more important than the actual quality of the show. It boosted the drawing power and income of many of them when they took to the road.

The frequent airing of *Comic View* created an insatiable need for new comics, and the program often used comedians who weren't television-ready. "*Comic View* threw on every comic that submitted a tape in '98," said Darryl Littleton, author of *Black Comedians on Black Comedy*. "If it turned out that they weren't funny, the production staff dubbed in cricket sounds and showed an impassive audience staring at the performer in a state of disgust with a nasty phrase encased in a comic strip bubble inserted above the comedian's head." *Comic View* lasted a remarkable eight years, longer than any other entity of the Black comedy boom.

White comics, even those who were established, struggled to sustain themselves with stand-up gigs alone in the early 1990s. Louis C.K.,

Jon Stewart and many others started writing for television to cover their expenses.

Jon Stewart entered the business during the height of the Comedy Boom. His first gig in front of a live audience was working "disabled puppets" in an ensemble called the Kids on the Block. The group played school assemblies in an attempt to teach children empathy. Stewart said he operated "a cerebral-palsy puppet, a blind puppet, a deaf puppet, a hyperactive puppet—and a puppet who couldn't commit to a relationship."

He did his first stand-up gig at the legendary Bitter End, still a historic but no longer great comedy venue. Bitter End manager Paul Colby said Stewart "bombed atomically. It was terrible to watch." Nearby was the Comedy Cellar, the club later made famous by the FX series *Louie*. Stewart made it his homeroom. "I went on for two years at the Comedy Cellar at 2:30 or 3 A.M. as the last guy. It was me and the waitstaff and a table of drunken Dutch sailors. And in that place, I learned how to be myself."

His gigs improved. Stewart opened for veteran comedian Alan King, warmed up the crowd for a Showtime special and was Sheena Easton's opening act in Las Vegas. In 1989 he joined fellow comedians as a staff writer on *Caroline's Comedy Hour*, the four-season A&E stand-up program. It resembled most Boom-era stand-up shows, distinguished only by its scripted, interstitial sketches. Michael Patrick King, the writer who later shaped *Sex in the City*, oversaw the sketches. King assembled an impressive staff and at one point the writers room included Jon Stewart, Dave Attell, Susie Essman, Colin Quinn and Louis C.K.

When the show was canceled in 1993, King moved to the fledgling Comedy Central and brought Stewart along to write some of the flagship programs. Stewart was soon named host of the low-budget *Short Attention Span Theater*, a show that utilized old comedy footage from the Viacom library. That led to a hosting gig on a cheap MTV program. (Comedy Central replaced Stewart with comedy's future podcast champion, Marc Maron.)

In March 1993 Stewart was booked as a stand-up on *Late Night with David Letterman*. Stewart was the last of many comic stars to get a break from Letterman's NBC show before its run ended. Letterman's production company expressed interest in Stewart, and because of that MTV started treating him more seriously and green-lit Stewart's idea for a talk show.

The Jon Stewart Show premiered on MTV on October 25, 1993, and it was soon second only to *Beavis and Butt-Head* in channel popularity. A few months later, when comedian Arsenio Hall announced he was leaving his syndicated talk show, the *Stewart* program was revamped for syndication, expanded to an hour and hustled in Arsenio's former markets. Comic Howard Feller was the sidekick on *The Jon Stewart Show*. "Jon Stewart was seen as this rising star and was doing fairly well on MTV. Arsenio Hall left. They needed a replacement, but a lot of the African American audience loyal to Arsenio wasn't going to watch Jon Stewart. It didn't get the black audience, although it probably *would have* if not for us replacing Arsenio. It almost looked like Jon Stewart kicked Arsenio off the air."

Stewart's writing staff at various points included comedians Dave Attell and David Cross and former Comedy Channel hosts Dave and Steve Higgins. Airing four nights a week for nine months, the program was frequently described in the press as a talk show for Generation X. When it was canceled on June 23, 1995, and a newbie named Conan O'Brien remained on the air over on NBC, critical backlash said it should have been the other way around.

New York magazine ran an article titled "The Man Who Should Be Conan" and chronicled Stewart's cancellation: "*Stewart* staff members, busy boxing up their belongings, blamed the cancellation on everything from lame promotional support by the show's syndicator . . . to the inevitable internal debates about whether *Stewart* should be a talk show with comedy sketches or a comedy show with talk, to Stewart's coming across as just too damn nice." Rumors speculated that Stewart would move to one of the major networks, but in the end they proved wrong. He figured his career was over. "I'm compiling rationalizations now," said Stewart. "It's hard not to take it as a personal rejection. I was looking for a hug—and America spit in my face."

*   *   *

From the ashes of the Comedy Boom came a DIY scene on both coasts, a new forum for comedians with a creative impulse. Alternative Comedy was an early 1990s antidote to the brick-wall conformity symbolizing stand-up in the 1980s. Innovative television like *The Larry Sanders Show, Late Night with Conan O'Brien, The Ben Stiller Show, The Dana Carvey Show* and *Mr. Show* was cast from the ranks of the Alternative Comedy scene.

The phrase "Alternative Comedy" was an offshoot of the 1990s record store category "Alternative Music," the catchall under which you'd find Nirvana and Pearl Jam cassettes. The difference between alternative comics and regular stand-up comedians usually had to do with the venues where they performed—alternatives to commercial comedy clubs.

"You would go to the Improv, which was, supposedly, a place you could work on material," says comic Dana Gould. "But every night Jim McCawley from *The Tonight Show* was there or the president of show business was there. You couldn't work on stuff because if they saw you bomb they thought, 'Oh, he's not very funny.' We wanted a place where you could go and bomb, a place to do new material. There was a real cool place on Beverly Boulevard called the Big and Tall Books. It had a loft, a little upstairs room, that seated forty people. We started to do shows there and devised a thing where you couldn't do material you'd already done—everything had to be new. It was a magical time—like when the grunge scene came together in Seattle. A bunch of things coalesced, a lot of great comedians: Andy Kindler, Janeane Garofalo, Bob Odenkirk, David Cross, Patton Oswalt, Julia Sweeney, Taylor Negron, Andy Dick. Beth Lapides would book the show and it became the cool night out." Surrounded by the alternative literature that defined the decade, like Peter Bagge's *Hate*, Alternative Comedy became a legitimate genre that attracted a cerebral audience.

Ben Stiller was the son of comedy team Stiller & Meara. Anne Meara and Jerry Stiller played the hip Village venues of the 1950s and 1960s as part of the New Wave comedy scene. Now, thirty years later, Ben Stiller was part of the like-minded Alternative Comedy world. "I met Ben Stiller through Janeane Garofalo in New York," says Gould. "Then Ben moved to Los Angeles and I introduced him to Judd Apatow. Janeane knew Bob Odenkirk. Judd knew Andy Dick. It was a social group."

Judd Apatow was contributing material to the stand-up acts of Jim Carrey, Garry Shandling and Roseanne while performing his own material on shows like *An Evening at the Improv*. "I used to tour a little bit with Jim Carrey. I wrote for Roseanne—wrote her stand-up act with her. I would take brief gigs here and there." After Gould introduced them, Apatow and Stiller started to collaborate. They sold comedy sketches that MTV aired between music videos, and that led to a deal with Fox for *The Ben Stiller Show*. It signaled the end of Apatow's stand-up career and the start of his life as a writer-producer. "When *The Ben Stiller Show* was picked up, I realized there was no way for me to do stand-up three or four nights a week and run this television show with Ben. So that was the moment." The program had a cult following during its only season and was the first steady TV gig for Andy Dick, Janeane Garofalo and Bob Odenkirk. As with David Letterman's morning show ten years before, it won an Emmy after cancellation.

Bob Odenkirk was shepherded into professional showbiz by Robert Smigel, a key *Saturday Night Live* writer best known today for his caustic puppet Triumph the Insult Comic Dog. In 1985 Smigel was hired with future *Kids in the Hall* members Bruce McCulloch and Mark McKinney to write on *SNL*. It was an impressive writers room that included Al Franken, Tom Davis, A. Whitney Brown, Jim Downey, Jack Handey, Carol Leifer, George Meyer, Don Novello, Herb Sargent and John Swartzwelder. Within two years Smigel was upstaging most of them. "He wrote a lot of sketches that were definitive for our time, for our generation," said Odenkirk. "The *Star Trek* sketch from 1986, in which William Shatner tells the Trekkies to 'get a life.' 'Da Bears' was his idea. He gave that show the strongest and smartest sketches that it had for a couple of years."

Odenkirk was working at Second City and fed Smigel ideas by proxy. "I would sort of work with him on the phone every week and pitch him ideas . . . sometimes they would do a joke of mine on *Weekend Update*. I came in and did an interview the following year, which was Robert's second year. I was hired a few months later."

SNL hired the writing team of Greg Daniels and Conan O'Brien for the 1987–1988 season, but that spring a Writers Guild strike brought the program to a halt. With nothing to do, Smigel and Odenkirk returned to Chicago, where the comedy scene was nurturing talents like Steve Carell, Stephen Colbert, Chris Farley, Jeff Garlin, Jane Lynch, Andy Richter and Amy Sedaris. "Bob and I decided to go back to Chicago and do a sketch show together," says Smigel. "We invited Conan to do it with us. Some famous sketches came out of that show, including 'Bill Swerski's Super Fans' and 'In the Year 2000.'" The latter became one of the signature segments on *Late Night with Conan O'Brien*. *SNL* returned the following season and won an Emmy. Robert Smigel, Bob Odenkirk and Conan O'Brien had their names on an Emmy Award—long before anyone had ever heard of them.

Late Night with Conan O'Brien was born out of a network crisis. Johnny Carson's retirement in 1992 and the battle between Jay Leno and David Letterman was big news, chronicled in detail by journalist Bill Carter in his book *The Late Shift*. When Letterman fled to CBS it left a vacancy in NBC's post–*Tonight Show* time slot. NBC needed to appease advertisers and affiliates across the country.

The affiliates were pleased with *Saturday Night Live*, which had become a very profitable franchise. The success of a film based on one of its sketches, *Wayne's World*, made Lorne Michaels a powerful mogul. When it came time to fill the post-Letterman void, NBC looked to Michaels for guidance.

"They had to sell the late night time slot to their affiliates before they were able to put a show in place," says comedian Paul Provenza. "They didn't have anything—they just had the time slot. So their idea was to make a deal with Lorne Michaels and make him the star of the time slot for the buyers."

Conan O'Brien was by then writing on *The Simpsons* and punching up the screenplay for *So I Married an Axe Murderer*. He heard about the opening before anyone else. His sister tipped him off. "I was working at William Morris," said Jane O'Brien. "[I] had access to the confidential e-mail when it was announced that Lorne Michaels was given the *Late Night* time slot. I called Conan and told him. I just knew it was his."

NBC president Warren Littlefield wanted comedian Garry Shandling for the job. *Late Night with Garry Shandling* looked like it might happen, and Michaels even asked O'Brien to produce it. "I wasn't interested," said O'Brien. "I did not think, 'No! Not Garry Shandling. Me!' But I told Lorne I wanted more performance." In reality, Shandling didn't even want the job, but used the offer to frighten HBO into implementing demands he had regarding *The Larry Sanders Show*.

Shandling gone, others tested for the job. Dana Carvey, Drew Carey, Michael McKean, Paul Provenza, comedian Rick Reynolds (whose stand-up special on Showtime had just got an Emmy nod), Ray Romano, Jon Stewart and O'Brien all auditioned. Using the *Tonight Show* set in Burbank, they were required to do a mock interview for NBC executives. NBC asked Jay Leno for his input, and he leaned toward Provenza, who was doing a talk show on Comedy Central called *Comics Only*. Provenza says, "NBC was holding out for me. Lorne Michaels was really offended that NBC used Jay Leno as a consultant. Because of that there was no fucking way anyone Jay suggested would get signed."

Dana Carvey became the front-runner. "Lorne wanted Dana to do it," says Robert Smigel. "Dana talked to me about it. Carvey knew how much I loved to work with Conan. He said, 'Yeah, you guys could both be featured players!' I immediately formed a lot of ideas. I pictured a late night sketch comedy show with characters and guests—and guests who were characters." Carvey ultimately changed his mind, deciding the grind would be too stressful and time-consuming.

Lorne Michaels used his persuasive powers, and NBC went with the least experienced candidate: Conan O'Brien. Smigel desperately wanted to be part of the project. "I weaseled my way into doing the show with him. I was one of the senior writers at *SNL* and Lorne didn't want me to go. To me, it was a dream. I knew who Pat Weaver was and I cared about that kind of thing. My dream was creating the show. Conan's dream was hosting the show."

Michaels had O'Brien tape two weeks of practice shows to assure NBC it wouldn't be a disaster, while Smigel went through the process of assembling a staff. Comedian Jeff Garlin recommended Andy Richter, whom Smigel knew through Chicago sketch comic Beth Cahill. O'Brien and Richter met at Canter's Delicatessen in Los Angeles, and their chemistry was immediate. Jeff Garlin further recommended Louis C.K. "We watched Louis's stand-up and watched two of his short films," says Smigel. "Jeff Garlin recommended him and [comedian-writer] Dino Stamatopoulos pushed hard for him, so Conan and I went with it."

Louis C.K. was reeling from the implosion of the Comedy Boom at the time. "I was going broke. I was just devastated. I wasn't making a living. I remember calling Marc Maron, who was living in San Francisco. I was up until dawn talking to him on the phone. I was so fucking depressed. And then I got a phone call out of nowhere from Robert Smigel. He said, 'I'd like to take a chance on you. I'm writing for Conan.' I didn't even know what that was."

Michaels sent Smigel on a scouting mission to Second City, in particular to check out the buzz surrounding a kid named Steve Carell. "We went to a Second City show and Steve Carell wasn't even there that day," says Smigel. "There was an understudy doing his part. I thought, 'Oh, well.' I saw the show and I thought the understudy was hilarious! The understudy was Stephen Colbert."

Smigel arranged a meeting with O'Brien and Colbert, expecting the same chemistry he'd enjoyed with Andy Richter. "I wanted him to meet Colbert. It was just the three of us at a bar, but there wasn't anything comfortable about it like when he met Andy." Colbert said, "We met at a bar, had a couple of beers, talked. I submitted some jokes—and didn't get hired."

Late Night with Conan O'Brien premiered on February 13, 1993, and Louis C.K. quickly put his stamp on it, creating recurring pieces that were used for years. "Louis was the most prolific and probably the best writer on the show," says Smigel. "I created a fair amount, but Louis created more than anyone. He created bits that were done for years, like 'Actual Items,' 'Staring Contest,' 'Bad Fruit Theater' and 'Patterns.' He was super-strong."

Smigel created a signature bit that was done the first week on the air. O'Brien conducted phony "via-satellite" interviews with people like President Clinton, in reality a photo with Smigel's human lips superimposed over the mouth, a takeoff on the low-budget *Clutch Cargo* cartoon of the 1960s. "We did the *Clutch Cargo* bit on the second show. The audience laughed so hard—it was such a thrill. Everything I wanted was happening. We were doing something different from any other talk show."

The program's comedy was decidedly weird. While the people responsible for it would become critical favorites in another fifteen years, reporters at the time were dumbfounded. They dismissed *Late Night with Conan O'Brien* as a lousy Letterman knockoff and dismissed O'Brien as an inept personality. Rick DuBrow at the *Los Angeles Times* wrote, "In the wee hours after Letterman and Leno, NBC's new Conan O'Brien series was an awkward, fumbling yawn." Tom Shales at *The Washington Post* wrote, "O'Brien's show just lies there, as lifeless and as messy as road kill." *TV Guide* said, "[Conan is] a twitching frat boy who thinks he's much cuter and funnier than he actually is." The bad press affected the studio audience itself. "December 1993, our first winter, was the worst time I will ever have," said O'Brien. "I'd go out to do the warm-up and the back two rows of seats would be empty."

Late Night with Conan O'Brien remained on the air against all odds, a testament to the power of Lorne Michaels. Critics did not let up. "They hated it the whole time I was there," said Louis C.K. "We just fought to stay on the air, constantly faced with extinction. Every Friday the word would come, 'This is probably our last week,' and everybody would call their agents."

New hires were signed to hesitant thirteen-week contracts and writers quietly inquired about other gigs. Louis C.K. continued to do stand-up. "We'd be there until three in the morning working something out. So I'd literally say, 'I'm gonna go to the bathroom,' and I'd go downstairs, hop on my motorcycle, run to the Comedy Cellar and do a set, then come back and try and play it off like I took a big shit."

Late Night with Conan O'Brien cast many of its sketches using people out of the Upright Citizens Brigade, a new sketch collective that was considered hipper than its precursors. Founded by Amy Poehler, Ian Roberts, Matt Walsh and Matt Besser in Chicago in 1991, it acted as an alternative to Second City, which was by then touting itself as a tourist destination. "We had no respect for any other comedy enterprise in Chicago," said UCB member Horatio Sanz. When the collective moved to New York in 1996, members started to show up with regularity on *The Daily Show* and *Late Night with Conan O'Brien*. "They were like a repertory company for us," says *Late Night with Conan O'Brien* writer Brian Stack. "The first sketch I wrote at *Conan* was called 'Andy's Little Sister,' and Amy Poehler starred in it."

While critics complained about *Late Night with Conan O'Brien*, David Letterman was impressed. He told the staff, "The more I watch the show, I realize you guys do an incredible amount of comedy, and the stuff that is produced is at a very high level. The volume and quality of the stuff just knocks me out."

So much so that Letterman wanted Louis C.K. for his own. "I was trying to get on *Letterman* as a comic," said C.K. "My manager approached Letterman's show for the fiftieth time. They said, 'Would he write here? 'Cause that would really make us interested.' And we said only if I could do stand-up. I didn't want to write on *Letterman*. I hadn't even been on the show yet and I'm meeting David Letterman. He said, 'Look, I saw your *Conan* reel. You're really, really great. We really feel like this show needs to go somewhere new. So the idea of having you come here and shaking things up is exciting to me. So will you write for me?' He just asked me point-blank. And I just said, 'Yeah.' What am I gonna do? And it was a miserable three months. I had a rotten time there. So I quit."

Meanwhile Smigel left *Conan* to write a "Da Bears" screenplay with Bob Odenkirk. It was commissioned by Paramount, but the studio shelved the project. Dana Carvey was going through an equally frustrating period. After having passed on his late night opportunities, his intention was to make quality comedy films, but those hopes were quickly dashed by studio interference. Carvey recalled, "After these horrible movie experiences I said, 'Oh, man, I really would love to do something with Smigel, who I enjoyed so much. Maybe we'll do a variety show somewhere.'"

Carvey, C.K. and Smigel joined forces and devised a sketch comedy program. "I had really wanted to do it on cable, HBO," said Carvey. "Robert and other people really believed, 'You have the face for prime time. You should be with a big audience.'" In order to cast *The Dana Carvey Show*, Smigel acquired the rejected audition tapes from *Saturday Night Live* and went through them. Among the people he looked at were Jimmy Fallon, Ana Gasteyer and Tracy Morgan.

Out of the tapes only comedian Jon Glaser was hired, as his weird sensibility seemed to fit. "My celebrity impression was the head coach of the Detroit Lions and my political impression was King Hussein of Jordan," says Glaser. "I didn't get *SNL*, but Robert Smigel liked my King Hussein and told me he wanted me to do it for *The Dana Carvey Show*."

At Second City, Stephen Colbert had been Steve Carell's understudy and Jon Glaser had been Stephen Colbert's understudy. Smigel hired all three of them.

Adding to the roll call of future giants was a taciturn writer named Charlie Kaufman. It was the first job for the man who went on to write *Being John Malkovich*, *Adaptation* and *Eternal Sunshine of the Spotless Mind*. "His writing submission was not fantastic," said Smigel. "[It] was up and down, but kind of interesting. There was one sketch that was a very meta treatment of *Unsolved Mysteries*. It was one of the most brilliant sketches I had ever read, and it was enough for me to hire him."

With future giants like Louis C.K., Stephen Colbert, Steve Carell and Charlie Kaufman all involved, how could it miss? *The Dana Carvey Show* premiered on ABC on March 12, 1996. Within seven weeks it was canceled.

The Dana Carvey Show had Tim Allen's high-rated sitcom *Home Improvement* as its lead-in. For anyone else this would have been an asset, but unfortunately these two programs had completely different temperaments. *The Dana Carvey Show* was on Disney-owned ABC, but its approach was more in line with Carvey's initial HBO ambitions.

The very first sketch of the series featured Carvey playing President Bill Clinton, telling the American people he "felt their pain" as the "compassionate president" and would nurture them. He then opened his shirt, exposing six nipples and breast-feeding a litter of kittens. "The president breast-feeding was probably the worst decision I've ever been involved in," said Smigel. "It was Louis C.K.'s idea. I foolishly got very excited about it, and Louis even said, 'You know what's great about this? We'll be able to really draw a line in the sand for people. Are you with us or aren't you?' For some insane reason, just a purely naïve moment of thinking about nothing but making myself laugh, I agreed with him. I was so stupid. I didn't even watch *Home Improvement*. I should've taken a second to watch five minutes of it. I'd heard Tim Allen had done coke and gone to jail. Then, about five shows into it, after a horrendous ratings drop-off, with every week getting worse and worse, I finally tuned in to *Home Improvement*. I was absolutely mortified. Not just for myself, but for the audience to whom I'd subjected *The Dana Carvey Show*."

Louis C.K. lamented that it was an "amazing pool of talent and we just couldn't turn it into anything. And the network hated us. I was so depressed."

CHAPTER THIRTEEN

THE NEW MILLENNIUM

Comedy entered the new millennium. George W. Bush was sworn in as the forty-third president of the United States, and some felt it was great news for comedians. One could get laughs by simply running clips of the president's malapropisms, without any additional joke writing required. But if President Bush was good for comedy, the events of September 11, 2001, had the opposite effect, and some wondered if it spelled the end of comedy as we knew it. How could one laugh amid such tragedy and devastation? How could one possibly find anything funny about it? Comedians were at a loss for what to say and how to say it.

All the late night comedy programs from *Letterman* to *The Daily Show* happened to be on hiatus the week of September 11. They were scheduled to return the following week, but the writers who usually wrote the jokes about the week's events were paralyzed. Comedy was a futile pursuit as the smell of charred bodies lingered in the air.

David Letterman, Conan O'Brien and Jon Stewart all did their comedy programs from New York. No one was quite sure how to proceed. Even the process of worrying filled them with a sense of guilt. "We were all walking around feeling dazed, not knowing if we should bother to write anything," says *Late Night with Conan O'Brien* writer Brian Stack. It seemed superficial to concern oneself with a comedy show while other New Yorkers were searching for lost relatives. Vinnie Favale, vice president of CBS's late night programming, says, "I didn't even think we could do television again."

"There were definitely mixed feelings," says Guy Nicolucci, a former writer for both O'Brien and Stewart. "There were a lot of people who felt that we shouldn't go on the air yet. It was very clear, however, that all the *hosts* wanted to go on the air." Former *Late Night with Conan O'Brien* writer Jon Glaser remembers, "I questioned why we were going back. It was strange and it didn't seem right. Why do we care? It seemed meaningless."

Late Show with David Letterman returned to CBS on September 17, 2001. "It was very hard, because it was a comedy show," says Favale. "Letterman had the license to go serious. He didn't need anyone by his side to come up with that first show after 9/11. It was honest and raw."

Late Show with David Letterman opened cold, without its normal theme song. Letterman sat behind his desk and addressed the camera. "Welcome to the *Late Show*. This is our first show on the air since New York and Washington were attacked. I need to ask your patience and indulgence here . . . If we are going to continue to do shows—I just need to hear myself talk for a couple of minutes . . . It's terribly sad here in New York City . . . You can feel it. You can see it. It's terribly sad. Terribly, terribly sad. Watching all of this, I wasn't sure that I should be doing a television show . . . So to come to this circumstance that is so desperately sad—and I don't trust my judgment in matters like this—but I'll tell you the reason I am doing a show, and the reason I'm back to work is because of Mayor Giuliani."

Letterman spoke for eight minutes about the city and the bond of sorrow uniting the country. He added one sentence of levity: "Thank God Regis [Philbin] is here so we have *something* to make fun of." Much of the commentary was devoted to Mayor Rudolph Giuliani, whom Letterman mentioned seven times in eight minutes.

Both before and after the tragedy Giuliani could be a polarizing figure, but he was the voice of the city during its season of grief. When *Saturday Night Live* returned to the air on September 29, 2001, the mayor was there. *SNL* opened with Paul Simon singing his song "The Boxer" while emergency workers stood around him. The segment ended with Mayor Giuliani and Lorne Michaels having a brief on-camera conversation. "We needed some moment to sort of give us permission to start again," recalled Michaels. "So we did a joke with Mayor Giuliani where he talked about what had gone on and the importance of what we do for a moment. I said, 'Can we be funny?' And he had this joke we'd given him, 'Why start now?'"

Late Night with Conan O'Brien returned to the air the night after *Letterman*. "We went into work," says former *Conan* writer Michael Koman. "Everyone was very silent. It was this general sense: 'What do we do? Does this even happen anymore? How do you put on a comedy show?' I felt everything was going to *end*. My feeling was less that it was dishonorable to return than what reality are we even writing from?" There was no opening monologue for the first couple weeks. The writers whose specific job was to write the monologue wondered if they would ever write another. *Conan* writer Brian Kiley says, "We couldn't do any jokes for a while. When we did there would be an *ooooh* and you'd feel the audience tightening up. This was a real scar."

Late Night with Conan O'Brien opened without a theme song, and O'Brien addressed the camera from his desk: "I will be very honest with you. I have no idea how to do what we've been doing— tonight. I have no idea tomorrow. I have no idea how to do it the rest of the week. I have no idea how we're going to get back to doing this again . . . I have never ever felt more unsure or more at a loss than I do tonight."

Jon Glaser remained skeptical about the choice to return, but then a friend of the show visited the set. "There was a guy named Chris Edwards, a retired fireman and policeman. He became an actor and we used him a lot. He showed up with another fireman and they were dressed to go to a funeral. The whole staff—fifty or sixty people—gathered around him. He said, 'It's so great you guys are back on the air because every day we're down at Ground Zero or at a funeral. At the end of the day we go back to the firehouse and watch your show.' It made me feel better. Most of the time it was just a stupid show, but this gave it meaning."

The Daily Show with Jon Stewart returned on September 20, 2001. One anonymous staffer claims it was a selfish decision. "Stewart went on that Friday and said, 'I can barely stand to be on the air . . .'

The son of a bitch *rushed* on the air to show how heartfelt he was because he needed to have a piece of the spotlight."

The Daily Show began like the others, with a "cold open," Stewart addressing the camera from his desk. "Good evening and welcome to *The Daily Show*. We are back. This is our first show since the tragedy in New York City and there's no other way really to start the show than to ask . . . are you okay? We pray that you are and that your family is. I'm sorry to do this to you. It's another entertainment show beginning with an overwrought speech of a shaken host . . . It's something that unfortunately we do for ourselves so that we can drain whatever abscess is in our hearts and move on to the business of making you laugh."

Comedy returned, but it was a struggle. "After 9/11 I couldn't think about anything else for months," says Robert Smigel. "I couldn't write comedy about anything. *SNL* did that first show and there was a benign recurring sketch going on. The prop guy said, 'I'm not ready to watch this.' And I understood that. That's how I felt. I couldn't think of anything but the tragedy. I tried to write some things, and they just didn't fly."

Television avoided comedy about the attacks, but satirical newspaper-turned-website *The Onion* devoted its next issue to 9/11. Headlines like "American Life Turns Into Bad Jerry Bruckheimer Movie" and "God Angrily Clarifies 'Don't Kill' Rule" resonated with readers. *The Onion* also managed to convey the feelings of comedy writers with the headline "Report: Gen X Irony, Cynicism May Be Permanently Obsolete." It earned the admiration of comedy writers across the board. "They did it quickly and they had the absolute perfect tone," says Smigel. "It wasn't remotely offensive. It was heroic."

The 9/11 attacks affected comedians in personal ways and changed the approach of some. Dennis Miller had always held a combination of liberal and conservative views, but September 11 turned him into a vocal jingoist. "9/11 changed me," he said. "I'm shocked that it didn't change the whole country, frankly. I stepped up after 9/11 to a more serious approach to protecting this country." His stand-up act became a platform for not just comedy, but pronounced opinion. Tom Smothers, clinging to his 1960s credentials, stormed out of a Miller stand-up gig in 2002. "I went and saw his act and I kinda started heckling because I couldn't believe it. And my wife said, 'Just shut up and get outta here.' I walked out. I was so upset. It was just, 'Bomb everybody, those ragheads, people in mud huts, they don't have a country, they're a bunch of stupid assholes.' 9/11 turned a lot of people around."

Jay Leno considered himself a liberal guy, but 9/11 made him cautious about his jokes. "During 9/11, I gave Bush a pass. And I remember about two months had gone by, and then one day I sensed that maybe people were ready. I said, 'Folks, if you don't laugh at this joke, that means the terrorists have won.' And it got a huge laugh. And it wasn't that funny. But they sensed that, now that it looks like the administration is using this as a crutch, it's okay to come in slowly with the jokes and roll them in. I remember that joke was a turning point. When it's obvious to the audience what's happening, then it works."

ABC failed to renew the program *Politically Incorrect* after host Bill Maher made a controversial comment about the 9/11 hijackers. Politicians referred to the hijackings as a cowardly act and Maher responded, "*We* have been the cowards lobbing cruise missiles from two thousand miles away. That's cowardly. Staying in the airplane when it hits the building—say what you want about it—it's not cowardly."

Politically Incorrect had debuted on Comedy Central in July 1993. When it moved to ABC in January 1997, Comedy Central filled the vacated time slot with a different news-oriented program—*The Daily Show*.

The Daily Show premiered on Comedy Central on July 22, 1996, hosted by sportscaster Craig Kilborn. Stephen Colbert and comedian Lewis Black were contributors, although neither had much stomach for Kilborn and his smug demeanor. Colbert later said Kilborn's only strength was reading the teleprompter. Kilborn accepted an offer with David Letterman's production company, and Jon Stewart took over *The Daily Show* in January 1999. Over the next several years the program gained momentum and was rivaled only by *SNL* for its star-making capacity. Thanks to regular *Daily Show* appearances, Lewis Black and Demetri Martin became major stand-up draws, John Hodgman and Kristen Schaal procured an enormous fan base, Steve Carell became a movie star and Stephen Colbert, John Oliver and Larry Wilmore got their own programs.

The Colbert Report, starring Stephen Colbert, debuted on October 17, 2005, cocreated by Colbert and Allison Silverman, a former writer with *The Daily Show* and *Late Night with Conan O'Brien*. It was the rare political satire that didn't alienate mainstream viewers. Colbert's character was impish and pixie-like, likable despite making horrible, pompous statements. His character was such a moron he could hardly be blamed for the things that came out of his mouth. Based on reactionary pundit Bill O'Reilly, Colbert's comedy was largely inspired by Don Novello, the former *SNL* contributor best known for his character Father Guido Sarducci. Colbert said, "I loved Novello's stuff so much I wanted to ape it."

Colbert's commitment was so total and so convincing that his character often appealed to the very people he was ridiculing. The bookers of the White House Correspondents' Dinner didn't see a contradiction when they booked him to perform on April 29, 2006, in front of a Republican president whom he routinely eviscerated Monday through Thursday nights on Comedy Central.

Political comedians like Will Rogers and Bob Hope had ribbed politicians for years, but it was a superficial roasting, one that poked fun at their golf game rather than their policies. Mort Sahl attacked Washington from the nightclub stage and Pat Paulsen did so from the safety of a television studio, but no comedian had ever dared criticize the president to his face. Colbert did just that, making an audience of Washington power players extremely uncomfortable. Appearing at the Correspondents' Dinner, he stood behind a podium and compared the administration to the exploding *Hindenburg*. When he criticized the Iraq War, the audience sat cringing in silence, unsure how to respond with the president of the United States sitting right there on the dais, squirming before their eyes. Several of the president's aides walked out in protest, claiming,

"Colbert crossed the line. I can see that [President Bush] got that look that he's ready to blow."

"A group of writers worked on that speech together," said Allison Silverman. "This is the type of material we write every night. It never occurred to me that it would affect the audience so intensely. So when I witnessed the reaction, I was shocked. *Shocked.* The speech definitely wasn't getting a great response. He just kept committing to it, plowing forward. We had no idea how the speech would be perceived. Even later, when we did find out, we were surprised by the strength of response. The reaction to that speech was a lesson on how many people wanted a voice of criticism at that time."

The morning papers, for the most part, ignored Colbert's performance. Reports focused on the other comedian at the function, Steve Bridges, who did a crowd-pleasing impression of the president. *The New York Times*, the *Chicago Tribune* and CNN failed to mention that Stephen Colbert was even there.

But in the days and weeks that followed, the performance gained traction. The C-SPAN website offered two separate feeds—one of Colbert's twenty-minute roast in its entirety, and the other focused solely on the reaction of a visibly annoyed president. When the video was uploaded to a brand-new website called YouTube, it reached nearly three million people in just forty-eight hours. The audio became one of the top downloads on iTunes for the next five months. And after several months of reflection, *New York* magazine assessed it as "a controversial, possibly very funny, possibly horribly unfunny, possibly bravely patriotic, and possibly near-seditious monologue." It was one of the earliest examples of the Internet's turning an otherwise passing comic moment into something lasting.

The Internet changed everything. Although uploading a video hardly guaranteed an audience, the Internet was a key tool in the comedy careers of Dane Cook and Louis C.K. Cook marketed his tours directly to fans on Myspace in the early 2000s. He endeared himself by being accessible over the Internet, and soon he was selling out arenas without ever having had major television exposure. He was the most popular comedian in America for a while, just as Myspace was one of the most popular websites. Cook had invented a modern way of marketing comedy, and the comedians who had worked harder and longer using the old-fashioned model were stunned. "With Dane Cook, I just don't see it," said Robert Klein. "He made a career for himself on the Internet. I just don't get it."

Louis C.K. entered a new level of popularity around 2005, when he started ridiculing his own children for being assholes. It hit a nerve with frustrated parents, and his career gained momentum. Then, with a bit of Internet luck, C.K.'s career hit new heights. C.K. did a panel segment on *Late Night with Conan O'Brien* in autumn 2008, talking about an entitled generation in which "everything's amazing, but nobody's happy." The segment aired on NBC and did fine, but when a random YouTuber uploaded the video a full nine months later, it was circulated widely around Facebook and other websites. It introduced C.K. to droves of new people.

His next bout of good press came when he offered his latest stand-up special as an affordable, direct download, skipping the traditional television route. A couple years earlier he reflected, "They don't put that much of a premium on comedy specials anymore. The new model for doing a special is that you get a company to shoot it with you, they bankroll it, and then you own the video rights. Then a place like HBO shows it for a pittance, just to advertise it, and then you sell it on DVD and you make money that way. But you don't make a special to make money in my eyes." When he skipped TV altogether and made his latest special available on his website for five dollars at the end of 2011, it made him over $1 million. Comedians copied his successful business model, but no one pulled in the same kind of audience. The business model of comedy was changing, but the most important variable was the same as ever: good luck.

Comedy had come a far way since the days when a cussword could land a comic in jail. Comedy veterans held a variety of views on the contemporary climate. Former Marx Brothers scriptwriter Irving Brecher observed in 2008, "Comedy these days takes on subjects that have some sort of importance. Now a writer can talk about abortion, the death penalty, immigration. I don't even know if I would have wanted to deal with the abortion issue when I was writing, but it would have been nice to know that I could have touched on something real if I had wanted to."

Rebels of the 1970s like Chevy Chase and Lorne Michaels were absorbed by the mainstream, and *SNL* is now just another stop on the corporate promotion train. *SNL* head writer James Downey said the reasoning behind the show's musical bookings has changed over the years. "Nowadays the choice of the music [is] entirely about getting kids to watch or earning a big rating. And in the old days, that's the kind of thing that would have prompted a full-scale staff revolt."

George Carlin was extremely critical of what *SNL* had turned into. "This group of people, who were once considered radical and revolutionary, has become just another fucking Hollywood celebrity club." He went so far as to call Lorne Michaels "a fucking hands-and-knees cocksucker."

It was a vulgar statement, and indeed Carlin said he adjusted his persona during his final twenty years to be angrier and more profane just in order to compete with modern comedians. Robert Klein believes there has been a devolution in comedy and its patrons. "I personally believe that comedy audiences have become less cognizant of the world around them, less well read, and generally expect more vulgar and gratuitously cruel humor than the ones I started with in the late 1960s."

Many of comedy's giants abandoned stand-up during their nightclub primes. It's interesting to imagine what the stand-up acts of Woody Allen, Albert Brooks and Larry David would have looked like if they had stuck with it all these years. None have returned to the nightclub stage since their formative years, but all three have considered it. Woody Allen said in July 2013, "I'd like to get back onstage and do stand-up again. I've just been toying with the idea. I would love to see if I could."

Larry David recently said, "If I had an act, it seems like it would be good. I've been trying to write some material. I have it in notebooks. The idea of putting the whole thing together fills me with dread."

Albert Brooks wonders about it. "I think about it. I think I'd enjoy it more now. I have less to lose. Tweeting is almost stand-up, the basis of it. All I have to do is show up somewhere and read them."

Twitter was the perfect medium for the short-form joke. Being limited to 140 characters instilled a joke-writing discipline and gave a comedian a platform on which to test jokes instantaneously. If a Twitter feed hit the right nerve, it could boost a comedian's career. Comedian Todd Barry earned a new following of people who had no knowledge of his stand-up act, but loved his Twitter persona. He saw a boost in stand-up ticket sales as a result. The comic tweets of Rob Delaney led to a following of over a million people. Delaney had never done stand-up, but his steady stream of jokes led to a book deal, a television pilot and a special award from Comedy Central. These success stories gave Twitter-using comics the same kind of hope that Johnny Carson's *Tonight Show* once gave to struggling comedians.

Twitter was a conduit for the written joke. Simultaneously a new audio vehicle became essential for online comedians. Podcasting existed at the turn of the millennium, but didn't spread until simplified software was provided free in Apple's June 2005 version of iTunes. Over the next several years comedians Scott Aukerman, Greg Behrendt, Doug Benson, Bill Burr, Adam Carolla, Greg Fitzsimmons, Todd Glass, Chris Hardwick, Pete Holmes, Jay Mohr, Jimmy Pardo, Greg Proops, Joe Rogan, Paul F. Tompkins and Aisha Tyler would take advantage of the technology, cultivating a loyal cult of listeners as hybrid comedian-broadcasters. Part comedy, part talk show, podcasts helped sell tickets when their stars traveled the country doing stand-up. *The Onion*'s website A.V. Club made a nice analogy, comparing the new podcast proliferation to the comedy record craze of the early 1960s.

In March 2010 Scott Aukerman and a Wall Street investor founded Earwolf, the first "podcast network." It provided the space and equipment and produced individual comedy podcasts for a variety of talents under one catchall banner. Comedian Chris Hardwick followed the concept and hit paydirt with his Nerdist Industries, a podcast network targeting superhero, tech and video game culture. The audience for each podcast is a fraction of what a network television series would bring in, but unlike with so much of television, the audience is not there accidentally. Podcast fans seek out favorites and remain loyal. In the new, atomized world of Internet show business, a cult following is a sustainable achievement.

Marc Maron's podcast was the primary success story of the genre. It inspired scores of comedians to start their own podcasts, hoping to emulate his popularity. Maron had started stand-up in 1986 and did long stretches in Boston, Los Angeles, New York and San Francisco. He became a staple along the Alternative Comedy circuit in the early 1990s and was the most frequent guest in *Conan O'Brien* history. But by 2009 he felt as if he had hit a career bottom. He started his podcast just for the sake of it. Once he became a DIY broadcaster his career climbed at an incredible rate, bringing him the fame he had craved for two decades.

WTF with Marc Maron launched in September 2009 and after twenty-four months had been downloaded twenty million times. One of the first episodes that gained wide attention was Maron's two-part investigation into charges that comedian Carlos Mencia was a joke thief. It was required listening in the comedy community. A few months later Maron interviewed Gallagher, the popular prop comic of the late 1970s, and it descended into a tense shouting match. Maron confronted Gallagher about xenophobic statements he had made and Gallagher stormed out of the interview in anger. It was a seminal moment that proved *WTF with Marc Maron* was not just a simple interview show, but often a compelling drama.

Maron's twenty-plus years as a stand-up gave him an informed point of view when he interviewed fellow comedians, an understanding that most interviewers did not possess. He achieved an intimate dynamic not unlike that of Tom Snyder's old *Tomorrow* show. At its best *WTF with Marc Maron* was hypnotic. Any comic with success in podcasts owes him a debt of gratitude.

Marc Maron trekked up to the Napa Valley with his podcasting equipment to speak with Robin Williams in 2011. Williams spent the hour talking about his anxiety, depression and fear. Four years later Williams succumbed to them and took his own life. "There was a humanity to Robin Williams," Maron said after his death. "The spirit of pure comedy ran through this guy . . . There's never been a comedic artist like this guy. And there's no more painful realization that the other side of whatever comic genius is—is sometimes this. That with that sensitivity, that with that perception, that with that empathy, that with that love, that with that mental agility, comes a heart too heavy to live."

It was not widely known that Williams suffered from depression. For fellow comedians, it was not surprising. The best comedians were sentient beings, men and women with powers of perception, sensitive to life's absurdities—and its cruelties. While the "tears of a clown" concept may be greatly exaggerated, sensitivity is a common trait of the artist—and it is frequently accompanied by depression.

Williams said he emotionally bottomed out around 2002, overcome by a feeling of dread that could not be rationally explained. He felt uncontrollable anxiety about his life and an intense fear of the future.

His cocaine and alcohol use during the late 1970s and early 1980s was well known, and his twenty years of sobriety since then was a source of pride. In 2003 Williams relapsed, making a decision to start drinking again in order to alleviate his uncontrollable anxiety. What started as a weeklong binge turned into three years of alcohol dependency.

Williams had no specific explanation for his relapse. The man who seemed to have everything was in deep suffering. "It's not caused by anything," said Williams. "It's just there. It waits. It lays in wait for the time when you think, 'It's fine now. I'm okay.' Then, the next thing you know, it's not okay."

The manic presence Williams had onstage was that of a man burning off all those anxieties, all the depression, all that fear. "Going onstage is the one salvation," said Williams. "I'm not going to stop."

ACKNOWLEDGMENTS

Thank you to Marc Maron for bringing my work to a wider audience. Thank you to those who, like Marc, helped me gain legal status in the United States: Jerry Beck, Brent Bambury, Brent Butt, Mark Evanier, Drew Friedman, Zach Galifianakis, Lana Gay, Howard Gewirtz, Leonard Maltin, Jenni Matz, Guy Niccolucci, Lisa Jane Persky, George Schlatter, Jim Windolf and Andy Zax.

Thank you to the comedy experts for their enthusiasm and all that comes with it: Jeff Abraham, Wayne Federman, Jim Gentile, Dan Pasternack. Thank you to the first interview subjects of my career, Tom Smothers and Steve Martin; their generosity sent me on an obsessive path.

Thank you to my parents, whose preference in comedy began and ended with *Hee-Haw*. Thank you to the Cinefamily Theater and its stewards Hadrian Belove, Bret Berg and Tom Fitzgerald for allowing me to present Mel Brooks and George Schlatter on its stage. Thank you to Jim Pitt and the staff at *Conan* for putting me in the same room with Mel Brooks in the first place. Thank you to Mel Brooks for being Mel Brooks.

Thank you to those that did the grunt work: my agent Daniel Greenberg, my editor Jamison Stoltz, photographer Jim Herrington and my lawyer Marc Veitenheimer, who desperately wanted a mention of the W. C. Fields film *Million Dollar Legs* in the book—so here it is.

Thank you to those who lent so much moral support through the entire process, which really started way back in 2007 when I was doing stuff online with no clear purpose. Thank you for your kindness, Victoria Fasano, Sara Bynoe, Brie Eileigh, Alana Purcell, Kristen Rattray, Illeana Douglas—and especially WFMU's Ken Freedman, for allowing me full creative freedom to grow as a writer, researcher and artist.

ILLUSTRATION LIST

p. 5, top, left: NBC Television/Wikimedia Commons

p. 5, top, right: CBS Television/Wikimedia Commons

p. 5, bottom: © NBC, courtesy of Photofest

pp. 6-7: © Al Hirschfeld. Reproduced by arrangement with Hirschfeld's exclusive representative, the MARGO FEIDEN GALLERIES LTD., New York. www.alhirschfeld.com

p. 8, top: Photograph by Allan Grant/The LIFE Picture Collection/Getty Images

p. 8, middle: Courtesy of the Pauly Cohen Collection

p. 8, bottom: Photofest

p. 9, top: © CBS, courtesy of Photofest

p. 9, middle, right: Photograph by James Kriegsmann/Fredana Management/Ashley-Steiner Famous Artists, courtesy of Wikimedia Commons

p. 9, middle, left: Wikimedia Commons

p. 9, bottom: Photograph by Herman Hiller, courtesy of the New York World-Telegram and the Sun Newspaper Photograph Collection/ Library of Congress, Prints & Photographs Division [LC-USZ62-121425]

p. 10: Dooto Records

p. 11, top: ABC Television/Wikimedia Commons

p. 11, middle: NBC Television/Wikimedia Commons

p. 11, bottom: © ABC, courtesy of Photofest

p. 12, top: Examiner Press/Wikimedia Commons

p. 12, middle: William Morris Agency/Wikimedia Commons

p. 12, bottom: © CBC Still Photo Collection

p. 13, top: Verve/Library of Congress, Motion Picture, Broadcasting And Recorded Sound Division [Verve V-15031]

p. 13, middle: © Bettmann/CORBIS

p. 13, bottom: CBS Television/Wikimedia Commons

p. 14, top: © CBS, courtesy of Photofest

p. 14, middle, right: CBS Television/Wikimedia Commons

p. 14, middle, left: © NBC, courtesy of Photofest

p. 14, bottom: Photofest

p. 15, top: © NBC, courtesy of Photofest

p. 15, middle, right: © NBC, courtesy of Photofest

p. 15, middle, left: © NBC, courtesy of Photofest

p. 15, bottom: Courtesy of Larry David

p. 16, middle: © Comedy Central, photo by Norman Jean Roy, courtesy of Photofest

p. 16, bottom: © CBS, courtesy of Photofest

NOTES

3   "Their virtual monopoly": Stein, pgs 110, 214

3   "I toiled when I first started": Academy of Television Arts and Sciences, interview with Milton Berle

3   "It was dollar-and-a-half": *Harpo Speaks* by Harpo Marx with Rowland Barber, pg 99

3   "It should have been spelled": *World I Lived* by George Jessel, pgs 19-20

3   "The vaudeville seasons": *Marx Brothers Scrapbook* by Richard J. Anobile, pg 13

3   "the dressing rooms were unclean": *Moe Howard and the Three Stooges* by Moe Howard, pgs 48-50

4   "the most miserable [time]": Stein, pgs 248-249

4   "If they ran off": Ibid.

4   "There never seemed to be": Allen, pgs 186-187

4   "Looking back": Stein, pg 286

4   "along with midgets": *King of Comedy* by Mack Sennett and Cameron Shipp, pg 27

4   "prostitutes, pimps, touts, beggars": Ibid., pg 38

5   "You could buy anything": Laurie Jr., pg 283

5   "Late night work made me": *Variety*, May 28, 1924

5   Narcotics addiction was so common: *50 Years of American Comedy* by Bill Treadwell, pg 14

5   "but none of the imitators": *Pittsburgh Press*, March 7, 1915

5   Ray Ripley was: *Variety*, July 8, 1921

5   Comic Joe Perryfi dealt: Ibid., May 21, 1924

5   "Prohibition posed great problems": Allen, pg 221

6   "alcoholics of all sizes": Stein, pg 257

6   "burlesque people, pimps": *Bud and Lou* by Bob Thomas, pg 53

6   Abbott started the Columbia Wheel: Ibid., pg 25

6   "would be mauled": *The American Burlesque Show* by Irving Zeidman, pg 182

6   "rampaging husbands and racial caricature": Ibid., pgs 202-203

6   "The old vulgar gag": Treadwell, pgs 20-21

6   "The aggravation we had": *Minky's Burlesque* by Morton Minsky and Milt Machlin, pg 30

7   "Mayor Jimmy Walker": *Show Biz: From Vaude to Video* by Joe Laurie Jr. and Abel Green, pg 348

7   "on the Sabbath": Stein, pg 325

7   "A man with a hoop": *Raised Eyebrows* by Steve Stoliar, pg 78

8   "We were pelted with sticks": Stein, pg 286

8   **"Sunday Nite—Amateur Nite"**: Laurie Jr., pg 272

8   **"consisted of several cats"**: Stoliar, pg 78

9   **During one performance**: *My Wonderful World of Slapstick* by Buster Keaton and Charles Samuels, pg 22

9   **"What most burned up Pop"**: Ibid., pg 33

9   **"There was not one word"**: Ibid., pg 32

10 **"Hide your children"**: *Let 'Em Eat Cheesecake* by Earl Wilson, pg 46

10 **"nobody took exception"**: Laurie Jr., pg 81

10 **"The Sandy McPhersons"**: Laurie Jr. and Green, pgs 7-8

11 **"We knew we had three strikes"**: Stein, pg 286

11 **"There were the hate towns"**: *Come Backstage with Me* by Benny Rubin, pg 199

11 **"But it wasn't like"**: Laurie Jr., pg 139

11 **"I missed the streetcar"**: *John Barbour Show*, December 1975

12 **"I loved his style."**: Academy of Television Arts and Sciences, interview with Milton Berle

12 **"We did a thirty-foot dive"**: Howard, pg 21

12 **"That was the Three Stooges"**: Academy of Television Arts and Sciences, interview with Milton Berle

12 **"Not only was the Gardens"**: Howard, pg 36

12 **"Mr. Healy is one"**: *New York Times*, May 22, 1927

12 **"While under the influence"**: Howard, pg 103

13 **"What the hell"**: Jessel, pg 85

13 **"We found Ted"**: Howard, pg 57

13 **"Drinking up a storm,"**: Ibid., pg 103

13 **"chronic alcoholism"**: *The Three Stooges* by Jeff Forrester and Tom Forrester, pg 67

13 **"Police are not investigating"**: *The Fixers* by E. J. Fleming

13 **"It can't be"**: Forrester and Forrester, pg 69

14 **"Fay pioneered the emcee"**: *No People Like Show People* by Maurice Zolotow, pg 213

14 **"Fay needs a good"**: Ibid., pg 210

15 **"I learned that"**: Treadwell, pg 230

15 **"I never attack"**: *No Applause—Just Throw Money* by Trav S.D., pg 233

15 **In a business**: *The Jack Benny Show* by Milt Josefsberg, pg 314

15 **"I reached out"**: *An Autobiography* by Milton Berle, pg 101

15 **"The last time"**: S.D., pg 234

16 **"Fay forgot to mention"**: Zolotow, pg 211

16   **"He was just a sensational man"**: *John Barbour Show*, December 1975

16   **"That's where Harpo appeared"**: Anobile, pg 14

16   **"It was a real dump."**: Ibid.

17   **"As a result"**: Marx with Barber, pg 130

17   **"She was impressed"**: *Sunday Nights at Seven* by Jack Benny and Joan Benny, pg 11

17   **"We weren't very close"**: Anobile, pgs 13, 44

17   **"For thirty solid weeks"**: Marx with Barber, pg 138

17   **"The thing was"**: Anobile, pg 44

18   **"Too late, we learned"**: Marx with Barber, pg 155

18   **"His humor was based"**: *The Palace* by Marian Spitzer, pg 25

18   **"The thing that impressed me"**: *Laughter Is a Wonderful Thing* by Joe E. Brown, pg 175

18   **"Evidently he has seen Julius"**: "It Happened Last Night," Earl Wilson, March 29, 1963

18   **In order to appease them**: Benny and Benny, pg 17

19   **"Benny says that he is"**: *Written By*, April 2002

20   **"egotism and aloofness."**: *Natural Selection* by Gary Giddins, pg 28

20   **"If a comedian was original"**: Allen, pgs 246-247

20   **The vaudeville term**: Spitzer, pg 97

20   **"Before the members vacated"**: Allen, pg 248

21   **"The raids on vaudeville talent"**: Laurie Jr. and Green, pg 160

21   **"Ziegfeld loathed comedians"**: *Life*, July 26, 1948

21   **Comedy writer Gene Buck**: *Banjo Eyes* by Herbert G. Goldman, pg 52

21   **"Cantor's humor is painted"**: *B.S. I Love You* by Milton Berle, pg 92

21   **"I can replace every one"**: S.D., pg 11

21   **"best Negro comedian"**: *The Way I See It* by Eddie Cantor, pg 113

22   **In 1911, when Walker died**: Goldman, pg 59

22   **"Before I got through"**: Stein, pg 242

22   **"This was made evident"**: Laurie Jr. and Green, pg 325

23   **"beautiful lobbies with oil paintings"**: Laurie Jr., pg 346

23   **"Sometimes, at the five o'clock"**: *Gracie* by George Burns, pg 73

24   **Phil Baker got five thousand**: *There's Laughter in the Air* by Jack Gaver and Dave Stanley, pg 235

24 **It was a time:** US Government Census, 1923-1926

24 **"Movies, vaudeville, burlesque":** Burns, pg 86-87

24 **Weekly attendance was:** Stein, pg 371

24 **"It did away with cumbersome":** *I Looked and I Listened* by Ben Gross, pg 74

24 **"born of military establishment":** *Tube of Plenty* by Erik Barnouw, pgs 56-57

25 **His masterwork:** Treadwell, pg 166

25 **"They flocked to watch":** Laurie Jr. and Green, pg 355

25 **"Most of the houses":** *American Burlesque Show* by Irving Zeidman, pgs 238-239

25 **"This was no living":** *This Laugh Is On Me* by Phil Silvers, pg 44

CHAPTER TWO: RADIO

26 **"Possibly because there was":** Ohmart, pg 49

26 **"Eddie Cantor was very important":** *It's Good to Be King* by James Robert Parish, pgs 28, 237

27 **"Laughs were mystifying":** Ohmart, pg 49

27 **In response Gross and Greenberg:** Gross, pg 136

27 **"The cast of the Eddie Cantor":** *Jack Benny* by Irving Fein, pg 129

27 **"He begged for laughs":** *Raised on Radio* by Gerald Nachman, pg 44

27 **"And he liked to goose":** Goldman, pg 232

27 **"He was chasing women":** Nachman, pg 43

28 **"The world's greatest professional":** Ohmart, pg 49

29 **"The owners always thought":** *Laugh Crafters* by Jordan R. Young, pg 8

29 **He was a marginal figure:** *Variety*, January 15, 1945

29 **"The Vallee fans":** Gross, pg 80

29 **"That was none of his doing":** Young, pg 31

29 **"He had absolutely no talent":** Ibid., pg 106

29 **"We once wrote":** *Laughs, Luck and Lucy* by Jess Oppenheimer with Gregg Oppenheimer, pg 100

30 **"He got so scared":** *Ed Wynn's Son* by Keenan Wynn, pg 89

30 **"When I was on *Kate Smith*":** *Fresh Air*, interview with Henny Youngman, 1992

31 **"They were working in burlesque":** *Take My Wife . . . Please!* by Henny Youngman as told to Carroll Carroll, pg 154

31 **"Lou Costello was one"**: *Bud and Lou* by Bob Thomas, pg 11

31 **"While minstrel-style wordplay humor"**: *The Original Amos 'n' Andy* by Elizabeth McLeod

32 **"Similar protests have been received"**: *Radio Digest*, June 1930

32 **"I am glad to know"**: *Inside Facts of Stage and Screen*, May 23, 1931

32 **"gross libel on the Negro"**: *Cold War, Cool Medium* by Thomas Doherty, pg 77

33 **"His client wanted"**: Benny and Benny, pg 40

33 **Canada Dry eventually objected**: Josefsberg, pg 322

34 **"He may be the only"**: Giddins, pg 25

34 **Eddie Anderson was hired**: Benny and Benny, pgs 100-101

34 **"Jokes of that insensitive sort"**: Josefsberg, pg 85

34 **"During World War II"**: Benny and Benny, pg 108

34 **In the 1960s**: Giddins, pg 35

35 **"He was at the center"**: *Vanity Fair*, December 6, 2012

35 **"Jack and I were charged"**: Burns, pgs 230-231

35 **"his name at the moment"**: *Los Angeles Times*, December 14, 2008

36 **"pale and nervous"**: U.P., January 11, 1939

36 **"They kept talking"**: Benny and Benny, pg 171

36 **According to Benny**: Josefsberg, pg 377

36 **"They were very tough"**: Young, pgs 278, 282

37 **The American Tobacco Company**: Goldman, pg 187

37 **"After the conclusion"**: FBI internal correspondence, April 10, 1939

37 **"murderer, kidnapper"**: Goldman, pg 198

37 **"We are all of the opinion"**: Nachman, pg 45

37 **"that even those in"**: *New York Times*, March 13, 1933

37 **Cohn was so impressed**: *Movies and Methods, Volume Two* edited by Bill Nichols, pg 103

38 **They formed RAM**: *Variety*, October 7, 1937

38 **"As our trademark"**: *Hollywood Speaks* by Mike Steen, pg 370

38 **"I gave a large party"**: Ibid., pg 370

38 **"red and gold metal cloth"**: *Variety*, September 29, 1937

38 **"from a business and diplomatic"**: Ibid., October 7, 1937

38 **Charlie Chaplin, Joan Crawford**: Ibid., October 9, 1937

38 **Mussolini's trip was cut short**: Ibid., October 7, 1937

38 **However, when the United States**: Ibid., February 9, 1938

38 **"a good dictator"**: Steen, pg 369

39 **"I had a very large"**: Anobile, pgs 174-176

39 **"So suddenly there was"**: King with Chase, pg 33

39 **"For this reason a lot"**: Marx with Barber, pg 416

41   "You Americans are such children": *Radio and Television Mirror*, June 1949

41   "I never for a moment": Ibid., April 1935

41   He sent word back to Boston: *Variety*, February 5, 1935

41   The film studio had plans: Ibid., April 9, 1936

42   In spring 1936: *Los Angeles Times*, May 31, 1936

42   A romance blossomed: *New York Times*, February 8, 1937

43   Originally a summer replacement: *Variety*, August 9, 1945

43   It featured fine comic actors: Ibid., October 22, 1947

43   "It's funny. Not inspired": *Billboard*, November 1, 1947

43   He checked in to Cedars: *Variety*, August 28, 1947

43   "All he intended to do": *Radio and Television Mirror*, June 1949

43   He invested in: *Variety*, November 15, 1946

43   He incorporated an independent: Ibid., February 10, 1947

43   He partnered with New York philanthropist: Ibid., July 10, 1947; August 7, 1947

43   He planned a record: Ibid., April 29, 1947

44   "He was so sick . . .": *Vanity Fair*, January 2013

44   Inactive, he took up coin: *Variety*, November 14, 1946

44   Jackie Gleason: Ibid., January 4, 1956

44   Tony Martin: Ibid., June 7, 1954

44   George Raft: Ibid., January 25, 1956

45   "Put his head down!": Ibid., November 26, 1958

45   "He was beside himself": *Mean*, May-June 2000

46   "He could have died": Ibid.

46   "Radio is a repugnant medium": Zolotow, pgs 270-271

46   "a bitter, frustrated and unhappy": Nachman, pg 108

46   "The worst thing that ever happened": Ibid., pg 103

47   "The only way": Ibid.

47   "Radio comedy is the most painful": Zolotow, pgs 270-271

47   "Fred was better": Young, pg 167

48   "The main thing in radio": *Ace*, 1959

48   "More and more things": *There's Laughter in the Air!* by Jack Graver and Dave Stanley

48   "Men who ran oil companies": *Treadmill to Oblivion* by Fred Allen, pg 13

48   "Practically everything is taboo": Nachman, pg 105

48   "immoral overtones": Zolotow, pg 273

48   "Radio's slogan is": *Variety*, September 30, 1948

48   "Their gags were more": Laurie Jr. and Green, pg 538

49   "Little or no regard": Ohmart, pgs 153-154
49   Morgan was as much : *Variety*, November 6, 1940
49   "If children eat enough": *Life*, April 14, 1947
50   "[He] did a goofy yarn": *Variety*, November 6, 1940
50   "Thank goodness the contract": Ibid., January 29, 1941
51   its version of Henry Morgan: Ibid., January 29, 1941
51   "a female Henry Morgan": Ibid., February 17, 1943
51   "in the Henry Morgan fashion": Ibid., February 19, 1947
51   When future *Match Game* host: Ibid., April, 14, 1948
52   in February 1948: Ibid., January 7, 1948
52   "He was very difficult": Nachman, pg 121
52   "I grew up thinking": Ibid., Nachman, pgs 121-123

CHAPTER THREE: NIGHTCLUBS

53   "If they didn't": Jessel, pg 83
54   "A horrendous blow struck him": *The Joker Is Wild* by Art Cohn
54   "Jack [McGurn] sent me": *Double Cross* by Sam Giancana and Chuck Giancana, pg 168
56   "[Mobster] Marty Krompier": Berle, pg 133
56   "His penis had been cut off": *The Show Business Nobody Knows* by Earl Wilson, pg 133
56   "In my time": *George Raft* by Lewis Yablonsky, pg 246
57   "When a well-dressed guest arrives": *Life*, March 3, 1941
57   "No small part": *52nd Street* by Arnold Shaw
57   He honed his insult shtick: *Variety*, November 26, 1969
58   "the first Don Rickles": Rubin, pg 63
58   "Every time someone like Frankie": *New York*, September 1985
61   It called for an investigation: *Kefauver* by Joseph Bruce Gorman, pg 74
61   The committee started work: *Cold War, Cool Medium* by Thomas Doherty, pg 108
61   Florida governor Fuller Warren refused: Gorman, pg 81
61   "is an ambition-crazed Caesar": Ibid.
62   It flourished during the war: *Variety*, June 27, 1945
62   "Two staffers in the Chicago office": Ibid., January 9, 1974
63   "I heard this gruff-sounding voice": *Jerry Lewis in Person* by Jerry Lewis, pgs 156-157
63   "The bull slowly rose": Ibid.

64   "I have made considerable headway": *Variety*, August 19, 1959
64   "No one wants to": Ibid.
65   "You could identify": Rose, pg 229
65   "By the time I joined": *Where Did I Go Right?* by Bernie Brillstein with David Rensin, pg 42
66   "The hoodlum burst": Berle, pg 24
66   "If they like you": *Fresh Air*, inteview with Henny Youngman, 1992
67   "excess law enforcement": *The Agency* by Frank Rose, pg 160
67   "the show violates": *New York Times*, November 3, 1942
67   "an affront to public morals": *Variety*, June 19, 1946
67   "for using blue material": *Billboard*, December 30, 1949
68   "Under the present attitude": *Variety*, November 14, 1956
68   The comedians playing his club: Ibid., December 5, 1956
68   "with lewd conversation": Ibid., March 6, 1957
68   "I'd heard plenty about B. S.": *It's Not Easy Bein' Me* by Rodney Dangerfield, pg 43
69   He and the club operator: *Variety*, November 4, 1942
69   He was put on trial: *New York Post*, November 1, 1946
70   "obscene and vulgar references": *Variety*, May 19, 1965
70   "Bourbon underwent a sex change": Ibid., August 1, 1956
71   "obscene and profane": Ibid., August 16, 1956
71   "Much of it was risqué": *Baby, I Don't Care* by Lee Server, pg 46
72   "for staging an obscene show": *Variety*, September 21, 1955
72   "A curious anomaly": *Billboard*, March 27, 1961
72   "on suspicion of performing": *Variety*, Janaury 9, 1961
72   "lewdness and immoral activity": Ibid., August 2, 1961
72   "If it's breaking the law": Ibid., January 30, 1963
72   "corrupted them morally": *Miami News*, January 14, 1964
73   "an area of maybe fifty": Youngman and Carroll, pg 89
73   "The Borscht Belt was a community": Academy of Television Arts and Sciences, interview with Jerry Lewis
73   "All he wanted to do": Lewis, pg 11
73   "Every summer, as the comedians": *Caesar's Hours* by Sid Caesar, pg 33
74   "originated in pre-caveman": *Collier's*, November 1950
74   "It was there": Caesar, pg 32
74   He circumvented war rationing: *Variety*, June 17, 1942
74   "He sends his acts rushing": Wilson, *Cheesecake*, pg 204

75   **"stood on stage"**: *How Dare You Say How Dare Me!* by Pat Cooper, pg 185

75   **"'Country Club' was an appellation"**: *Amorous Busboy of Decatur Avenue* by Robert Klein, pg 117

76   **"At times they would throw"**: Ibid., pg 119

77   **"Don't get lost"**: Spitzer, pg 139

77   **According to New York columnist**: *Knows* by Earl Wilson, pg 32

77   **"There was nothing artistic"**: Rubin, pg 197

78   **The Paramount was arguably**: *Variety*, November 7, 1947

78   **Harry Kalcheim of William Morris**: Ibid., January 8, 1941

79   **In his place producers cast**: Ibid., November 13, 1975

79   **"Jean Carroll, a single"**: Ibid., March 1, 1944

79   **"Jean Carroll gives a hint"**: Ibid., April 12, 1944

80   **One tally had it**: *The Kid* by Richard Gehman, pg 103

80   **"It was in a downstairs café"**: Ohmart, pg 140

81   **"He hasn't even bothered"**: *Bud and Lou* by Bob Thomas, pg 153

81   **"The response was almost orgiastic"**: *Everybody Loves Somebody Sometime* by Arthur Marx, pg 142

81   **"This is a nothing act"**: Ibid., pg 64

82   **"Jerry, who was supposed to be"**: Ibid., pg 135

82   **"Then Jerry would do them"**: *The Box* by Jeff Kisseloff, pg 328

82   **He fired them**: Marx, pg 166

82   **"The greatest performers"**: *Been There, Done That* by Eddie Fisher with David Fisher, pg 26

83   **"Everybody would drop in"**: Henny Youngman and Carroll, pgs 133-134

83   **Marlon Brando and fellow actor**: *Variety*, June 7, 1939

84   **"At night in Kellogg's"**: *From Gags to Riches* by Joey Adams, pg 299

85   **"It was where [gangster] Arnold Rothstein"**: *Variety*, January 7, 1970

85   **"Songwriters, song pluggers"**: *Longest Street* by Louis Sobol, pg 422

85   **"One seldom sees him"**: Gross, pg 125

86   **"Lindy's was where"**: *Variety*, January 7, 1970

86   **"It's a small place"**: *I Kid You Not* by Jack Paar, pg 6

87   **"Max is a man"**: Ibid.

89   **"I didn't get one"**: Nachman, pg 399

89   **"I asked Tommy"**: *Honey* by Honey Bruce with Dana Benenson, pgs 148-149

90   **"It is a city where"**: *Time*, June 25, 1951

90 "One night in Kellogg's Cafeteria": Dangerfield, pg 115
92 "According to James J. Kelly": *Long Island Star-Journal*, October 22, 1955
94 Rodney claimed to have picked: *The Jack Benny Program*, January 4, 1942

CHAPTER FOUR: TELEVISON

95 "a device that permits people": Nachman, pg 116
95 "Radio was a much more": Josefsberg, pg 59
96 Two hundred different advertisers: *Radio Annual*, 1948, pg 1047
96 "For nine months": *Ed Wynn's Son* by Keenan Wynn, pgs 193-194
96 "I think the audience": Kisseloff, pg 317
97 "Parlaying the best": *Variety*, June 9, 1948
97 "In 1948, [William Morris]": Kisseloff, pg 511
98 A classic Joe E. Lewis joke: Adams, pg 153
98 "He started inserting old jokes": Young, pgs 56-57
98 "The rehearsals became": *NBC Book of Stars* by Earl Wilson, pg 40
98 "being stuck in an air raid": *This Is Your Life*, June 6, 1956
99 "I don't like being on": Howard, pg 165
99 "That whistle got me": Berle, pg 274
99 "Milton is a coward": Kisseloff, pg 307
99 "I was under pressure": Academy of Television Arts and Sciences, interview with Milton Berle
100 "arrogant, demanding": Rose, pg 145
100 "It will be the first": Kisseloff, pg 304
100 "Jackie Miles, Lenny Kent and": Adams, pg 304
101 "I got the idea": Berle, pg 99
101 "impersonating a woman": *WFMU: Murder in Mink* by Kliph Nesteroff
101 "Knocked Berle off": Silvers, pg 208
101 "I felt drained, finished": Berle, pg 3
102 "one of the most likeable": *Variety*, February 18, 1956
102 He immediately entered negotiations: *Collier's*, May 11, 1956
102 "immensely impressed": *Variety*, September 1, 1954
102 "Don't get into that": Silvers, pg 201
102 "He's going to be": *Variety*, May 17, 1955
103 "*My Little Margie* was stupid": Kisseloff, pg 336

103 **"Sgt. Bilko holds up"**: *By the Way: In Conversation with Jeff Garlin*, January 2013

103 **"He nursed me along"**: Silvers, pg 44

103 **Coke-bottle glasses:** *Variety*, January 8, 1958

103 **"He did not realize"**: Silvers, pg 218

103 **"Without me, the *Bilko* show"**: *WFMU: King of Slobs* by Kliph Nesteroff

104 **"Their sketch was painful"**: Silvers, pg 218

104 **"Someone apparently didn't have much"**: *Variety*, September 21, 1955

104 **"[The president] has been"**: *Variety*, May 16, 1956

104 **"That ruined his life"**: Kisseloff, pg 336

105 **He wrote most of:** *Variety*, October 7, 1959

105 **"I'm getting out"**: Ibid., July 31, 1957

105 **Hiken met with Carl Reiner:** Ibid., May 29, 1957

105 **"You son of a bitch"**: Fein, pgs 175-76

106 **"Every week that summer"**: Kisseloff, pg 309

106 **In less than twenty minutes:** *Billboard*, February 5, 1949

107 **In the dressing room:** *It's Good to Be King* by James Michael Parish, pg 61

107 **Roy Atwell, Admiral's answer:** *Billboard*, February 5, 1949; Caesar, pg 76

107 **"Fundamentally the weakness"**: *Variety*, February 2, 1949

107 **In addition, he was fielding:** Ibid., June 8, 1949

107 **When those sketches appeared:** Ibid., April 11, 1949

108 **called *Great Caesar*:** Ibid., January 11, 1950

108 **"There was an enormous"**: Nachman, pg 111

109 **"The very first day"**: Kisseloff, pgs 312, 316

109 **"For nine years"**: Caesar, pgs 119, 131-132

110 **"When I was listed"**: Parish, pg 86

110 **"We wanted him to do"**: Kisseloff, pg 310

110 **"I was aggressive"**: Parish, pg 93

110 **"Sometimes once a day"**: Caesar, pg 133

110 **"Caesar running out of material"**: *Collier's*, November 11, 1950

111 **"then Sid Caesar is"**: Ibid.

111 **"Sid Caesar doesn't steal jokes"**: Ibid.

112 **"He calls me upstairs"**: *Fresh Air*, interview with Henny Youngman; 1992

113 **"They were worried"**: Burns, pg 97

113 **"in an age"**: *New Yorker*, February 20, 1978

114 **"He didn't need":** Kisseloff, pg 322

114 **"Canned laughter and applause":** Barnouw, pgs 247-248

114 **"I told them":** Burns, pg 257

114 **Further use of laugh tracks:** *Variety*, April 7, 1965

114 **"It got to the point":** Academy of Television Arts and Sciences, interview with Carroll Pratt

115 **"If it wasn't funny":** Arce, pg 30

116 **Fielding couldn't find work:** Ibid., pgs 58-59

116 **"That I bowed to":** Ibid., pg 87

116 **"Lou felt very strong":** *Lou's on First* by Chris Costello with Raymond Strait, pgs 195-196

116 **"We have to keep taxes":** Thomas, pg 175

117 **Grant quit and stormed:** Costello with Strait, pg 197

117 **"I will be dying":** Steve Allen FBI File, October 1960

117 **Morgan was one of 151 people:** Barnouw, pg 122

118 **"Whatever happened to Henry Morgan?":** *Variety*, January 2, 1952

118 **"Besides the newsletter":** Kisseloff, pg 409

118 **"The guys who came":** Ibid., pg 410

118 **"Nevertheless we decided":** Ibid., pg 411

119 **"On the early *Tonight* shows":** Nachman, pg 171

119 **"Pat Weaver came down personally":** Kisseloff, pg 416

119 ***Red Channels* was confused:** Doherty, pg 30

119 **Before she was cast:** Kisseloff, pg 339

119 **Male lead Philip Loeb:** Nachman, pg 245

120 **"He sent for me to talk":** Kisseloff, pg 427

120 **While it was no surprise:** *Empire of Dreams* by Scott Eyman, pg 414

120 **"The entire industry":** Kisseloff, pg 403

120 **"Kirkpatrick has sat in":** Barnouw, pg 212

120 **"I'm an internationalist":** *New York Herald Tribune*, January 8, 1953

121 **"I will be proud":** *Champagne Before Breakfast* by Hy Gardner, pg 2

121 **"While the House Committee":** Doherty, pg 52

121 **"Lucille Ball announces":** Ibid.

121 **a protest against *I Love Lucy*:** FBI memorandum, Lucille Ball file, 1953

121 **"The investigation is continuing":** Doherty, pg 54

121 **"my favorite redhead":** Ibid., pgs 55-56

122 **"They feel that when":** Ibid., pgs 57-58

122 **"The blacklist is one":** Ibid., pg 33

122 **"most important people":** *WFMU: The Early Woody Allen* by Kliph Nesteroff

123 **"It's either him":** Parish, pg 97

123 **"I wanted my own show":** Kisseloff, pg 313

124 **"Do you know the competition":** *And Here's the Kicker* by Mike Sacks, pgs 329-330

CHAPTER FIVE: LATE NIGHT

125 **"embarrassingly pedestrian":** *Variety*, May 30, 1950

126 **Lester was promptly fired:** Kisseloff, pg 213

126 **"He wrecked the place":** Ibid., pg 117

126 **Lester hosted Tuesday, Thursday:** *Variety*, August 23, 1950

127 **"It wasn't like the late-night":** Kisseloff, pg 117

127 **Eventually NBC hired Cal:** *Variety*, August 23, 1950

127 **"I went down to the Greyhound":** Kisseloff, pg 118

127 **"That one really got":** 7 *Dirty Words* by James Sullivan, pgs 16-17

128 **Feeling slighted, Amsterdam quit:** *Variety*, November 22, 1950

128 **"but wrote great memos":** *P.S. Jack Paar* by Jack Paar, pg 99

129 **NBC put his name:** Nachman, pg 185

129 **The guests were Wally Cox:** *Inventing Late Night* by Ben Alba, pg 59

130 **During a broadcast:** *Variety*, September 8 and 15, 1954

130 **"I'd have six million people":** Nachman, pg 171

130 **Premiering June 24, 1956:** Alba, pg 279

131 **"looking ill at ease":** *Variety*, January 30, 1957

131 **"a disaster from the first":** Wilson, *Knows*

132 **"I met and became friendly":** Paar, pg 55

132 **"This Jack Paar was":** *I Kid You Not* by Jack Paar, pgs 44-45

133 **"patterned too closely after":** *Variety*, June 16, 1947

133 **"I hope he is as funny":** Wilson, *Knows*, pg 358

133 **"He hired and fired":** Josefsberg, pg 271

133 **"Did you ever have":** Paar, *I Kid*, pg 59

133 **"Three hours a day":** Paar, *P.S. Jack*, pg 96

133 **He shone and was hired:** *Variety*, June 20, 1956

133 **"This looks like the last":** Ibid., July 31, 1957

134 **"Their main thought":** Paar, *P.S. Jack*, pg 100

134 **Of 131 different programs:** *Variety*, April 7, 1958

134 **Boston, Cleveland, Houston:** Ibid., September 11, 1957

134 **"Junkie Mark Twain":** *A Funny Thing Happened to Me on My Way to the Grave* by Jack Douglas, pg 142

135 **"Steve is the greatest":** Paar, *I Kid*, pg 66

135 **"The experience of his helmship"**: *Variety*, June 4, 1958

135 **"a mystery comedy"**: Ibid., October 5, 1959

135 **By the end**: *Life*, March 9, 1959

135 **"get a doctor's certificate"**: *Variety*, September 17, 1958

135 **In protest Paar vacationed**: Ibid., February 19, 1959

135 **For a substantial raise**: Ibid., June 8, 1959

136 **He had the most profitable**: *Life*, March 9, 1959

136 **"I felt the implication"**: Paar, *I Kid*, pg 227

136 **"They said, 'No, no'"**: *WFMU: Late Night Distemper of Our Times* by Kliph Nesteroff

137 **"Bob Hope and Jack Benny"**: Paar, *P.S. Jack*, pg 116

CHAPTER SIX: THE EMERGENCE OF LAS VEGAS

138 **"By 1953, forty-five citations"**: Gorman, pg 95

138 **"Those were the Ben [Bugsy]"**: King with Chase, pg 62

139 **"He had absolutely no voice"**: *Las Vegas Is My Beat* by Ralph Pearl, pgs 92-93

139 **By 1952 Joey Bishop**: Wilson, *Knows*, pg 5

140 **"I'd watch Lewis come"**: Pearl, pg 48

141 **"When the first two blasts"**: UPI, September 25, 1952

141 **"He wouldn't take out patents"**: *TV Radio Mirror*, November 1956

142 **"Lenny couldn't wait"**: Bruce with Benenson, pgs 177-178

142 **"You're a fine comedian"**: *TV Radio Mirror*, November 1956

142 **"with the different humorous aspects"**: *Variety*, October 25, 1961

143 **He bought a ranch house**: *TV Radio Mirror*, November 1956

143 **Comedy writers William Friedberg and**: *Variety*, May 2, 1956

143 **"Hackett is a good comic"**: Ibid., September 26, 1956

143 **"Liebman was too strong"**: *Woody Allen* by Eric Lax, pg 121

147 **"One explosive night"**: *Hollywood Is a Four Letter Town* by James Bacon, pg 50

149 **"represented what I thought"**: Larry King, interview with Don Rickles, 1986

151 **"That's where my style came"**: *Rickles' Book* by Don Rickles with David Ritz, pg 56

151 **Rickles appealed to have**: *Cangold v. Don Rickles*, Supreme Court of New York, February 2, 1959

151 **"He died heartbroken"**: Pearl, pg 99

152 **"The dolt and the dullard"**: *Miami News*, December 20, 1957

152 **"Frank Costello called me":** *Mickey Cohen: In My Own Words* as told to John Peer Nugent, pgs 117-118

153 **"He was so wrong":** Guy MacPherson, interview with Don Rickles, October 6, 2006

Chapter Seven: Stand-Up's Great Change

156 **"For twenty years":** *Life*, November 12, 1956

156 **"Every joke ever written":** Treadwell, pg 205

156 **Orben later became:** *A Critical History of Television's* The Red Skelton Show, pgs 89, 148

156 **"The end of World War II":** Laurie Jr. and Green, pg 537

157 **"What it did for me":** *Comic Insights* by Franklyn Ajaye, pg 84

158 **It was where Bruce met:** *Trials of Lenny Bruce* by Ronald K. L. Collins and David M. Skover, pg 87

158 **"It blew my mind":** Bruce with Benenson, pg 217

160 **"I constructed a network":** *Impolite Interviews* by Paul Krassner, pg 156

160 **"to show we weren't":** Nachman, pg 9

160 **He did impressions:** Ibid., pg 56

160 **"Then I got up onstage":** Ibid., pg 59

160 **"I was afraid no one":** Ibid., pg 61

160 **"In my case":** *Late Night with David Letterman*, January 20, 1988

161 **"funny without being much fun":** Nachman, pg 59

161 **"the wrong associations":** Ibid., pgs 71-72

161 **"There was a need":** Ibid., pg 68

161 **"Who wants a comic":** Ibid., pg 52

161 **"as important in the history":** Ibid., pg 11

162 **"One night through the ventilator":** Ibid., pg 416

162 **Welk threatened Bruce:** Ibid., pg 392

162 **"His act was a mixture":** *Show Me the Magic* by Paul Mazursky, pg 142

164 **"As opposed to Mr. Bishop":** Krassner, pg 13

164 **"Through the title":** *Backing Into Forward* by Jules Feiffer, pgs 243, 217

164 **"Opening night witnessed":** *Variety*, March 16, 1960

165 **"He continues to preach against":** *Billboard*, April 14, 1962

165 **"Everybody has to have some":** *Playboy*, March 1961

165 **"But I was in":** Ajaye, pg 247

165 "He was a revolutionary": Nachman, pg 240
165 "Every night he became": Ibid., pg 256
165 "He came out and": Bacon, pg 61
165 Banducci had to call: Nachman, pg 254
165 "He began the show": Mazurksy, pg 140
166 He wandered to the wharf: Nachman, pg 243
166 "It was a mental breakdown": Bacon, pg 57
166 Doctors suggested Winters accept: Nachman, pg 256
166 "You gotta say goodbye": Ibid., pg 255
168 "What kind of a comedian": *It Only Hurts When I Laugh* by Stan
    Freberg, pg 111
168 "As a result, CBS": Ibid., pgs 117-118
168 "Art for money's sake.": Ibid., pg 131
169 the *Harvard Lampoon*: *Revel with a Cause* by Stephen E. Kercher,
    pg 128
169 "Suddenly there was this place": *Something Wonderful Right Away*
    by Jeffrey Sweet, pg 47
169 "The wedge was Shelley": Ibid., pgs 52-54
170 "It wasn't a well-matched": Ibid., pg 219
170 "I wanted to make": Kercher, pg 162
170 "I thought I might": Sweet, pg 143
170 The Compass called it home: *Variety*, February 26, 1964
170 "St. Louis was a very hip": *Married to Laughter* by Jerry Stiller,
    pg 168
171 "We performed for fifty hipsters": Mazursky, pgs 136-137
171 "We joked around": Academy of Television Arts and Sciences,
    interview with Fred Willard
172 "innate sense of the absurdity": *Cue*, volume 31, 1962
172 "We had an ending piece": Academy of Television Arts and Sciences,
    interview with Fred Willard
172 "One time we were on": Ibid.
173 the Inquisition in Vancouver: *Variety*, October 23, 1963
173 the King's Club in Dallas: Ibid., August 19, 1964
173 "A wildly funny comedy duo": Ibid., October 10, 1962
173 "I was kind of": *Second City Unscripted* by Mike Thomas, pg 32
175 "I always had a progressive": *Comedy at the Edge* by Richard Zoglin,
    pg 22
175 "I kind of learned": *WFMU: Early George Carlin* by Kliph Nesteroff
176 "The pope sucks": Sullivan, pg 43

176 **"He called us 'a cerebral'"**: *Last Words* by George Carlin with Tony Hendra, pg 80

176 **"The defiance inherent in"**: Ibid.

177 **"too hip for general run"**: *Variety*, August 23, 1961

177 **They were booked**: Ibid., February 14, 1961

177 **"Peter, Paul and Mary"**: *Playboy*, January 1982

177 **"When Jack and I"**: Nesteroff, *WFMU: Early George Carlin*

177 **"His texts are generally"**: *Variety*, September 5, 1962

178 **"the degrading things"**: *WFMU: Early Woody Allen* by Kliph Nesteroff

178 **"He was arrogant and hostile"**: Lax, pg 130

178 **"This is crazy"**: Ibid.

178 **"Woody was terrified"**: *Woody Allen: A Biography* by John Baxter, pg 79

179 **"When I first started out"**: Nachman, pg 95

179 **"Woody Allen is such a"**: "The Voice of Broadway," Dorothy Kilgallen, December 3, 1962

179 **"He was quite outraged"**: *The Dick Cavett Show*, October 4, 1977

179 **"It is because of you"**: Ibid.

181 **"Dick Cavett came in 1964"**: *The Bitter End* by Paul Colby, pgs 77-78

182 **"They auditioned sixty ladies"**: Sweet, pg 287

182 **"I was never truly happy"**: Ibid., pg 291

182 **"Visibly nervous at the start"**: *Variety*, August 5, 1964

183 **"That kept me going"**: Zoglin, pg 185

183 **"I learned later that Totie"**: *Still Talking* by Joan Rivers with Richard Meryman, pg 52

184 **"I never believed"**: Ajaye, pg 273

185 **"America's Smartest Colored Shows"**: *New York Age*, December 29, 1934

185 **"The slightly off-color gags"**: Ibid.

185 **"It's a real bladder"**: *Milwaukee Journal*, July 17, 1968

186 **"You don't need blackface"**: *Timmie Rogers: Forgotten Pioneer of Comedy*, YouTube documentary

186 **"A lot of people"**: *WFMU: Last Man in Blackface* by Kliph Nesteroff

187 **"She liked me"**: *Redd Foxx, B.S.* by Joe X. Price, pg 110

187 **His car was searched**: *Variety*, September 7, 1949

187 **"Fellow entertainers often wondered"**: *Black and Blue* by Michael Seth Starr pg 33

187 "display more care with": *Variety*, October 31, 1951

188 "I remember going over": Price, pg 115

188 "The walls are painted": *New York Times*, May 15, 1961

189 "White audiences would not": *Jet*, November 28, 1957

189 A production company even packaged: *Variety*, April 12, 1961

189 "The Negro is an original": *Ebony*, October 1960

189 "I went in with Maynard": Price, pgs 76-77

190 "White comics can insult": *Ebony*, October 1960

190 "the brightest aspect": *Billboard*, November 20, 1961

191 "Hey, what was that": Starr, pg 52

191 "I had no idea": Price, pg 115

191 He paid each comedian: *Black Comedians on Black Comedy* by Darryl Littleton, pg 86

191 "I should have never": Ibid., pg 87

192 "Redd had a big influence": *Cheech and Chong* by Tommy Chong, pg 59

192 It had been recorded: *Billboard*, October 27, 1958

193 The Los Angeles Sheriff's Department: *Variety*, January 20, 1961

194 "they gave information": Ibid., September 20, 1961

194 While the albums were hardly: *Los Angeles Times*, April 23, 1952

194 In November 1963: *Variety*, November 27, 1963

194 Warner Bros. released Newhart's: *Variety*, April 13, 1960

195 "I was coming to work": *WTF with Marc Maron*, ep 332

195 "A disc jockey friend": www.pbs.org/wnet/makeemlaugh/episodes/history/comedy-lps/38/

195 The recording sold two hundred: Kercher, pg 136

195 "make more money than me": Nachman, pg 366

195 Dan Sorkin, the man who: *Broadcasting*, September 2, 1963

195 "All I knew as I left": Parish, pg 118

196 "Take a hundred small round tables": *Variety*, October 29, 1963

196 It sold two and a half: Kercher, pg 233

196 "One of his assets is": *Variety*, September 12, 1962

197 It was left to: Ibid., November 21, 1962

197 The Jenkins Music Store: Ibid., November 28, 1962

197 Eight separate pressing plants: Ibid.

198 "are deprecating the nation's leader": *Billboard*, March 23, 1960

198 "With cigars we retired": Paar, *P.S. Jack*, pg 134

198 "Meader Bombs": *Variety*, January 16, 1963

198 "sat stonily as George Carlin": Ibid., December 13, 1961

199 **"Joseph Kennedy called Enrico Banducci"**: Nachman, pg 80
199 **"I've been told that"**: Ibid., pg 82; Kercher, pg 243
200 **The television show *Hootenanny*:** *Variety*, December 4, 1963
201 **"He began drinking"**: *Life*, January 21, 1972

CHAPTER EIGHT: PERCOLATION IN THE MID-1960S

202 **"declare war against"**: Kercher, pgs 175-176
203 **"very disturbing"**: Ibid., pg 266
204 **"While I was in New York"**: Sweet, pg 261
204 **"Bill Alton was the head"**: Ibid., pgs 335-336
204 **Susskind promoted the cast"**: *Variety*, September 27, 1961
205 **"We were getting the uptown"**: *Second City Unscripted* by Mike Thomas, pg 23
205 **"The reason we didn't make"**: Sweet, pg 198
206 **"a dreary affair"**: *Variety*, June 20, 1962
207 **"Fifty new banks"**: Ibid., September 20, 1963
207 **"The desk at which Jerry"**: *King of Comedy* by Shawn Levy, pg 297
207 **"It's a little nauseating"**: *The Jerry Lewis Show*, November 6, 1963
208 **"It's truly amazing"**: *Variety*, September 25, 1963
208 **"ABC has . . . the apparent"**: *Time*, October 18, 1963
208 **"Lewis was agreeable"**: *Variety*, October 18, 1963
208 **The ad was surrounded:** Ibid., November 20, 1963
209 **"as a result of Mason's"**: Ibid., October 21, 1964
209 **"maliciously and wickedly contrived"**: Ibid., February 24, 1965
209 **"Everyone who's discussed it"**: *Miami News*, October 21, 1964
210 **"*The Ed Sullivan Show*"**: *Newsday*, October 11, 1987
210 **"Jackie Mason was one"**: *Cue the Bunny* by Alan Rafkin, pgs 129-130
210 **The assassination attempt:** *Variety*, November 9, 1966
210 **"Those bullets [that were] supposed"**: "It Happened Last Night," Earl Wilson, November 17, 1966
210 **The attacking car fled:** *Variety*, November 22, 1966
210 **"He was hit eight"**: *St. Petersburg Times*, February 14, 1967
211 **"As soon as I walk"**: Nachman, pg 37
211 **"the wealthiest of"**: Ibid., pg 310
213 **"If it happens too fast"**: Ibid., pg 312
213 **"He was temperamental"**: Ibid., pg 313
213 **"I actually suggested"**: *Vanity Fair*, May 2011
214 **"Never before until Hefner"**: Ibid.

215 **"an albino Negro"**: *Nigger: An Autobiography* by Dick Gregory with Robert Lipsyte, pg 105

215 **"hit them hard and fast"**: Ibid., pg 101

216 **"Twelve o'clock I was still"**: Dick Gregory interview, www.visionary project.org/gregorydick/

216 **When it came around**: *Variety*, April 5, 1961

216 **"One reason that there is"**: *Ebony*, October 1960

216 **"And with it, the tacit"**: *Playboy*, August 1964

216 **"I needed eighty percent *white*"**: Kercher, pgs 291-292

217 **"There was a battle"**: Ibid., pgs 296-297

217 **"one million in travel expenses"**: *New York Times*, March 17, 1968

217 **"A roadblock had"**: Gregory with Lipsyte, pgs 172-174

218 **"Never in the history"**: Kercher, pg 297

218 **"No nightclub owner has ever"**: *Playboy*, August 1964

218 **"Can't afford not to"**: Ibid.

219 **Coulter was a historian**: *The Free Lance-Star*, April 23, 1964

219 **"I'm a Negro *before*"**: *Playboy*, August 1964

219 **"It doesn't seem to be"**: Krassner, pg 171

219 **"As we marched"**: King and Chase, pg 129

220 **"There were troops"**: Sullivan, pg 110

220 **"I didn't respond with rage"**: Carlin with Hendra, pg 137

220 **"In case you don't know"**: *New York Times*, March 17, 1968

220 **He renamed it**: *Variety*, Feburary 20, 1967

221 **"I was playing white audiences"**: *Jet*, January 18, 1962

221 **an insult to comedy"**: Ibid.

222 **"Let's hear it for him!"**: *Stormy Monday* by Helen Oakley Dance, pgs 130, 133

222 **"I was in heaven"**: Chong, pg 54

223 **"He wanted to be"**: Nachman, pg 570

223 **"The Tarriers are a sparkling"**: *Variety*, August 22, 1962

223 **"It was like he'd already"**: Nachman, pg 563

223 **"I didn't want to be"**: Ibid., pg 572

223 **"He was a poor imitation"**: Ibid., pg 571

224 **"When I first began telling"**: Ibid.

224 **"Allen and Cosby are both"**: *Village Voice*, December 20, 1962

224 **His routine about karate**: *Variety*, August 21, 1963

225 **"I became associated in"**: *Milton Berle's Mad Mad Mad World of Comedy*, TV special, 1974

225 **"Chicago is the largest Catholic"**: *Variety*, May 12, 1965

225 **"If he ever speaks":** *Trials of Lenny Bruce* by Ronald K. L. Collins and David M. Skover, pg 149

226 **"In the days that followed":** Sullivan, pg 57

226 **The prosecution was immediately reminded:** Collins and Skover, pg 158

226 **Where do you stop":** *Los Angeles Times*, March 25, 1963

226 **"fressing, schmuck, putz":** Collins and Skover, pg 101

226 **"signs of growing obesity":** *Los Angeles Times*, March 24, 1963

227 **When his screenwriter friend:** *Ladies and Gentlemen, Lenny Bruce!!* by Albert Goldman, pg 591

227 **"He didn't appear in clubs":** Carlin with Hendra, pg 108

228 **"I'll never forget":** *Playboy*, January 1989

229 **"a quiet, intense young man":** *Variety*, October 15, 1965

230 **"Is he going to get":** Zoglin, pg 47

230 **three thousand dollars a week:** *Variety*, October, 4, 1967

230 **"It was Mickey Mouse material":** *Tuscaloosa News*, July 7, 1976

230 **"I told neat little inoffensive":** Price, pgs 84-85

230 **Legend has it:** Zoglin, pg 48

230 **"Entertainment director Dick Kanellis":** *Variety*, October 4, 1967

231 **"And I kept watching Redd":** Price, pg 18

CHAPTER NINE: HIPPIE MADNESS AT DECADE'S END

232 **Mobsters Johnny Roselli and:** *The Last Mafioso* by Ovid Demaris, pg 120

233 **Johnny Roselli, T. Warner Richardson:** *Variety*, July 14, 1968

233 **Roselli was found guilty:** Demaris, pg 229

233 **He phoned another Vegas contact:** *Next to Hughes* by Robert Maheu and Richard Hack, pg 126

233 **"I was terribly shocked":** *New York*, July 21, 1975

233 **"What the fuck is wrong":** Giancana and Giancana, pg 247

233 **"He cowered in the corner":** *Rat Pack Confidential* by Shawn Levy, pg 132

234 **"chase out the hoods":** *Variety*, January 3, 1968

234 **"I wish the anti-racketeering":** Ibid., July 3, 1968

234 **"spiritual kinship between the operations":** *City of Nets* by Otto Friedrich, pg 259

235 **"Gamblers' junkets, which hauled":** Wilson, *Knows*, pg 19

235 **"Banks and insurance companies":** Bacon, pgs 200-201

236 **"That was in 1965":** YouTube Channel of Randolfe Wicker

237 "I'd been on the network": *New York Times*, February 24, 1965

237 "Mr. Crane is something": Ibid., November 12, 1964

237 Only after the Mummy: *Variety*, August 27, 1969

238 "Brando doesn't say anything": *My Life with Regis and Joey* by Trustin Howard, pg 112

238 The police slapped him: *Variety*, June 16, 1971

238 "If a station licensee let": Barnouw, pg 271

239 By law *The Joey Bishop Show*: *Variety*, October 25, 1968

239 The Peace and Freedom Party filed: Ibid., November 6, 1968

239 "Consider the use of": *Official and Confidential* by Anthony Summers, pgs 383-384

240 "We keep voting for": *New York Times*, March 17, 1968

240 "I'm a very good friend": Joan Rivers, UCLA lecture, November 15, 1972

241 "Nor did they promote it": *TV Guide*, July 7, 1973

241 They adopted the name: Kercher, pg 251

242 "charades in a Quaker": Ibid., pg 253

243 "I went down to Los Angeles": Chong, pg 78

244 "a perverse delight": Sullivan, pg 145

244 "What kind of LSD": *The Comedians* by Tedd Thomey and Norman Wilner, pg 33

244 "I went in and turned": A.V. Club, April 13, 2011

244 Groucho Marx was cast: Roger Ebert, March 8, 1970, via RogerEbert.com

245 "Groucho was concerned": *Confessions of a Raving, Unconfined Nut* by Paul Krassner, pg 124

245 "The guy [Preminger] cost us": *The Kid Stays in the Picture* by Robert Evans, pgs 122-123

246 "Pot and to some extent": Chong, pgs 51, 133, 156-157

246 "I know exactly when": Carlin with Hendra, pg 142

247 "We didn't realize how": *Canyon of Dreams* by Harvey Kubernik, pg 133

248 Despite the kibosh: *Variety*, May 28, 1971

248 "There were all these": *We Killed* by Yael Kohen, pg 48

248 "It went thirty-two shows": *Satiristas* by Paul Provenza and Dan Dion, pg 49

250 Paulsen ran a comedic campaign: *Variety*, July 23, 1968

251 "an obvious infringement": Ibid., March 8, 1972

251 "Pat ran his campaign": Colby, pg 139

252 "A musical background": *Billboard*, June 7, 1969

252 **Initially he worked at MCA:** *Variety*, November 18, 1965

252 **"The D.A. came and":** *Earth vs. the Sci-Fi Filmmakers* by Tom Weaver, pgs 238-258

253 ***The Third Ear*:** *Variety*, June 10, 1964

253 **"You will do anything":** Ibid., April 8, 1968

254 **He, Ken Fritz and:** Ibid., July 31, 1968

254 **They bankrolled the:** Ibid., January 13, 1970

254 **"I was a head":** Provenza and Dion, pg 49

256 **"I'd found a list":** Brillstein with Rensin, pg 102

257 **Sentenced to four years:** *Variety*, April 18, 1973

257 **"All that happened afterward":** Carlin with Hendra, pgs 112, 114

257 **"Nothing seemed to upset him":** Ibid., pg 122

258 **"I was in the depth":** Academy of Television Arts and Sciences, interview with George Carlin

258 **"I was playing the biggest":** Carlin with Hendra, pg 126

258 **"From when I was a kid":** Academy of Television Arts and Sciences, interview with George Carlin

258 **"He looked to be":** *Variety*, November 26, 1969

258 **Coming down from his psychedelic:** Ibid., December 12, 1969

259 **"All of my friends":** Ajaye, pg 83

259 **"Down the street Buddy Hackett":** Carlin with Hendra, pg 146

259 **"offensive and abusive language":** *Variety*, September 29, 1970

259 **Carlin adopted a confused look:** Sullivan, pg 111

259 **"and management feared":** *Variety*, December 2, 1970

259 **"couldn't believe [his] ears":** Sullivan, pg 133

259 **The grievance was later thrown":** Carlin with Hendra, pgs 168-169

260 **"seems lost on the":** *Spartanburg Herald*, April 17, 1973

261 **"Jack Benny had two writers":** Young, pg 117

261 **"There is a tendency":** *The Dick Cavett Show*, October 4, 1977

262 **"They've got it all backwards":** Gaver and Stanley, pg 38

262 **"fringe groups that are trying":** *New York Times*, October 4, 1970

263 **"We hate writing":** Ibid., October 4, 1970

263 **"looked into the Kent State":** *Life*, January 29, 1971

263 **The Black cast member:** *Variety*, January 7, 1970

263 **"When they filmed us":** *Rolling Stone*, March 20, 1980

263 **"President Nixon asked me":** *New York Times*, October 4, 1970

264 **"I hear you are interested":** *Variety*, December 30, 1970

264 **"Older pros such as":** Ibid., September 2, 1970

264 **"lunatic fringe that gets":** *Life*, January 29, 1971

264 **"I am neither a Democrat":** Fein, pg 130

265 **"I think the only hope"**: *Nixon's Shadow* by David Greenberg, pg 101

266 **The FBI reopened**: *Confessions of a Nut* by Paul Krassner, pg 129

266 **"Townspeople said to hide"**: Anobile, pg 42

266 **"They would only put"**: *The Dick Cavett Show*, October 4, 1977

267 **Nothing was found**: *Dangerously Funny* by David Bianculli, pg 327

268 **"He phoned me"**: *The Agenda with Steve Paikin*, April 2012

268 **"Done every day"**: *Here's the Thing* with Alec Baldwin, interview with Lorne Michaels

269 **"My father, Bob Schiller"**: *Live from New York* by Tom Shales and James Andrew Miller, pg 19

269 **"The writers would write"**: *Here's the Thing* with Alec Baldwin, interview with Lorne Michaels

270 **"a field which"**: *Variety*, October 1, 1969

270 **Their initial contract**: Ibid., July 16, 1969

270 *Hart and Lorne* **was the matrix**: *The Agenda with Steve Paikin*, April 2012

271 **"I spent a huge chunk"**: *Here's the Thing* with Alec Baldwin, interview with Lorne Michaels

271 **"We want to continue"**: *Ottawa Citizen*, October 16, 1970

272 **"A TV special"**: Brillstein with Rensin, pg 126

272 **"About ten days"**: Kohen, pg 54

272 **"[Cowriter] Jane Wagner"**: Shales and Miller, pg 18

273 **"They really were looking"**: Ibid., pg 38

273 **"I coproduced with"**: *Here's the Thing* with Alec Baldwin, interview with Lorne Michaels

273 **"[NBC executive] Herb Schlosser"**: Ibid.

273 **"I'd been offered four"**: Shales and Miller, pg 97

273 **"Writing was zilch"**: *Variety*, September 10, 1974

CHAPTER TEN: THE FIRST COMEDY CLUBS AND THE 1970S

275 **"He was well respected"**: Zoglin, pg 88

276 **"Robert Klein came along"**: *Mohr Stories*, interview with Jay Leno

277 **"It was a lot of"**: *The Last Laugh* by Phil Berger, pg 398

277 **"He'd ask me afterward"**: Zoglin, pg 131

277 **"At Beverly High"**: *Vanity Fair*, January 2013

278 **"had the rhythms"**: Zoglin, pg 109

278 **"Al Einstein is still"**: *Variety*, June 21, 1967

278 **"He knew about this"**: *Vanity Fair*, January 2013

279 **"His best moments suggest"**: *Variety*, July 6, 1973

279 **"I had to come out"**: Zoglin, pgs 117-118

280 **"While the two outfits"**: *Dancing at Ciro's* by Sheila Weller, pgs 158-159

282 **"It is my gift"**: *Variety*, April 12, 1972

284 **"There were nights"**: *The Warm-up* by Sammy Shore, pg 68

284 **"*Vegas* clinched it"**: Ibid., pg 66

284 **"the best thing that ever"**: *Black Is the New White* by Paul Mooney, pg 136

285 **"Gathering for our first reading"**: *Warm Up the Snake* by John Rich, pg 115

285 **"It was a strange sight"**: *My Father, Uncle Miltie* by William Berle with Brad Lewis, pg 146

285 **"He [Paar] was ensconced"**: *Variety*, January 10, 1973

286 **"up to his old campaigns"**: *WFMU: Fairies and Communists* by Kliph Nesteroff

286 **"One of the reasons"**: Paar, *P.S. Jack*, pg 50

287 **"Guests often delivered"**: *Dino: Living High and Dirty* by Nick Tosches, pg 414

287 **"Many of the people"**: Audio recording, November 10, 1977

287 **"He's at the dentist"**: Ibid.

288 **"Milton Berle's penis"**: *Let Me In, I Hear Laughter—A Salute to the Friars Club*, Showtime documentary

288 **"Go ahead, Milton"**: Berle, pg 142

288 **"He parts his bathrobe"**: Shales and Miller, pg 165

288 **"This is the best TV"**: *Variety*, January 13, 1971

289 **"Pryor dismissed his boss"**: *Flip* by Kevin Cook, pg 163

289 **"loved to help people"**: Sullivan, pg 115

289 **"It's an opportunity"**: Ibid., pg 126

290 **"the new Richard"**: Mooney, pg 137

290 **"Pretty much every comedy"**: Kohen, pg 82

290 **The show proved successful**: *Black and Blue* by Michael Seth Starr, pg 140

290 **"Redd was born"**: Price, pg 21

290 **"That Redd Foxx on"**: Starr, pg 150

291 **Elvis Presley was a fan**: Shore, pg 50

291 **"in my opinion"**: Chong, pg 86

291 **"They would get stoned"**: Rafkin, pg 56

291 **"He would come into"**: Starr, pg 145

291 **"Finally I set up"**: *Billboard*, January 7, 1978

292 **Drozen's second act:** Littleton, pg 140

293 **"He had to have it":** Ibid., pg 137

293 **"We believe our album":** *Billboard*, January 7, 1978

293 **"In the middle of":** Littleton, pg 88

294 **"They knew how to sell":** Ibid., pgs 87-88

294 **"In those days":** *Piers Morgan Live*, May 29, 2012

295 **"I started working":** *Los Angeles Times*, May 20, 1979

296 **"I can't tell jokes":** Ibid.

296 **"I used to do these":** *Fresh Air*, interview with Jay Leno, 1996

297 **"He had enough chutzpah":** *Dyn-O-Mite* by Jimmy Walker, pg 74

297 **"James combined these two":** Chong, pgs 159-1960

298 **"except that when I":** *WFMU: Early David Letterman* by Kliph Nesteroff

299 **"And he not only":** Zoglin, pg 163

300 **"Home Box Office":** *Variety*, March 10, 1976

300 **"So I did, without telling":** Brillstein with Rensin, pg 359

301 **"We respect your decision":** Zoglin, pg 34

301 **"*The Richard Pryor Show* is over":** Mooney, pg 178

302 **"The Unknown Comic, I loved him":** *A Special Thing*, interview with Louis C.K., 2006

305 **"It was a book about":** *Entertainment Weekly*, June 28, 2013

Chapter Eleven: The Stand-up Comedy Boom

306 **"This is a good way":** *Variety*, October 20, 1976

306 **"He was behaving like":** Zoglin, pg 196

307 **"Shelley Berman works":** Mooney, pg 194

307 **capitalize on the vacuum:** *Variety*, July 11, 1979

308 **"Once the unions are involved":** *Los Angeles Times*, May 10, 1979

308 **"It feeds on hate":** Zoglin, pg 151

308 **"kind of a sick culture":** Ibid.

309 **"The Comic Strip was lame":** Ibid., pg 218

310 **"Kenny Kraemer [*sic*], a gangling":** *Variety*, April 28, 1976

310 **"I had a series of jobs":** *KPCS193*, interview with Larry David

310 **Jerry Seinfeld said David:** *The Howard Stern Show*, June 26, 2013

310 **"right out into the street":** Shales and Miller, pg 335

311 **"Occasionally I would do":** *KPCS193*, interview with Larry David

311 **Despite the many stories:** *Fresh Air*, interview with Larry David, 1992

311 **"He complained about it":** *Make 'Em Laugh* by Jeffrey Gurian and Richie Tienken, pg 38

312 "It never occurred to me": Berle and Lewis, pg 209

313 "Without much ado": *Boston Globe*, January 31, 1980

314 "an infectious rash": Carlin with Hendra, pg 206

316 "The drugs were free": *I Killed* by Rich Shydner and Mark Schiff, pg 176

316 "What do you mean?": *Los Angeles Times*, March 7, 1982

316 Belushi convinced Brillstein: Shales and Miller, pg 263

316 "Whenever a new shipment": Ibid., pg 270

317 "It was the most exciting": *Los Angeles Times*, August 23, 1979

317 By the time he got: *Variety*, February 1, 1980

317 "Of the newest personalities": Paar, *P.S. Jack*, pg 27

318 Letterman forced Stewart to resign: *New York Post*, June 18, 1980

318 The management team: *Variety*, July 1, 1980

318 "a disgustingly pert, cheery": *Los Angeles Times*, June 27, 1980

318 Some affiliates, like KYW: *Variety*, July 30, 1980

318 Four major markets: *Globe and Mail*, August 19, 1980

318 It was consistently the lowest-rated: *Variety*, September 29, 1980

319 "Dinah's makin' an omelet": *Los Angeles Times*, June 27, 1980

319 They considered using Letterman: *New York Times*, September 27, 1980

319 "opening remarks": *Mohr Stories*, ep 95

320 "It was the greatest fog ever": Ibid.

320 "The ludicrous quinella NBC": *Palm Beach Post*, June 26, 1979

320 "*Late Night with David Letterman* has become": *New York*, May 30, 1983

321 "But here are the facts": *Born Standing Up* by Steve Martin, pgs 125-126

321 "In the era that": *WTF* with Marc Maron, ep 254

322 "Jim didn't understand": Zoglin, pg 152

322 "McCawley's close personal interest": *Los Angeles Times*, November 1, 1983

322 "He bullied people": Zoglin, pg 153

322 "That's all you heard": A.V. Club, July 17, 2012

323 "So if they put a": Kohen, pg 156

323 "It was financed by": Berger, pg 450

324 "One of the reasons": *New York Times*, October 29, 1987

325 *The New York Times* reported: Ibid.

326 "I found that highly reassuring": Sullivan, pg 202

326 "Sam Kinison was the only": *Fresh Air*, interview wth Chris Rock

326 "I've known Dice": *Los Angeles Times*, December 25, 1990
327 "I knew Andrew before": Ajaye, pg 124
327 He was booked: *Variety*, August 27, 1990
327 "I was really going through": Shales and Miller, pgs 358-359
327 "do for comedy what MTV": *Variety*, December 24, 1985
328 "very unlikely they can": Ibid., May 24, 1989
328 In October 1990 Viacom: Ibid., October 30, 1990
328 "misled by the Comedy Boom": Ibid., July 25, 1994
328 They became known as CTV: Ibid., May 16, 1991
329 "Every club in the city": *A Special Thing*, interview with Louis C.K., 2006

Chapter Twelve: The 1990s

330 "After I came out": Littleton, pgs 158, 160
330 "Anybody who says different": Shales and Miller, pg 403
331 "I just came in": Gurian and Tienken, pg 58
331 "This whole thing happened": Ibid., pg 61
331 "To me one of": Alba, pg 319
332 "The black comedy boom": Shales and Miller, pg 405
332 "On *SNL*, I either had": Ibid., pg 418
332 "I used to get": *Difficult Men* by Brett Martin, pgs 50-51
332 "When it was mentioned": Littleton, pg 197
333 Hughley was a cut above: Ibid., pg 206
333 "They were telling me": Ibid., pgs 209-210
333 "If it turned out": Ibid, pg 214
334 "a cerebral-palsy puppet": *New York*, January 10, 1994
334 "bombed atomically": Colby, pg 144
334 "I went on for two years": *Los Angeles Times*, October 5, 2008; *Philadelphia Daily News*, November 2, 1994
334 His gigs improved: *People*, April 4, 194
335 "*Stewart* staff members": *New York*, July 1995
335 "It's hard not to take": Ibid.
337 "I used to tour": A.V. Club, March 1, 2011
337 "When *The Ben Stiller Show*": Ibid.
337 "The *Star Trek* sketch": Sacks, pg 132
338 "I would sort of work": Shales and Miller, pg 335
339 Conan O'Brien was by then: *Los Angeles Times*, January 31, 1993
339 "[I] had access to": *Rolling Stone*, September 19, 1996

339 "I did not think": *Spin*, February 1994

339 In reality, Shandling didn't": *Los Angeles Times*, April 19, 1993

339 Dana Carvey, Drew Carey: *WTF with Marc Maron*, ep 418

340 "I was going broke": *A Special Thing*, interview with Louis C.K., 2006

340 "We met at a bar": *GQ*, August 2011

341 "In the wee hours": *Los Angeles Times*, April 16, 1994

341 "[Conan is] a twitching": *New York Times*, September 25, 1994

341 "I'd go out to do": *Playboy*, February 1998

341 "We just fought to stay": *A Special Thing*, interview with Louis C.K., 2006

341 "We'd be there until three": Ibid.

342 "The more I watch": *New York Times*, September 25, 1994

342 "My manager approached Letterman's show": *A Special Thing*, interview with Louis C.K., 2006

344 "amazing pool of talent": Ibid.

Chapter Thirteen: The New Millennium

347 "So we did a joke": HRTS, conversation with Lorne Michaels, April 16, 2013

348 "I'm shocked that it didn't": Associated Press, February 1, 2004; www.firstliberties.com/dennis_miller_right.html; February 5, 2004

349 "I went and saw his act": Guy MacPherson, interview with Tom Smothers, July 22, 2006

349 "During 9/11, I gave Bush": *LA Weekly*, September 16, 200

349 Colbert later said: *Angry Optimist* by Lisa Rogak, pg 84

350 "I loved Novello's stuff": Provenza and Dion, pgs 26-28

351 "Colbert crossed the line": *U.S. News & World Report*, May 1, 2006

351 "This is the type of": Sacks, pg 242

351 "a controversial, possibly very funny": *New York*, October 10, 2006

352 "He made a career": Standup.com, December 2006

352 "They don't put that much": *A Special Thing* message board, Louis C.K. interview, 2006

353 "Comedy these days takes": Sacks, pg 114

353 "Nowadays the choice": Shales and Miller, pg 488

353 "a fucking hands-and-knees": Carlin with Hendra, pg 268

353 "I personally believe": Klein, pg 323

353 **"I'd like to get back":** *New York Times*, July 17, 2013

354 **"If I had an act":** *By the Way, In Conversation with Jeff Garlin*, January 10, 2013

354 **"I think about it":** *CBS Sunday Morning*, December 25, 2011

357 **"It's just there":** *ABC News*, October 2, 2006

INDEX